Nigel West is a military historian specialising in security matters, and is the European Editor of the *World Intelligence Review*. He has written several controversial histories of Britain's intelligence organisations, including *A Matter of Trust: MI5 1945–72*; *Molehunt: The Full Story of the Soviet Spy in MI5*; and *The Friends: Britain's Post-War Secret Intelligence Operations*. The *Sunday Times* has commented on his books: 'His information is often so precise that many people believe that he is the unofficial historian of the secret services. West's sources are undoubtedly excellent. His books are peppered with deliberate clues to potential front-page stories.'

COUNTERFEIT SPIES

Genuine or Bogus?

An Astonishing Investigation into
Secret Agents of the Second World War

NIGEL WEST

ST ERMIN'S
PRESS

A *St Ermin's Press* Book

First published in Great Britain in 1998 by St Ermin's Press
This edition published in 1999 by St Ermin's Press
in association with Little, Brown and Company

Copyright © 1998 by Westintel (Research) Limited

The moral right of the author has been asserted.

A CIP catalogue record for this book
is available from the British Library.

ISBN: 0 7515 2670 3

Typeset by M Rules in Century Old Style
Printed and bound in Great Britain
by Clays Ltd, St Ives plc

St Ermin's Press
in association with
Little, Brown and Company (UK)
Brettenham House
Lancaster Place
London WC2E 7EN

'Myths about espionage die hard.'

Leopold Trepper in *The Great Game*

By the end of the Second World War, Trepper had been imprisoned in Palestine by the British, in Paris by the Nazis, and in Moscow by the NKVD. He is, therefore, one of the best documented spies of all time.

In Memoriam

Dedicated to the memory of Lieutenant-Colonel T. A. Robertson OBE (1909–94), who was one of the most intuitive intelligence officers of the Second World War, and was the architect of the organisation of controlled enemy agents which became known as the double-cross system.

Contents

Acknowledgments and Illustrations

My thanks are due to the many *cognoscenti* in the intelligence field who expressed doubts about particular books and the claims made for them by their authors. In particular, I should like to express my gratitude to Colonel Hayden Peake, whose encyclopaedic knowledge of the subject was invaluable; David Stafford and Tim Naftali, who have done much work on Sir William Stephenson; Professor R. V. Jones for clarifying details of the Oslo Report; the British Army Records Centre at Hayes, Middlesex, which verified the biographical data of some dubious characters; Brian Garfield for patiently answering so many of my queries regarding *The Paladin*; Peter Green for the use of his facilities in Canada; Camilla Keith for her research in Spain; Colonel Edward Edlmann's son, John, for his help in tracing his father's story; Colonel T. A. Robertson and Rodney Dennys, former members of the Security Service and the Secret Intelligence Service respectively; and numerous other members of the intelligence and security community who prefer not to be identified publicly.

Illustrations

1. Quentin Reynolds, a war correspondent of great distinction. (Popperfoto)

2. The original OSS report written by Aline, Countess of Romanones, when she was a cipher clerk in Madrid with the codename *Butch*.

3. Johnny Nicholas, the mysterious black OSS agent who is alleged to have parachuted into France and worked undercover in Paris in 1943. (Courtesy of Hugh Wray McCann)

4. The postcard Johnny Nicholas is alleged to have sent from the concentration camp Buchenwald to his brother in Paris, one of the few items to confirm that such a person really was held by the Nazis. (Courtesy of Hugh Wray McCann)

5 & 6.   A comparison between MGM's film *School for Danger*, released after the war, and the photos in *A Man Called Intrepid* prove that the latter pictures came from the movie and not from a secret wartime archive, as claimed by the author, William Stevenson (Imperial War Museum/Weidenfeld & Nicolson Archive)

7. Sir William Stephenson. (Associated Press)

8. John Cottell lecturing at Wichita State University in 1992, holding what he claimed to be his wartime parachute suit. (Keith Melton Collection)

9. The dustjacket of one of Josephine Butler's books, *Cyanide in My Shoe*.

10. Roxane Pitt in 1957, publicising her book *The Courage of Fear*. (Keystone)

11. A respected historian, Leonard Mosley invented a bogus Nazi spy, codenamed *The Druid*, to link separate incidents mentioned in other books. (Topham Picturepoint)

12. The X Troop: a group photo which was taken in May 1943, when *Nimrod* could not have been included, as the historian James Leasor claimed.

Abbreviations

BCRA	Gaullist French Intelligence Service
BSC	British Security Co-ordination
CEMA	Council for the Encouragement of Music and the Arts
CIA	American Central Intelligence Agency
DST	French Security Service
ENSA	Entertainments National Service Association
FANY	First Aid Nursing Yeomanry
FBI	American Federal Bureau of Investigation
GCCS	Government Code and Cipher School
GCHQ	Government Communications Headquarters
ISLD	Inter-Services Liaison Department
KGB	Soviet Intelligence Service
MI5	British Security Service
MI6	British Secret Intelligence Service
MI9	British Escape and Evasion Service
NKVD	Soviet Intelligence Service
OKW	Wehrmacht High Command
ONI	US Office of Naval Intelligence
OSS	American Office of Strategic Services
PWE	Political Warfare Executive
RASC	Royal Army Service Corps

RCAF	Royal Canadian Air Force
RHSA	Reich Security Agency
SD	Sicherheitsdienst, Nazi Security Service
SDECE	French Intelligence Service
SHAEF	Supreme Headquarters Allied Expeditionary Force
SHAPE	Supreme Headquarters, Allied Powers Europe
SIM	Italian Military Intelligence Service
SIME	British Security Intelligence Middle East
SIS	British Secret Intelligence Service
SOE	Special Operations Executive

Introduction

Since the end of the Second World War, many hundreds of books have been published about the exploits of secret agents who operated behind enemy lines. Some have been written by the men and women who risked their lives to fight the Nazis and survived to give first-hand non-fiction accounts; others have collaborated with journalists to produce versions that often have been less than accurate pictures of the clandestine war. A few have been based on nothing more substantive than a fertile imagination, a gullible publisher and, in a surprisingly large number of cases, access to some very dubious historical records. Several of these more implausible tales have, however, gained some verisimilitude and wide circulation, and a few have even been endorsed by respectable historians and supposedly expert commentators. The real difficulty lies in distinguishing between the wheat and the chaff for, as Professor M. R. D. Foot has pointed out, during the war there were any number of genuine 'eccentrics, the social oddities who got attracted to irregular and clandestine units'. So who are the hoaxers and the fakes?

Certainly publishers are not entirely free of guilt in promoting some works of fiction as authentic accounts of real events. One particular publisher, Geoffrey Faber, who was to receive a knighthood in 1954 in recognition of his secret contribution to the war effort, provided journalistic cover to British Secret Intelligence Service (SIS) personnel and, in June 1941, collaborated in the fabrication of what purported to be the moving memoirs of a tragic twelve-year-old Dutch child from Rotterdam who had endured the Nazi occupation of his country. For a publisher who based himself at All Souls, Oxford, and hitherto had produced a rather austere list of English literature, Faber's decision to move into this particular field, and his astonishing ability to obtain apparently limitless quantities of paper, which was then in very short supply, raised eyebrows among his colleagues. In reality, the entire book, entitled *My Sister and I: The Diary of a Dutch Boy Refugee*, by Dirk van der Heide, was a plausible forgery designed for the purpose of assisting Britain's anti-Nazi propaganda, and Faber had acted as a willing front for the intelligence establishment. 'Dirk van der Heide' never existed and, as the publisher observed in the introduction, perhaps with a deliberate hint of irony, 'sometimes his writing seems abnormally mature'. The same book was released in the United States by Harcourt, Brace & Co. and was a phenomenal success. By March 1942, it had already gone into its eighth printing.

Because so many wartime records remained classified for so long after the end of hostilities, it was only to be expected that hoaxers and fraudsters would take advantage of the public's apparently insatiable appetite for war stories describing episodes of extraordinary courage and endurance. At one time there was a thriving international trade in bogus Nazi memorabilia, including documents purporting to be the letters of Hermann Goering, the diaries of Josef Goebbels, and even poetry composed by Hitler. For a while, dealers paid high prices for counterfeit Gestapo medallions, although the sums involved were trivial when compared to the millions of dollars invested by *Stern*, *Newsweek* and Rupert Murdoch's News International newspapers in the notorious Hitler diaries in 1983. The CIA reminds its own staff of the skill of forgers by offering a display at its headquarters at Langley, Virginia, of apparently authentic material identifying General Bill Donovan, the wartime head of the Office of Strategic Services (OSS), as a Nazi spy. Whilst it is futile to deny that over the years many experts have been duped, the true scale of the deception has never previously been documented.

Inevitably there have been instances of exaggeration, most often of commentators dressing some disclosures in hyperbole with the intention of making them more attractive and saleable. This may be the explanation behind *A Spy for Churchill*, written by Robert D. Vacha, himself a wartime intelligence officer before he joined the *Daily Mail*. He tells of a British officer named Craig, who, for a period of nearly two years, was substituted for a German officer on Rommel's staff and communicated Rommel's intentions to Cairo. In a similar vein is *With My Little Eye* by Edward G. Edlmann, a wartime British officer who claimed to have donned a German uniform in 1940 to perform numerous secret missions before he successfully masqueraded as a Fascist supporter of Mussolini in Italy before the surrender. In *The Year of the Rat*, Mladin Zarubica took a similar theme and described how an Allied agent had taken the place of a Wehrmacht major-general and had planted a fake plan of the D-Day landings on the enemy. The proposition that the amphibious assault in June 1944 was accompanied by nefarious deception schemes is not new, but some of the participants purported to have played key roles most definitely are. One hitherto undisclosed agent, identified by James Leasor as Stefan Rosenberg in *The Unknown Warrior*, even succeeded in duping Field Marshal Rommel only hours before the invasion of Normandy began. The claims of all four authors will be examined in the pages that follow.

Since the end of the Second World War, a remarkable mythology has developed around what has been termed the French resistance. When the Comte de Marenches returned to Paris after the Liberation in 1944, having spent the previous three years in London organising de Gaulle's fledgeling intelligence service, he remarked that he had had no idea there had been sixteen million Frenchmen in the resistance. He might also have said that some of the characters who were later to claim to have participated in the underground had very strange credentials. One, a Canadian air-force officer named George DuPre, persuaded the distinguished war correspondent Quentin Reynolds that he had operated in Normandy in the guise of a deaf mute, whereas actually he had spent almost the entire war in Canada. His tale of dangerous clandestine missions in enemy-occupied territory turned out to be complete fiction, although it fooled Reynolds and numerous others. Similarly, an American congressman, Douglas Springfellow, was forced to resign his seat in Utah when it was discovered that his supposed war record, as an agent for the OSS, was entirely bogus. Martin Gray, allegedly a survivor of the Warsaw ghetto uprising and a decorated member of the Soviet partisans, whose moving book *For Those I Loved* was a bestseller in 1971 and was dramatised for television in 1991, turned out never to have been an inmate of the Treblinka concentration camp as he claimed.[1] As for Albert Haas, his account of his work as a prisoner physician in Dachau,

Flossenberg and Mauthausen, *The Doctor and the Damned*, has a ring of authenticity, but his tales of espionage on the Côte d'Azur prior to his capture bear no detailed scrutiny .

Post-war accounts of what happened during the occupation of France have tended to stereotype the Germans as murderous thugs who enjoyed torturing their victims, usually beautiful but doomed women who defied the Gestapo and were murdered in horrific circumstances. One classic example must be the case of Violette Szabo, the heroine of Special Operations Executive (SOE), whose story was told by the novelist and playwright Rubeigh J. Minney in *Carve Her Name With Pride*. The book, and the film of the same name which was released a year later in 1957, described the 'most atrocious torture' Szabo underwent at the hands of the Gestapo. In fact, there was never any evidence that Mrs Szabo suffered maltreatment before her execution and Minney's tale was 'completely fictitious'. Yet Minney himself was a distinguished biographer, film producer, wartime editor of *The Strand* magazine and twice a Parliamentary candidate for the Labour Party. However, as Professor M. R. D. Foot discovered when he researched the activities of SOE in France, the truth was somewhat different. Indeed, in the first edition of his official history, *SOE in France*, he declared that there was no evidence that any of SOE's women agents had been tortured by the enemy: 'The allegations of fiendish brutality towards these women by the Germans that are freely and frequently made are by no means all of them borne out by the facts.'[2] After having made this bold and iconoclastic statement, Foot found himself on the receiving end of a legal action brought by Odette Churchill GC (*née* Sansom), who dismissed the report of a medical examination she had been given upon her release from Ravensbrück in 1945, recovered from SOE's archives by the historian, and forced him to rewrite several passages in *SOE in France*. The threat of litigation also obliged Foot to delete in subsequent editions the sentence in which he wrote that 'the ghastly imputations about what happened to these girls have been freely inserted by sensation-mongers',[3] identifying Minney as having been responsible for 'particularly bad examples'.

Although vulnerable to criticism as authentic accounts of work behind enemy lines, authors like Minney and Barry Wynne, who wrote *Count Five and Die* about Allied deception schemes in Holland, escaped serious challenge and had their books accepted as genuine by all but a handful of *cognoscenti*. Wynne also wrote *The Empty Coffin*, a further story of

secret agents operating in enemy-occupied territory, but that too
escaped the searching analysis that would have revealed it to be bogus.
While Wynne was apparently taken in by the rather tall tales revealed to
him by William Eliscu and Alain Romans respectively, some other
authors claimed to have had first-hand experience of hazardous clandestine operations.

Elizabeth Gibbs, writing under the pseudonym of Elizabeth Denham,
wrote *I Looked Right*, an astonishing memoir of what she claimed to be
the dozens of clandestine missions she had undertaken into occupied
France for an unidentified British secret service.[4] She alleged that each
week she had been slipped across the Channel to rescue Allied servicemen and guide them home. Her cover had been maintained, so she said,
by returning to her family's country home each weekend. The title of her
extraordinary book was taken from an incident in which she asserted
that she had been arrested by the Germans because a sharp-eyed
Gestapo agent had spotted her looking in the wrong direction for traffic
before crossing a busy road. In reality, her tale was wholly untrue, but
nevertheless this particular episode was to become well-established in
the mythology of the wartime French resistance. In fact, Elizabeth
Gibbs, who was then married to a British diplomat based in Washington,
and was later to marry Sir Humphrey Clarke Bt, never left England at
any time during the war, as her family knew. Nevertheless her story
was accepted as genuine when it was published in 1956 and was serialised in the *Daily Express*. Indeed, it was even believed by Maurice
Buckmaster, who had headed the French Section of SOE. Two years
after the release of Elizabeth Denham's book, Buckmaster included a reference to her tale in his somewhat fanciful account of SOE's activities,
They Fought Alone. In his version Colonel Buckmaster recalled that

> One of our girls landed in France in 1943 and successfully
> reached the large town where she was due to rendezvous with
> the local Resistance man. In the middle of the town she was
> obliged to cross a main road. As she went to cross it she looked
> right to check that the road was clear; this of course is the natural
> thing to do if the traffic drives on the left hand side of the road.
> Seeing the road clear, she started to cross; a howl of brakes and
> curses of a lorry driver revealed her mistake.[5]

Buckmaster's memoirs, which included some other embarrassing gaffes which were politely overlooked by SOE's subsequent historians for fear of reopening a simmering controversy over his competence, thus had the effect of authenticating Elizabeth Denham's entirely false tale. If Buckmaster, who died in April 1992, had been allowed access to SOE's records, he would have realised that only twelve women had been sent to France by his section in 1943. Denham had not been among them, nor had she ever worked for SOE or any other secret wartime organisation. A check in the archives would have confirmed that none of them had been arrested as a consequence of the road-crossing episode she had described so vividly. However, by her fertile imagination, and aided by Buckmaster's unwitting support, the Denham story subsequently received wide circulation and is now accepted as a true chapter in SOE's tangled and tragic history.

Lady Clarke was by no means the only woman to invent a clandestine wartime career for herself, or to write an autobiographical account of her adventures and then succeed in persuading others of its veracity. Another classic example must be that of Roxane Pitt, a Classicist from the University of Milan, whose book *The Courage of Fear* was endorsed by some impressive public figures, including Sir Robert Bruce Lockhart, formerly the Director of the Political Warfare Executive. Miss Pitt's success in 1957 encouraged her to produce a second volume eighteen years later, appropriately entitled *Operation Double Life*, and still she escaped detection, even though she had fabricated aspects of her life that were ludicrously easy to check, and contradicted herself on many significant occasions when giving her two very different versions of what she claimed had been her secret wartime assignments. Another authoress who could not resist a second bite of the cherry was Madelaine Duke, who in 1955 wrote a highly fanciful tale about her late brother, who, she asserted, had operated undetected as a British agent in Berlin throughout the war. Perhaps encouraged by her ability to dupe her readers, she embarked on another biography two years later, her new subject being an SOE officer named 'Jan Felix'. Once again, her book was received uncritically although Felix's story was not quite as she told it.

Rather less lucky in avoiding challenges to her recollections is Aline, Countess of Romanones, who worked for OSS in Madrid for the latter part of the war. In three best-selling volumes of her autobiography, she has graphically reconstructed her hair-raising adventures while working under cover in Spain. Unfortunately, the declassification and release of OSS's files reveal a rather more prosaic life for the self-styled secret agent.

Nor is it only the agents themselves who have been known to falsify their achievements. George Borodin, the author of no less than sixteen books, who described himself as one of the pioneering plastic surgeons of his day, made entirely spurious claims about what he alleged was his wartime work for the secret services, altering the appearance of agents about to undertake missions behind enemy lines. In fact, as we shall see, his war memoirs, *No Crown of Laurels*, were entirely manufactured. Curiously, none of his bogus stories was ever challenged, even when compelling evidence emerged years later in another of his books, *Secret Surgeon*, which he wrote under another name.

With the relative paucity of wartime records it must have been a temptation for the unscrupulous to embellish their own spies. There can be little other explanation for Leonard Mosley, who invented a German agent, *The Druid*, who supposedly outfoxed MI5; or for the American team of Hugh W. McCann, David C. Smith and David Matthews, who produced some ostensibly plausible material to support their extraordinary story of a black OSS agent who had been captured by the Gestapo in Paris in 1943. As we shall see, the odds for this adventurer ever having existed are infinitesimal.

A common strand running through some of these tales is the figure of Winston Churchill, who, so three separate Walter Mitty characters would have the public believe, ran his own private intelligence service in deliberate isolation from the more conventional agencies that so much has been written about. Christopher Craig, hero of *The Paladin*, asserts that the organisation was known as M Section and was run by the late Sir Desmond Morton. In *Churchill's Secret Agent*, Dr Josephine Butler states that, codenamed *Jay Bee*, she was one of twelve members of the 'Secret Circle' headed by Professor Lindemann (Lord Cherwell). The self-styled Lieutenant-Colonel John E. Cottell MVO OBE MC insists that he was codenamed *Badger* and worked directly for Churchill personally. His astonishing story, ghost-written by Arthur Gordon, a former staff writer on *Reader's Digest* and author of fifteen books, is entirely bogus, as is his claim to his military rank and numerous decorations.

Not quite so phoney was Sir William Stephenson, a genuine intelligence officer with a wealth of bona fide experience, who, dissatisfied by two biographies, opted to assist a third writer. The resulting farrago, *A Man Called Intrepid*, was deeply flawed, but none the less sold sixteen million copies around the world. Certainly its influence should not be underestimated for it was the author of this particular book who not only authenticated *The Paladin*, but also endorsed Leonard Mosley's fictitious spy *The Druid*! Similarly, Alain Romans, whose own adventures as portrayed in *The Empty Coffin* are open to considerable doubt, authenticated Roxane Pitt's fabricated memoirs.

As for George Borodin, why did his account of plastic surgery performed on wartime secret agents bear such a close resemblance to the autobiography of Dr George Sava, published twenty-nine years later? What follows is the story of how the myths were created, and how some of the counterfeit spies were detected.

1

The Man Who Wouldn't Talk

'Nothing seemed impossible to this incredible organisation called so prosaically the BIS.'[1]

In 1953, the distinguished American war correspondent Quentin Reynolds, whose book *Dress Rehearsal* was to be regarded as the standard work on the ill-fated raid on Dieppe, announced an astonishing coup: he had persuaded a quiet, reserved businessman from Calgary to relive the horrors he had experienced during the war. George Cyril DuPre, the branch manager of Commercial Chemicals Ltd, was a respected member of the local community who led the Boy Scout troop, taught at Sunday School and always attended the monthly meeting of the Canukeena Club, a group of ex-servicemen. Word of his wartime exploits had reached Reynolds following a speech made by DuPre during a lunch held by some businessmen in Toronto. Reynolds, a regular contributor to *Life* magazine, flew up to Toronto to meet DuPre and the result was 'The Man Who Wouldn't Talk', a long article in the November 1953 issue of *Reader's Digest* heralded as 'the heroic true story of the gentle spy'. This was followed by a full-length book of the same title, published by Random House, which was an instant success, becoming the number one non-fiction bestseller in New York. Reynolds himself, perhaps somewhat immodestly, described it as 'the greatest spy story to come out of the Second Great War'.

George DuPre was apparently a reluctant hero. When he had returned home to Winnipeg in August 1946, in the uniform of a flight lieutenant of the Royal Canadian Air Force (RCAF), his wife Muriel, whom he had married in 1935, had been astonished to discover that her husband, then aged forty-one, had aged dramatically and his hair had turned prematurely white. It was only much later that she persuaded him to reveal what had really happened to him. Between the time he had volunteered for the RCAF in 1940 and his reappearance five years later, he had not been based at various RAF stations across England – as had been suggested by the total of fifty-five letters he had written home – but had in fact been selected for intelligence work soon after his arrival in London and had spent most of the war operating as a secret agent in enemy-occupied territory.

DuPre's story was remarkable. At the age of thirty-six he had been too old for combat duties, so, after his initial training in Toronto, he had been assigned to an intelligence section. When, six months later, he had been posted to England, he had been invited to an interview at a Whitehall address with a civilian who demonstrated a detailed knowledge of his background. He knew that DuPre's name was Huguenot in origin and that he had been born in Poona, India, where his father, Peter DuPre, had been a colonel in the Royal Artillery. George had been educated at Harrow and Cambridge, and then had moved to Canada, where he had worked for thirteen years in the Arctic for the Hudson Bay Company, first on ships and later as the manager of a million-acre muskrat ranch in Manitoba.

At the conclusion of this, his first encounter with the British Intelligence Service, DuPre was posted to 'the Oxford Home for Convalescents', a baronial mansion outside Oxford set in 500 acres of woodland. This 'was actually one of the really top secret installations in England; it was the training school for British agents', where the course lasted nine months and where

> he would study short-wave radio operation, the architecture of French bridges and viaducts, the strength, the vulnerability and the operation of French railroads; he would learn how to manufacture and handle explosives of all kinds; he would be taught how to care for and use pigeons as messengers; he would learn everything there was to learn about French automobiles; he would take a course on French police procedure, and would be trained in the art of parachuting from a plane.[2]

DuPre's mission was to be on behalf of the British Escape and

Evasion Service known as MI9, and he was to run an escape line for aircrews from a headquarters in the village of Torigni, not far from St Lô, masquerading as a certain Pierre Touchette.

The selection of this particular Frenchman as the identity to be adopted by DuPre was unusual. His background was explained to DuPre by Colonel William Baker, the training school's commandant: Touchette 'was born in the village of Torigni on August 10, 1903. Your parents, Marcel and Madeline Touchette, really never should have married. . . . They were first cousins and they thought the discredited law of consanguinity caught up with them. You – their only child – turned out to be feeble-minded.'[3]

Having been reassured that the Touchettes had left Torigni in 1934 and had all been killed in the early days of the war, DuPre accepted his bizarre assignment. He was to be parachuted into Normandy, where arrangements had been made for him to live with a local farming family, Joseph and Madeline Thibaut, and work in a garage owned by Georges Lavalle.

DuPre's training included a course on silent killing, shared with a group of six young men who were to seize an enemy radar station on the French coast, and many hours with Johnny Peterson, a man with the mind of an eight year old who taught DuPre to play with building blocks and model trains so as to prepare him for his role. There were twenty-seven other students at the convalescent home, taken from various walks of life, including a pair from a divinity school. Two of those named were Archie Steele, who was to impersonate a dead Frenchman, and Samuel Rosen, who was to adopt the identity of a German then in an officers' prisoner-of-war camp. Both were despatched on their missions prior to DuPre.

At the three-quarter moon in February 1941, the agent graduated and climbed aboard an aircraft on the strip attached to the school. 'Neither the pilot of the single-engined Lysander nor his radio man said much to George DuPre as the plane slipped casually through a star-speckled night. George was in the rear gunner's cockpit.'[4] Once over the dropping zone, at a height of 1,200 feet, DuPre leapt from the aircraft and moments later was on the ground, gathering up the black silk of his parachute. He had landed in a field beside the Thibauts' farm and, having quickly established himself with the family, made contact with members of the local resistance, but 'of these only Thibaut, his wife, the priest and Georges Lavalle knew that George was a British agent'.[5]

During the next two years, DuPre, while acting the role of the village idiot, secretly organised the resistance in the vicinity of Torigni and was responsible for many acts of sabotage, destroying bridges and blowing up trains. In addition, he 'managed to save about a hundred RAF airmen'[6] and maintained a regular contact by radio with London. There were routine supply drops every Friday night and members of the resistance, the *réseau*, were paid a weekly wage. Despite his participation in numerous operations, DuPre was never detected by the Germans, although on one occasion in late 1943 he was arrested by the Gestapo, together with sixteen other villagers. Over a period of several days he was tortured terribly, suffering beatings, scalding with boiling water and the injection of sulphuric acid into his rectum. Three of the prisoners died of maltreatment, but DuPre was eventually released.

Soon after his recovery, DuPre received instructions from London to make contact with René Godbout, the leader of the resistance in the town of Bernay. His new assignment was to infiltrate a U-boat factory in Hamburg which had recently been damaged in an air raid. The local Gestapo had been ordered to seize sixty men as slave labourers in the villages around Bernay as replacements for those killed in the bombing, and DuPre was successful in ensuring that he was one of them. The huge, heavily protected plant, which was partly underground, was located on the River Elbe and employed 'four thousand skilled technicians'.[7] DuPre's first task was to discover the names and addresses of two diamond experts responsible for assembling precision instruments. Once obtained, the information was relayed to London, and their suburban homes, 'two houses on Wilhelmstrasse, just off Bruckenallee',[8] were destroyed by Mosquito fighter-bombers in a skilfully planned attack. Other key specialists were picked off in the same way, and the submarines themselves were also sabotaged: 'The last two subs to be launched had made their final dives, but in each case something had gone wrong with the surfacing apparatus and both subs and their crews had been lost.'[9]

In February 1944, after DuPre had been in the plant for 'nearly ten months',[10] he was handed a capsule of a chemical which enabled him to persuade the factory doctor that he had contracted pneumonia and was therefore unfit for further work. He was promptly discharged and made his way home, across Germany and France, to Torigni, where he arrived 'late in March, 1944'.[11] His contribution to D-Day was to organise the theft of fifty-six SS uniforms, but on 1 July he was summoned back to

London. Three nights later, a single-engined aircraft flew him to Bournemouth; after a brief stop for a meal, he was taken in another plane to RAF Northolt and then driven to a suite in the Savoy Hotel, London.

DuPre was welcomed home by a Canadian, Brigadier Matthew Penhale, who introduced him to 'two Brigadiers and a Colonel of British Intelligence', who debriefed him and also gave him a warning:

> You may live to be a hundred, DuPre. . . . Even if you do, never mention the town in which you operated. Never mention the names of the eight Resistance men and women with whom you worked. Never mention the code we used in communicating with each other. . . . We're an old service. . . . There is a continuity about our end of it. We work in peace and in war. You can tell your story. You can tell it all, but disguise the name of the village and the eight who worked with you. May seem a bit overcautious but . . . we made this rule back in the Boer War days and it's worked out pretty well in the long run.[12]

The damage to DuPre's body inflicted by the Gestapo was repaired by a plastic surgeon at a small hospital the service maintained 'at Taplo-on-Thames near Maidenhead',[13] and by April 1945 his health had been restored. Now 'the MI-5 boys' were anxious to deploy DuPre to catch high-ranking Nazis suspected of masquerading as Allied prisoners of war. 'Those who speak English well get hold of British, American or Canadian uniforms,' the Brigadier explained. 'With or without the connivance of prison officials they get into the compounds where they pass themselves off as Allied officers.'[14] DuPre's task was to infiltrate Stalag 3, near Berlin, and detect the suspected Nazis among the authentic prisoners. This he achieved with the help of two other Canadians, 'Flight Lieutenant Theodore "Tug" Wilson and Flying Officer Fred Hutchinson'. Together they flew in a Lancaster to a field near the camp and simulated a crash landing. The crew were promptly captured by the Germans and escorted to the prisoner-of-war camp, where they met the chairman of the escape committee, Squadron Leader Bushell. DuPre quickly caught out one suspect prisoner, and

> during the next three weeks DuPre and his Canadian colleagues turned in a dozen names to the Squadron Leader of men they had

caught in contradictions or lies. In all, the Squadron Leader had a
list of twenty-two Germans who had resorted to this unorthodox
method of escaping the consequences of their war crimes. . . . All
were rounded up and all stood trial at Nuremberg later on.[15]

Four weeks after his arrival, the Americans liberated the camp and
DuPre was flown back to England, where he underwent a further operation on his nose, which had been broken by the Gestapo in St Lô; he then
went to recuperate at the home in Derbyshire of the Marquis of
Kedleston. There he suffered a breakdown and an 'ambulance came
and sped him back to Taplo. . . . For five days he lay there unconscious,
part of his mind fighting madly to reassert the personality of Pierre
Touchette, while the other fought to re-establish George DuPre'.[16] Some
weeks of psychiatric care followed, and finally he was sent home to
Winnipeg.

Once back in Canada, he went to work for Commercial Chemicals and
became branch manager in Edmonton. In 1949, when Alberta's oil boom
was starting, DuPre was hired by the Minister of Mines, Nathan E.
Tanner, but three years later he was back with Commercial Chemicals in
Calgary. This was where he met Quentin Reynolds, to whom he told his
remarkable story.

Reynolds appears to have accepted DuPre's tale uncritically for he certainly overlooked a number of clues that ought to have alerted him to the
possibility that the 'gentle spy' was not all that he seemed. As regards the
mission itself, DuPre's account of his flight to France must have been in
error. The Lysander aircraft was an unarmed two-seater, and had neither
radio operator nor rear gunner. Nor was it possible to parachute from it,
and no agent ever did during the war. Also, whilst there were special
training establishments in the Oxfordshire countryside where agents
learned wireless techniques and other clandestine skills, such as Water
Eaton Manor (STS 50), Fawley Court (STS 54A) and Thame Park (STS
52), none fitted the description of the Oxford Home for Convalescents.
Because of the degree of secrecy still preserved in 1953 regarding
wartime secret operations, Reynolds may have been unable to conduct
the kind of checks that might have raised his suspicions. However, there
are still a few significant contradictions in the text that suggest all is not
well. Take, for example, DuPre's chronology of events. Although vague
about the exact timing of many episodes recounted in *The Man Who
Wouldn't Talk*, it is possible to calculate, from the date given for his flight

to France in February 1941, that his nine months of training must have commenced in May 1940. This is itself a little strange because at that time Normandy was not yet under German occupation, and the Touchette family was presumably still living together in their village. Elsewhere in the book there is a further contradiction, with the assertion that 'George . . . had arrived in 1940'.[17] There is a further oddity in DuPre's claim to have been a prisoner of the Gestapo in St Lô in late 1943, and in February 1944 to have been working in Hamburg for the past ten months. This latter statement would have placed DuPre in Germany from April 1943 onwards, precisely when he was supposed to have been operating for the French resistance around St Lô.

Apart from the chronological inconsistencies which make DuPre's story difficult to swallow, there are some other rather strange aspects to it. Why, for example, should MI9 have decided to select a Canadian with a poor knowledge of French, who had never lived in that country, for a long-term secret mission in Normandy? And if he was to be given a false identity, why that of someone who had really existed? And if there was some overriding reason to adopt an authentic identity, with all its attendant dangers, why that of a man known to be simple-minded?

Despite his distinguished credentials as a journalist, Reynolds was evidently so enchanted with DuPre's story that he failed to make the most rudimentary checks, by verifying whether any George DuPre was educated at Harrow and Cambridge, or even whether his father had held a commission in the Royal Artillery. Of those named in the book, only Brigadier Matthew Penhale was identified sufficiently to be traced. He had been GOC Western Area between 1947 and 1951, and when interviewed by Reynolds he explained that, although he had no recollection of the incident in which he was described as having debriefed DuPre at the Savoy Hotel in London, he certainly had met DuPre once or twice in Edmonton after the war and was prepared to rely on his memory. Reynolds also made contact with the British Embassy in Washington DC to confirm DuPre's credentials, but an unnamed spokesman said that 'MI5 does not comment on book material concerning former members'. When asked whether this reply amounted to a clearance, the spokesman suggested that the author 'used his own judgement'.

According to DuPre, by late 1943 he had helped '152 British and American airmen'[18] to reach safety, an astonishing total that, if true, made DuPre easily the single most successful organiser of any escape route in northern France at that time. The doubts only began to emerge when no aircrew came forward to confirm DuPre's assistance on their journey. Indeed, the only air-force officer to comment on him was someone who had served with him during the war . . . in Canada.

George DuPre was eventually exposed as a fraud by an RCAF officer who had worked alongside him at an airfield in Victoria, British Columbia, and who possessed proof in the form of a group photograph of six officers, including DuPre, taken on 9 June 1942. The picture, signed 'C. G. DuPre', had been taken at the very moment when he was supposed to have been operating undercover in France. Soon afterwards, another airman came forward with a menu card of a dinner held aboard the SS *Bayano* in mid-Atlantic on 4 March 1943. Like his RCAF colleagues accompanying him, DuPre had been on his way to attend an advanced RAF intelligence security course in England, and there was a record of his subsequent return to Canada in July 1943. Later, he was posted to England for a second time, in the role of an intelligence officer based at an airfield at Topcliffe, near Thirsk in Yorkshire, interviewing fliers who had returned after landing in enemy territory. Topcliffe was the main operating base controlling two other RCAF stations at Dalton and Dishforth and, although Topcliffe was a training centre for bomber crews, operational missions were flown from the neighbouring airfields. In December 1945, DuPre was posted to Winnipeg before his final discharge in February the following year.

However, until this startling evidence of DuPre's duplicity was uncovered, by a *Calgary Herald* journalist named Doug Collins, few questioned his story, in spite of the numerous flaws it contained. Collins had compared the Reynolds version of DuPre's activities in France with a newspaper report of a talk given by DuPre to the United Services Institute in Calgary in October 1951. In his original account, DuPre had mentioned that he had returned to London after his arrest and release by the Gestapo, and Collins's suspicions had been aroused by the change in chronology, which was not an insignificant one. He knew from his own wartime contacts with various branches of British Intelligence that no agent would have been allowed to return to operational duties after having been interrogated by the Gestapo. He reckoned that the Germans would only release an agent they had succeeded in turning, or someone whom they could keep under surveillance in the hope of being led to other conspirators. Either way, it would have been an appalling breach of security for the British to have allowed DuPre his liberty in France after his ordeal, and Collins had been mystified by the apparent lapse. When analysed in detail, other components of the tale failed to stand up to scrutiny.

Firstly, there was the issue of what British organisation had been able to infiltrate an agent into France in 1940, particularly when SOE had been unable to despatch anyone until May 1941. By December of that year, SOE had only succeeded in establishing twenty agents in France, all of them well documented. It certainly could not have been MI9, which was very late into the field and was unable to handle anything like the number of fliers suggested by DuPre until at least 1943.

Upon closer examination, very few of the details of DuPre's training or mission had sounded authentic. Most agents in preparation for their assignment received specialist training at several different locations, each a school concentrating on a particular skill. Thus, after a preliminary paramilitary course in the Highlands of Scotland, candidates were taught wireless telegraphy at a centre such as Thame Park, and tradecraft at an establishment known as a 'finishing school', which, for those destined for France, was located in Hampshire around Beaulieu. Parachuting was practised at RAF Ringway, outside Manchester. In DuPre's unique case, however, all these different disciplines had been accommodated on one site. The description of his fellow students, twenty-seven in all, was also rather odd. He recalled that six of them were to capture 'a radar set on the French coast', and while there was just such an operation, it did not take place until 1942, two years after the men supposedly had completed their training. There was also doubt about Archie Steele, another agent on the course, who, allegedly, was to adopt the identity of a dead Frenchman. Not only was there no record of any agent of that name, but none was despatched to France during 1940. And as for Samuel Rosen, another potential agent whom DuPre described as an estate agent in civilian life, and who supposedly was to be 'dropped into Germany'[19] to impersonate a German officer, no British agent was infiltrated into Germany until 1944.

Leaving aside the flaws in DuPre's account of his training, his arrival in France was certainly very unusual. Parachute operations over enemy-occupied territory fell into two categories: the so-called 'blind' drops, where agents landed in a predetermined area without any prearranged assistance on the ground; and the agreed rendezvous, where a reception committee was on hand with marker flares to prepare a dropping zone and flash a recognition signal to the approaching aircraft. Both procedures had their attendant advantages and risks. However, DuPre claimed to have been dropped within a matter of yards of his destination, but without any assistance from the ground. This would have been an extraordinary accomplishment, for navigation by night, even at the full moon, was a notoriously inaccurate undertaking in 1940, and blind drops were often scores of miles off target. To have achieved a blind drop into the exact field designated would have been improbable, if not impossible.

When DuPre's hoax was exposed, there was widespread dismay in Canada and the United States. Quentin Reynolds, when told at his home in Bedford Village, New York, said that he was 'shocked and appalled' by his friend's duplicity. Staff at the *Reader's Digest* headquarters in Pleasantville, New York, were equally surprised by the news and declared themselves to have been impressed by DuPre's 'sincerity, integrity and modesty'. Meanwhile, Random House relabelled the book as fiction and offered to refund the purchase price to disappointed customers. There were few takers, but Quentin Reynolds's reputation never recovered fully from the humiliation. DuPre swiftly disappeared from Calgary and was last heard of living quietly in retirement in Victoria, British Columbia. However, as the first significant fabricator of a tale of wartime espionage, he had achieved a memorable, if dubious, first.

For those who were later to argue that no one would be foolish enough to make extravagant claims about their wartime activities for fear of being denounced by officialdom, DuPre's experience demonstrated that, however absurd the story, traditional British secrecy can be relied upon to prevent any public comment, positive or negative, from Whitehall sources. In the absence of any kind of denial, the hoaxer can flourish, and in subsequent years there were to be numerous examples of authors making completely bogus claims to having participated in secret operations.

Indeed, DuPre took quite a risk fabricating his story so soon after the end of the war, when he must have realised that there were still plenty of people around who had been in a position to have known the true facts of his wartime service. However, in later years this risk lessened, with memories fading and the number with first-hand knowledge diminishing. The problem of explaining to friends, family and former colleagues how an individual came to be in two places at once, typically undertaking dangerous missions abroad while apparently fulfilling a rather more mundane task in an office, is sometimes explained by what might be termed the 'double identity' phenomenon. In DuPre's case, it was quite unsophisticated, with the spy covering his absence abroad by writing dozens of letters to his wife, which, he asserted, had really been written in advance and then posted at regular intervals by his employers. In fact, this practice was not uncommon, but the letters were usually very banal, comprising one or two lines intended to reassure a family of an agent's continued good health. Poor co-ordination occasionally allowed such a message to be mailed soon after news of an entirely different kind had been broken to the family, that of his (or her) death.

Most of the stories manufactured by the fantasists contain some common denominators, the principal one manifested by DuPre being the appalling torture he says he underwent. He gave a graphic description of his maltreatment at the hands of the Gestapo in St Lô, in which he suffered a broken nose in a beating and the fracture of an index finger snapped in a carpentry vice. Portraying the Gestapo as brutal sadists merely conformed to a well-established stereotype, and even when certain atrocities proved impossible to verify, few were willing to query the detail. In DuPre's account, he mentioned a certain 'Oberst Franz Genthner of the Gestapo', someone who could not have been a member of that notorious organisation with a Wehrmacht rank. In reality, if Genthner had ever existed, he would have held the rank equivalent to colonel, or obersturmbanführer.

As we shall see, the fabricators are invariably exhorted by their superiors on the subject of secrecy, and use this motive as an excuse to conceal vital components of their stories, which, if revealed, would probably expose the fraud. Usually the figures who demand pledges of lifelong secrecy are major historical characters, typically Winston Churchill, but they may also be men of lesser stature whose names have appeared in an intelligence context in recently published books. In this respect, DuPre was the odd-man-out, mentioning only Brigadier Penhale by his correct name and rank. Curiously, though in a position to do so, Brigadier Penhale was unwilling to denounce DuPre, perhaps because he did not wish to be the only person to undermine a man perceived then as an unsung hero, Canada possessing few enough of that precious commodity. However, such inhibitions may have encouraged others to follow DuPre's example. In any event, the combination of a ubiquitous, ruthless British intelligence service, the Gestapo's atrocious misconduct and a continuing need for absolute secrecy were to be recurring themes in subsequent stories, all presented as absolute fact.

Not long after the DuPre affair, Quentin Reynolds was back in the news, embroiled in another controversy. Reynolds had participated in the ill-fated Dieppe raid in August 1942 as an observer, and subsequently had disclosed that an electronics expert named 'Professor Wendell' had undertaken a secret mission while Canadian troops had engaged the enemy on the beaches. The syndicated columnist Westbrook Pegler denounced the Reynolds story as 'a quirk of your mind, a falsification of your own vivid imagination'.

Despite the damage his reputation had sustained because of the DuPre fiasco, Reynolds sued for libel and won $175,000 in damages when Colonel Jock Laurence, a former member of the Combined Operations staff, not only confirmed that there had been a scientific aspect to the raid, but also identified to the judge the name of the technician involved. As we shall see, this particular episode was to be of some significance in demonstrating that another account of the same operation had been fabricated by another author.

2

Count Five and Die

'If he were caught by the Gestapo or the dreaded Milice all he
had to do was to bite on the button, swallow, count five and
die.'[1]

In 1958, intelligence literature was very limited, and relatively little had
been published about the wartime exploits of secret agents. A few personal memoirs had been written about SOE, but the survivors of that
organisation had not yet been engulfed by the controversies that were to
surround them when details of the more successful German penetra-
tions in France and Holland were disclosed. Nor had there been any
authoritative accounts of the work of the British Security Service in
rounding up enemy spies and turning them into double agents. As for
strategic deception, the entire topic remained classified. This, then, was
the relative vacuum in which the author Barry Wynne produced *Count
Five and Die*, a non-fiction account of a wartime espionage case in which
a senior member of the US Office of Strategic Services, Colonel William
Eliscu OBE, had participated. Its publication in England and Canada
coincided with a Twentieth Century-Fox movie of the same title directed
by Victor Vicas.

In the foreword to *Count Five and Die*, the author stated that 'this is a
true account within the dictates of public security of a principally
American operation to deceive the enemy in the three months prior to
the landings in Normandy' based on material supplied by Colonel Eliscu,
'one of General Donovan's aides'.[2] The story itself opened in the spring
of 1943 and described how a lissom blonde Abwehr agent named Hannie

Herodsen had succeeded in cultivating many indiscreet American friends in Algiers, and had learned enough from men of the 26th 77th OSS Group stationed at the Villa Magnol to transmit a signal warning the Abwehr of the imminent invasion of Sicily. Aged twenty-eight, vivacious and intelligent, Hannie posed as a Dutch refugee from Amsterdam and had become a regular guest on the American cocktail-party circuit in Algiers, where she had met a young lieutenant-colonel.

> It is not suggested, of course, that this colonel had willingly passed on any vital information, but the fact that he drank heavily and had probably in those unguarded moments fallen victim to the sensuous attraction of this 'Dutch' girl did not relieve him of his responsibilities to his country.[3]

When the X-2 counter-intelligence branch of OSS became suspicious of Hannie's activities, the local head of the Secret Intelligence division, described as 'Stephen Martinelli, a cold calculating American of Italian descent'[4] and a lawyer by training, initiated an investigation into her background. However, before any action could be taken, Hannie disappeared, taken at night by Arab dhow to a U-boat and returned to the European mainland, where she caught a flight to Berlin.

By March 1944, Hannie had been assigned a new mission by her Chief, Ernst Kaltenbrunner: she was to go to England by submarine to discover what she could about the Allies' invasion plans. She was put 'ashore in a collapsible dinghy close to the little town of Winchelsea'[5] in Kent. On the beach she was met by her contact, a commercial traveller and Welsh Nationalist named Jimmy Foster, who drove her in his van to a London flat he had rented for her in Clifton Villas, Maida Vale. Hannie was to continue to masquerade as a Dutch refugee and for the benefit of her landlady was to pretend to be Foster's fiancée. She was also to take command of an existing spy network, which included Foster and at least two others: a businessman named Bruno Baber, who ran a pharmaceutical company in the East End of London, and Kurt Radmin, a radio operator who 'since the early thirties had rented a consulting room in Wimpole Street'.[6]

At this stage Barry Wynne explained the current position of the security authorities in London:

There were a number of enemy agents operating in London and

various parts of the British Isles who were permitted to continue functioning, working on the theory that the devil you know is better than the devil you don't know. By tapping their 'phones and keeping them under constant surveillance, they guided us to many spies who had, up to that moment, remained undetected. When new German agents came to Britain they were virtually forced to contact one another. . . . But, as it happened, Jimmy Foster was unknown to MI5 or, in fact, the CID.[7]

It should be remembered that this explanation was given in 1958, *fourteen years before* Sir John Masterman released his seminal work on the Security Service's manipulation of double agents, *The Double Cross System in the War of 1939–45*.[8] Thus, the references to MI5 had rather more than a ring of truth to them, even if some of the details were, as we shall see, slightly inaccurate. However, although MI5 had failed to notice Baber, it knew of Radmin's 'activities and preferred to let him continue'.[9]

When Wynne returned to the narrative, he explained that Hannie had been given a complicated cover story to explain her absence in Germany between her departure from Algiers and her recent arrival in London. She was to pretend that she had driven across the length of Africa to Cape Town, where she had acted as a nanny to a French family, and had then taken a passage in a Dutch ship to Liverpool. The author pointed out that 'the greatest weakness in her story was the fact that she had never been to Cape Town',[10] so as a precaution she had been coached by a German who knew the city well, and her name had been inserted into a ship's manifest by a German agent. This, however, did not really deal with what presumably was a much greater hazard, the absence of any of the customary landing documentation from the authorities in Liverpool to authorise her arrival in Britain.

Despite the apparent handicap of no official stamps in her passport, within ten days of her arrival in London Hannie had acquired an interpreter's job in an unnamed ministry located near Tottenham Court Road. She also found herself invited to a party by an OSS officer who shared an office with Stephen Martinelli, the intelligence officer from Algiers, who, coincidentally, had been posted to General Eisenhower's headquarters in London. He was 'one of only three men in London' to know that Hannie was 'in fact a top German agent',[11] and an elaborate deception scheme was prepared for her benefit 'as it was now obvious that Herodsen was out to crack the date and place of Operation Overlord'.[12]

The plan required an unsuspecting OSS officer, Captain Dan Russell, to become intimate with her and then to use him as a conduit through which to pass her inaccurate information about the imminent invasion to the enemy. 'There was very little time to lose. Although the actual date of Operation Overlord was not then known, it was almost sure to fall some time during the first two weeks of June, where the moon and tide phases were right.'[13] The method chosen to boost Russell's standing with Hannie was to send him on a five-day mission to occupied France to brief resistance leaders on their role in the invasion. He was 'to contact several groups in order to find out just to what state of preparedness they have managed to reach and tell them that within the next few months an invasion will be launched from Britain'.[14] Russell was told that he was to be parachuted near to the town of Laval, and the same evening he promptly passed on the news of his mission to Hannie, who in turn relayed it to Berlin .

Russell's instructions took him to an RAF field in Suffolk for 'a Jedburgh' flight to France in 'T for Tommy',[15] one of twelve Lancaster bombers due to raid the docks at St Nazaire. En route the aircraft would be diverted over Laval so that Russell could be dropped to the local *maquis*. Once on the ground Russell was met by a resistance leader named Gaston, who introduced him to 'the highly important Maurice Camus' at Chantilly. 'To culminate his series of meetings, he met Colonel Passy just outside Paris'[16] and then returned to England by Lysander, having been collected from an airstrip near Fougères.

Thanks to Hannie's tip, Ernst Kaltenbrunner knew about Russell's trip to France very quickly, and he received 'confirmation from the Gestapo headquarters in Paris that an American had been in contact with the *maquis* in Chantilly not twenty-four hours previously'.[17] Similarly, 'a message had reached OSS headquarters from one of their permanent agents in Cherbourg that apparently all local Gestapo in northern France had been warned to watch out for the possible landing of an American agent in their area',[18] which seemed to Martinelli to confirm neatly that Hannie had indeed supplied the enemy with details of Russell's mission.

Russell's safe return enabled him to participate, albeit unconsciously, in a further scheme, Operation STAMPEDE. This sophisticated deception required a special Dutch liaison office to be opened under commercial cover so that Hannie, who had become Russell's mistress, could be employed as a translator and be given access to plans for an Allied invasion of Holland. The intention was to employ an SOE officer, a peacetime lawyer named Major Julian Howard, to head the unit, which would be disguised as 'Arista Productions Limited', a documentary film company with premises on the top two floors of 69 Wardour Street. As well as six Dutch nationals who were to be engaged on the preparation of propaganda material, the unit would maintain a short-wave link to the Dutch resistance and conduct briefings for its members, who would be brought over to London for indoctrination.

That this was a risky enterprise was apparently appreciated by Martinelli and Howard, who knew that 'for something like twenty months the Germans actually ran the SOE operations in Holland. They captured forty-odd agents, worked their radios',[19] and penetrated the Allied networks, but OSS was undeterred. As a first step, a key resistance leader named Henk Janssen was brought by motor launch to Harwich and escorted to Arista's offices by Russell. There he was informed that Holland was to be D-Day's target, and he 'not only became completely convinced but also highly enthusiastic'.[20] Janssen was described as a businessman from Amsterdam and, after he had been briefed, he was introduced to the other members of Russell's unit, including Hannie Herodsen. This apparently caused Howard some anguish, especially when Russell asked whether Janssen had been supplied with a suicide capsule before he embarked upon his return journey. Prudently, Russell had queried the wisdom of Howard's intention 'to send this man back into Holland with all the information he's been given without the safe-guard of a cyanide pill'.[21] Howard's dilemma apparently centred on Hannie's treachery:

It was a hideous thought, for, if Hannie Herodsen told Berlin, there was a good chance that Janssen would be picked up. On the other hand, the Germans might prefer to leave him free in order to see what was afoot. It was a hard decision, a soldier's decision, and Howard wished that he could shirk it. But time wasn't on their side. Soon, thousands upon thousands of British, American, French and Dutch soldiers would be storming ashore and his job was to deflect part of the opposing army. This could not be done without sacrifice.[22]

Evidently Dan Russell's worst fears were realised, for two days later he was informed by Howard that Janssen had been arrested by the Germans 'the day after he arrived'.

It was not until after the war that the full tragedy of Janssen was revealed. He had withstood the torture for eight long and dreadful hours before finally giving in. He talked and the Germans received their first inkling of the Allied intention.[23]

As a footnote to this grisly episode, Wynne recorded that Janssen's family 'received a monetary settlement from the United States of America'[24] as compensation for their loss. Thus the bogus Allied intention to launch the invasion of Europe across the North Sea to Holland was conveyed to the enemy, and the almost identical operation was repeated again soon afterwards. Apparently undeterred by the loss of Janssen and the confirmation that Operation OVERLORD had been compromised, a second agent was brought to London, this time by Lysander aircraft 'to a tiny airfield near Crawley Down'.[25] There Russell met Jan Bakker, a *Havenmeester* from near Rotterdam, who had been recommended by Janssen as 'a man who had intimate knowledge of the coast and dockside installations, both at Rotterdam and other Dutch seaports'.[26] Although not 'an active member of a resistance group',[27] Bakker was driven to London and interviewed by Howard, who, having discovered that the harbourmaster spoke practically no English, arranged for Hannie Herodsen to act as their interpreter. It was at this stage that Howard himself had some second thoughts:

Surely he wasn't expected to send another man to his death? What on earth would Russell say? Surely he would become suspicious. He was an intelligent man, he'd soon put two and two together, to realise that we were in fact anxious that the Germans should learn of our supposedly secret plans for the invasion of Holland.[28]

Howard's solution was to despatch the awkward Russell to an invasion planning conference at Dover Castle while Bakker was debriefed by two American naval intelligence officers. Then, having reassured Russell that Bakker would be equipped with cyanide before his departure, Howard escorted the Dutch harbourmaster back to the airfield for a flight home, but not without experiencing a sense of foreboding:

He had an intuitive feeling that the fate that had met Janssen was only round the corner for his travelling companion. It was an indescribable way to send a man to his death. The following

Sunday, before he had even got back to his work, Jan Bakker was seized by the Gestapo and taken to Mauthausen. . . . He was a stubborn man but they had eventually succeeded in making him talk. He admitted having just returned from London and virtually confirmed all the details extracted from Janssen. It was apparent that he had supplied the enemy with considerable information regarding coastal defences.[29]

With Janssen and Bakker's information, extracted after 'nearly eleven hours of persuasion before they finally broke down',[30] the Germans proceeded to reinforce their defences in the Netherlands. 'The following day in May 1944, orders were given to send extra troops to Holland. Some of them came from as far away as Novara in Northern Italy', and units of the Waffen SS were redeployed from the Russian Front, 'so Operation Stampede began to have effect and the sacrifices were not in vain'.[31] To emphasise the point, Wynne identified some of the enemy forces that had been moved into Holland during May, apparently in response to STAMPEDE:

The 347th Division were put in to defend the coast between Helder and Alkmaar in Noord Holland. The 719th Division were centred on Haarlem and the 165th Division defended the coast at The Hague. The 19th Panzer Division and the headquarters of the German Air Command were located in the centre of Holland. The 16th GAF [German air force] were located to the north and to the west of Amsterdam and still additional troops were being sent in by the German High Command. The 1st SS Panzer Division was just south of the Dutch border and there was also a strong concentration of troops in the Scheldt Estuary. Besides these active infantry divisions, there were thousands of troops garrisoning the rest of Holland and the OKW [the Wehrmacht High Command] Reserve, consisting of another four panzer divisions, were being re-fitted across the borders in Germany, having been withdrawn from the Eastern Front. As the last days of May rapidly drew to a close, there were upwards of a hundred thousand troops within the borders of Holland.[32]

It is at this stage that Barry Wynne's story takes a bizarre twist. Notwithstanding the counter-measures allegedly taken by the Germans

to repulse the expected Allied offensive, Hannie's two contacts took the
initiative on 31 May and kidnapped the daughter of Dr Mulder, described
as a professor of history at the University of The Hague who had been
recruited into Dan Russell's deception team. Radmin and Baber snatched
the young Gerda Mulder on her way home from school and imprisoned
her in Radmin's consulting rooms on the first floor of 25 Wimpole Street.
Using her as bait to lure her father into a trap, Radmin took them both to
a house in Bray, Berkshire, leaving Baber behind to receive an OSS
search party. In the struggle that followed, Baber was shot dead. Another
raid was then mounted on Southdown Cottage, Bray, an address that had
been disclosed by Baber before he received his fatal wound. Although Dr
Mulder was rescued, Radmin was shot dead and Gerda was found to
have 'died of a weak heart accelerated by shock'. However,

> Poor Dr Mulder was completely broken and utterly inconsolable.
> He had now lost not only everyone he had in the world but also
> his pride, for he had betrayed the supposed secret of the D-Day
> landings and thereby in his own eyes he was a traitor to his coun-
> try and all that he held dear.[33]

Meanwhile, at news of the fracas in Berkshire, Hannie had returned
to her flat in Clifton Villas and transmitted a signal to Germany on an
ingenious wireless concealed inside a small box of chocolates. This
remarkable apparatus, rightly described by Barry Wynne as 'a feat of
engineering', encoded the text on to a magnetised wire tape and then
broadcast it 'in three-fifths of a second'.[34] Her message alerted the
Germans to an imminent Allied landing on the coast north of The Hague
and an airborne assault in the Utrecht area.

Despite the loss of Radmin and Baber, Hannie apparently continued to
work for Russell's deception unit and even scored one final coup: the theft
of the Allied plans for D-Day from Howard's private safe. Using a 'key to
the safe that had been manufactured in Berlin from a wax cast'[35] and a
Minox camera, she slipped into his office on 2 June 1944 and 'hastily
photographed, page by page, the official plans from SHAEF [Supreme
Headquarters, Allied Expeditionary Force] for the invasion of Holland'.[36]
Then she transmitted a final signal to Germany from her flat before fleeing
the country. Wynne concludes his story by relating that Hannie Herodsen
'was executed three weeks after her arrival home on the personal orders
of Kaltenbrunner'[37] because her information had been proved inaccurate

when the Allied invasion occurred in France, not Holland. Dr Mulder eventually returned to Holland with a liberal pension, but subsequently hanged himself in a country barn. As for Dan Russell, who had been living with Hannie for 'three or four months',[38] he was decorated for his contribution to the success of STAMPEDE and shipped home.

At the time Wynne's book was released, very little had been published on the subject of wartime intelligence operations, although the existence of SOE and MI5, of course, had been acknowledged publicly. However, only a tiny amount of material relating to strategic deception or German espionage had been made public. In fact, the open source literature (as opposed to the classified histories locked in secret archives) was really confined to the individual memoirs written by various participants. In this genre were the recollections of Maurice Buckmaster, head of SOE's F Section, recounted in *Specially Employed*[39] and *They Fought Alone*,[40] and of some of his agents, particularly Peter Churchill, Ben Cowburn and George Millar. However, not all the stories conformed to the stereotypical adventures of brave secret agents dropping into enemy territory and avoiding capture by the Gestapo. In parallel a more critical tradition had developed, with researchers delving into the murky depths of the enemy's counter-intelligence operations. Details of SOE's disastrous activities in Holland had been disclosed already by Peter Dourlein, who wrote *Inside North Pole*[41] in 1953, and by Herman Giskes, who produced his own version of the same episode, but from the Abwehr's standpoint, entitled *London Calling North Pole*,[42] in the same year. Both had described how SOE's Dutch Section had been duped by the Germans and had been persuaded to send dozens of young men straight into the enemy's hands. The catastrophe had prompted at least two internal enquiries in London, the results of which have never been published, as well as a comprehensive investigation conducted over two years by a Dutch Parliamentary Commission soon after the cessation of hostilities. At the conclusion of the latter, the Netherlands Government accepted that, despite the rumours, there was no evidence of treachery at SOE's headquarters, and that there had merely been a series of mistakes, each serving to compound the next. The Foreign Office in London issued a terse statement which indicates the gravity of the accusations: 'The suggestion that the lives of Dutch patriots were deliberately sacrificed in the interests of other objectives, in the Netherlands or elsewhere, is considered repugnant by HM Government and the British people.'[43] Nevertheless, the controversy continued, with a suspicion that the

Germans had succeeded in planting a spy inside SOE's London headquarters.

This was an especially sensitive issue, and the British security authorities went to considerable lengths to discover whether there was any foundation for the belief that penetration really had occurred. Certainly SOE had not been immune to the attentions of hostile intelligence agencies, and a member of the Hungarian sub-section, Captain Ormond L. Uren, had been arrested in September 1943 and imprisoned for passing SOE's secrets to the Soviets. But had the Germans achieved the same degree of success? This was the issue that MI5 had attempted to resolve by bringing captured senior Abwehr personnel, including Colonel Giskes, to London for interrogation. None had admitted having recruited any useful sources, but, regardless of the lack of evidence, the rumours persisted.

One reason for the apparent willingness of the Dutch to ascribe their losses to treachery rather than to incompetence was their pre-war experience at the frontier post at Venlo, an incident that had compromised the neutrality of the Netherlands and had left a Dutch intelligence officer dying of wounds. The tragic affair had happened in November 1939 while two SIS officers, Sigismund Best and Richard Stevens, attempted to rendezvous at the border with a man whom they believed to be a disaffected Luftwaffe general. The preparations for the meeting had been made in conjunction with the Dutch military intelligence service, which had provided the operation with a liaison officer named Dirk Klop. However, at the appointed time, when Best, Stevens and Klop had approached the boundary between Holland and Germany, a group of well-armed Germans had burst through the frontier and seized the two Britons. In the *mêlée* that followed, Klop had been shot and the SIS men had been dragged back across the border into Germany, where they eventually re-emerged five and a half years later. The entire episode had been a profound embarrassment to the supposedly neutral Dutch, and evidence accumulated after the war from captured enemy documents had demonstrated that the Abwehr had always possessed a very detailed picture of SIS's activities in Holland, to the extent that they had taken photographs of virtually all SIS's Dutch assets and had collated a vast amount of biographical detail on personnel operating from its various cover addresses in Amsterdam, Rotterdam and The Hague. But how had they acquired such a comprehensive understanding of what the British had been up to, and had the degree of clandestine Anglo-Dutch collaboration compromised the country's neutrality?

The Dutch were understandably sensitive on this issue, and various candidates were suggested as those responsible for the intelligence failure, which, in the judgment of some, had continued seamlessly from the fiasco at Venlo to SOE's loss of many brave agents later in the war. The fact that British personnel known to have been compromised at Venlo had been retained as Dutch experts by the British intelligence services was regarded as either foolhardy or, worse, a manifestation of calculated treachery. For example, Lionel Loewe, the SIS liaison officer who had actually been in the office of the Dutch Director of Military Intelligence when news of the Venlo incident had first reached The Hague, had subsequently transferred to SOE, where he had played a leading role in the Dutch Section. Similarly the Hooper brothers, one of whom was widely (but wrongly) thought to have been a source for the Abwehr pre-war, had been employed in an intelligence function as an interrogator in London throughout the war. Neither of these appointments was calculated to inspire Dutch confidence in the British authorities, especially when Herman Giskes alleged that after the war he had seen John Hooper at MI5's detention centre in London. The implication was that Hooper had been a prisoner, undergoing interrogation, but in fact Hooper had been an inquisitor on the staff there. As well as Hooper and Loewe, whose activities received wholly unjustified criticism, there was further vilification for the more senior SOE management who supervised the Dutch Section. In particular, Seymour Bingham and Charles Blizard, both successive heads of the section, were castigated for their role in what the Germans termed '*Der Englandspiel*' and Operation NORTH POLE.

Dutch paranoia on the subject of treachery had also been fuelled by mischievous suggestions that, far from being a tragic miscalculation, the double-cross operations run so successfully by the Germans had in fact been part of a sophisticated deception scheme masterminded from London by especially ruthless practitioners of the art, who had deliberately sacrificed Dutch lives in a misguided attempt to lend their Machiavellian project added credibility. Although there had never been any evidence to support such a proposition, there were those who were inclined to believe the very worst of the British Secret Service and who were entirely prepared to accept that perfidious Albion's most nefarious warriors had been willing to further their Byzantine plots by deliberately sacrificing pawns . . . especially foreign pawns. In the film version of *Count Five and Die*, there is no ambiguity whatever regarding the sensitive topic of agents being despatched to their certain death by their British case officer, Major Howard. Two Dutchmen, armed with disinformation, are sent into the enemy's hands without the customary suicide pill.

In contrast to the relative wealth of information publicly available about SOE, which finally had been wound up in June 1946, not much was known in 1958 about MI5 or SIS. Both agencies continued to exist, which was the reason for the policy of non-disclosure, but there had been a few references to what is now termed strategic deception. Indeed, Churchill himself commented briefly on the elaborate invasion cover plans, a point noted by Barry Wynne, who reproduced this relevant passage from Churchill's *The Second World War*: 'Our deception measures both before and after D-Day had aimed at confused thinking. Their success was admirable and had far-reaching results on the battle.'[44]

It was into this vacuum of knowledge about Allied deception measures taken in preparation for D-Day that in 1958 Barry Wynne dropped his tale of Hannie Herodsen, a story supposedly authenticated by a senior American officer who boasted the credentials of first-hand experience of the OSS and a respected British military decoration. As an authoritative account of the deliberate manipulation of an enemy spy, and the intentional despatch of two Dutch patriots to certain death, *Count Five and Die* confirmed the worst fears of the conspiracy theorists who had long suspected that Holland's losses had not been entirely accidental.

Clearly *Count Five and Die* purports to raise some important issues about the ethics of wartime intelligence operations, but upon further research the author's principal source, 'Colonel William Eliscu OBE', is not quite what is claimed. Although Captain William Eliscu did serve in the 267th Regiment, the OSS cover unit in the Mediterranean theatre, there is no record of his promotion beyond the rank of captain nor of his ever having received any British award, and certainly not an honorary Order of the British Empire. To the Veterans of OSS, an organisation based in New York which looks after the interests of the agency's survivors, Bill Eliscu is a well-known and colourful character who has variously promoted a film series about OSS's exploits, worked for Madame Nhu in the Far East and, most recently, attempted to franchise private hospitals in Texas and obtain financial backing for a movie based on the Shah of Iran from his widow, a venture that ended with claims of civil fraud in the California courts by the Robert Armao Company and with Eliscu being declared bankrupt. In short, Eliscu is an unlikely candidate as a reliable source for Wynne's remarkable work of what purports to be non-fiction. Thus the question remains: how much of Wynne's story is really true? Did Hannie Herodsen exist, and were Dutch agents deliberately sent to their deaths to enhance an Allied deception scheme?

As to whether a German spy arrived in England in 1944 undetected and remained in control of an undiscovered network of enemy agents, it is possible to be quite emphatic because, although little had been written on this topic in 1958, a great deal of relevant material has since been released from official sources. In 1972, Masterman's *The Double Cross System in the War of 1939–45* disclosed the very comprehensive nature of the Security Service's control over such German spies that ventured to these shores. Far from allowing a few agents their liberty so that their activities could be monitored, MI5 had wisely adopted a policy of detaining and interrogating every suspect, and freeing only those who had demonstrated their willingness to collaborate. Even then a very strict regime of supervision had been imposed, and the record shows that only two agents of German origin had been allowed any measure of freedom. They were Wulf Schmidt (codenamed *Tate*) and *Dragonfly*, who was born in London of German parents. *Gander*, a parachute agent who operated for only a few weeks in October 1940, had remained in custody throughout his brief term of usefulness, as had the other double agents with close family connections to the Reich.

It could, of course, be argued that the details of Hannie Herodsen, Bruno Baber and Kurt Radmin had been omitted from Masterman's book because they had remained uncontrolled, and although supposedly used as a conduit to convey disinformation to the enemy, they had never fallen into the category of double agents handled by MI5. However, if this were truly the case, one would at the very least expect to find references to them in the official history of the wartime Security Service. Certainly there were agents who had rowed ashore on the coast of Kent, but the five who arrived in 1940 had been caught within a matter of hours of their arrival. None, so far as is known, had slipped on to the beach in 1944. It is also true that there were several Abwehr spies who had established themselves in London before hostilities, but all had become known to MI5 by means of the control the counter-espionage branch exercised over certain key agents, notably Arthur Owens. This Welsh Nationalist had been appointed the Abwehr's principal asset in England in 1939 and, during the months that followed, he had been able to alert his MI5 case officers to several other German spies. However, none resembles the description given of Baber or Radmin. Nor were two German spies killed in any shooting incidents in England during the war. Although some popular writers have hinted at secret executions, the full process of the criminal law was applied to all those who were sentenced to death, even if their trials (and one court-martial) were held *in camera*. Meticulous records were kept of each, and death certificates were issued in every case. But even if the actual details were inaccurate, was it true that Hannie Herodsen had infiltrated Britain at a crucial time and then had evaded capture? Had Bill Eliscu told Barry Wynne a slightly garbled version of the work of MI5's double agents?

Admittedly in 1958 no word had yet filtered out from official circles about the degree of success achieved by MI5 in countering enemy espionage. Masterman's account, though in existence, was not to receive wide circulation for a further decade. Yet Wynne confidently asserted, correctly, that a number of Abwehr agents had fallen under MI5's control, and that among them had been a Welsh Nationalist, the spy known to Hannie Herodsen as Jimmy Foster. In reality, if Foster was supposed to be Owens (codenamed *Snow* by MI5), Eliscu must have skewed the story further, because in 1940 the Welshman had been regarded as unreliable and had been imprisoned and kept in strict isolation. Thus, when Hannie Herodsen was allegedly meeting her Welsh Nationalist contact near Winchelsea, Owens was actually languishing on Dartmoor and had been abandoned by the Abwehr.

It seems likely that although Eliscu may have heard something of what MI5 had accomplished, he had been obliged to rely on guesswork for Wynne's reconstruction. There may be a similar explanation for Operation STAMPEDE, a deception which appears nowhere in any of the recently declassified official papers. Whilst there is a wealth of evidence concerning the scheme codenamed FORTITUDE, which was intended to divert enemy attention away from Normandy and persuade the Germans that the long-expected invasion was destined for the Pas de Calais region, there was no parallel plan to promote Holland as a target for an amphibious or airborne assault. Once again, it is clear that Eliscu must have heard that some ingenious arrangements had been made to dupe the German High Command about Allied intentions, as indeed had been the case, but apparently he had been insufficiently well-placed to learn of the measures taken to enhance the conclusions reached by the enemy's intelligence analysts who had plumped for the shortest route across the Channel as the most likely Allied plan.

On the basis that there was a limited amount of truth behind Wynne's confident assertion that double agents had been manipulated to convey misleading information concerning D-Day to the enemy, and that the Allies had indeed conducted a skilful deception operation to conceal their true intentions, what value should be placed on the most damaging proposition, that at least two Dutch agents had been deliberately sacrificed?

The suggestion that Allied commanders were occasionally obliged to wrestle with their consciences while brave men were sent to their graves in support of an objective of greater significance is a theme that has entered the mythology of the Second World War. The claim that Churchill had received a warning that the city of Coventry was to be attacked by the Luftwaffe on 14 November 1940 is a classic of the genre, a *canard* initially (and inadvertently) created by Group Captain F. W. Winterbotham in *The Ultra Secret*,[45] and subsequently embroidered by many others. Similarly, the journalist Anthony Cave Brown perpetuated the legend that advance notice of the disastrous Bomber Command raid on Nuremberg in March 1944 had been leaked deliberately so as to increase the status of a particular British double agent.[46] The idea that individual agents had been supplied with disinformation in the hope that they would fall into enemy hands and reluctantly disclose their knowledge is equally controversial and has been pursued on several occasions, most recently by Robert Marshall, who opined in *All the King's Men*[47] that SOE had been misled into supporting a deception scheme in 1943. The theory, hotly disputed by historians, rests on the idea that an entire SOE network in France was discarded in a futile attempt to persuade the enemy that a second front was imminent, and thereby relieve the Wehrmacht's pressure on the Soviet Red Army. The accusation that the PROSPER *réseau* had been the unwitting victim of a Machiavellian scheme was originally proposed in 1959 by Charles Wighton in *Pinstripe Saboteur*,[48] and was followed up two years later by Jean Overton Fuller in *Double Agent?*.[49] Professor Foot for one has strong views on the matter and in his official history, *SOE in France*, states: 'it is undoubtedly the case that no use was made of SOE's work in France for any purposes of deception,' adding, perhaps revealingly, that 'no one trusted the agents enough for such delicate tasks'.[50] However, in an apparent contradiction, Foot himself had previously cited an example of how SOE's French Section had indeed been used in a deception scheme in 1943:

Twice that autumn the BBC broadcast warning messages to
every active SOE circuit in France, indicating that the invasion
would come within a fortnight; but the action messages that
should have followed, on the night of the landing, were not sent.
The warnings formed a small part of the deception plan that covered the Italian surrender and the Salerno assault (8 and 9
September). No doubt word that these warnings had gone out
was passed round, too far for the safety of resistance circuits, so
that the Germans heard of it; for this the indiscretions of local
sub-agents were responsible.[51]

Foot clearly understood the import of this allegedly unique incident,
for he commented: 'The staff concerned with deception relied on indiscretion, and might have thought more about safety,'[52] indicating that he
believed such behaviour placed lives at risk for a relatively trivial objective. Evidently the planners had thought that if they failed to send the
second signal, calling the *résistants* to immediate action, there was little
harm in the initial transmission, which might accomplish what was
intended. This rationalisation, of course, took no account of conditions in
the field, where individual circuit members might be willing to attempt
the foolhardy, safe in the mistaken knowledge that Allied deliverance
was imminent. Whether this occurred in the example of the SCIENTIST
organisation, cited by Foot, is unknown, but his rebuke is unmistakable,
even if he was less critical of the circumstances in which some French
SOE agents are known to have perished.

The French tragedy had occurred in June 1943, when the Gestapo
had attempted to communicate with London on no less than four captured transmitters. The 'wireless game' (*funkspiele*) was detected by
SOE's headquarters staff, and the decision was taken to exploit the radio
link by making the Germans believe that their ruse had been successful.
Colonel Robert Bourne-Paterson, who refers to this episode in his secret
account of F Section's activities in France written in 1946, says only that
the enemy 'were encouraged to believe that we were unaware of the
extent of their penetration', but confirms that 'deliveries of stores were
continued to circuits known to be Gestapo-operated'.[53] This astonishing
admission, that SOE had deliberately supplied networks known to be
enemy-controlled, amounts to a deception scheme, whatever definition of
the term is used. Foot himself concedes the point, observing that 'it was
in fact a quite sound piece of deceptive activity'.[54] However, the situation

was to get out of hand, for the Germans had been rather more adept at deception techniques than the British had given them credit for, and their control of F Section circuits had extended far beyond the four captured radios, to the *réseaux* known as PHONO, BUTLER and ARCHDEACON. Because SOE had failed to spot the German penetration in time, several agents had been delivered straight into the hands of the Gestapo, which had manned reception committees to greet the parachute agents. In recording these events, Foot insists that 'it was certainly never any part of F Section's intention to send them straight to their death; nor indeed were their deaths intended by anybody else on the Allied side',[55] and this is an important distinction. These 'unfortunates' were victims of an all-too-successful enemy deception, which had gone unnoticed by SOE, rather than part of a deliberate scheme ruthlessly masterminded in London. So although F Section agents had been dropped accidentally to the Gestapo, none had been despatched with the intention that they should be captured. Whereas it might have been possible, in Barry Wynne's scenario, to convey some item of disinformation by sacrificing one or perhaps two low-level, unimportant agents, the catastrophe that had befallen SOE's circuits in 1943 had involved some very senior personnel. France Antelme (*Antoine* of DONKEYMAN), Lionel Lee (*Mechanic* of PHONO) and Alec Rabinovitch (*Arnaud* of BARGEE) were all experienced agents who had already operated successfully in occupied territory. All had fallen victim to the German double game, as had Madeleine Damerment (*Solange* in BRICKLAYER), and they had all perished in Nazi concentration camps.

In retrospect, it would seem that SOE's involvement in deception schemes had invariably left the organisation at a disadvantage, and there can be little doubt that the Allied planners at the very least had contemplated using SOE as a component of FORTITUDE, the main deception strategy for D-Day. This is conceded by M. R. D. Foot, who confirms SOE's role immediately after the invasion had started,

> to prolong the enemy's hesitation, care was still taken after NEP-TUNE began to encourage him to think that another and larger landing was to be made further east, and in this major deception plan called BODYGUARD (later FORTITUDE) SOE also had some part to play. That part was to have included sending some organizers into the immediate hinterland of Calais in the spring; here common sense fortunately prevailed. . . . The proposal to

send SOE teams to so unsuitable a spot shows how much these plans smelled of the lamp, and how little some of the planners were in touch with fact.[56]

From Foot's account, it is fair to conclude that although a proposal had been made to involve SOE in FORTITUDE, the idea had been vetoed and therefore was never executed, which rather leaves Wynne's version of STAMPEDE as something of an orphan. Foot confirms that although 'SOE had expected in its early days to perform itself' for deceptive purposes on D-Day, it 'had not succeeded in establishing itself as trustworthy enough in the eyes of the deception planning staffs'.[57]

Major Julian Howard, the senior British officer in Wynne's tale and the person referred to as being in command of STAMPEDE, was described as having been 'attached to Special Operations Executive',[58] and the arrival of the first Dutch agent, Henk Janssen, 'had probably been arranged by SOE',[59] which disposes of the defence that *Count Five and Die* was not based on an operation run by SOE, but another secret organisation. According to Professor Sir Michael Howard, who published the official history of British wartime deception, no project like STAMPEDE ever existed and, furthermore, the Germans never believed that there was any Allied intention to land on the Belgian or Dutch coasts. Strategic deception schemes, intended to divert enemy forces from vital locations to insignificant ones, are highly complex undertakings, and if they are to be executed in the expectation of any degree of success, they must be supported by a range of components. Certainly SHAEF would never have contemplated, or been authorised to allow, the preparation of an isolated plan for the invasion of Holland, especially one that might contradict, and thereby jeopardise, the sophisticated project which had started life as BODYGUARD and had later become FORTITUDE. This scheme had taken months to develop and had received support from double agents, fictitious military units and bogus radio signals, all judged to be essential if the master plan was to have any hope of accomplishing something positive. Certainly none of these measures was taken for STAMPEDE, and there is no reference to STAMPEDE or any similar operation in the mass of declassified material relating to FORTITUDE.

A key component of any practical deception scheme is the enemy's predisposition to accept that the actual operation could be plausibly mounted. The unquestioned success of FORTITUDE lay in the German appreciations that had recognised the Pas de Calais region as the most obvious and likely target for an Allied amphibious assault. This is in sharp contrast to the enemy's opinion of the likelihood of an attack on Belgium or the Netherlands. It is clear, both from enemy documents captured after the war and from communications intercepted at the time, that the Germans never thought the Dutch coast was an Allied objective, and Field Marshal Jodl made this clear to the Japanese naval attaché in Berlin during a briefing on 3 June 1944, the day after Hannie Herodsen's signal. In his subsequent report transmitted by an insecure cipher to Tokyo, and intercepted by the Allies en route, the naval attaché quoted Jodl as having said that

> Reports of preparations for large enemy landings on the Mediterranean coast of southern France appear to be largely deliberate propaganda reports by the enemy. We are prepared for landings in the vicinity of Bordeaux and on the coast of Belgium and the Netherlands, although there is little possibility of such landings.[60]

The Japanese Embassy's communications with Tokyo had provided GCHQ (the Government Communications Headquarters) at Bletchley Park with a rich vein of intelligence, and much of the data had been highly relevant to the Allied deception plans. As early as November 1943, the Japanese Ambassador, General Oshima Hiroshi, had undertaken a tour of the Atlantic Wall and had concluded that 'the Strait of Dover is given first place in the German Army's fortification scheme and troop dispositions'.[61] He had received confirmation of this on 23 November 1943 from Hitler himself, who told Oshima, during a private conversation, that 'beyond any doubt the most effective area would be the Strait of Dover'.[62] On 27 May, almost on the eve of D-Day, Oshima had discussed the subject again with Hitler, who had repeated his prediction that the Allies would open 'an all-out Second Front in the area of the Straits of Dover'.[63] Because Oshima's telegrams were being decrypted and translated at Bletchley Park within a matter of hours of their transmission, the Allied intelligence analysts possessed both a reliable guide to Hitler's current strategy and a highly effective method of judging FORTITUDE's efficacy. Considering this remarkable insight into the enemy's mind, and the obvious acceptance by the German High Command of FORTITUDE's basic principle, that the invasion was destined for the Pas de Calais, it is difficult to see why anyone in the Allied camp would have seen the need for STAMPEDE, let alone execute it.

According to Barry Wynne, one indication of STAMPEDE's success was the enemy's deployment of formations in Holland that might more usefully have been assigned to areas nearer the Normandy bridgehead. In particular, he cites the 19th SS Panzer Division as an example of how the Germans had sent some of their crack units to the Netherlands, presumably in preparation for an invasion. In fact, the 19th SS Panzer Division had been sent to Holland from Germany as a replacement for the 1st SS Panzer Division, which had been despatched to Normandy from Belgium soon after D-Day. As for the others mentioned, none amounted to evidence of a significant concentration of military force as implied by Wynne. A closer look at the units mentioned by the author demonstrates the element of embroidery in his presentation of the German order-of-battle in Holland, the subject of intense study by MI-14, the War Office unit dedicated to this specific task. Wynne's exaggeration may also have been the provenance of the claim made at the conclusion of the film version of *Count Five and Die*, which asserted that when the Allies invaded Normandy *ten* enemy divisions had been moved 'out of the line' and sent to Holland. However, Wynne's assertions do not coincide with what MI-14 knew of the situation. As well as the conventional sources of intelligence, MI-14 received regular decrypts from Bletchley Park, including the texts of messages from the Japanese Embassy in Berlin, which gave detailed appreciations of the German forces in the occupied countries.

Wynne identified three Wehrmacht infantry divisions in the Netherlands: the 165th, the 347th and the 719th. In fact, there were really only two: the 347th and the 709th (Limited Employment Division), which was to be withdrawn and was later captured at Cherbourg. The third division was the 16th Luftwaffe Field Division, based at Haarlem, which was to move to France to join the 86th Corps within a fortnight of D-Day. The Wehrmacht commander of these forces was Air General Friedrich Christiansen, who had been a naval officer in the First World War and then a naval pilot, before joining the Luftwaffe in 1933. General Dr Hans Speidel, who was Rommel's Chief of Staff, described him as 'a bluff, simple seaman [who] did not have the experience and education, and mental qualities to lead an army; he knew very little of land warfare'.[64] In Speidel's view, 'these divisions were useless for modern warfare',[65] and he had no doubt that the prospect of an Allied invasion north of the Somme was 'unlikely because of the terrain, and for strategic and tactical considerations'.[66] Clearly Speidel gave no credence to the proposition that Holland was a probable invasion target, and the selection of Christiansen as the local commander suggests that the Chief of Staff was not alone in considering the Netherlands a low-risk area.

The 165th Infantry Division, which was under the separate command of Field Marshal Rommel's Army Group 'B', was located on the Dutch–Belgian border, but was in the process of refitting at the time of the D-Day landings and was therefore not a force of any significance.

Setting aside the contentious issue of whether STAMPEDE, or any similar deception scheme centred on Holland, ever existed, is there any evidence that the Germans received Hannie's warning on 2 June and took measures to strengthen their defences in Holland at that critical time? If so, as we have seen, the news was not imparted to the Japanese naval attaché. In fact, the evidence is that no special alert was issued to the German Command until 0730 on 10 June 1944, four days *after* the D-Day landings had begun, when the Fifteenth Army had been placed on the highest, or second highest, level of readiness. On that day, Field Marshal Rommel reported that 'every German soldier and man is standing by night and day for defence'.[67] Indeed, examination of the Wehrmacht's official War Diary indicates that the only tip regarding a threat to the Fifteenth Army area had come from a report which had been studied by the OKW on the evening of 9 June and which had suggested an imminent landing in the Pas de Calais area, perhaps in Belgium. The provenance of this particular message is unusually easy to trace because it was recovered at the end of the war and was presented to the OKW's Chief of Intelligence, Colonel Friedrich-Adolf Krummacher, then in Allied custody, who had recognised it and had pointed out where Jodl had underlined a particular sentence, and where there was a mark indicating that it had been shown to Hitler. The text had proved to be identical to a signal that had been transmitted by the MI5 double agent *Garbo* just after midnight the previous evening, 8/9 June. In it *Garbo* had predicted a second assault, which 'may very probably take place in the Pas de Calais area',[68] and had described the recent Normandy landings as 'a diversionary manoeuvre designed to draw off enemy reserves'. Krummacher had emphasised this crucial information and added that it 'confirms the view already held by us that a further attack is expected in another place (Belgium?)'.[69] Thus, there is compelling evidence that Holland had never been regarded by the Germans as a likely target, and the belief that a second amphibious landing was to take place in the Pas de Calais region had been the consequence of a concerted Allied deception campaign based on messages fabricated by *Garbo*.

Barry Wynne acknowledges the existence of FORTITUDE in a remark attributed to an American intelligence officer, who, in discussing STAMPEDE's objectives, refers to another deception scheme: 'The British have got one worked out for the Pas de Calais and we might be able to link up ours with theirs, but, of course, Holland would be the ideal place.'[70] In reality, deception operations cannot be mounted in isolation from each other or, indeed, independently of authentic plans, so none of the Allies had been permitted to launch their own projects, and FORTITUDE was itself eloquent testimony to the high degree of integration that had been achieved by SHAEF's joint deception staff.

Despite Wynne's assertion that his was 'a true account', there was very little in the story that was even remotely authentic, so how did he come to write *Count Five and Die*? No doubt William Eliscu played some role, but exactly where the blame lies is difficult to determine. Eliscu now lives in the Quai des Bergues in Geneva and continues to use his bogus British decoration.

As for Barry Wynne, he later wrote two books on the clandestine war. The first, *The Empty Coffin* (1959),[71] told the supposedly authentic story of Alain Romans, a pianist of Polish origin who escaped to Gibraltar from the South of France and subsequently parachuted into Brittany in December 1941 with a team of five other Frenchmen from SOE's F Section. They were betrayed soon after their arrival near St Malo, arrested by the Germans and shot in a wood close to St Servant. Miraculously, Romans apparently survived the execution and was rescued by a priest administering the last rites. He recovered from his wounds, but was arrested again and sent to a camp in Lithuania. He escaped, found the Russian lines and was repatriated to Newcastle.

Like *Count Five and Die*, *The Empty Coffin* presents considerable problems for the historian. Only two of the companions who had supposedly accompanied Romans on his mission to Brittany were named, but there appears to be no trace of 'Georges Letitre' and 'Kristian Laville' and their names do not appear on the memorial at Valençay to the SOE personnel who lost their lives in France. Nor, indeed, is there any trace of them or their mission in SOE's records, or, for that matter, of Romans himself. According to the SOE Adviser at the Foreign Office, who is the guardian of SOE's archives, no agents at all were dropped into France in December 1941, which rather casts doubt on Wynne's story. The author identified St Servant as the village near St Malo where the SOE agents were shot, but no such place exists. There is a St Servan-sur-Mer, also on the estuary of the river Rance, and effectively a suburb of modern St Malo, but there is no local record of the tale spun by Wynne. In a curious twist to the story, as we shall see, Roxane Pitt, who is another self-styled secret agent, claimed in both her not entirely reliable autobiographies, *The Courage of Fear*[72] and *Operation Double Life*,[73] to have played a part in a very similar episode involving 'Alain Roman [sic]', who had been left for dead on the banks of the Seine by a Nazi execution squad.

Barry Wynne's other book on wartime espionage, *No Drums, No Trumpets*,[74] is an authentic account of the Comtesse de Milleville, the English-born nurse Mary Lindell, who built the MARIE CLAIRE escape route in France for Allied evaders and survived imprisonment at Fresnes and Ravensbrück. She twice experienced interrogation at the hands of the Gestapo and in October 1942 was delivered back to France by Lysander after having escaped to England via Spain, disguised as an elderly governess. After the war, she was able to provide damning evidence against some of the concentration-camp staff, and then returned home to Paris with a Croix de Guerre.

Wynne, who had been born in Eastcote in 1929 with the name Robert Wynne-Roberts, and claimed to have served in the Special Air Service Regiment (although the regiment has no trace of him under either name), wrote several other books, including *Music in the Wind*, *Angels on Runway Zero 7*, *The Spies Within*, *The Sniper* and, most recently in 1969, *The Day Gibraltar Fell*.[75] He then turned to corporate security and began training bodyguards in unarmed combat techniques. He was appointed chief executive of J. Donne Holdings Ltd, a company that in 1977 was criticised for entering into contracts with the Libyan Government. Since that time there has been no trace of either Wynne, who lived at Stokenchurch in Buckinghamshire, or his company, which was registered at 10 Golden Square in London.

There is no obvious explanation for how Wynne succeeded in peddling two books of non-fiction which have no foundation in fact, but nevertheless *Count Five and Die* and *The Empty Coffin* were not only received uncritically, but were used as a source of supposedly authentic detail by another unscrupulous author.

3

Aline, the Countess from New York

'In the course of lecturing over the past eight years, I've discovered that people enjoy (and need) authentic first-hand information about espionage, a topic on which reliable information is (understandably) difficult to come by.'[1]

Born in Pearl River, a town some forty miles north of New York City, Aline Griffith was working as a fashion mannequin when she volunteered to join General Donovan's Office of Strategic Services at the age of twenty, as a code clerk. Her first assignment was to the US Embassy in Madrid, where she worked for the OSS station chief.

In 1985, Aline produced her first volume of memoirs, *The Spy Wore Red*, in which she gave an account of her experiences as an OSS agent in Madrid. The book was an instant success. In an Author's Note, she confirmed that 'the core of the story is accurate', while conceding that she had 'changed the names of some of the characters . . . and in a very few cases, where a name change did not sufficiently conceal a character's identity, a composite character was created'.[2] According to her version, she had been recruited into OSS in September 1943 by an officer code-named *Jupiter* and had been sent to a training camp outside Washington DC, 'the first school of espionage in the United States . . . RTU-11, also known as the farm'.[3] Her adventures were presented as an authentic, non-fiction account of her wartime work and started with her being assigned a codename and number, '*Tiger* – 527'. She recalled that as an introduction she had been given a briefing on OSS and its structure:

OSS has five sections, MO, Mobile Operations, coordinates agent activities behind enemy lines. There's the propaganda section. R & A, Research and Analysis, collects and sifts strategic war data. CE, counterespionage, deals with gathering foreign intelligence while overseas. And SI, Secret Intelligence, handles agents assigned special missions in countries abroad.[4]

During training she underwent 'about ten days of close-combat classes' on a course that lasted three weeks without a break. One section of the course was weapon assembly, supervised by an instructor known only as 'Sphinx':

Blindfolded, I groped and fumbled with the revolver, disassembling it piece by piece, hammer, barrel, muzzle, heel. It had an acrid, metallic smell. When it was completely disassembled, Sphinx scattered the parts around me. Then, trying to put it back together as fast as possible, I dropped the empty clip – it banged on the wooden floor. Groping sightlessly while Sphinx looked on, I finally retrieved it and proceeded.[5]

Having completed her training, Aline was given the details of her mission by Whitney Shepardson, OSS's Chief of Secret Intelligence:

A contact inside the Gestapo in Berlin informs us that Himmler has one of his most capable spies operating out of Madrid, running a network – a particularly effective one – for uncovering Allied plans related to Operation Anvil. Your mission is to discover who that person is. Our Berlin agent has given us the names of four people in Madrid, one of whom he believes is the person we're looking for. All move at a level of international society which precludes easy surveillance. We need an agent who can fit into that group.[6]

Having received her orders for what was to be designated 'Operation BULLFIGHT', she was despatched on Christmas Eve 1943, via a flying-boat, to Lisbon. One of the other passengers on the plane was, by coincidence, William Casey, the OSS's head of Secret Intelligence in Europe, and later a Director of Central Intelligence during Ronald Reagan's Presidency. The journey was eventful, for during Aline's first evening in Portugal a guest in the Estoril casino was stabbed only yards away from her. Her companion, Larry Mellon, who had also escorted her across the Atlantic, examined the body to confirm that he was dead.

A little shaken by the murder, Aline arrived in Madrid on New Year's Eve and spent her first night in Spain dancing with her OSS contact, Edmundo Lassalle, codenamed 'Top Hat, one of the best agents we've got'. Ostensibly Lassalle was a Mexican working as 'the representative of Walt Disney in Spain', and during their night-clubbing he was able to identify various enemy personnel to Aline, including Constantin von Weiderstock, 'a favourite disciple of Admiral Canaris, who controls the Abwehr'.[7] Having recovered from her partying, the following morning Aline presented herself to the Oil Mission of the USA, where Phillip Harris, the local OSS Station Chief codenamed *Mozart*, described the difficult conditions his staff had to endure:

> We're understaffed since a triple agent burned half our group –
> and the ambassador does all that's possible to make it difficult for
> us to get recruits. That damned agent was working for the
> Germans, the Spaniards, and us, all at the same time.[8]

Far from being a neutral backwater, Madrid was apparently a centre of operations, supervising air drops into occupied France from air bases in Algiers. 'A radioman always advised us in Madrid if all went well and set up the date and hour for the next radio contact.'[9] Harris explained to Aline that the success of Operation ANVIL, the imminent invasion of France from the Mediterranean, would depend

> principally on intelligence provided by OSS Madrid. Some of our
> information on German troop movement is brought here by
> agents coming across the Pyrenees. Also we receive reports
> through our radio rigs. Our transmitters, although small, reach
> Madrid. We relay on to headquarters.[10]

Having been initiated into the complexities of OSS's operations in Madrid, and issued with a .25 Beretta, an 'L-pill' and a generous 'OSS hazardous duty salary',[11] Aline established contact with, and maintained a watch on, the suspected traitors. She was helped by another OSS agent, François Ferronière, codenamed *Pierre*, with whom she had trained at the farm, and narrowed the list of possible enemy agents to the beautiful Countess Gloria von Furstenberg, originally from Mexico and then Hollywood, who was married to a German officer fighting on the Russian Front (she was alleged to have 'seduced General Wolff of the SS for an exit permit from Germany to Spain');[12] Prince Nikolaus Lilienthal, a pro-Nazi Czech industrialist using a Liechtenstein passport; and Hans Lazaar, the press attaché at the German Embassy.

In the course of her investigations, she spotted Gloria von Furstenberg dining with Heinrich Himmler in a Madrid restaurant, and was offered help by Mimosa, the elderly Marquesa de Torrejón, who was promptly strangled. René Blum, the French leader of the orchestra at the Pasapoga night-club, was another of *Top Hat*'s agents, and he too was found dead in mysterious circumstances, his body dumped in a Steinway piano. Aline, who was at the centre of these events, was herself twice the target of an attempted murder. On the first occasion, in a case of mistaken identity in April 1944, a Basque woman sleeping in her bed was shot dead: on the second occasion, in June, Aline was attacked by a chauffeur, but succeeded in shooting him and making her escape unscathed. Undaunted, her exploits continued breathlessly: she uncovered a plot to assassinate Franco and a scheme masterminded by Karl Wizner, the Gestapo chief at the German Embassy, to smuggle looted works of art to Buenos Aires. In addition, she was entrusted with a mission to Malaga in May to deliver a microfilm containing the names of Spaniards willing to help OSS agents who had been infiltrated into the country. On this operation, she was to act as courier for another OSS officer, codenamed *Blackie*, who had recently arrived by boat from Algiers, and she was also to carry a specially constructed suitcase containing a Colt automatic and a concealed transmitter. However, as she had no travel permit, she was arrested on the train and, although imprisoned for more than twenty-four hours in Malaga, was never searched. Freed by the American consul, she attended the rendezvous and delivered the microfilm and suitcase.

Soon afterwards, at the end of July 1944, Aline was selected to carry another microfilm to the port of Lloret de Mar, near Barcelona. This time she was to deliver it to a private yacht for onward transmission to an American PT boat. Having accomplished the mission, she returned to Madrid, in time to be entrusted on 8 August with vital information that she had to convey to Pierre:

His orders are to move his subagents to the Marseilles area.
They should be in a position to assist our troops when they land.

He must act surreptitiously with his own people. Information on the location of the landing is so secret it cannot be leaked, cannot be made known, even to those who have been risking their lives for us these past years.[13]

Aline gave *Pierre* his instructions and then accompanied *Top Hat* on a raid on a dress shop in Madrid, where Gloria von Furstenberg had 'a huge radio transmitter. Overwhelming in comparison to anything we had.' The beautiful Gloria confessed to working as a Gestapo agent for Karl Wizner and 'for Schellenberg, for Himmler',[14] and agreed to hand over all future communications to OSS.

Finally, François Ferronière was exposed as a Nazi spy and as the nephew of the Marquesa de Torrejón, whom he had murdered. His father, Josef Ferronière, was a known Fascist sympathiser in Nice, but this had not prevented François from obtaining 'a minor clerical position with the US Consulate in Vichy'.[15] Later, in November 1942, he had moved to Algiers and had then attended the OSS course in Washington. He had been dropped into France for the first time in December 1943 and had then turned up in Madrid 'at the beginning of February' 1944. As was explained to Aline,

After surveillance, Pierre's guilt became more obvious and he was called to Madrid with the pretext of overseeing agents' crossing the frontier. In actuality he was being kept there to be used at the proper time to feed false information to the Germans on the Anvil landing location.[16]

Thus, *Pierre* had been identified as a traitor and then manipulated to deceive the enemy. The scheme had been entirely successful, and Aline received praise for her unconscious part in the operation. 'The importance of your contribution is incalculable,' she was told.

We were manipulating others to confuse the enemy at the same time, but personally, I think the decisive information that convinced the enemy was that which you passed on to Pierre. Obviously he never suspected you would give him false information. And fortunately the Germans had full confidence in him.[17]

Aline 'continued to do undercover work in France and Switzerland until 1947',[18] when she resigned from OSS to marry the Count de Quintanilla, who later inherited the title Count de Romanones. But that was by no means the end of the story, for in 1984 she unexpectedly encountered *Pierre* in a hotel in El Salvador, where he claimed not to have murdered his aunt and René Blum forty years earlier, placing the blame on Hans Lazaar and Karl Wizner. Despite being wanted for war crimes, he had lived in Milan, where he had changed his name, worked for the KGB and then moved to Miami.

At first blush there seem to be one or two chronological details that tend to undermine the author's extraordinary tale. The original proposition was that a dangerous German spy was at liberty in Madrid and was threatening to endanger Allied plans for ANVIL. This was the version given to Aline in December 1943 by Whitney Shepardson when she was assigned to Spain with the specific purpose of identifying the traitor. If this was indeed the case, the spy referred to could not have been *Pierre*, for he had been on Aline's training course and only dropped back into France at the end of the course, on an unspecified date in December 1943. Therefore, the original tip, allegedly from a Gestapo source in Berlin, could hardly have been related to *Pierre*. However, even accepting that there were two dangerous enemy spies operating simultaneously inside OSS's network in Madrid, there must be some doubt whether *Pierre* was used as a conduit for disinformation, for there is a curious discrepancy in dates regarding ANVIL. Aline describes being given *Pierre*'s instructions upon her return from Barcelona on 8 August 1944, but later goes on to give a detailed account of his arrival in the *South of France at midnight on 1 July*. Thus, according to her version, *Pierre* parachuted into France without the key information he was intended to deliver to the enemy. The invasion itself, of course, actually took place on 15 August 1944. When Aline heard that the landings had taken place near St Tropez and not Marseilles, her reaction was one of astonishment: 'I couldn't believe my ears. Saint-Tropez was near Cannes – far from Marseilles.' In reality, St Tropez is virtually equidistant between Marseilles and Cannes, but in any event there was never any deception scheme to promote Marseilles as a cover plan. The point of Aline's surprise was her realisation that she had been duped into believing in *Pierre*'s bona fides when he was really working for the Nazis.

There is also a slight confusion over exactly where *Pierre* was parachuted, whatever the exact date. The objective was to deliver *Pierre* so that he could 'move his subagents to the Marseilles area'.[19] Aline refers to a 'dangerous drop in southern France' and mentions that 'the Germans had powerful anti-aircraft searchlights placed all along the coast'.[20] The clear implication is that the drop was to take place in the vicinity of Marseilles, and this is confirmed by the timescale of the account Aline gives of the night of the operation, 1 July 1944. *Pierre* was due to land at midnight, and forty minutes earlier Aline says that he was 'in a plane over the Mediterranean', which fits perfectly. However, when Aline and *Pierre* subsequently meet, Aline asks: 'What happened to you after you parachuted into Pau?'[21] This is a curious question, for Pau is nowhere near Marseilles or the Mediterranean; it is in fact located in the foothills of the Pyrenees in Gascony. This may be another example of Aline's limited grasp of French geography, or more evidence that the flight never happened.

Further analysis of *The Spy Wore Red* reveals some other significant inconsistencies. During a training session at 'the farm', Aline was certainly misinformed about OSS's structure. Whilst the organisation did consist of five branches, the components were not as described; MO was not 'Mobile Operations' but Morale Operations, and there was no separate propaganda unit. Counter-espionage was not a separate branch but a subsection of Secret Intelligence. No mention was made of Special Operations, arguably OSS's most important division, and the Research & Development unit was a technical group concentrating on new weapons and communications technology, with no responsibility, as alleged, for the collection and study of 'strategic war data'. Nor is Aline's memory of 'RTU-11' or 'the farm', which definitely existed and was the advanced training school officially designated ' Rural Training Unit 11', entirely accurate. It was located in Maryland, twenty miles outside Washington DC, on a 100-acre estate leased from Andrew R. Berger, a rich industrialist from Pittsburgh. Her recollection of the weapons training she says she underwent there is also dubious for on five occasions in *The Spy Wore Red* she mistakes an automatic for a revolver. No revolver contains a magazine, and it would be wholly impractical to teach any agent to dismantle and reassemble a revolver. A knowledge of how an automatic works, on the other hand, and how its parts fit together and are cleaned and oiled, would be essential for anyone contemplating using such weapons, which are always susceptible to jamming if not properly maintained.

Aline's inability to distinguish between a revolver and an automatic brings into question whether she ever went to RTU-11, which was an advanced fieldcraft course for those intended for operational duties in the field in Europe. Clerical or cipher personnel invariably underwent a fortnight's basic orientation training at a separate location, known as 'Area E', which certainly did not include a weapons course. One of the few women to serve in OSS as an officer, and who operated in Berne, recalls that her code clerk, Eileen Sullivan, went on the same training course as Aline, and that the subjects taught were limited to OSS orientation and some work with one-time pads. She is emphatic that neither Eileen nor Aline were taught any tradecraft.

On the assumption that Aline really did complete her training and was assigned to Madrid, she must have embroidered the stories of the murder in the Estoril casino on Christmas Day 1943, and of the killings of René Blum, the Marquesa de Torrejón, the Basque woman and the homicidal chauffeur, for there is no other record of these events. Indeed, because of the enormous sensitivity of the work undertaken by cipher clerks, and the implications for the entire organisation if one fell into enemy hands, few, if any, were ever allowed to place themselves at risk. Certainly Aline could not have received the briefing she described from the OSS Station Chief, whom she identifies as Phillip Harris, having supposedly disguised 'the man codenamed *Mozart*'.[22] In fact, his true name was H. Gregory Thomas, but he was to be removed from his office for incompetence and a rather greater crime, getting the US Ambassador's daughter pregnant.

The OSS mission in Madrid was never entrusted with any important information, not because, as supposedly alleged by 'Harris', it had been compromised by a triple agent, but because it was the subject of harassment by the notorious *Seguridad* following the BANANA fiasco. This was a joint SIS/OSS operation which had been conducted in September 1943, involving the infiltration into southern Spain of mainly Republican agents trained at the OSS camp at Oujda, outside Algiers, and equipped with American weapons. The Spanish police arrested a group of agents on a beach near Malaga on 23 September 1943 and subsequently took a total of 261 suspects into custody, of whom twenty-two were executed. The aptly named BANANA incident, which was one of a series of infiltrations codenamed APPLE, ORANGE and GRAPEFRUIT, caused such embarrassment that Robert Solborg, the regional OSS/SI Chief, was relieved of his command and returned to Washington, and two other senior OSS officers in North Africa, Arthur Roseborough and Donald Downes, were transferred to the Middle East. Downes later recalled that 'the sparks flew in Washington. General Donovan was on the mat. State Department was indignant. Inter-departmental protests and demands for scalps flew around Washington.'[23]

This was the true environment into which Aline was thrust, and it is unimaginable that she could have been unaware of these matters which had so preoccupied her Chief, the late Greg Thomas. Certainly her account of what OSS undertook in Madrid hardly accords with what is known about the Station's activities, which were severely circumscribed for fear of further political blunders. For example, the assertion that Madrid exercised control over, and was in radio contact with, operations in the South of France seems open to doubt. Quite apart from the inherent improbability of running paramilitary operations from an embassy on neutral territory, OSS was not allowed independent wireless contact with its agents in France and depended entirely upon the British for both ciphers and radio facilities.

This tends to leave open to question the claim that OSS had despatched the agent codenamed *Pierre* into France in December 1943 from North Africa. Quite simply, there were no air operations of that kind in that month. In fact, the only OSS agents parachuted into France from Algiers during the whole of 1943 were Peter J. Ortiz, who was flown to France by SOE in June 1943, and the two-man PENNY FARTHING team, which actually flew to France indirectly, via England, in July 1943. By January 1944, only a handful of OSS agents had been dropped into France. They were Ernest Floege (*Alfred*), André Bouchardon (*Narcisse*), Owen Johnson (*Gael*) and Claude Arnault (*Neron*). In addition, two other OSS officers, Lieutenants G. Demand and Victor Soskice (*Solway*), participated in SCULLION II, an SOE raid on the shale oil refinery at Le Creusot in August. All of these operations are well documented and none of the individuals conforms to the description of *Pierre*.

Since *Pierre* is such a key figure in *The Spy Wore Red*, it is worth examining him a little more closely. Aline confirmed, after all, that although 'the man I call Pierre has been disguised . . . there was a Pierre',[24] whom she had met as recently as 1984. She allegedly inspected his OSS dossier in which his biographical details were recorded, from his birth in Nice in 1916 to his work for the US Consulate in Vichy, and his parachute drop into southern France in December 1943. This would not be an entirely improbable course of events, discounting the question mark over the flight from Algiers, were it not for other clues to his movements contained elsewhere in *The Spy Wore Red*. For example, the Countess von Furstenberg described having met *Pierre* in Paris in 1942, when theoretically he had been working in Vichy. Paris was, at the time, in German-occupied territory and travel across the demarcation line was prohibited. This is not a minor detail, for Aline quotes Gloria von Furstenberg on the subject of *Pierre* and she places him in Paris in 1942:

> We met in Paris two years ago. He used an exotic title, Comte de la Perla, although I always suspected it was false. Francisco likes to impress people. So handsome, and Paris in 1942! We had a glorious time for ten days. Then he disappeared.[25]

Quite how a clerk at the US Consulate in the unoccupied zone could find ten days to masquerade as an aristocrat and romance the wife of a German officer in 1942 in the occupied capital is unexplained. Equally unexplained is the absence of this potentially crucial data from *Pierre*'s OSS file.

There should also be doubt about the authenticity of two cables which were received from London and decoded by Aline. Both are described as having arrived on 27 March 1944, and the first concerned a British double agent, codenamed *Garbo*:

TO MOZART FROM CHESS STOP BRITISH IMPRISONED SPANIARD WORKING AS
GERMAN AGENT UNDER CODE NAME GARBO STOP GARBO CHANNELLED
MESSAGES TO BERLIN THROUGH GUILLERMO IN MADRID STOP[26]

It so happens that *Garbo*, who was known to the Abwehr as *Arabel*, is one of the best-documented double-agent cases in counter-intelligence history, and if this signal was ever sent it was not just a grotesque breach of security, it was hopelessly misinformed. At no time, for example, did the British ever imprison *Garbo*, who was the Security Service's star asset. He had arrived in Britain in April 1942 and, under MI5's continuous supervision, had been maintaining a regular radio schedule with his Abwehr contact in Madrid, Karl-Erich Kuhlenthal, ever since. Proof of this is that *Garbo*, whose real name was Juan Pujol, could not operate a Morse key or a wireless, but relied upon a British nominee, Charles Haines, to transmit every message. Each signal was acknowledged from Madrid using the callsign CENTRO, and relayed to Wiesbaden, so the reference to *Guillermo* in the OSS text makes no sense. So where did it come from? None of the standard textbooks on wartime intelligence and deception operations mentions *Guillermo*, but, by an interesting coincidence, it is the codename attributed by Leonard Mosley to Alcazar de Velasco, the journalist who worked at the Spanish Embassy in London as secretary to the press attaché. In *The Druid* (see Chapter 16 below), Mosley refers to *Garbo*, incorrectly identifying him as Luis Calvo, the London correspondent of the Spanish daily *ABC*, but rightly does not connect the two. How Aline has been able to do so is, at first glance, something of a mystery for certainly *Garbo* had no connection whatever with Alcazar de Velasco, apart from sharing the same nationality. The solution to this conundrum is to be found in Ladislas Farago's *The Game of the Foxes*,[27] the only other book to attribute the German codename *Guillermo* to de Velasco. What seems to have happened is that Aline read these two books for background information, not realising that, although Farago was a fairly reliable source on the Abwehr, Mosley's book had been largely invented. Accordingly, Aline's identification of Alcazar de Velasco as *Guillermo* was quite straightforward, but she ought to have noticed that Farago never attempted to give *Garbo*'s true name. The next part was a little more complicated and went awry. Farago had correctly documented the fact that de Velasco had fled London late in 1941, when the journalist had detected that he had been placed under intensive surveillance by MI5. In his place, de Velasco had appointed Luis Calvo as a German spy, who was subsequently arrested early in 1942, following his return to London from a routine visit to Madrid. Calvo was to spend the rest of the war in MI5's custody, but in 1981 Mosley had mistakenly named Calvo as *Garbo*. Upon reading this – and there is only one other possible source, which was only published in England and was swiftly withdrawn because of legal action – Aline must have thought that as Calvo had been reporting to de Velasco, she could safely construct an authentic-sounding text linking *Garbo* (i.e. Calvo) to *Guillermo* (i.e. de Velasco). Unfortunately, the whole pack of cards collapses when one realises that Calvo was not *Garbo*. Aline's error, apart from trusting Mosley, was to have missed *Garbo*'s own memoirs, published in 1985. The inescapable conclusion, therefore, is that under close scrutiny the fairly innocuous text of Aline's purported OSS cable can be shown to be a highly revealing clue to her embarrassingly inept choice of sources.

Even if there is, ostensibly, a puzzle about the reference to *Guillermo*, could *Garbo* have sent this text, or one like it? It is perfectly possible to check *Garbo*'s movements by tracing his radio messages. In March 1944, he was in London, having recently returned from a tour of England's south coast. At 1920 on 28 March 1944, twenty-four hours after Aline states she deciphered a message confirming *Garbo*'s arrest, *Garbo* was on the air to pass on a message he had received from his sub-agent *Benedict* in Dundee. The text described two military units in the area, one of which was identified as the 52nd Lowland Division.

Clearly the reference to *Garbo*'s imprisonment has been fabricated, so what about the rest of the cable? One clue is the mention of *Guillermo*, to whom *Garbo* allegedly sent his messages in Madrid. As befitting his status as an enemy intelligence personality, and not a source of information, Karl-Erich Kuhlenthal was never attributed this codename in Allied official files, or any other codename, so where did it come from? Certainly not an official cable, and it is quite likely that, far from recalling the text of an authentic cable from March 1944, Aline's text was concocted from material gleaned from much more recent publications. Thus it is highly improbable that OSS received any signal of the kind described by Aline. Similarly, there must be much doubt about the contents of a second cable received on the same day and allegedly reproduced verbatim:

HITLERS ORDERS TO WEHRMACHT AS FOLLOWS QUOTE SABOTAGE AND TERROR TROOPS WHETHER ARMED OR UNARMED IN OR OUT OF UNIFORM ARE TO BE SLAUGHTERED TO THE LAST MAN STOP THIS INCLUDES ENEMY AGENTS IN NEUTRAL COUNTRIES STOP [28]

This extraordinary signal appears to be a version of Hitler's notorious directive concerning the treatment of captured commandos issued on 18 October 1942, immediately following Operation BASALT, an SOE raid on Sark in the Channel Islands, during which a German prisoner, with his hands tied behind his back, was stabbed through the heart. However, the original directive, which was a matter of some controversy at the Nuremberg war crimes trials, and which was discussed during Field Marshal Jodl's cross-examination, was issued as an official Wehrmacht communiqué and broadcast from German radio stations in plain language:

In future, all terror and sabotage troops of the British and their accomplices, who do not act like soldiers but rather like bandits,

will be treated as such by the German troops and will be ruthlessly eliminated in battle, wherever they appear.[29]

As can be seen, this order dealt only with Allied irregular forces and,
significantly, made no mention of 'enemy agents in neutral countries'.[30]
One possible motive for the addition of this puzzling statement is an
attempt to demonstrate that OSS personnel in neutral countries were in
some personal danger, which, of course, they never were. Indeed, there
is no known case of a single American or British intelligence officer
experiencing anything worse than indigestion or a hangover in Madrid;
quite why OSS should choose to circulate an inaccurate version of an
enemy order that was seventeen months old is unclear.

In addition to the problems posed in *The Spy Wore Red* in regard to the
events portrayed, there is some difficulty in accepting some of the personalities involved. Many of the Spanish characters are authentic
individuals, but some of the others are not. The German intelligence personnel, for example, pose particular difficulties, even on the basis that
their names have been changed. Constantin von Weiderstock, who is
referred to as controlling the Abwehr in Madrid, is a case in point. He is
described as 'a young fellow' and 'a favourite disciple of Admiral Canaris',
who also happens to be his godfather.[31] This is odd because the senior
Abwehr officer in Madrid at that time was a naval contemporary of
Admiral Canaris during the First World War, whose name was
Commander Gustav Leisner.

Quite apart from the chronological difficulties presented by Aline's
recollection of events, there is a further factual obstacle to be overcome
if *The Spy Wore Red* is to be taken as a work of non-fiction. According to
Aline Griffith's personnel file, recently declassified at the US National
Archives in Washington DC, she was never codenamed '*Tiger* – 527' and
she did not operate as an intelligence source at all during 1944. Aline's
official OSS dossier reveals that her true codename was *Butch*, and her
reports started on 1 February 1945 and continued for just five and a half
months until 13 July 1945. Nor is there any evidence in the file to substantiate any of the claims in *The Spy Wore Red*, apart from a single
reference to Gloria von Furstenberg, who in the book is denounced as a
dedicated Nazi spy intimate with Walter Schellenberg of the
Sicherheitsdienst, SS General Karl Wolff and Reich Marshal Heinrich
Himmler. Yet Aline's original report dated 2 May 1945 portrays the same
von Furstenberg as a victim of Nazi persecution and concludes: 'Subject

is not actually considered suspect although known to have various German connections in the German Embassy in Madrid.'[32] So, far from having operated as a dangerous German spy, and having been coerced into working for OSS, it is clear from *Butch*'s cable that the woman, who had a young son and a daughter with her and travelled on a Mexican passport issued in her maiden name of Gloria Rubio, was entirely innocent of any espionage:

> On April 26th, 1945 subject left Madrid with two children and nurse for Irun (Address: GLORIA RUBIO, HOTEL TERMINUS, IRUN) where she will rent a home for the children for the summer months. Subject will then proceed alone to Paris; she has her papers arranged to leave Irun for Paris, May 12th. In Paris she will immediately contact her friend AKHMED FAHKRY, son of Egyptian minister to France and Spain. Her plans are to obtain divorce from FURSTENBERG in France and to marry PRINCE FAHKRY. Subject has Mexican passport in name of GLORIA RUBIO, Nr 8/469, issued by Mexican Consulate in Lisbon.[33]

In fact, despite Gloria Rubio's marriage to a German officer, she was herself entirely anti-Nazi and in 1951 married Loel Guinness, formerly the Conservative Member of Parliament for Bath. She died in 1980, long before the book's publication, but Guinness, who died in 1989, was enraged by Aline's tale of his late wife's espionage. However, he was powerless under British law to take any legal action to protect her reputation. Coincidentally, Gloria's German husband, Franz von Furstenberg, was captured by the US army in 1944 and subsequently became a liaison officer in Wiesbaden for the Intelligence Division of the Control Commission for Germany. He died in 1976, unaware of what Aline intended to write about his former wife, but his post-war employment indicates that there was never any suspicion that he had been a Nazi.

All the other entries in Aline's official file reveal her activities as those of collecting gossip about how prominent German families resident in Spain intended to export their assets, and retailing inconsequential stories about Spanish café society gleaned from dinner parties in Madrid and lunches hosted by the local Associated Press correspondent. Of special interest to Aline was Prince Max Hohenlohe, whose daughter's wedding in June 1945 merited a breathless, four-page

cable describing his 150-room palace, his 300 servants and his wine
cellar, which stretched for half a mile. Aline was one of an intimate
group of 250 guests, 'the best and wealthiest families in Spain', but was
disappointed to find that there was only 'a sprinkling of Germans'[34] present. From other entries in the Hohenlohe dossier compiled by Aline
one can see that she was keen to identify the names of his friends in
Mexico, where he also owned an estate. Not long after the wedding
Aline reported:

> I learned yesterday from one of HOHENLOHE's sons that they
> had recently heard from their friend the PRESIDENT of Mexico
> and that he had told them that if one of the sons could get to
> Cuba he would send over a private plane to bring him to
> Mexico.[35]

As for agents run by *Butch*, it is clear from the OSS archive that she
was responsible for handling only two active sources: a secretary, codenamed *Column*, working for Orto S.A., a German-owned advertising
agency, and *Flamenco*, a typist in a Spanish publishing company whose
owner, Herbieto Serra, was suspected of pro-German sympathies. His
firm, Editorial Biografica Española, was engaged in compiling an edition
of *Who's Who in Spain*, a project Aline considered highly suspicious,
particularly since Señor Serra often worked late at night, and some of the
information he collected duplicated the research methods used by OSS's
counter-intelligence staff to collate counter-espionage data on card-index
files:

> At about 8:00 PM everyone in the office including the maid leave
> the building. Sr SERRA seems to have arranged this for more
> secrecy for his nightly visits and work. The cards which list the
> biographical data of persons who are to be used in QUIEN ES
> QUIEN are in very much the same form as our CE cards. The
> name in the upper left-hand corner, then a space about 1 inch
> square for the picture and below all the data on the person. When
> SERRA requests biographical data from a client he always asks
> for a picture. All the information he asks for is very detailed;
> birth place, date, nationality, if the person happens to be a writer
> or a speaker he asks where each speech was made, what was the
> topic of each speech etc. The cards which the typists type during

the day are taken from them every evening by SERRA and are never seen again in the office. He seems to keep all the cards in a special file in his office. They are sent to the print shop and returned in an unknown way to the offices of E.B.E. These trips between the printer's shop and the offices of E.B.E. must be made during the night since no one in the office ever goes to the printer or does any messenger from the printer ever come into the office. Also the address of this particular printer is kept completely secret.[36]

The overwhelming majority of the other documents to be found in the *Butch* file are in a similar vein, innocuous observations of figures in Spanish society who were deemed to have been pro-Axis during the war. The files are laced with enthusiastic offers to discover further information about Aline's friends, but for the most part they have been declassified in full, with only two or three surnames deleted, a clear indication that none of the material was regarded as sensitive. Accordingly, one must conclude that there is nothing in the *Butch* file to justify Aline's exaggerated claims.

Despite the obvious flaws in *The Spy Wore Red*, Aline was unabashed and went on to produce three sequels, *The Spy Went Dancing, The Spy Wore Silk* and *The Well-Mannered Assassin*.[37] Each present the same problems as the first book in that they are hard to accept as authentic accounts of true events. In the first, Aline describes searching for lost art treasures at the end of the war for OSS, and then helping the CIA identify a KGB source in NATO in 1966 who subsequently defects to an Eastern Bloc country. All that can be said about this tale is that no official record exists to substantiate any part of it. Nor, indeed, is there any reason to believe that a senior American army officer defected in 1966. The only noteworthy item in the book, which contains photographs of the author at a number of social gatherings, is a picture of *Jupiter*, the OSS officer who recruited her in 1943 and subsequently maintained contact with her for the CIA. Although named as 'John Derby' in the text, his true identity is unquestionably that of Frank Ryan, but Ryan was never a CIA officer as alleged by Aline. In OSS, he headed the Iberian desk in Washington DC and later in the war was based in Madrid. After the war, he ran World Commerce, a global trading organisation which participated in the Marshall Plan.

Similarly, with *The Spy Wore Silk*, published in 1991, which is woven around the purported defection of Serge Lebedev, identified as the KGB *Rezident* in Morocco in 1971, there is no reason to suppose that it is anything other than fiction, for whilst there were two defections from the KGB to the West in 1971, neither Oleg Lyalin nor Vladimir Sakharov had any connection with Morocco, and the character of Lebedev must be imaginary, even though both he and 'John Derby' reappear in Aline's most recent offering, *The Well-Mannered Assassin*, which is the first of her self-styled memoirs to be published as a novel. Yet despite the publisher's classification of fiction, the author insists that she has 'developed a fictionalised story that was nevertheless based on actual facts'. In a preliminary note, Aline explains that she had known the notorious terrorist called Carlos the Jackal, and her book, released in August 1994, was an account of their relationship, having 'changed names of people and places for security reasons'.[38]

Aline alleged that she had come to know the Jackal, actually Ilich Ramirez Sanchez, when he had worked for her husband's insurance business as a salesman in Madrid for eight months in 1977. Her timing was certainly impeccable, for her book went on sale a week or so after Sanchez had been arrested in Khartoum and flown to Paris to face a long list of murder charges. Under interrogation the arrogant Sanchez cheerfully acknowledged his crimes, but as the details emerged, few seemed to match the version produced by Aline. Indeed, some very stark contradictions materialised which suggested that either Aline had invented her encounter with the Jackal, or her sources had been wholly unreliable. Virtually every aspect of the Jackal's career, as described by Aline, is incorrect, even though she says that during her research she examined a classified dossier prepared by the CIA. The file documented Sanchez's role in the kidnapping of the OPEC representatives in Vienna in December 1975 and included two other items, a diary written by a DST (the French Security Service) informer, 'Michael Moukharbal',[39] who was subsequently shot by Carlos, and the terrorist's own version of his attempted assassination of Edward Sieff, which was purportedly discovered in a notebook found in his flat. Aline also mentioned two other incidents, one at Orly airport in which an Israeli aircraft had been the target of a rocket attack, and the other the bombing of a Jewish bookshop in Paris, which had killed a woman and injured six others.

A comparison with the true facts of the Jackal's handiwork reveals that Aline had been misinformed on virtually every issue. Certainly Sanchez led the OPEC abduction, and he also killed Michel Moukharbel in a bloody encounter in the rue Toullier in June 1975. Two unarmed counter-intelligence officers from the DST's B2 Arab anti-terrorist section, Raymond Doubs and Jean Donatini, were also shot, and Commissaire Jean Harranz was wounded as they attempted to confront Sanchez with Moukharbel, the head of the PFLP's operations in Europe who had been in the DST's hands for four days. Instead of incriminating Sanchez, Moukharbel was shot dead, allowing the Jackal to make his escape. As for Moukharbel's diary and the Jackal's scribblings, as described by Aline, neither ever existed. Certainly the attack at Orly airport happened, but there was no grenade thrown into a Jewish bookshop. Actually, in August 1974 Sanchez had bombed Le Drugstore, a popular Jewish-owned café on the Boulevard St Germain on the Left Bank, killing two and injuring thirty-four.

Sanchez had been linked to the attack on Sieff when the Browning pistol used to shoot him was found in a former girlfriend's flat in Bayswater, London. Horrified by her discovery, she and her new boyfriend had informed the police, and Sanchez became the world's most wanted terrorist, responsible for the attack on Sieff and an ineffective assault on an Israeli bank in the City of London .

The account of the attack on Edward Sieff demonstrates the contrast between what really happened and Aline's version. In December 1973, Sieff was in the bathroom at his house in St John's Wood, north London, when a hooded gunman burst in, pushed a servant aside and shot the elderly financier in the face. It was an unexpected and unprovoked attempt on the life of a man who had never had any connection whatever with Sanchez. Yet according to Aline, Carlos had sent 'Edouard Sieff'[40] a box of Cuban cigars and, having been invited to join him for a drink at his Mayfair apartment, masquerading as a student named Steiner, took Sieff by surprise, pulled a gun and shot him. Aline's version, though detailed, is completely at odds with what is known of the incident, although Sieff, who died in November 1982, cannot demand the appropriate corrections. Carlos, however, has given his story to the British journalist David Yallop, who reproduced it in *To the Ends of the Earth*,[41] and confirms that every one of Aline's details is incorrect. Sanchez had driven alone to Sieff's unguarded house in north London and had burst in without warning. Aline's elaborate tale of an appointment was sheer invention.

In July 1976, seven months after his raid on the OPEC meeting, Sanchez masterminded the hijacking of an Air France jet, during a scheduled flight from Athens to Paris, to Entebbe, but his plans went wrong when the Israelis made a dramatic intervention and wiped out eight of his gang. Sanchez had intended the plane's passengers and crew to be exchanged for members of the Baader-Meinhof leadership imprisoned at Stammheim in Germany, but when the Jackal's scheme misfired, they committed suicide. By now publicly acknowledged as responsible for half-a-dozen incidents, Sanchez's notoriety restricted his movements to the Middle East and Eastern Europe, and he was not seen again in the West for nineteen years until his arrest in the Sudan. The proposition that immediately after the Entebbe disaster the ruthless but incompetent terrorist had found a job as an insurance salesman in Madrid was too preposterous, but then Aline could not have known that Sanchez had gone to ground in Damascus, only to become a public figure again, just as her book *The Well-Mannered Assassin*, glamorising him as a charmer, was being distributed to bookshops across America.

So if Carlos was not in Spain in 1977, where was he? According to David Yallop, the only person to have cross-examined Sanchez at length and with his consent, the terrorist started the year in Algeria under the alias of George Osharan, ostensibly a professor of archaeology, with the full protection of President Houari Boumédienne. Yallop has researched Carlos in meticulous detail and has reconstructed his travels from his safehouse, a villa in Oran, where he was under the sponsorship of the head of the Algerian military security service, Commander Taihibi. Because of his involvement in the shooting of the three DST officers, and his subsequent conviction for murder *in absentia*, both French intelligence agencies took a close interest in Sanchez, and their agents often reported seeing him in the company of senior Algerian security staff at a night-club owned by President Boumédienne's brother. During 1977, Carlos's movements included some extended visits to Baghdad, where he established an apartment, but his principal sanctuary remained Algeria, where he had fled in July 1976. In September 1976, he had visited Yugoslavia and had accompanied one of his lieutenants, Hans Joachim Klein, on an unsuccessful recruiting tour to Italy, Austria and Germany, before returning safely to Oran. In the months that followed, Sanchez flew to Iraq, Yemen and the Gulf to extort cash from vulnerable Palestinian sympathisers who preferred to pay protection money rather than risk abduction. His permanent move to Baghdad took place in April 1978, to attend the funeral of Dr Wadi Haddad, the terrorist leader of the PFLP, who had died in Berlin of leukaemia. Thereafter, Sanchez made a bid to assert himself as Haddad's successor, but by then he had become too closely associated with failure to attract backers. Nevertheless, an impressive mythology had developed about the terrorist, and his name had achieved much notoriety, often being linked to incidents, such as the massacre at Lod airport in May 1972, and at the Munich Olympic Games in September the same year, or to the Lufthansa hijack at Mogadishu in October 1977, in which he had played absolutely no part.

Sanchez has been the subject of one full biography, *Carlos: Portrait of a Terrorist* by Colin Smith,[42] and has been featured in numerous other studies of international terrorism, including *The Carlos Complex* by Ronald Payne and Christopher Dobson,[43] and Claire Sterling's *The Terror Network*.[44] However, upon closer analysis it becomes clear that none of these books are particularly reliable, and that anyway Aline appears to have ignored them as sources for her material on the Jackal. Certainly Sanchez often promoted an image of himself as a ruthless but cosmopolitan sophisticate, who was committed to the Palestinian cause, but in reality he was a cowardly mercenary who revelled in his own publicity. No doubt the prospect of being lionised by Aline de Romanones would have appealed to his vanity, if not to the families of his many victims.

Of course, all four of Aline's books should be regarded as fiction, and nothing more, whatever her protests to the contrary; her books serve as an unusual example of declassified documents providing eloquent testimony to an author's remarkable imagination.

4

The Search for Johnny Nicholas

'As an aspiring actress Florence didn't mind stories. But a girl did like to know fact from fiction in a love affair. And that was her problem with Johnny.'[1]

Of all the books to be written about the adventures of wartime agents, perhaps the strangest is the one compiled by two Detroit journalists, Hugh Wray McCann and David C. Smith, which they described as 'the greatest untold mystery of World War II'.[2] Their research began in 1968, when they undertook a joint project with David Matthews, a lawyer from South Bend, Indiana, who, at the end of the war, had served with the 7708th War Crimes Group, a US army unit investigating breaches of the Geneva Convention. During the course of Matthews's duties, he had participated in the prosecution of several Germans accused of the horrific murder of Allied prisoners of war and innocent civilians at Gardelegen, near Nordhausen, during the last days of the war. Those responsible for the atrocity, in which more than a thousand men had been herded into a barn and massacred, had been brought to justice in August 1947, and Matthews had been intrigued by testimony from a handful of the survivors which mentioned that among the prisoners had been a single American serviceman. Furthermore, he had been a *black American spy*.

The story of Johnny Nicholas was an important scoop, not just because of his colour or the privations he had experienced at such notorious concentration camps as Buchenwald, Dora, Sachsenhausen and Ravensbrück, but because of the secrecy that had surrounded his case. This is evident from what the publishers said of the book:

Operating in Paris under the cover of a downed US air pilot,
'Major John Nicholas' was the only known black American
Intelligence agent in Nazi-occupied Europe during World War 2.
His story has not yet been told because some say he failed. He
broke the first commandment of his trade – by falling in love.[3]

In the years following his military service, when he had returned to
his practice as an attorney, David Matthews considered writing the story
of the Nazis' negro victim for *Reader's Digest*, but it was not until he met
the two journalists in Detroit in September 1968, and the three agreed to
pool their resources, that *The Search for Johnny Nicholas* became a reality. The result of their research, published in 1982, provoked great
interest in the United States, particularly among the black community,
for not only was their subject an authentic black American war hero, but
he had also operated as an undercover agent in occupied Paris before his
arrest by the Germans in November 1943.

The Search for Johnny Nicholas tells the extraordinary story of a
Haitian who had been educated in France, at the Aristide Briand School
in St Nazaire, and who had subsequently joined the French navy as a
cadet. No mention is made of his recruitment and training by the OSS,
but in the book's acknowledgments the authors express their gratitude
to an individual 'without whose assistance and advice it might never
have reached fruition: Thomas G. Cassady, former head of Secret
Intelligence for the OSS in France'.[4] Instead, the book concentrates on
his experiences in German captivity, first at Fresnes and Port Lieu in
Paris, and later at Buchenwald, Ravensbrück and Mittelbau, the notorious V-1 rocket factory under the Harz mountains known as Dora. At
Buchenwald, where he was incarcerated between January 1944 and
1945, Nicholas had been registered as prisoner number 44451. During
their research, the three authors had acquired a mass of compelling evidence about the black American, who apparently had pretended to have
been part of a USAAF bomber aircrew, but occasionally had confided to
his fellow prisoners that his tale of being an evading pilot was merely a
cover for his true role as a spy who had been infiltrated into Paris masquerading as a medical student in order to gather intelligence.

The authors had managed to piece together Nicholas's remarkable
story from a handful of Holocaust survivors, who well recalled the tall
black man with medical knowledge who had treated several of them in
the *revier*, the concentration camp's sickbay. Certainly Nicholas was

easy to remember, for he had been the only black among the 40,000 captives at Dora, and his name had first been mentioned by Wincenty Hein in the preparations for the Nordhausen war crimes trial of August 1947. Originally a lawyer from Krakow, Hein had served as a clerk in Dora's *revier* and had known Nicholas well. He had been interviewed by Captain Robert G. McCarty of War Crimes Investigation Team 6822 in April 1945 and had been shown a card-index file referring to prisoner number 44451: Nicholas, Johnny; Nationality: American:

> Johnny Nicholas, a Negro, appears from the card to have been born on 5 October 1918. He was an acquaintance of mine at the camp. He was very conspicuous because he was the only Negro there. He was a tall man about six feet in height. I met him in the first part of November 1944, although he had been present at the camp for a period of what he told me (was) one year prior thereto.
>
> At the time I became acquainted with him he was working as a doctor in the hospital (at Dora), and I worked for him. He told me that he had parachuted from a damaged American plane into France, where he had a secret service assignment to perform in the nature of setting up a medical practice in Paris, communicating information to the Allies.
>
> He also told me that after landing he was arrested by the Germans but later released, and that he did establish in Paris a medical office which he operated for a period of time that he did not disclose to me.
>
> I did not ask Nicholas what sort of plane he was in at the time of parachuting into France or in what part of France he landed. I never questioned his story, although he indicated to me that his original arrival in France was prior to the entry of the United States into the European war. . . .
>
> From Dora he was transferred to Rottleberode in the first part of January (1945), and that is the last I saw of him. . . .[5]

This account was the very first to refer to the single American prisoner at Mittelbau, and Hein's testimony was to be used by the Chief Prosecutor, Colonel William Berman, when the trial of fifteen SS personnel (and four other Germans) opened at Dachau on 7 August 1947.

According to the authors, Nicholas was 'the first Negro spy to parachute into Occupied territory in World War II',[6] and this historic event apparently took place near Orléans on an unspecified date in 1943, or perhaps earlier, when he had been welcomed to France by a reception committee. His arrest had occurred in November 1943, when the Gestapo had called early in the morning at an elegant fifth-floor apartment in the Avenue de Lamballe, close to the Eiffel Tower, where he lived with Florence, his wealthy blonde girlfriend. Florence was a beautiful, blue-eyed aspiring actress, whose career had been interrupted by the Nazi occupation. Now she was part of a well-established escape line, 'a link in a chain of thousands of French women whose cunning and courage were daily saving American and British pilots shot down over France'.[7] Ostensibly Nicholas had joined the line as an evader, seeking to be smuggled across the Spanish frontier, but unlike the other aircrew he had lingered in Paris. His lack of determination to return home had aroused some doubts among his contacts in the resistance, who had been unable to extract from the flier the details that could be confirmed over a radio link to London. 'What's wrong with telling us the name of your unit and the type of aircraft you flew?' Florence had pleaded. 'Give it to us and we can radio London and complete the verification and you can be on your way to the Spanish frontier in a few days.'[8]

Nicholas, who had been in bed when the Gestapo agents had arrived, had drawn his Colt automatic with the intention of making his escape, but the lovely Florence had not only betrayed him, but had also removed the magazine from his gun. Unarmed, the American had been quickly overpowered by the Germans, handcuffed and escorted to the notorious interrogation centre in the rue des Saussaies.

Initially Nicholas had been unconcerned about his arrest, for it had not been his first encounter with the German authorities. He had apparently been befriended by a Major Gardemann before the war when he had been 'military attaché to the German Embassy in Haiti',[9] and this officer was now working in Paris, as Colonel Schmidt, on the personal staff of 'the most powerful German in Paris: General Hans von Boeineberg-Lengsfeld, the commandant of Greater Paris'.[10] In the following months, Nicholas and Schmidt had been frequent companions, driving around the city in a Wehrmacht staff car. Indeed, through Schmidt, 'Nicholas had obtained a car, gasoline coupons and his own personal Ausweis'.[11] Equipped with 'a large Citroen',[12] Nicholas had been able to perform invaluable duties for the resistance. On one occasion, he had driven a wounded American airman, Lieutenant Pete Edris, across Paris from a safehouse that had fallen under German surveillance to the home in the Champs-Élysées of a medical student, Jacques Coicou. Nicholas 'had shared an attic room' with Edris at the address 'for several months'.[13] The reason for Schmidt's generosity was Nicholas's knowledge of his pre-war marriage to an exotic Haitian woman, who had borne him 'three children'.[14]

About a month after Edris had recovered from his wounds, the apartment had been raided by the Gestapo and Edris, Coicou and his wife were taken into custody; 'a couple of days later',[15] Nicholas was also caught. Then, 'miraculously', all four had been released. Coicou knew that Nicholas 'was a frequent visitor at German Army headquarters; that he associated with German officers and had been seen riding around with them in their staff cars'.[16] Accordingly, he had credited his unexpected freedom, and that of his wife, to Nicholas's intervention and had been suspicious. His fears had increased when he discovered that Nicholas had moved from his old lodgings, and he had tracked him eventually to a small office in a modern block in Les Batignolles. There he found Nicholas working as a doctor and masquerading as a gynaecologist with a medical qualification from Heidelberg University.

Under questioning by the Sicherheitsdienst during his second period of detention, Nicholas had admitted to a prepared cover story, that he was an American airman who had baled out of his bomber. This explanation apparently had been accepted by his captors. They had moved him first to Fresnes, and later to barracks at Port Lieu near Compiègne, which acted as a transit camp for prisoners destined for deportation to Germany. He had hoped for Colonel Schmidt's intervention, but unfortunately the compliant Abwehr officer had been transferred to the Russian Front and, therefore, was unavailable to exercise his influence for the prisoner. On 25 January 1944, Nicholas was shipped to Germany in a railway cattle truck on a journey to Weimar that was to last three days and end by lorry at Buchenwald.

Once in the concentration camp, Nicholas confided to other prisoners that he held the rank of major in the USAAF, but he was apparently shunned by the other Allied prisoners:

There were no other Americans, so he had no one to buddy up with. Except the British POWs. But the British were a tight-lipped, close bunch themselves and their innate snobbery about all things American forced Nicholas into an outsider's role even with his English-speaking fellow prisoners.[17]

In March 1944, Nicholas's elder brother, Vildebart, who lived at 135 rue de Charonne in Paris, received a postcard from him, a photo of which is reproduced in *The Search for Johnny Nicholas*. In it he asked for food and shaving equipment, and the message was rubber-stamped with the command 'reply in German'.[18] Vildebart and his wife had only seen Johnny 'two or three times a year'[19] when he had been at liberty in Paris, and when asked what he was doing the younger man had been evasive and had mentioned studying medicine at the University of Paris. Until he received the card, Vildebart had had only minimal contact with his brother.

On 11 May 1944, Johnny Nicholas was transferred from Buchenwald to Dora, a labour camp some fifty miles away near Nordhausen. The camp's main function was to supply a workforce for an underground factory located under the Kohnstein in the Harz mountains. Here, in what had once been a calcium-sulphate mine operated by the huge industrial combine of I. G. Farben, a sophisticated factory had been constructed for the assembly of V-weapons. Dora was one of more than thirty labour camps in the region which provided the human slaves to burrow into the hillside and drill forty-eight separate but parallel chambers connected at each end by two long tunnels. The size of the underground accommodation was unprecedented and designed to provide the bombproof facilities that had been lacking at Peenemünde, which had been destroyed by the RAF in an air raid in August 1943.

By pretending to be a physician Nicholas obtained an assignment to the *revier*, the camp sickbay which was sited inside the underground factory, and ministered to the ill and dying until December 1944, when he was transferred to another of Dora's camps, Rottleberode. On 4 April 1945, together with the rest of the prisoners, Nicholas was evacuated to the village of Niedersachswerfen, where freight trains met them and took them on a 100-mile journey to Mieste. Because of the frequent air attacks by Allied planes, the nightmare journey lasted three days. On arrival, they began to march to Gardelegen, escorted by their SS guards, but as soon as an air raid started Nicholas seized the opportunity to run into the woods. Within yards of making his break he was wounded in the leg by a Volkssturm volunteer armed with a shotgun and forced to rejoin the column of emaciated prisoners. When they reached the outskirts of

Gardelegen, they were marched into the Luftwaffe airfield and then herded for the night into a large empty warehouse. The doors were locked and grenades were lobbed in by the SS guards. Altogether 1,000 prisoners were massacred, their remains buried nearby in shallow graves by the few survivors. However, another group of prisoners escaped this fate because there was insufficient room for them in the building, and they were marched a further sixty miles to Sachsenhausen. Among them was Nicholas.

The details regarding Nicholas's last months in Nazi captivity were pieced together from testimony given during the war crimes trials conducted in Germany immediately after the war. During the prosecution of SS personnel at Dora, which started in August 1947 at Dachau, mention was made of the tall American negro, and there was sworn evidence to suggest that he survived temporary imprisonment at Sachsenhausen and was subsequently transferred to Ravensbrück. The camp was liberated on 30 April, and Nicholas was found soon afterwards by a US army unit. Diagnosed as suffering from tuberculosis, he was moved to the Lariboisière hospital in Paris, where he was visited by his brother Vildebart. Shocked by his condition, Vildebart had him moved to the St Antoine hospital, where he died on 4 September 1945.

The moving story of Johnny Nicholas is essentially the biography of Jean Nicolas, a Haitian who enlisted in the French navy in Martinique in 1937 and was arrested in Paris in November 1943. The problem concerning *The Search for Johnny Nicholas* is the assertion that at the time of his imprisonment by the Nazis he was an agent for the OSS. Despite the apparently painstaking research to trace Nicholas's movements, and the detailed description of his eighteen months of captivity, moving from one concentration camp to another, there is a mystifying gap in the chronology between his departure from Haiti and his final arrest in Paris.

A close analysis of the text reveals some surprising discrepancies in Nicholas's tale. For example, the authors recall Jean Nicolas, aged twenty, leaving his home in Port au Prince to join the French navy:

> Late in the fall of 1938 word came that the French naval vessel had finally docked at the island of Martinique. He grabbed his bags and hopped aboard the inter-island ferry for the 100-mile trip. . . . A few weeks later he was aboard the training ship *Courbet*. Later he was transferred to the *Ocean*, totally challenged and excited by the life of a sea cadet.[20]

Thus Nicolas left Haiti late in 1938, yet this version is contradicted by his mother: 'The last time she saw him was in 1937 when he left for Martinique to enlist in the French Navy.'[21]

Clearly there is some confusion about exactly when Nicolas left his home, but what of his movements thereafter? The authors say that he accidentally fell from the *Ocean*'s rigging and was badly injured, so that in March 1939 he was handed a Certificate of Good Conduct and informed that he was unfit for military duties. It is at this moment that the chronology becomes a little fuzzy. Initially he 'closeted himself at 97 Boulevard Diderot', but only 'weeks later' he 'snatched the allowance his mother had lodged in the bank for him'[22] and set off for the riviera, where 'Jean Marcel Nicolas of Port-au-Prince had become Johnny Nicholas of Boston, USA'.[23]

How did a penniless Haitian naval cadet make the transformation to 'an urbane host, a witty conversationalist and – for an American – unbelievably facile among the international set with his command of French, German and Spanish'?[24] Somehow he found a job as a consultant to a film producer and was paid half a million francs, but the rest of his period in France, until he reappeared on a parachute, is left to the imagination of the reader. Nor is it known exactly when this particular event took place, and this omission is important. The single firm date supplied by the authors is 23 November 1943, which is when he was betrayed by his girlfriend, Florence. Working backwards from that, it is clear that Nicholas must have been in Paris for at least six months. The chronology is like a jigsaw puzzle, but, when assembled in reverse order, one can determine three separate episodes, each of which is described as either weeks or months apart.

Before his final arrest, Nicholas had been practising as a gynaecologist in Les Batignolles. Prior to that he had experienced his first arrest, when his release, and that of his three friends, had been engineered by his Abwehr contact, Colonel Schmidt. So how much time had elapsed between his appearance at the office in Les Batignolles and his release? There are no exact dates in the text, but there is a single clue. Two Haitian medical students, Hans Pape and Jacques Coicou, had been prompted to look for Nicholas after his release from German custody and 'when the weeks lengthened into months' they had started to search for him. From this reference one can deduce that there was a gap of at least two months between Schmidt's intervention and Nicholas being found by his friends masquerading as a doctor with a bogus medical qualification. The crucial event prior to his arrest was the period Nicholas spent with Paul Edris. The authors say that the arrests happened 'about a month later when Lt Edris was fully recovered'.[25] Therefore, another month can be added to the previous two referred to.

Since it is known that Nicholas shared the attic of Coicou's apartment on the Champs-Élysées with Edris 'for several months',[26] one can make a conservative estimate and conclude that between his initial introduction to Edris, at a safehouse in Passy, and Nicholas being traced by his friends, a period of at least six months must have elapsed. Having established the minimum time gaps, in reverse order between Les Batignolles, the arrest of Edris and the rescue of Edris from Passy, what are the earlier episodes that are recounted, and when did they take place? One should add the unspecified number of months that Nicholas spent in Colonel Schmidt's company:

> Nicholas emerged with Colonel Schmidt and they'd driven off in a staff car. In the months that followed, the guards became used to seeing the tall black civilian come and go at headquarters, sometimes with the colonel, sometimes without him. . . .[27]

The implication is, therefore, that Nicholas was at liberty in Paris for rather longer than a year. This proposition seems to be supported indirectly by a reference to the frequency of the meetings between Nicholas and his brother Vildebart. The authors say that 'he and Vildebart didn't see much of each other. Two or three times a year at most. But in Johnny's line of work that was to be expected.'[28] On the assumption that the 'line of work' was an allusion to espionage, one is left with the impression that Nicholas may have been in Paris for up to two years. The number of visits Johnny made to Vildebart and his wife is unknown except that

> they'd tried to pump him on his first few visits; when he didn't tell them anything they finally gave up. Other than saying that he was taking some medical courses at the University of Paris, he kept them in the dark. It annoyed Vildebart, but in wartime Paris the less you knew about a friend's or relative's activities, the better it was for everyone.[29]

There is one further item which supports this rather lengthy timescale. Florence is described as having betrayed him 'after a year of ardent passion'.[30] Having gleaned all the clues from the text, one can reasonably conclude that Jean Nicolas, alias Johnny Nicholas, spent at least a year, and probably two, operating in Paris after his arrival by parachute. The problem with this, or indeed the contention that he only dropped near Orléans sometime in 1943, is that, according to OSS records, the organisation did not have any agents in occupied France prior to June 1943. Furthermore, the handful that were despatched between June and November are fully accounted for, and none bears any resemblance whatever to Nicholas. In other words, if Nicholas was in Paris in 1943, he certainly was not there on behalf of OSS.

The question then arises, what evidence is there that Nicholas was ever connected with OSS? The authors are clearly convinced that he was an agent, for they describe the flight he took across the English Channel on the way to a dropping zone manned by a reception committee of the French resistance. They also record his unsuccessful attempts to convey details of the V-weapons he had seen at Mittelbau to another Allied agent imprisoned at Buchenwald, Wing-Commander Yeo-Thomas, from SOE's RF Section. Nicholas was unwilling to confide the nature of his secret orders to Florence, who believed him to be an evading US airman, and it would seem that the first time he entrusts a version of the truth to anyone is on his arrival at Buchenwald, when he tells an unnamed fellow prisoner: 'I'm not a Frenchman. I'm an American. A major in the United States Army Air Corps.'[31] He gives a similar response to the other prisoners who challenge his air-force credentials and ask whether he is really an Allied agent. Nicholas declines to answer, saying only that he dropped into France by parachute, thereby leaving the strong impression that he is indeed a spy. When he was at Dora, he was more forthcoming to Wincenty Hein, the Polish prisoner who gave sworn testimony to war crimes investigators in May 1945:

> He told me that he had parachuted from a damaged American plane into France, where he had a secret-service assignment to perform in the nature of setting up a medical practice in Paris, communicating information to the Allies.[32]

Astonishingly, despite the impressive pages of source notes and appendices listing the many intelligence experts who had assisted the research for *The Search for Johnny Nicholas*, virtually the entire story is predicated on the statement made by Hein, that the black prisoner in Dora had told him that he had been on a secret mission at the time of his arrest. The authors had ignored the reference to the aircraft having been damaged, which would give more weight to the theory that Nicholas had been a fairly straightforward case of an evading airman, and built the more exotic story of an American intelligence operation on these rather flimsy foundations. The only connection Nicholas had with OSS is the appearance in the appendices entitled 'principal sources and references' of various senior US intelligence personnel. But did they confirm that Nicholas had served in OSS? If so, there is actually no evidence anywhere in the text.

There must be considerable doubts about Nicholas, both in his role as an airman and as a secret agent. If he were an authentic agent, why was he so reluctant to admit his true status to Florence, who was, after all, a member of an active escape line? If Nicholas really had been a spy, and had been trained as one, it is certain that he would have been able to distinguish between the considerable difference in weight of an empty automatic and one loaded with a full magazine. Yet when the Gestapo arrived to arrest him, he allegedly produced his Colt and pulled the trigger three times, not realising that Florence had removed the magazine. Whilst the proposition that OSS recruited and trained a black agent is improbable, the organisation would have been guilty of appalling negligence if it had even contemplated dropping one into territory occupied by the Nazis. Philippe de Vomécourt, one of the architects of SOE's networks in France, well recalls the attitude of the Germans to Negroes:

For coloured men in France, a 'safe-house' or false identity papers were an impossibility. To be a coloured man in a district occupied by the Germans was to know that death was near. When the Germans first overran France, reaching as far south as Bordeaux before the cease-fire, they took prisoner all the coloured men they met. They made no distinction between those in uniform and those without it. All were taken. Some were shot, some 'died' in captivity. Others just disappeared. None of the men taken prisoner were ever seen again. The truth is that they were all put to death. The Germans had a pathological fear and hatred of coloured men; they could not conceive of living in the same country with them.[33]

The disappointing truth is that there probably was a single black prisoner at Buchenwald and Dora, and he may even have told some of his fellow prisoners that he was a spy, but, whatever his background, he was never an American intelligence agent captured on a secret mission to Paris.

5

George Borodin,
Surgeon Extraordinary

'It would be all right in a thriller, but this is real life, and these things can't be done.'[1]

Born in Baku in 1903, George Borodin came from a military family, but was given the opportunity after the 1917 revolution to study medicine. He came to London and, according to his publishers, was regarded in 1950 as one of Britain's 'most famous plastic surgeons'.[2] As well as a celebrated medical practitioner, Borodin was a man of letters. His success with *Pillar of Fire* and *Cradle of Splendour*[3] gave him considerable status as a writer, and he was later to publish books on an astonishing variety of topics, ranging from biography to travel, music and ballet.

The book that qualifies Borodin for mention in these pages is *No Crown of Laurels*, an unusual account of his wartime work as a plastic surgeon, operating on Allied agents for British Intelligence. The author concedes that, in the interests of security, he has given 'imaginary names to the leading characters',[4] but confirms that during the war he 'actually operated on various resistance leaders, who had been smuggled into this country, so that they might return to carry on their arduous duties unrecognised by friends and relations or, more important still, by their enemies in the Gestapo'.[5]

Borodin's story opens as he is asked by a man who calls at his Harley Street consulting rooms in September 1940, representing himself as an executive of a film company, to perform surgery on the face of a young man. The proposal is to disfigure a perfectly good-looking face and

Borodin refuses on ethical grounds. He is then summoned to the War Office, where a 'Colonel X' explains the background of his putative patient: 'He's a Norwegian, a patriot working in the underground movement and a very reliable agent of ours. We want to drop him behind the lines in his own country to do some vital work for us.'[6]

The Colonel outlines the operation. The Norwegian is to adopt the identity of a Gestapo officer who is in British hands, and Borodin's task is to alter the features of the agent, giving him scars and a broken nose, so that he can 'play the part of a Nazi thug'.[7] Borodin agrees the commission, and within two weeks the Norwegian is transformed at a small country hospital. However, this is far from the end of the case for his patient returns to visit Borodin 'three times during the course of the next year'.[8] Borodin refers to him as 'Erik A' and reveals that the German for whom he is to be substituted is 'Otto Leichenhauser, who is now in the keeping of the British Government'.[9] After his wounds have healed and Erik has completed 'no more than three practice drops in England',[10] he is parachuted into Norway with instructions to 'report to a small Norwegian village where a new submarine base was to be constructed'.[11] Here he was 'attached to one of the Gestapo squads who were supervising the gangs of forced labour building pens and other structures for the submarine base'.[12] After several weeks of gathering information, Erik was granted leave and was ordered back to London for further instructions. He started the journey across the North Sea by a small fishing boat, but was soon intercepted by a Coastal Command Sunderland which carried him the rest of the way.

Erik's second mission was to be dropped by parachute near Oslo and report for duty, as Otto Leichenhauser, to a new aerodrome still under construction. He spent several months at the airfield before being transferred to another important project. 'Now he was on the coast once more, his unit supervising work on a small port that was being reconditioned and enlarged for service and equipment of German destroyers and surface raiders.'[13] Borodin recalls that he received no further visits from Erik after he had been despatched on his second mission and the explanation from Colonel X was simple: Erik had been shot dead by the Norwegian resistance while he had been helping them to sabotage the port. On this occasion he had been compromised and, in order to prevent him from falling into German hands, Erik had been shot dead 'by Erik's finest friend'.[14]

Borodin's second patient had an equally harrowing experience to relate.

He was a schoolteacher from eastern Poland, who had pretended to be a
Nazi sympathiser. He had been smuggled to England in October 1940 for
training in sabotage techniques, but had been badly injured by a grenade.
He had obtained permission from the occupation forces to be away for
only six weeks, ostensibly to travel to see his sick mother, so there was
only a limited amount of time before he was to be parachuted home.

> That afternoon, he would make a practice parachute drop. The
> next day he would set out on a flight that would be a very long
> one, over enemy territory for its greater part, and with constant
> threat of interception. It was 1940, and pinpointing targets had
> not reached the level of perfection it afterward attained in the Air
> Force.[15]

Borodin never saw the Pole again, but, according to Colonel X, the
agent had previously visited England in 1939 when he had been
recruited. After his return home, for the second time, he participated in
the sabotage of a dam that had been built near his village to power a
chemical plant. The teacher destroyed the dam, but also flooded much of
the village. Later, 'he gave the warning about the concentrations against
Russia, and from that moment his name was passed on to the Soviets as
that of a very reliable agent who could be trusted in every way.
Throughout 1942, he was more in touch with the Russians than the
British.' His fate was unknown, but 'it was early in 1943 that his reports
suddenly ceased. . . . Rather against the usual procedure, the department
put through an enquiry to Moscow. The Russians, came the reply, had
heard from Vaslav about a week after the date of his last despatch to
London.'[16]

Borodin's third patient was another Norwegian, a captain in the
Norwegian army who had gone underground after the British with-
drawal. 'Edvard was already famous as a fighting patriot – too famous for
his safety.'[17] He had come to England in 1941 to be transformed and,
after his operation, had been parachuted into the neighbourhood of his
native village, where he was well known. The transformation had to 'be
so complete that not even a close friend or even a relation'[18] could recognise him. He was to be appointed the guide to a party of a dozen German
mineral prospectors led by a Professor Ziedermann on a search in the
Norwegian mountains for uranium. Once the mission had been completed, Edvard had returned to London to prepare for a further

assignment, which he evidently survived as he exchanged letters with Borodin after the war.

Borodin's next patient, later in 1941, was a Dutchman named Dirk, who had escaped from a labour camp and was wanted by the Germans. He had been flown out of Holland and the surgeon was to alter his very prominent features so that the man could return home in safety. Colonel X confided to Borodin that Dirk 'had brought certain information about some curious structures the Germans were putting up near The Hague'.[19] After treatment and his insertion back into enemy-occupied territory, 'he'd picked up the trail that led to one or two other places and in the end led us to Peenemünde'.[20] Dirk later volunteered to work for the Germans and was sent to an aircraft factory making jet engines. Then, 'after two months, he was transferred to one of those secret underground factories, and ... gave us some quite imposing information about how the Germans were tooling up the place for the production of V2s'.[21] Although initially considered unpromising, Dirk had 'developed into one of the most resourceful and energetic and determined agents we had'.[22]

During the summer of 1941, Borodin operated on the eyes of Pierre, a Free French *résistant* from the South of France hunted by the Nazis. The shape of his eyes made him easily recognisable and, once altered, he announced that 'the Royal Air Force will fly me to the Southern Alps and there I will descend into the heart of my own country'.[23] Six months later, Pierre was back in London with a broken leg and Borodin heard more of his patient's background. He had been dropped successfully, but soon afterwards he had been arrested by the Gestapo and sent to a concentration camp. However, on his way to Germany he had escaped, but had broken his leg in the process. Undaunted, and helped by sympathisers, he travelled to the French coast, a journey which had taken 'over two months',[24] and then crossed the Channel in a small motor launch. When Pierre's leg had mended, Borodin performed a second operation to change his face again, and the Frenchman returned home and survived to see the Liberation as a leader of the resistance.

Another patient of Borodin's in 1942 was a German intellectual named Heinrich, who had fled the Nazis in 1935. After his face had been changed, he returned to Germany and was engaged 'stirring up trouble and doing a spot of sabotage organisation right inside Krupp's place itself in Essen'.[25] Not surprisingly, he was denounced to the Gestapo, but he survived incarceration at the Belsen concentration camp and was able to undergo another restorative operation at Borodin's hands after the war. By that time, Heinrich reportedly had obtained a job in the Allied Military Government.

The next patient was Philip, a young Englishman 'known to practically all the underground leaders in Europe',[26] who had recently emerged from a mission to Austria. Unfortunately, the Gestapo had seized his forged German passport so they possessed a detailed description of him. Astonishingly, Borodin performed five separate operations on Philip, transforming him into, consecutively, a beer-soaked Bavarian; then, three months later, into 'a mild-looking man who might have easily passed for a professor of some obscure subject in a minor university'; then, six weeks later, into 'a far from prepossessing peasant. His face was surly with a touch of stupidity'; then into a Dutch collaborator; and finally into a Prussian officer. He played a key role in the liberation of Belgium, Holland and France, and Borodin saw him 'last in the early months of 1945'.[27]

In the case of the left-wing Dutchman named Piet, Borodin was to make him resemble his older cousin Jan, a Nazi sympathiser. Jan had been killed by the resistance in Amsterdam and Piet was to take his place. As well as altering his face to fit that of his Fascist cousin, Piet was also given flat feet so that he could duplicate Jan's characteristic walk. Borodin never discovered whether the mission was a success or not, because 'from the moment his parachute left the aeroplane in Holland, nothing more was ever heard of him'.[28]

A well-known rising young Dutch actress was Borodin's first woman patient referred to him by Colonel X. In 1940, Wilhelmina had fled to London from Rotterdam with her mother and three sisters. Now she proposed to return and find a job as a radio announcer, and the surgeon ensured that, despite her previous fame as a star of the theatre, she would go unrecognised. 'No one would have suspected that this plain-looking girl was the striking actress who had first walked into my consulting rooms,' he recalled.[29] Her mission was to pretend to be a collaborator in order to secure her post as a broadcaster, and then make a particular announcement at a certain time. As Colonel X pointed out, 'as soon as the Germans realise what she is doing, the engineers will cut her out, and next morning, probably, she'll be before a firing squad. It is certain death for her.'[30]

After he had performed the necessary operation and Wilhelmina was despatched on her mission, Borodin often tuned into the Hilversum station and heard her broadcasts. He could not speak Dutch and could not make out what she was saying, but the voice was 'quite unmistakable, speaking across the ether'. However, 'it was during the last great drive into Germany that the end came' and Wilhelmina simply disappeared without trace.[31]

The penultimate case Borodin describes is that of Gaston, an electrical engineer who had been sabotaging supply lines since 1940. 'For years his name had been one of the bright lights of the French resistance.'[32] By 1944, he had achieved some notoriety both within the resistance and among the German authorities, and his assistant, named Jean, had volunteered to be captured so as to reduce the pressure on Gaston. Borodin's task was to turn Jean 'into the perfect counterpart of Gaston',[33] and this he accomplished to perfection. Later, he heard that 'Jean had blown up a small power station of some importance to the German Army and he had been caught making his escape. They were completely taken in, and announced that the famous *franc-tireur* and Red Terrorist, Gaston, had at last been brought to stern Nazi justice.'[34] This left the way clear for Gaston to blow up 'an electrical plant that was a key point for the German field repair system' a week before D-Day. He did so, but apparently perished in the explosion.[35]

Borodin's final case was that of Hilde Gartner, a Viennese Jewess whose obtrusive nose required reconstruction if she was to return home under cover and avoid the attention of the Nazi racial experts. After the rhinoplasty had been completed, Hilde was dropped over Austria with a new identity, that of Hilde Kintzler. She found work in a local factory, but after nine weeks she was recognised, despite the improved shape of her nose. Under interrogation she admitted only to her Jewish origins and was sent to a concentration camp. Just as she was about to be transferred to an extermination camp, a German major-general on an inspection tour obtained her release, tried to rape her and then sent her to a garrison as a nude dancer in a cabaret entertaining the officers' mess. After two months, the unit was sent to the Eastern Front and Hilde escaped, promptly falling into the hands of Russian partisans. She now became 'a recognised agent of the Soviets'[36] and accompanied them back to Vienna, where she described her experiences in a letter to Borodin.

Borodin does not reveal the branch of the War Office which sponsored his patients, but it can reasonably be assumed that, on the basis that the organisation was operating before the war, and SOE only came into existence in July 1940, it must have been SIS. But if that were the case, why should SIS require the services of a plastic surgeon when it ran its own medical facility at a country house at Tempsford? Borodin recalls the inconvenience of having to deceive the nursing staff at a country hospital to obtain treatment for his patients and suggests a rather lame excuse for the choice: 'Military hospitals were ruled out, because any military establishment is a very clear hunting ground for spies.'[37] This is odd logic on two grounds: SIS did not know, as the author asserted, 'German agents to be extremely busy – and efficient'[38] in September 1940. In fact, the reverse was true and by then the Security Service had come to the realisation that the only German spies still at liberty in Britain were double agents under MI5's control. Secondly, why bother with finding a new medical establishment when Tempsford Hall, run by the redoubtable Dr Henry Hales, was fully staffed and operational? Thus there is some doubt about exactly which branch of British Intelligence made the approach to Borodin, and attention should turn to his two intelligence contacts. The first was the film company representative whose original approach in Harley Street Borodin had rejected. 'This man must remain in these pages cloaked behind the rather unconvincing and certainly unsatisfactory label of "Mr Z", for he remains, as he was at the time, one of the most capable and accomplished members of the British Intelligence Service, to identify whom would be a crime even now peace has come.'[39]

At first Borodin had denounced 'Z' as 'jovial looking and a little flamboyant. I took an instant dislike to him.' However, he later found him to be 'a man of culture':

> His dress was perfect as only the dress of an English gentleman
> can be. Every detail of it seemed inevitable – even the carnation
> in the buttonhole, the one touch of colour in an outfit that was
> otherwise a paragon of sober propriety. Perhaps, with his butter-
> fly collar and restrained, striped trousers, he would have passed
> as a prosperous City man – but for an air of authority about him
> that suggested rather a survivor of one of the dying feudal British
> ruling caste.[40]

This description might be thought to fit two senior British intelligence officers. The first is Sir Claude Dansey, who at the outbreak of war headed a highly unorthodox branch of SIS known as the 'Z Organisation'. Dansey himself was known as the 'Z-1'. and his subordinates were identified by similar Z numbers, and several pretended to work for a film company, London Films, as a convenient cover. However, Dansey can probably be discounted in that he died in June 1947 and, therefore, could hardly have been known to Borodin to be active at the time of his book's publication, in 1950. The second candidate is Major Lawrence Grand, the first head of SIS's Section D, who habitually wore civilian clothes and sported a red carnation in his buttonhole, but he fell out of favour with SOE and had been transferred to India by the end of 1940. Nor was he to rejoin SIS after the war, which also tends to rule him out. Despite the difficulty of putting a name to Z, the combination of that choice of letter, his customary buttonhole and the use of a film company as cover all sounds like the genuine article.

Borodin's book contains in total the stories of ten different secret agents, but upon detailed study it emerges that each of them contains a sufficiently serious flaw to undermine its authenticity. Take, for example, his first patient, the Norwegian patriot named Erik, who adopted the identity of the Gestapo officer Otto Leichenhauser. There is no record of any Gestapo official being taken prisoner in Norway in 1940. Nor is there any trace of a Norwegian who was parachuted twice into that country in 1940. Indeed, there were no agents parachuted into Scandinavia in 1940 by any British intelligence organisation. As Sir Frank Nelson, the first head of SOE, complained at the time, 'we have at the moment literally no one in the field at all'.[41] Quite apart from the above, Erik's exfiltration from enemy territory in a boat must be fictional as there were no Sunderland aircraft deployed across the North Sea in the autumn of 1940. Nor was there any significant sabotage of a German naval installation in 1942, as alleged by the Colonel, and his achievement, by masquerading as a Gestapo officer for months at a time, strains reason and credulity.

Closer examination of the other stories reveals similar inconsistencies and contradictions. In the case of the Polish teacher, he is described as having been recruited in England in 1939, which is entirely plausible. However, Borodin then says that Vaslav was exfiltrated to England and returned to east central Poland by parachute, all in a period of six weeks in 1940. Apart from the time factor, the problem here is that the RAF flew no parachute missions into Poland in October 1940. Nor is it likely that SIS would willingly surrender the identity of its star agent to the Soviet NKVD, a proposition about as likely as a patriotic Pole willing to switch his allegiance from the British to the hated Soviets.

When one turns to Edvard, the Norwegian officer who parachuted into Norway in 1941 to assist in a German geological survey for uranium, further problems emerge. There was no air mission of the kind described in 1941, and there were generally very few flights of this type to Scandinavia because the mountainous terrain made parachute jumps very hazardous undertakings. During 1942, the first year in which a Special Duties Squadron flew to Norway, there were only eleven missions. Understandably, both SIS and SOE preferred the more reliable sea route from Shetland, especially during the winter months of long nights which protected them from enemy fighters and reconnaissance aircraft. There must also be some doubt about the likelihood of a German search for uranium, particularly as the enemy's atomic research programme had acquired a plentiful supply in Belgium. Strangely, Borodin comments that Edvard's assignment is proof that British Intelligence was monitoring German atomic research at an early date:

> The attack on the Norsk Hydro heavy-water plant was to be made by some other intrepid Norwegians and thus set back German progress irredeemably – to our own salvation. That was in 1943. This was in 1941, showing how early the Germans were at work – and also how soon our own Intelligence got wind of their intentions.[42]

In reality, we now know from declassified documents that the British were aware of the progress made by German nuclear physicists much earlier, and that a Norwegian scientist at Trondheim, Professor Leif Tronstad, who had access to Vermork, was keeping SIS informed of developments from the earliest days of the Nazi occupation. Borodin's conclusion that the sabotage at Vermork in 1943 'set back German progress irredeemably' is a slight exaggeration. In fact, the attack took place on 27 February 1943 and production was restored to normal levels by mid-August. It also transpired that the commodity known as heavy water was not the crucial ingredient of the fission process as had previously been believed.

Whether the Dutchman named Dirk really alerted SIS to the existence of V-weapons in 1941 is also somewhat contentious. Certainly there is no evidence from official sources that the identification of 'curious structures'[43] in The Hague ever led British intelligence analysts to Peenemünde, which had been identified as a rocket development site nearly two years earlier, in November 1939, when it was included in the famous Oslo Report. This document, delivered anonymously to the naval attaché at the British Embassy in Oslo, described the V-1 prototype and was studied by SIS's scientific adviser, Professor R. V. Jones, who recalls that

The German Navy was said to have developed remote-controlled rocket-driven gliders of about three metres span and three metres long, with radio control for launching by aircraft against enemy ships. The experimental establishment where this work was being carried out was Peenemünde – the first mention we had ever heard of this establishment.[44]

The original translation made of the Oslo Report was declassified and released in 1979, and it definitely contains a reference to Peenemünde. In fact, the direct reference was quite detailed: 'The testing range is at Peenemünde, at the mouth of the Peene, near Wolgast, near Greifswald.'[45] Clearly Dirk cannot be credited with helping SIS find Peenemünde, so what of the 'strange structures' at The Hague? One explanation might have been the navigation antennae used by the Luftwaffe to guide its bombers to targets over Britain at night. These strange devices were sited along the coast from Cherbourg to Denmark, but they were entirely unconnected with the V-weapons and were the subject of close surveillance from both agents and aerial reconnaissance from the moment they first appeared, in 1940.

If Dirk really existed, and he is alleged to have become 'one of the most resourceful and energetic and determined agents'[46] of all, it is surprising more is not known about him. Much the same could be said for Pierre, the hero of the resistance, 'who had terrorised the Germans in the South of France ever since they marched in'[47] and who was caught by the Gestapo in 1941. His tale, of being flown by the RAF from England into southern France, is hopelessly flawed on two counts: the RAF did not possess aircraft with sufficient range to fly to the South of France from England, and the Germans did not 'march in' to the South of France until November 1942.

If the accounts of Dirk, Edvard, Vaslav and Erik appear unlikely, what of the rest? Heinrich, the intellectual factory worker at Krupp's, who survived Belsen, sounds strange, although it is true that X Section of SOE attempted to infiltrate agents into Germany. None survived, yet Heinrich apparently did. In any event, none was parachuted as early as 1942, as claimed by Borodin. Philip also sounds too good to be true. He emerged unscathed at the end of the war, having operated undercover in at least four different European countries, including Austria. Any Briton accomplishing such a feat would be sure to have been decorated, but there is no record of any person resembling him receiving an award for his heroics. Colonel X suggested to Borodin that Philip's life story merited a book, and if only half his exploits are true it is astonishing his biography has not been published. None of his many guises strike a chord with historians of the European resistance movements and, therefore, the claims made on his behalf should be treated with some scepticism, particularly the fanciful idea that this Briton had posed 'as a Dutch collaborator . . . and found himself under suspicion, but he got his own back – so the colonel told me – he went back next time to the same place with the face of a Prussian officer and laid an information against the same Dutchman who was now no more and started a hue and cry.'[48]

Could the story of Piet the Dutchman be true? He was the young anti-Fascist who adopted the identity of his older collaborator cousin. Borodin maintains that Piet simply disappeared after he had been parachuted into Holland, but this is where his story becomes even less credible. So many Dutchmen lost their lives while operating for the Allied clandestine services that after the war the Netherlands Government established a Parliamentary enquiry to investigate the circumstances of each. Meticulous care was taken to document every agent who vanished from sight and, although Borodin omits any dates in his account, it is possible to be quite emphatic that no agent despatched to Holland by SIS, SOE or any of their Dutch counterparts conforms to the details supplied by Borodin.

Another Dutch case that seems upon examination to be doubtful is that of Wilhelmina, the actress who returned to Holland to become a radio announcer. As with Piet, there is no trace whatever of any person resembling her. There is no reference to her in the Dutch Parliamentary investigation and the Dutch broadcasting authorities, which are still located at Hilversum, have also denied knowledge of her.

Having disposed of so many of Borodin's patients, one is left with Gaston and Hilde. The engineer who was a hero of the French resistance is a curious fellow, for he is described as 'a very successful leader' who has 'been with us since 1940'.[49] Supposedly, 'he's organised some of the strongest groups in France' and enjoyed unprecedented prestige among the *maquis*. 'There are plenty of engineers among the *maquis*. But not one of these men combines his specialised knowledge with great powers of leadership.' For years, according to Borodin, 'his name had been one of the bright lights of the French resistance',[50] but he had disappeared a week before D-Day and was presumed to have died while sabotaging a key electrical plant in France.

This scenario, the loss of a famous French hero around 31 May 1944, is inherently unlikely, for none of the many histories of the French resistance, or the accounts of D-Day, refers to such an event. If Gaston existed, he could never have achieved the celebrity Borodin credits him with. Bearing in mind that his friend Jean had already sacrificed himself to allow Gaston a measure of freedom, one might reasonably expect the story to have received wider circulation and acceptance.

Finally, we turn to the remarkable ordeal of Hilde Gartner, the Austrian from Vienna, who had fled to England before the war to escape the Nazi persecution of the Jews. What makes her story so exceptional is the fact that, like Heinrich, she survived not just a concentration camp, but capture on the Eastern Front by Russian partisans, who rarely wasted time by taking prisoners or an opportunity to despoil someone who, according to Borodin, looked 'like a goddess from a Wagnerian Valhalla'.[51] The Soviet Red Army was not renowned for discriminating between Austrian and German camp followers, and the Russian irregulars attained an even less appealing reputation when it came to their treatment of the enemy's womenfolk. Accordingly, if Hilde really did exist and survived her traumatic experiences, she at least had a story worth telling.

It may be reasonably concluded that George Borodin may have allowed his imagination a little too much rein when he was writing *No Crown of Laurels*, so it should be asked what has become of him. According to the British General Medical Council and the British Association of Plastic Surgeons, no doctor of that name ever practised medicine in Britain. However, further research reveals that Borodin is a pseudonym, and that the author's true name is George Alexis Milkomanovich Milkomane, the son of General Ivan Alexandrovitch and the Countess Maria Ignatiev Milkomane. He studied medicine in Florence and Rome before the war and became a naturalised British subject in 1938, six years after his arrival in England. In 1939, he married June Hollingdale, an Australian artist. He has written more than 120 books under a variety of pen-names, including George Braddon, George Alexis Bankoff, Peter Conway, Alec Redwood and George Sava. This last name is of some considerable interest as this was the name he used in 1979 to write *Secret Surgeon*,[52] an account of the author's experiences as a plastic surgeon during the Second World War.

No one reading *Secret Surgeon* would have any hint that George Sava was not the author's true name, for he lists only three previously published books and omits *No Crown of Laurels*. However, since *Secret*

Surgeon and the title published twenty-nine years earlier cover an identical period in the same author's life, it is worth making a brief comparison. The results are really quite surprising for there is a distinct similarity between the two. Indeed, the familiar characters of Erik, Edvard, Dirk, Heinrich, Philip, Wilhelmina, Gaston, Piet, Hilde, Gustav and Pierre are all there, but the story of each has been told in slightly different terms. Furthermore, instead of 'Colonel X' and 'Mr Z', Sava was introduced to his secret work by two Scotland Yard detectives, Detective Inspector Holmes and Sergeant Robert Mansfield of the Special Branch. They had tested his loyalties with an elaborate charade, using a woman pretending to be a Nazi sympathiser to invite him to join a meeting of anti-Communists. Instead, Sava had reported her approach to the police. It quickly transpired that the proposal had been made to establish his bona fides before 'Colonel Wilson (not his real name) from MI5 of the War Office' began to bring him patients requiring his special talents. His first case, in September 1940, was Pierre Newchamp, whose story is almost identical to that of the other Pierre in *No Crown of Laurels*, except for two significant changes. In the original version, Pierre was not Borodin's first patient, and he was treated in the summer of 1941. Yet in every other respect the story is virtually the same. A comparison between these two passages, where Pierre explains why the shape of his eye needs to be altered, is typical of the remainder:

'I come from the south of France, m'sieur,' he explained. 'It is a part of my country to which, in the course of her long and glorious history, many races and many people have come. I do not know but perhaps in me flows the blood of one of these peoples. Look at my eyes, m'sieur. They are slanting. There is in them something of the East. By them alone I might be recognised among a thousand.' I had already noticed his eyes, but I now made another and more careful inspection.[53]

This was the dialogue that took place between Borodin and Pierre 'from the South of France', which is not dissimilar to the remarks made by Pierre Newchamp, who had been 'born in a small town in Alsace-Lorraine',[54] which, geographically, is about as far from the South of France as possible, to George Sava some nine months earlier:

'My eyes, Monsieur Sava. You know that I come from a part of

France where many people of different races had lived. I do not know, but perhaps in me flows the blood of one of these people. You have noticed my eyes, no doubt Mr Sava. They are slanting. There is in them something of the Orient. By them alone I'll be recognised in no time by our enemies.' I had already from the beginning of our friendship noticed his unusually attractive, slanting eyes. This time I made another professional examination.[55]

These passages bear a striking resemblance to one another, and there are dozens of similar examples throughout *Secret Surgeon*. Indeed, any reader of both books, understandably unaware that George Borodin of 1950 and George Sava of 1979 were the same person, might be forgiven for thinking that there could scarcely be a more blatant example of modern plagiarism. Virtually the only other difference between the two versions is the chronology, as is demonstrated by this comparison. In *No Crown of Laurels*, Borodin recalls Erik the young Norwegian, 'the first of these extraordinary cases . . . presented to me as a film actor':

The colonel had called him Mr A, but that is a clumsy and tedious name to keep repeating, whether in writing or in speech. . . . So let us call this Norwegian youth by the name of Erik. It may or may not have been his name.[56]

In *Secret Surgeon*, Sava contradicts Borodin and asserts that Erik was not the first of his kind, but in every other respect his description of the case is identical.

The young Norwegian who was brought to me by Colonel Wilson was not chronologically speaking the next case to follow Pierre. No, he was the sixth or seventh of the 'film actors' who required facial changes.[57]

When asked for an explanation in 1992, George Milkomane replied from his home outside Perth in Western Australia that *No Crown of Laurels* was intended 'purely as wartime propaganda'.[58] Whilst this certainly explains the book's fictitious content, one is still left wondering how the publication of *Secret Surgeon* could have been justified.

6

A Man Called Intrepid

'Nothing deceives like a document.'[1]

When, in April 1990, Sir William Stephenson died at his modest bungalow in Paget, Bermuda, news of his passing was delayed until after the funeral. Then his adopted daughter Elizabeth, who had first been hired to nurse him more than a decade earlier, released a brief public statement that reopened the speculation about a man who had often been dubbed the greatest spymaster of the Second World War.

The diminutive Stephenson had never been a professional intelligence officer. He was an entrepreneur by inclination, and it had been his knowledge of the Swedish steel industry that had, by chance in 1938, brought him into contact with an obscure branch of Whitehall known as the Industrial Intelligence Centre. Run by Desmond Morton, the IIC had collated commercial information relevant to Germany's strategic power and had been anxious to learn more about supplies of iron ore, an important raw material, destined for the Ruhr Valley. As a director of Pressed Steel and an investor with interests in neutral Sweden, the Canadian millionaire had been well placed to help Morton compile statistics about mineral exports to Germany.

Although well-intentioned, Stephenson's efforts to acquaint the British Government with what was happening in Scandinavia were to go badly wrong. According to his own testimony, he played a preparatory role in an ill-conceived scheme to survey and destroy some of the

Swedish installations used by the Germans. A team of SIS saboteurs, led by a journalist named Alexander Rickman, were arrested by the Swedish police as they prepared to place explosives in the port of Oxelösund, where much of the iron ore destined for Germany was stockpiled. Rickman and his collaborators received lengthy prison sentences and provided some embarrassing newspaper headlines in Stockholm, where the British Embassy tried unconvincingly to dissociate itself from the SIS men's mischief.

Despite this unfortunate setback, Stephenson remained on the periphery of the intelligence world and in May 1940 was selected for the post of SIS Head of Station in New York. His appointment was not without precedent, for in 1915 another Anglophile Canadian, Sir William Wiseman, had fulfilled much the same function. Although officially leader of the UK Purchasing Commission in the United States, the influential Canadian banker had been chosen to look after Britain's clandestine interests because he already commanded widespread respect in the North American continent and had the added advantage of 'speaking the language'. The decision to send Wiseman to Washington during the Great War had been an inspired one, and he had immediately gained the trust of the Federal authorities with whom he had to deal. The idea was to repeat the exercise in 1940 in the hope that Stephenson would prove as successful as Wiseman.

SIS's representation in the US had consisted of a baronet and veteran of the Royal Navy, Sir James Paget, who liaised with the FBI and maintained a small SIS office under Passport Control cover in the premises of an obliging shipping company in lower Manhattan. Stephenson replaced Paget and his first, most delicate task was to persuade Washington to enter into a lend-lease arrangement in which Britain would receive a number of much-needed American warships in exchange for the right of the US to operate bases in certain selected British territories in the Atlantic and the Caribbean.

That Stephenson played a key role in negotiating this historic agreement cannot be doubted, but after the war it was suggested that he had been instrumental in achieving much more. Indeed, one author went so far as to promote the idea that Stephenson had been the unacknowledged prime mover in the clandestine war conducted by the Allies against Nazi Germany. As we shall see, all such claims are entirely bogus, and after the cessation of hostilities the newly knighted Stephenson made several unscrupulous attempts to enhance his own reputation. That he should have wished to do so is odd, for his own unembellished story was quite remarkable.

As an industrialist Stephenson had contributed to the development of television through the Baird Company and had backed the London Broadcasting Company, the forerunner of the BBC. During the Great War, he had been gassed in the trenches as an engineer and, in 1918, had transferred to the Royal Flying Corps, winning the Distinguished Flying Cross in September 1918 and the Military Cross in June 1919. However, one subsequent biographer, William Stevenson, has claimed numerous other decorations on his behalf in *A Man Called Intrepid*, including the French Légion d'honneur 'and Croix de Guerre with Palm', but no record exists of either award. Nor is there any substance in the assertion that Stephenson was a fighter ace with 'twenty-six aircraft shot down' to his credit. Official archives confirm that during his brief service in the Royal Flying Corps with 73 Squadron, between March and the end of July 1918, he had claimed nine enemy aircraft destroyed, sharing two others with fellow pilots, and a further unidentified two-seater reported out of control, making a total of twelve planes claimed in combat reports filed by Stephenson, but not verified by other records. Of the two shared kills, the first was a Fokker DrI shot down on 21 July 1918 north-east of Oulchy-le-Château and claimed also by no less than eight other British pilots.

Stevenson also made the preposterous statement that Stephenson 'had won the interservice lightweight world boxing championship'. Quite simply, he did not. Nor did he 'hold his title of amateur lightweight boxing champion until he retired in 1928'.[2]

Stephenson first embarked on a campaign to publicise his own achievements in 1961, when he commissioned his Australian wartime deputy, C. H. (Dick) Ellis, to write his biography, together with that of Colonel 'Wild Bill' Donovan of the wartime OSS, entitled *The Two Bills: Mission Accomplished*.[3] In contrast to Stephenson, Ellis had been a professional intelligence officer since his recruitment into SIS in October 1923, and had served SIS in Paris and Berlin before his transfer in 1940 to New York. After the war, Ellis had continued his career and had retired in 1953 as SIS's Controller, Far East. To those of his acquaintances and friends who knew of his work for SIS, Ellis was the successful author, skilled linguist and discreet diplomat who had fought in the Russian Civil War (as recounted in *The Transcaspian Episode*)[4] and who had been re-employed after his retirement to 'weed' sensitive Foreign

Office documents before they were consigned to the archives. However, Ellis had a guilty secret, which a very limited circle of counter-intelligence personnel knew about: in 1967, he had confessed to having betrayed SIS's pre-war secrets to the Nazis for money. Ellis's superiors had decided to save him (and them) the humiliation of a public prosecution and instead cut him adrift without a pension. Thus, when Stephenson offered him the potentially lucrative task of compiling a favourable biography, Ellis, short of money, grasped the opportunity and omitted to mention his indiscretion. Ellis wrote two unpublished versions of Stephenson's biography. The first manuscript *The Two Bills: Mission Accomplished*, undated but probably written in the early 1960s, is 209 pages long. The second is slightly shorter, has been revised and contains a foreword contributed by Major-General Sir Colin Gubbins, the last wartime head of SOE. Ellis's version of Stephenson's life apparently did not meet his subject's approval for it remains unpublished and only one copy survives, which Stephenson himself refers to in the 1973 edition of *Who's Who* under the heading of relevant publications.

Stephenson's involvement with Ellis was to become extremely embarrassing for him, not least because the industrialist was never told that his wartime aide had been guilty of treachery, and when *A Man Called Intrepid* came to be released in 1976 Ellis's name was used at the foot of an authenticating 'historical note'.[5] Once Ellis's true role was revealed, initially by Chapman Pincher and Peter Wright in 1985, the choice of Ellis's name to endorse the Stevenson biography proved ironic.

After Ellis's apparently disappointing performance, Stephenson turned to another old friend, Harford Montgomery Hyde, to prepare a hagiography. Hyde was a distinguished barrister, biographer and politician, who had been the Unionist Member of Parliament for North Belfast between 1950 and 1959. In 1941, he had been posted as an intelligence officer to British Security Co-ordination (BSC), the cover title of SIS headquarters in New York, headed by Stephenson. Hyde was to spend three years as Stephenson's subordinate and was later to become a frequent visitor to his home in Bermuda. Hyde's account of Stephenson's war, entitled *The Quiet Canadian*,[6] was published in November 1962. It established his subject as a highly successful businessman and an influential figure, who had fulfilled a role similar to that of Sir William Wiseman in the Great War. Perhaps significantly, Ellis was not referred to, but one controversial name was mentioned: that of Major-General Sir Stewart Menzies, the SIS Chief who had retired a decade earlier and whose wartime role had never previously been publicly revealed. Hyde's disclosure gave his book much publicity and led to questions being tabled in Parliament by John Cordeaux, himself another SIS veteran. On 8 November 1962, he demanded that Hyde be prosecuted for the 'publication of a book that describes in detail the work of one of the head agents of the British Secret Intelligence Service'.[7] It also had the effect of ensuring that Stephenson became something of a national hero in Canada.

Exactly what prompted another Canadian, the journalist William Stevenson, to write *A Man Called Intrepid* is unknown. Hyde's own biography was largely accurate and had been well received. Was there room for another version? Hyde himself thought not, especially as he had been allowed to quote from *The BSC Papers*, the same document that Stevenson subsequently had acquired.[8] This remarkable private history had been commissioned by Stephenson at the end of the war and had been edited by another of his staff, Giles Playfair. The main body of the text had been compiled by three of his BSC subordinates: Professor Gilbert Highet, the novelist Roald Dahl and the radio broadcaster Tom Hill. Stephenson had retained a small number of privately printed copies and evidently had entrusted one to Hyde. According to Tim Naftali, who has undertaken a detailed comparison, of 'approximately 240 pages in *The Quiet Canadian*, about 200, or 85%, are either direct reproductions or faithful executive summaries of the sections dealing with intelligence, special operations and counterespionage in the Playfair document'.[9] Although throughout *A Man Called Intrepid* there are references to, and what purport to be quotations from, *The BSC Papers*, there is good reason to believe that Stevenson chose to ignore this uniquely useful source, written as it was by those who had enjoyed first-hand experience of BSC, so soon after the conclusion of hostilities; instead, he relied on some rather more dubious recollections and, indeed, not a few inventions.

A Man Called Intrepid was to prove a bestseller that sold nearly six million copies around the world, yet it was to be almost entirely fictional in content. To begin with, the title suggested that Stephenson had been selected for the BSC post personally by Churchill, who had conferred on him a special codename. In reality, there is no evidence that Churchill ever met Stephenson, and the name Intrepid was not the Canadian's codename but BSC's publicly registered telegraphic address in New York City. The claimed intimate relationship between Churchill and Stephenson was denied by two of the Prime Minister's private secretaries, Sir John Colville and Sir David Hunt, and it became clear that the three items of evidence cited by Stevenson to support his proposition were invented. The first was the reproduction verbatim of an invitation supposedly from Churchill addressed to Stephenson and signed 'WC'. However, for obvious reasons, the Prime Minister *never* used this abbreviation when signing notes and always initialled himself 'WSC'. Secondly, Stephenson is portrayed as having attended a dinner with Churchill at Lord Beaverbrook's home on the night France surrendered, Saturday, 22 June 1940. In fact, no such social gathering took place on that particular evening when the Prime Minister was preoccupied with the Cabinet, which sat from 9.30 p.m. to half-past midnight. Finally, a photograph of Churchill surveying the bombed-out ruins of the House of Commons in 1940 bears a caption identifying an indistinct silhouette in the foreground as Stephenson. In reality, the figure was that of Brendan Bracken MP, Churchill's Parliamentary Private Secretary.

Having disposed of the book's title and the allegedly close relationship between Churchill and Stephenson, critics turned to its 'historical note', attributed to Dick Ellis. According to the text, Ellis described himself as having 'been twenty years in the professional secret intelligence service'[10] in 1940, suggesting that he had joined SIS in 1920, yet there are no records to show that Ellis had been employed by SIS before 1923. How could Ellis have made such a mistake about his own career? A clue is to be found in the motive he purports to ascribe to his original participation in *A Man Called Intrepid*. Ellis asserts that he was advised that following the defection of Kim Philby, the authorities had decided that SIS was in need of some good publicity, so Ellis was given permission to break his silence. A plausible enough reason, one might think, for Ellis to assist his old wartime colleague Montgomery Hyde, except that Hyde's book *had already been published* when Philby had fled from Beirut in January 1963. Accordingly, what is presented as SIS's motive in assisting Ellis is sheer hokum. This fact, combined with the glaring error over the length of Ellis's career, makes it clear that whoever concocted the 'historical note', it could not have been Ellis, who, after all, had died on 5 July 1975, a year before *A Man Called Intrepid* was published. Unless what purported to be Ellis's preface had been written by him from beyond the grave, perhaps with the help of a clairvoyant, it must have been forged. Certainly it was not written before he died, considering the number of elementary mistakes contained in the short text, including details that Ellis might have reasonably been expected to remember.

If the 'historical note' to *A Man Called Intrepid* was bogus, how genuine was the remainder of the book? Stevenson credited Sir William with involvement in several important intelligence operations and described five in some detail. In particular, Stephenson is mentioned as having played a key role in the acquisition of a German Enigma machine in 1939; the assassination of Reinhard Heydrich in Prague in 1942; the attack on the Pourville radar station during the Dieppe raid in 1942; the ill-fated mission undertaken by an SOE agent, Noor Inayat Khan, code-named *Madeleine*, in 1942; and the sabotage of the Norwegian heavy-water plant at Vermork in 1943.

Taking a closer look at these separate operations, the first matter to be dealt with is the Enigma machine. This was the ingenious ciphering device which was adopted by all the German armed services and carried the bulk of the enemy's classified communications. It looked not unlike a hefty portable typewriter and at its heart was a series of moving rotors through which an electrical current passed. Two operators seeking to exchange messages simply set their rotors to an agreed identical sequence, one of many combinations, and encrypted a message by typing it on to a standard keyboard. As each letter was punched in, a corresponding letter would light up on a battery-operated panel. This was the cipher version. To transform the ciphered message back into plaintext, the receiving operator simply typed each letter on to the keyboard of his identically set Enigma. Provided both operators had taken care to ensure that their machines had started from the same rotor position, the original text would emerge. Although widely believed to be inviolate, Allied cipher experts based at Bletchley Park were able to decrypt a substantial proportion of the signals encoded by the Enigma. Each text transmitted by wireless was intercepted by monitoring stations located across the globe, analysed at Bletchley or one of its satellite stations, and subjected to a complex process which depended upon specially constructed devices to race through the likely permutations of the all-important rotor settings. To make the task more difficult, and the Enigma more secure, various additional features were incorporated, including extra wiring and a special plugboard. A fourth rotor was introduced for the Kriegsmarine, and more frequent changes in the starting position (or 'key') of the rotors were employed, with some units changing the key several times a day. Despite these precautions, the Allied cryptographers succeeded in identifying many of the keys and thereby defeating the machine. Once a plaintext had been obtained, it was translated and passed, in summary form, to a small group of indoctrinated commanders who knew the information to be wholly reliable. The summaries from Bletchley were granted a special codename, BONIFACE, and circulated as though they emanated from an especially reliable source. The special classification, ULTRA SECRET, surrounded by unprecedented security measures, was later introduced, as evidence mounted that military strategists were not giving sufficient weight to the Enigma-based material.

According to Stevenson, the Enigma machine was a combined cipher machine and wireless transmitter, and as a businessman interested in communications equipment, Stephenson had 'played around with the design of the first Enigma' in 1924,[11] and in 1933 had learned that 'the new portable Enigma was very different from the original'.[12] Stephenson had 'estimated it would take a month for one combination of the drums to be solved by a team of brilliant mathematicians'[13] and so resolved to gather together the experts needed to solve the Enigma's problem at a regular lunchtime meeting. The initial solution was 'the task of trying to build a replica',[14] but the first attempt, made by a Polish engineer in Paris working from memory, failed. Meanwhile, 'a professor of mathematics brought together the men and women who would interpret Enigma if it came their way. The professor was at this private luncheon, attended by civilians, who became the core of Stephenson's secret intelligence.'[15] Eventually, an authentic Enigma machine was acquired in Poland:

> Stephenson, using his knowledge of electronic transmission and cipher machines, provided more specifications and tracked down a German SS unit in the Danzig area where Poland's Secret Service could hope to recover cipher books. The new Enigmas were being delivered to frontier units and in early 1939 a military truck containing one was ambushed. Polish agents staged an accident in which fire destroyed the evidence. German investigators assumed that some charred bits of coils, springs and rotors were the remains of the real Enigma.[16]

Thus, a stolen original of the portable Wehrmacht Enigma machine, 'probably the most guarded mystery in Britain',[17] was brought to

Bletchley, via Warsaw, and then 'duplicated with copies from Stephenson's electronics labs'.[18] Having acquired the Enigma, Stephenson then suggested that 'a computer for Enigma could be mass produced in the United States. The prototype of such a computer had been made. What he wanted was a series of computers linked to banks of Enigma duplicates.'

> Stephenson argued for the acquisition of American brains while planning to solve mechanically the cipher and index problems that drained Bletchley's human energies. He proposed that British Tabulating be the cover for a computer to be called 'Colossus'. Smaller and better versions would then be constructed in the United States with expert British aid. Computers were something new. Computers powered electrically were unknown.[19]

With the aid of Stephenson's innovative genius, ULTRA gradually came on stream. Although ULTRA 'covered many sources on intelligence . . . its principal product came from the daily deciphering of German orders coded through Enigma machines'.[20] In practical terms, ULTRA 'demonstrated its effectiveness when British expeditionary forces escaped through Dunkirk'.[21] Lest there be any mistake about the impact of ULTRA, Stevenson emphasised the point:

> The Bletchley codebreakers, by a combination of familiarity with German military thinking, ULTRA's still incomplete retrieval of orders, and analysis of other German signals, were able to guess German intentions and even to predict some German operations prior to the fall of France.[22]

As well as assisting the British to withdraw from France, ULTRA apparently also played a crucial role in the Battle of Britain. Bletchley was by then taking 'readings of the Nazi mind, showing that waves of German bombers would try to complete the destruction of RAF defences by mid-September'.[23] According to Stevenson, 'On September 15 ULTRA revealed a statistical picture of preparations to invade Britain'[24] and, allegedly, even alerted Churchill to the Luftwaffe's intention to bomb Coventry. Stevenson says that 'in the second week of November in 1940, Bletchley obtained the German order to destroy Coventry. The name came through in plaintext. . . . The name of the target was in Churchill's hands within minutes of Hitler's decision.'[25]

When compared to the established historical fact, Stevenson's version is, to put it mildly, inaccurate. William Stephenson played no part whatever in the work undertaken by the British on the Enigma machine, which had been purchased legally by the Admiralty in 1928. There was no mystery surrounding its construction, and mere possession of a duplicate was of little help in solving the near-random ciphers it generated. No Enigma was seized by the Polish secret service, although it is true that the cryptographic advances accomplished by Polish codebreakers did enable Bletchley Park to achieve the breakthroughs that occurred later in the war. As for Stephenson's contribution to ULTRA, the account in *A Man Called Intrepid* is entirely false. The term ULTRA was not even introduced until June 1941, and Bletchley was unable to supply any significant data relating either to the fall of France or the bombing of Coventry. As for the significant date of 15 September 1940, it was not the date of an ULTRA decrypt revealing German plans for an invasion of Britain. On the contrary, it was the date of a signal sent over all German naval channels of identical length, which, though not decrypted at the time, was interpreted either as an order launching the operation, or as a cancellation. As the assault barges failed to materialise over the following forty-eight hours, it was correctly assumed to be a cancellation.

Clearly Stevenson not only invented a fanciful tale relating to the Polish cryptographic co-operation with Bletchley Park, inserting his subject William Stephenson into the plot at vital moments, but he also telescoped the work undertaken by the codebreakers, which took years, into a period of weeks. His proposition is that with Stephenson's help Bletchley was able to crack the Enigma, using a computer, within 150 days. In reality, the first ULTRA summaries were not distributed until June 1941 and the first Colossus computer was not installed at Bletchley until December 1943.

The second operation to preoccupy *A Man Called Intrepid* was the assassination of Reinhard Heydrich in May 1942. According to Stevenson, 'plans for the assassination of this man Heydrich were begun in New York, at the beginning of August 1941'.[26] These elaborate preparations included 'forging necessary documents and Camp X was reproducing conditions in which Heydrich was said to live'.[27] The assassins were also trained at Camp X, Stephenson's special training school near Toronto. 'The assassins, volunteers from the Czech secret resistance army, slipped out of their occupied homeland, were flown to Camp X, and there prepared for their mission.'[28] A special Moon Squadron flight had been arranged that 'secretly brought the assassins out of Czechoslovakia and, when they were ready, returned them'.[29] Having exfiltrated the volunteers from Czechoslovakia, the measures taken to prepare them for Heydrich's assassination were comprehensive: 'at Camp X a replica was made of the green Mercedes he used when not piloting himself to Berlin'.[30] Stevenson concludes his account with further compelling evidence: a series of seven photographs recovered from BSC's secret archive which portrayed the operation from the first stages through to a picture of the wreck of Heydrich's car.

Once again Stevenson's version is quite misleading. The entire operation, codenamed ANTHROPOID, was initiated and developed in England. The Czech volunteers were not smuggled out of Czechoslovakia on a clandestine flight, but chosen from among the Czech troops already billeted at Cholmondeley Castle in May 1941. They had originally fled as refugees to Poland and had then joined the French Foreign Legion, fighting on the Western Front in 1940. After the French collapse, they had moved to England to join the 1st Czech Brigade. Following their selection for parachute training in April 1941, at Ringway airport near Manchester, they attended various SOE schools in Scotland and Surrey, but they never left the shores of Britain until their final flight, postponed twice because of poor weather, eventually got under way in late December 1941. They were unable to initiate the main operation, the assassination, for a further five months and they decided upon an attack on Heydrich while he was being driven into Prague *after* they had arrived and after they had conducted a reconnaissance. Accordingly, Stevenson's entire story of volunteers being brought out of Czechoslovakia and preparations in Canada are without foundation. Indeed, the location identified by Stevenson as 'Camp X',[31] the special school where the assassins underwent their training, was actually better known to SOE under its designation STS 103. One chronological difficulty with Stevenson's version is that the land on which STS 103 was built was only purchased in September 1941 and, according to research undertaken by the Canadian academic David Stafford, it only opened for business two months later, in November.[32] The ANTHROPOID mission was originally intended to kill Heydrich on 28 October, the Czech national holiday, but poor weather caused the mission to be delayed. Thus, STS 103 was not even operational when the ANTHROPOID party was assembling for its first aborted flight. As for Stevenson's photograph of a scene purporting to be 'a scale model of the Prague area used in the planning and training', it is actually a movie still taken from a feature film made after the war.[33]

The raid on Dieppe mounted in August 1942 by a force composed chiefly of Canadian troops commands Stevenson's attention in *A Man Called Intrepid* because he contends that among its objectives were the acquisition of German radar secrets and the release of 'twelve French Resistance leaders'[34] held captive in the Gestapo's headquarters in Dieppe. Apparently, Stephenson had also played a role in the operation by training the Allied personnel intended to go on the raid:

> Two British radar experts were brought for special training to Camp X. They were introduced to the FBI man who would go with them to examine the enemy radar at Dieppe. The FBI man's job would be to shoot either or both of them dead if there was any danger of them being captured.[35]

Stevenson identified the FBI man as James Callaghan, who 'began working with the Toronto police in April, helping to test Camp X employees'.[36] One of those to undergo the training in Canada was 'Sergeant [Peretz] Rose, the chubby-cheeked specialist from the Jewish Agency, [who] had been flown from Camp X'.[37] His task was to blow up the Pourville 'radar control hut with plastic explosives'[38] after another electronics specialist, Jack Nissenthall, had removed the German instruments for examination in England.

> The two radar experts who were to go to Dieppe with them spent the final days studying relief maps and timing each phase of their own task. They carried slips of paper ordering the 'beachmasters' to give them absolute priority to commandeer transport. A Canadian Security sergeant had been secretly ordered to back up Callaghan. He would act ostensibly as the scientists' bodyguards. In reality he was to kill either or both if Callaghan failed to prevent them from falling into enemy hands alive. A team of Baker Street Irregulars was split up, each member attached to one of the regular Canadian military units. The Irregulars carried in their heads the details of the Gestapo jail where French Resistance leaders were being held.[39]

In his account of the raid itself, Stevenson records that Sergeants Rose and Nissenthall were escorted to the site of the radar station 'by two of Callaghan's colleagues from Camp X. They took the guards by surprise, slitting their throats with knives and thin copper wire.'[40] However, they were unable to penetrate the main building and retired, having cut the station's communications cables. Elsewhere, 'On the other side of town, men of Special Operations Executive broke into the local jail, which had been converted into a Gestapo interrogation center, and collected the French Resistance leaders.'[41] Stevenson concludes his tale with the footnote that 'the men on Baker Street Special Operations were not awarded medals, nor was their work disclosed after the war. Nissenthall was advised to change his name, for fear of German reprisals.'[42]

Unfortunately, almost every aspect of Stevenson's version of events is untrue, beginning with the claim that some of the participants in the Dieppe raid, codenamed Operation JUBILEE, had been trained at 'Camp X' in Canada. None had; nor was there a former FBI man involved, nor even a radar expert named Peretz Rose. Furthermore, SOE played practically no part in the operation, apart from sending three observers with a watching brief, and certainly no leaders of the French resistance were rescued from their alleged imprisonment.

The true facts are that Jack Nissenthall was the only radar technician sent on the raid, and his task was to remove whatever equipment he could dismantle in the limited time available. His presence was essential because he was considered sufficiently qualified to choose which items of hardware should be seized. If his task had simply been one of demolition, any sapper could have placed the necessary explosives. Nissenthall's interest was centred on the small German apparatus known as Freya, which had first been identified in 1940 as a surface radar intended to detect approaching ships in the Channel. No sentries were killed silently with knives, although three Germans were shot during a fierce firefight, during which Nissenthall managed to cut eight electrical cables leading from the station. There had been no plans to destroy the 'radar control hut with plastic explosives' as no plastic was taken on the raid, and the 'hut' was actually an almost indestructible blockhouse constructed of reinforced concrete. So what part did SOE play in the raid? The answer, quite simply, is a very limited one. SOE's involvement consisted of the handful of observers who had accompanied the raid, but of them, Jacques de Guelis never made it ashore, Lieutenant D. Wyatt did, but was left behind, later to be killed, and Captain P. Harratt, DF Section's beach landing expert, was wounded. As SOE's official historian recorded, 'that unfortunate operation was not SOE's involvement'.[43] Contrary to Stevenson's assertion, details of SOE's work were disclosed after the war and many of its personnel received decorations, including Captain Harratt, who received a Military Cross and the DSO.

One is bound to ask how Stevenson could have been so wrong in his account of the attack on the Pourville radar station, and one clue is to be found in James Leasor's *Green Beach*,[44] a well-researched study of the raid written with Jack Nissenthall's assistance and published a year before *A Man Called Intrepid* was released. The radar technician confirmed that he had been instructed to remove what he could from the Freya station, but in the event had been unable to enter the building. He also revealed that Sergeant Roy Hawkins of the Field Security Police had been assigned the task of accompanying him so as to ensure that he did not fall into enemy hands. Neither 'Peretz Rose' nor the FBI man 'James Callaghan' ever existed. The revelation that Hawkins had been ordered to kill Nissenthall to prevent him from being captured was obviously somewhat controversial, and evidently had been seized upon by Stevenson, but it was not until 1978 that SIS's scientific expert, Dr R. V. Jones, made a further disclosure which indicated that the controversial instructions received by Hawkins *had been given in error*.

Jones explained that during Operation BITING, the first Allied raid on an enemy radar station, at Bruneval in March 1942, the radar technician who had been responsible for recovering the German Wurtzburg apparatus, Flight Sergeant Cox, had not been the subject of any order regarding his safety resembling that subsequently issued to Sergeant Hawkins. However, that latter instruction had been given in the mistaken belief that Nissenthall had a knowledge not of British capabilities but, much more significantly, of *what the Allies knew of the enemy's radar*. It seemed that a certain Captain Manus, one of the Canadian officers responsible for planning the operation, had misunderstood the depth of knowledge possessed by the radar expert, and had even thought that it was to have been Dr Jones himself who was to go on the raid. As Jones later recounted:

Actually there was no more reason for him to be shot than there would have been for Cox in the Bruneval Raid, since they knew comparable amounts about our own radar, and only as much about

German radar as was necessary for dismantling captured equipment. It was the misapprehension of Major Manus regarding my own presence on the Raid that resulted in his dramatic order.[45]

In reality, Nissenthall's capture, though disagreeable for him, would not have meant the loss of invaluable secrets concerning British development of surface radar. This single error, which was faithfully recorded by James Leasor and gave his *Green Beach* rather more dramatic content than might have been expected for an operation that failed, was one that was embroidered with even greater enthusiasm by Sir William Stephenson's biographer. Accordingly, the version of the Pourville raid which appeared in *A Man Called Intrepid* was not only completely wrong in content, but also the premise upon which it had been constructed was itself ludicrously flawed.

Stevenson believes that one of his subject's more enduring achievements was saving the planet from the consequences of a German atomic weapon. Apparently, Stephenson was one of the first to recognise the destructive potential of atomic energy and, early in January 1940, had travelled to Norway with false papers to obtain information about the Norsk Hydro plant from Professor Leif Tronstad. Located near Vermork, the complex was producing a commodity known as heavy water, then considered a vital component in any atomic research programme. Stephenson received 'a copy of the Norsk Hydro plant layout'[46] from the scientist and then 'returned to Britain aboard a submarine that collected him near Narvik shortly before Germany struck at Norway'.[47] Once back in England, Stephenson wrote a visionary report on the subject of heavy water and, in April 1940, circulated it to, among others, President Roosevelt. Stephenson was later a key figure in the development of a scheme to deny the Germans the hydro-electric plant's much prized by-product, heavy water.

In Stockholm, a Baker Street/SIS station gathered information from Bohr and from Norsk Hydro. Copies of Stockholm bulletins went to Stephenson, who had started the training of agents and a new 'school for danger' in the Canadian wilderness, where saboteurs could prepare for a suicidal mission.[48]

Once a sabotage scheme had been prepared, 'Stephenson flew to Canada where agents of the Norwegian secret army were now in training',[49] and was also able to open a new line of communications with Nazi-occupied Norway. Stephenson went 'looking for American speedboats to run the blockade – eventually, they ran with clockwork efficiency between enemy territory and the Shetland Isles'.[50] Once trained, the Norwegian volunteers in Canada were assessed and from them a small group was selected for the hazardous mission. 'Out of these trainees a tiny handful were to be inserted'[51] back into Norway to destroy the Hydro. After an abortive attempt made by Combined Operations in November 1942, the successful operation was undertaken by SOE in February 1943. Nor was this the end of Stephenson's involvement with atomic weaponry. He also participated in a secret operation to persuade the Danish physicist, Niels Bohr, to escape to the Allies and collaborate with the Anglo-American project to build an atomic bomb. 'Stephenson understood Niels Bohr and the ticklish problem of persuading him to escape.'[52] The first invitation, sent to Copenhagen by clandestine means, was rejected by the scientist. 'His reply was read by BSC in New York with dismay,' records Stevenson.[53] Finally, Bohr agreed to flee and, on 7 October 1943, he was flown to an airfield in Scotland, where Stephenson was on the apron to greet him: 'Waiting on a desolate Moon squadron base near Edinburgh was the man who could persuade Professor Bohr to join the Allied attempt to build an atomic bomb – Bill Stephenson.'[54]

From Stevenson's account, a reader might be forgiven for thinking that his subject had indeed played a part in the sabotage of the Vemork works, and had even met Niels Bohr. In fact, neither was true and the saboteurs who participated in Operations FRESHMAN and GUNNERSIDE were all trained at Aviemore in Scotland. The participants in the first, ill-fated operation were all British volunteers from the 1st Airborne Division and not one of them ever visited Canada; nor did any of the smaller, GUNNERSIDE team which accomplished the sabotage. And as for Stephenson having been in contact with Bohr prior to his exfiltration, the version in *A Man Called Intrepid* is sheer fantasy, as is the scene in which Stephenson welcomed Bohr to Scotland after his hazardous flight across the North Sea on 7 October 1943. In fact, Bohr did not arrive until 12 October 1943.

The reality is that Leif Tronstad was in continuous contact with SIS throughout the German occupation and kept SIS supplied with statistical data from Vemork. However, he had always been reluctant to compromise the technical aspects of his work, which makes his encounter with Stephenson in January 1940, when he supposedly handed over a complete blueprint of the complex, unlikely in the extreme. In October 1941, Professor Tronstad fled to England, a fact omitted from Stevenson's account, and alerted SIS to a sudden rise in German demand for heavy water, a clear indication that Nazi scientists were concentrating on atomic research.

One of the more curious episodes to be included in *A Man Called Intrepid* is the account of the SOE agent codenamed *Madeleine*. According to Stevenson, this beautiful but tragic woman, whose real name was Noor Inayat Khan, had been brought up in India. 'Stephenson, who had met her in India before the war, sensed steel within her seemingly timid personality.'[55] The author described the circumstances of their first encounter:

> She had first met Bill Stephenson during one of her family journeys back to India. She was nineteen years old then, stunningly pretty, gifted with an innocence which he judged could never be corrupted. He was leading a mission of technical experts that in 1934 studied India's resources and potential for self-development. He met her on a tiger shoot arranged by her father's fellow Muslim Air Vice-Marshal Nawab Haji Khan, chief of the Chamber of Princes and Nawab of Bhopal. The pomp and ceremony of the jungle shikaris amused both the girl and Stephenson. They talked about a future India where the gap between rich and poor might be narrowed through love and compassion. The Nawab was a close friend of Stephenson's and later, on active service with the RAF, he learned that the Canadian kept a fatherly eye on the girl. It was in this way that Noor entered the world of Baker Street with credentials.[56]

Stevenson was emphatic about her suitability as an officer: 'Noor volunteered for the RAF. She was quick, intelligent and dependable. She would have made a good officer.'[57] He also described the role his subject had played in recruiting Noor into SOE in April 1942: 'Noor's international background, her familiarity with strange places and foreign languages encouraged BSC's attention – that and the girl's frankness. She was recruited in London.'[58] Having been accepted for training as a wireless operator by SOE, she was ready to participate in an operation, but she experienced the 'customary nerve-shattering delay. The moon was right, the weather was good, the reception committee had reported that a field had been prepared. But no aircraft was available.'[59] Eventually, she was flown by Lysander aircraft to an airstrip near Le Mans, but when her Lysander landed, there was no reception committee to ease her passage through the first awful hours in hostile territory. Why did the pilot not bring her back?'[60] Undeterred by this setback, *Madeleine* walked to the railway station at Le Mans and 'she arrived by train in Paris late on Thursday, June 17'.[61] Two days later, having established herself in a safehouse, her radio was delivered by parachute and she began work for the PHYSICIAN *réseau*. When she sent her first signal, less than forty-eight hours later, 'she became the first woman radio operator to transmit for the French secret armies'.[62] Unfortunately, noted the author, the network had already been penetrated by the enemy and two of its most recent arrivals, John McAlister and Frank Pickersgill, both Canadians, were to be captured on Monday, 21 June 1943, just four days after *Madeleine*'s arrival. Stevenson is highly critical of SOE's decision to send Noor to Le Mans when the organisation had already been warned of increased enemy activity in the area:

Less than a hundred hours before her departure the reception committee had radioed Bletchley that Nazi security forces were swarming through the reception area near Le Mans, and requested that all air operations be suspended. This was June 12, 1943. Yet supplies and agents continued to be dropped.[63]

Characteristically undaunted by the arrests, *Madeleine* 'began regular transmissions from the first week of July and she continued until October, when she was caught'.

She was working with a rebuilt circuit, a group of saboteurs, when arrested. The group had traced underground sewers in which the Germans stored torpedos to be shipped to the U-boat pens at Brest, and *Madeleine* had just conveyed their request to London for the new explosive known as marzipan because of its sweet smell resembling that of almonds.[64]

Madeleine was interrogated by the Gestapo and participated in two escape attempts, but was quickly recaptured on both occasions. She was sent to a concentration camp and shot at Dachau in September 1944.

Whilst a few of the basic details regarding *Madeleine,* as recounted in

A Man Called Intrepid, are accurate, one is bound to wonder why the story appears at all in the biography, for William Stephenson never met Noor Inayat Khan. They could never have met in India in 1934, for, despite her family origins, Noor only visited that country once, in 1928, when she was just fifteen years old. The proposition that she attended a tiger shoot and had engaged the middle-aged Canadian industrialist in a conversation about the future of India was entirely imagined. In 1934, the year when Noor supposedly met Stephenson, she was at school in Paris and spent her vacation in Spain. Nor did Stephenson assist her to join SOE. In fact, Noor experienced great difficulty in joining the Women's Auxiliary Air Force because of doubt over her citizenship, and her application for a commission was turned down. She was eventually accepted as a wireless operator, and it was only after she had completed her WAAF training that she transferred to SOE, in February 1943. Indeed, Noor's true story contained numerous facts at odds with Stevenson's version.

Noor was despatched to France initially in May 1943, but when her aircraft had reached the designated landing field near Compiègne, there had been no reception committee, so she had been flown home. On her second flight, a month later, she had been accompanied by Charles Skepper and two other women, Diana Rowden and Cecily Lefort. Accordingly, Stevenson's rhetorical question regarding the conduct of *Madeleine*'s pilot, and the implication that she arrived in France alone, are specious. Two Lysander aircraft were involved in the mission and a total of four agents were delivered, not to a point near Le Mans, but to a field just outside Angers. Furthermore, there was a sizeable reception committee awaiting their arrival, for there were five people to be flown back to England in the same pair of aircraft. They were Jack and Francine Agazarian, P. H. Lejeune and two French politicians. As the official account of the operation relates, 'In perfect conditions, Rymills and McCairns the pilots had not the slightest difficulty; everything went without a hitch.'[65]

If the official record states the operation 'went without a hitch', what about the warning received from the reception committee on 12 June, cited by Stevenson as evidence of SOE's folly? The answer is that there was no such signal. SOE's communications were not channelled through Bletchley and *Madeleine*'s reception committee was located at Le Vieux Briollay near Angers, a considerable distance to the south of Le Mans. Indeed, because the Germans were fully aware of this particular flight, which had been arranged by Henri Dericourt who was a Sicherheitsdienst asset, the enemy made elaborate arrangements to ensure that the SOE operation was not interfered with. From testimony given after the war by various Abwehr and SD personnel, it is clear that Dericourt, F Section's air movements controller in France, had effectively secured German consent to the operation. Thus, neither *Madeleine* nor her companions were ever in any danger of arrest as they landed in France.

Contrary to Stevenson's account, Noor never went anywhere near Le Mans, although that was where SOE had originally intended her to be based. Instead, she was escorted by Remy Clement to the railway station at Ettriche, whence they both caught a train to Paris, where Noor remained hidden until September 1943. In the middle of the month, she sent a single message to London, listing the agents still at liberty and, according to her official file, 'regular wireless contact was re-established by the end of the month'.[66]

Stevenson's reference to SOE's two Canadian agents is also curiously inaccurate, particularly in regard to Le Mans. According to his account, 'on the sixteenth, two Canadian agents were parachuted into the district: John McAlister and Frank Pickersgill',[67] and they were arrested on Monday, 21 June. In fact, the two men were caught at Dhuison on 18 June, having been dropped near Valençay two days earlier. However, the interesting point here is not so much Stevenson's error in identifying the place of their arrival and the wrong date of their arrest, but his incorrect spelling of John Macalister's surname. There is only one other published account of the two Canadians' story that makes the same mistake and that is contained in Jean Overton Fuller's biography of Noor Inayat Khan, entitled *Madeleine*,[68] which was released in 1952 and includes many passages similar to those reproduced in *A Man Called Intrepid*. When the author, who had been Noor's personal friend, noticed the similarities between her book and Stevenson's version, even to the typographical spelling error, she complained to Stevenson's publishers in London, who immediately agreed to delete the entire chapter so as to avoid a plagiarism suit. Strangely, the New York publishers, Harcourt Brace Jovanovich, did not feel obliged to do the same and as recently as 1989 have released a paperback edition in America which includes the offending passages.

Stevenson's attempt to link the stories of Pickersgill and Macalister to Noor Inayat Khan was equally misconceived. According to the author, the two Canadians were imprisoned in Paris at the same time as Noor. Allegedly she was kept 'on the top of the five-storey Gestapo headquarters at 84 Avenue Foch',[69] while the two men were incarcerated in 'torture chambers at 13-bis Place des Etats-Unis'.[70] In reality neither of the Canadians was ever in Paris at the same time as Noor. She was arrested on 13 October 1943, *after* Pickersgill had been transferred to the concentration camp at Rawicz in Poland. She was kept in Paris until 26 November 1943, when she was sent to Badenweiler for subsequent transfer to Pforzheim prison, and then to the women's prison at Karlsruhe. This was a full four months before Pickersgill alone had been flown back to Paris, in March 1944, from Rawicz. Thus Pickersgill was not in Paris when Noor was arrested, and by the time he was returned to Paris, Noor was in Germany, making Stevenson's assertion quite untenable.

The stark fact is that William Stephenson had no connection whatever with Noor, nor any of the other four operations described here. Indeed, most of the details relating to all five appear to have been taken not from Stephenson's memory, but from books written by other authors and reproduced without attribution. Not only was Stephenson linked to operations in which he had played no part, but even the illustrations in the book were misrepresented. Most were captioned as having been obtained from a secret wartime archive and purported to be authentic photographs of agents training before being dropped into enemy territory. In reality, they were movie stills taken from *School for Danger*, a film made after the war. Several other pictures were also incorrectly labelled, including one which claimed to be a photo taken of *Madeleine* shortly before her execution at Dachau in 1944. In fact, the photograph, of a naked woman with her head shaved crouching on the ground, was of a French prostitute who had been denounced as a collaborator after the Liberation.

Analysis of the five major episodes in which Stevenson alleged Sir William had been involved reveal that there was not even the most tenuous of connections between them: Heydrich's assassination was executed by an SOE team recruited in England who never travelled to Canada to train at Sir William's base outside Toronto; mere possession of an Enigma machine did not enable the Allies to break the enemy's codes; nor did Stephenson plot the destruction of the Norwegian heavy-water plant at Vermork. There is no doubt that Sir William Stephenson performed many services for his country during the Second World War, but few of his exploits are to be found in the pages of *A Man Called Intrepid*.

7

A Spy for Churchill

'One day, if security ever allows, the whole truth will emerge.'[1]

Robert Vacha is now retired and lives in the village of Woodhall Spa, Lincolnshire. In 1974, he published an extraordinary book, *A Spy for Churchill*, and the biographical details of the author suggested that he was eminently well-qualified to write what amounted to the story of a previously unsuspected British agent, a spy who had reluctantly volunteered to adopt the identity of a German prisoner of war and had penetrated Rommel's headquarters with astonishing success. At the beginning of the book there is a dramatic WARNING:

> Thirty years have gone by since the events related here took place, and every attempt has been made to keep the correct historical perspective. The names of the world famous personalities of the time have been included, as they had to be. But, for obvious reasons, parts of the main story and certain characters have had to be fictionalised. One day, if security ever allows, the whole truth will emerge. Until then, this is the closest you will ever get to it.[2]

Reading this statement, a reader might be expected to assume that the broad outline of the story that followed was true, but that details had been altered for reasons of security, presumably to protect the real participants from retribution. And what of the author himself? Vacha is described as 'a wartime Lieutenant-Colonel, Intelligence in the Middle East and Europe and later with the Foreign Office'.[3] Since 1954, he had been a staff foreign correspondent for various international newspapers, working finally for the *Daily Mail*. Although there is no record in the Foreign Office of his work there, his entry in the *Army List* for 1944, under 'Regular Army Emergency Commissions, Intelligence Corps, 2nd Lieutenants', shows Robert D. Vacha joining the army on 4 October 1942, commissioned in the rank of a war substantive second lieutenant six months later and being promoted to temporary captain on 4 January 1943. By coincidence his hero, named Robert Craig, was also a fluent German speaker, had been employed before the war in Berlin for 'several years' as a journalist for the *New York Times* and had also been commissioned in 1942.[4] This, however, is the moment to retell Craig's remarkable story.

In mid-May 1941, officer cadet Craig, aged twenty-four, was undergoing training at the Kasr El Nir barracks in Cairo when he received his commission (as a full lieutenant) and was posted to SOE.[5] When he reported to Colonel Brinton at SOE's headquarters, he was informed that he bore an uncanny resemblance to a major on the German staff of the 15th Panzer Division named Karl Hermann von Warnke, who had been attached to Rommel's headquarters when he had been captured a week earlier during the Afrika Korps' push to Alexandria. SOE's daring plan called for Craig to impersonate von Warnke, pretend to escape from British custody, return to the Axis lines and resume the German's position on Rommel's staff. The matter was urgent, Brinton confided, because Field Marshal Wavell intended to launch a counter-offensive, Operation BATTLEAXE, in just a few weeks:

> In other words, on June 15. Before that date we must have certain information as to how many tanks Rommel actually has. Our intelligence is a little scanty at the moment and not too reliable. We must be certain about the number of tanks and their types because the 7th Armoured is being re-equipped with tanks from the UK and we want to know what they'll be up against. That will be your first job and for the moment the most important.[6]

Craig was further informed by Brinton that 'only Churchill, the C.-in-C., the Director of Military Intelligence and myself know of this scheme and that's how it is going to stay'.[7] His briefing completed, Craig was taken to an interrogation centre in Heliopolis, where he was to spend three weeks listening to the unsuspecting von Warnke. The German had explained under questioning that he had been in North Africa for less than a fortnight before his capture. He had given his date of birth as 22 February 1917, which made him eleven months older than Craig, and had described some of his background. Six months earlier he had married a woman named Erika whom he had met in Berlin in 1939, and 'in anticipation of the Polish campaign he had been posted for training with the 7 Panzer Division under Rommel's command'.[8]

Having been indoctrinated into von Warnke's background, Craig was equipped with a codebook which bore the words in bright red letters, MOST SECRET – SPECIAL 'W' TYPE CIPHER, and placed in a prisoner-of-war camp at Burg el Arab, outside Alexandria. There he teamed up with three other young German officers, who, in the middle of an air raid, succeeded in escaping. With Hauptmann Schneider and Oberleutnants Lippmann and Reschke he stole a British RASC truck and drove across the desert to the German lines to be reunited with Rommel's staff, only sustaining a minor flesh wound on the way. While having his arm dressed in hospital Craig met von Warnke's sister-in-law, Hildegarde, and soon afterwards began a short romance with her during a visit to Benghazi. In the meantime, the substitute 'von Warnke' was re-established at Rommel's headquarters and succeeded in transmitting a 'safe-arrival' signal to the British as well as a coded message in a letter to a contact named Otto Rahmer, then living in the German town of Bielefeld. He was also able to give the British 'full knowledge of the Wehrmacht's strength, particularly in tanks, and exactly where they were' in time for the offensive which commenced on 15 June 1941.[9]

A month later, on 16 July, Craig flew to Berlin in a Junkers transport on a fortnight's leave and went straight to his second-floor apartment at 88 Joachimsthalerstrasse, where he met his wife Erika for the first time and discovered that, in his absence in Poland, France and the desert, she had been having an affair with another German officer. Craig then turned to her sister Hildegarde for solace and reported back to Sidi Rezegh for duty. Upon his return he was able to photograph 'Rommel's plan of attack for Tobruk . . . drawn in his own hand'[10] and scheduled for November 1942, which he conveyed to Otto Rahmer by an ingenious route. Hildegarde had made a second visit to see him and they had met in Tobruk, where she was killed in an Allied air raid. Her companion, an unsuspecting general named Weber, obligingly agreed to convey Craig's letter, containing the incriminating photograph, to Berlin and post it to Bielefeld.

Craig remained in the desert, attached to Rommel's retreating headquarters unit, into 1943, winning an Iron Cross first class for gallantry displayed at Ruweisât Ridge while undertaking liaison duties with the 15th Panzer Division in mid-July 1942.

Craig's adventure, blandly retold here without Vacha's narrative skill, lasted for twenty-one months, from June 1941 to February 1943, and was not without incident. Hildegarde had suspected his duplicity shortly before she was killed, and two of his fellow officers were shot by Craig to prevent them from betraying him. Major Uwe Seedorff was disposed of on 14 June 1941 in the middle of an air raid, following an argument over von Warnke's prowess at tennis, which Craig had been ill-prepared for, and Oberst Reimann was eliminated in November 1942 while they were both on patrol in an armoured car, after his discovery of Craig's codebook. Finally, on 11 February 1943, Craig made his escape from the 21st Panzer Division, where he had been posted as a security officer, and was captured by a reconnaissance section of the US 1st Armoured Division near Fondouk. After an initial interrogation by American personnel, he was transferred to British custody in Algiers, where he was reunited with Colonel Brinton. In his absence, Craig had been promoted to the rank of captain and had been decorated with the Distinguished Service Order.

All attempts to verify Vacha's extraordinary story have proved unsuccessful, not least because of the paucity of archival material relating to SOE's activities in the region. Most were either destroyed in a panic when Egypt looked likely to fall before the Afrika Korps, or were burned at the end of the war. There are, therefore, no records of any similar operation undertaken by SOE in North Africa and, as might be expected considering Vacha's initial declaration of caution, none of the British personalities mentioned in the text can be authenticated. As for the Germans mentioned, there is something a little awry with von Warnke's background, or at least enough to have given his British interrogators cause to wonder whether he had been entirely truthful about it. According to Vacha, von Warnke had mentioned being trained with the 7th Panzer Division in 1939, a unit which was alleged then to have been under Rommel's command. Yet most Allied intelligence personnel would have known that Rommel did not take command of the 7th Panzer

Division until *after* the Polish campaign. To be exact, he had accepted the command in Godesberg on 15 February 1940. If von Warnke had served with the 7th Panzers, his commanding officer would have been General Georg Stumme. In 1939, Rommel had been in command of the *Führergleitbataillon*, Hitler's personal bodyguard, which had protected him in March when the Wehrmacht marched into Prague. In August, Rommel had been promoted to major-general on the staff of Hitler's headquarters and had been responsible for his safety throughout the Polish campaign.

Von Warnke's interrogators would also have been intrigued by his claim to have been in the 15th Panzer Division, attached to Rommel's staff, for the 15th Panzers did not arrive in North Africa until mid-May 1941, and none of its units was deployed into forward positions until the end of the month. Since von Warnke was supposedly captured early in May, there must have been some doubt about what he had said because even the most mundane of details fail the accuracy test. For example, Erika von Warnke's address in Berlin's Joachimsthalerstrasse seems fictitious: there is no number 88, as the street merges with the Hardenbergplatz at number 42. For Craig's cover story, upon which his life would depend, to have been so fundamentally flawed tends to undermine Vacha's credibility.

Notwithstanding the above, Vacha does, however, cite two quotations to support the proposition that Craig, or someone similar, actually existed: the first being Churchill's own memoirs, in the third volume of which the Prime Minister had stated: 'At this time we had a spy in close touch with Rommel's headquarters, who gave us accurate information. . . .'[11] The second is a German source, *Die Wustenfuchse*:

> The reports of the experts on Rommel's staff show that an intelligent enemy Secret Service had plenty of opportunity to acquire valuable information. One man in the chain along which Rommel's plans was passed was in the pay of the enemy. Who was it? This question *still* remains to be answered.[12]

It was not until 1974, long after these observations had been made, and Eisenhower and Montgomery had written their autobiographies, and been hailed as brilliant military strategists, that Group Captain F. W. Winterbotham let the real cat out of the bag: a still classified Allied code-breaking operation centred at Bletchley Park in Buckinghamshire had been responsible for the interception and decryption of thousands of Axis signals during the war. Dozens of keys to the supposedly unbreakable Enigma cipher machine had been solved by a team of more than ten thousand cryptographers and traffic analysts, who had supplied intelligence of the very highest quality to a select group of Allied commanders in the field. All had been sworn to secrecy, and almost no word of what had been accomplished by the organisation known as GCHQ had leaked out. Winterbotham himself, who had been responsible for maintaining the security of the distribution of the decrypts to those authorised to receive them, had been prompted to give his version of events after having been interviewed by a journalist, Anthony Cave Brown. A professional researcher, Cave Brown had been tipped off to what was to become known as the ULTRA secret by a disgruntled American airborne officer, who had been granted access to the source and had been disciplined for flying in a combat zone, contrary to the regulations governing those who had been indoctrinated into 'special intelligence'. Under the very strict conditions laid down for all Allied personnel who knew of ULTRA's origin, no individual was allowed to jeopardise it by placing himself in a position where he might risk capture and interrogation by the enemy. This single officer gave Cave Brown the first inkling that a highly sophisticated codebreaking operation had been undertaken during the war with a breathtaking degree of success, and the author persisted in his demands for further details from Winterbotham, who had retired to Devon. But instead of contributing to what was to be published as *Bodyguard of Lies* in 1975,[13] Winterbotham opted to rush out his own account a few months earlier.

Contrary to popular opinion, Winterbotham's decision to publish his own recollection of the ULTRA programme, in a second volume of memoirs entitled *The Ultra Secret*, was not made in the teeth of official opposition.[14] In fact, the Ministry of Defence sanctioned the publication, and the then Chairman of the D Notice Committee attended Winterbotham's launch party on the day of its publication with several of his colleagues. Furthermore, the editor employed by Winterbotham's publishers, Weidenfeld & Nicolson, was Venetia Pollock, who had strong family connections with SIS, her brother-in-law then being a senior SIS officer, and she kept his office fully informed of Winterbotham's progress. This gave the same authorities, who, two years earlier, had persuaded Sir John Masterman to delete all references to Enigma decrypts from his book *The Double Cross System in the War of 1939–45*, the opportunity to exercise some control over what Winterbotham disclosed. However, the Government had not been prepared to give Winterbotham access to any official papers, so inevitably the book contained more than a few inaccuracies. Nevertheless, although incorrect on many points of detail, the broad thrust of the book, that much of the skill ostensibly manifested by Montgomery in the desert had been more a credit to the advance knowledge he was receiving of the enemy's intentions than to his own intuitive genius, was demonstrably correct. In particular, Winterbotham disclosed that the exploitation of Enigma-based decrypts had been of the greatest value in the North African campaign and had allowed successive commanders unprecedented insight into the enemy's staff decisions. Not only was Montgomery receiving copies of his opponent's communications from Berlin, on the Wehrmacht's Rome to Tunis radio link codenamed GOLDFINCH, but since January 1941 he had also been reading summaries of the more routine logistical traffic codenamed CHAFFINCH, which, when processed, revealed the enemy's complete current order of battle and its technical status. The position of each enemy component had been monitored, and the daily situation reports from the supply units had revealed the exact number of operational vehicles and of those held in reserve. In the desert theatre this vital intelligence had proved to be the crucial key to victory. The consequence, of course, had been to endow Montgomery with considerable powers of prescience.

As well as forcing historians to revise their estimates of the reputation of certain Allied strategists, the disclosure of the ULTRA secret clarified some previously opaque references to intelligence sources, and revealed a few examples of where elaborate cover stories had been invented to conceal the true nature of a sensitive item of signals intelligence. One of the more colourful spies largely manufactured during the war was Amy Elizabeth Thorpe, codenamed *Cynthia*. She had indeed been a British wartime agent operating among her husband's diplomatic acquaintances, but she had not been instrumental in extracting copies of the Italian naval code from the Italian naval attaché in Washington, Admiral Alberto Lais. This officer's affair with *Cynthia* really had occurred, but he had not been responsible for disclosing cryptographic details that, according to some sources, led to Admiral Cunningham's victory at the battle of Cape Matapan on 28 March 1941, when he surprised and sank three enemy cruisers, the *Fiume*, *Pola* and *Zara*, two destroyers, and torpedoed the Italian flagship, the *Vittorio Veneto*, all for the loss of a single

Swordfish biplane. According to Professor Hinsley, 'it was the first important operation in the Mediterranean to be based on Sigint'.[15] The Italian plan to deploy their fleet against Allied convoys in the eastern Mediterranean, after months of idleness, had been betrayed by the interception and decryption of Luftwaffe signals. The Italians had demanded German air cover before venturing from Spezia into the open sea and a rendezvous had been arranged south of Crete. However, instead of meeting friendly German fighters, the Italians had encountered aircraft from HMS *Warspite*, HMS *Formidable* and Admiral Cunningham's 1st Battle Squadron. Similarly, there was no agent codenamed BONIFACE to whom much of the early Enigma-based decrypts were credited. Sir David Hunt, who handled ULTRA material in the desert, recalls that this was the cryptonym for 'a supernaturally omniscient and highly placed agent in the German supreme command'.[16] When further disclosures were made about the extent of GCHQ's success against the enemy's ciphers, it emerged that another entirely notional spy had been created in Hitler's entourage so as to account for the quality of information supplied to the Russians prior to BARBAROSSA in June 1941.

In the light of the intelligence service's tendency to attribute Sigint material to fictitious spies, might there be a similar explanation for Churchill's remark about the Allies possessing an agent 'in close touch with Rommel's headquarters'? His choice of words is interesting, because he appears to have avoided stating outright that the spy was 'in Rommel's headquarters', instead preferring the slightly more longwinded description of being 'in close touch'. To this extent Churchill was entirely accurate. The Allied cryptographers *were* 'in close touch' with Rommel's HQ, and if they can be categorised as spies, the remark may not have been appropriate, but it was certainly accurate, as far as it went. The historical context of Churchill's cryptic comment is also significant. Vacha only quoted part of Churchill's sentence, ending it with the words: 'who gave us accurate information'. However, in the original text the full sentence reads: 'At this time we had a spy in close touch with Rommel's headquarters, who gave us accurate information of the fearful difficulties of Rommel's assertive but precarious position.'[17] This latter half of the sentence, omitted by Vacha, refers to the problems Rommel experienced at the end of April 1941, when his troops had surrounded Tobruk and had raced across the desert towards Egypt. Tobruk's Australian garrison was stubbornly resisting the Afrika Korps, and Rommel's lines of supply looked dangerously vulnerable to a counter-attack from Wavell. On 27 April, General Friedrich von Paulus arrived in Libya from Berlin to assess the situation and was appalled by Rommel's impetuous action. He called off the costly frontal assault on the beleaguered Commonwealth forces defending Tobruk and, on 2 May, sent a long report over the Luftwaffe's circuits to General Halder, the Wehrmacht's Chief of Staff. This momentous signal was intercepted by GCHQ, decrypted in full and circulated on 4 May to provide Churchill with an invaluable and informed assessment of Rommel's current and hitherto unsuspected weakness. Von Paulus stated that the Afrika Korps was low on fuel, ammunition, food and vehicles, and that the Italians were incapable of replenishing Rommel's dwindling stores by sea to Benghazi. Rommel's troops were 'thoroughly exhausted'[18] and lacking any reserves or secure bases of supply. Accordingly, von Paulus recommended caution and not only advocated a period of consolidation and reorganisation, but even opined that no further fresh troops should be despatched to the theatre until the situation had improved. Nor, he added, should Rommel's forces be allowed to advance any further towards Alexandria or mount even small-scale attacks on Tobruk.

It was this critical message, dated 5 May 1941 at 0405 Hrs, that Churchill referred to in his famous signal to Archie Wavell of the previous day:

> Have you read my telegram of 4th inst.? Presume you realise the
> highly secret and authorative character of this information?
> Actual text is more impressive than paraphrases showing enemy
> 'thoroughly exhausted' pending arrival of 15 Armoured Division
> to do more than hold ground gained at Tobruk . . . also definite
> forbidding of any advance beyond Sollum except for reconnais-
> sance without permission. . . .[19]

Wavell received the full summary of the von Paulus report, designated by GCHQ CX/JQ 914, on 7 and 8 May, and this 'directly influenced the character and planning'[20] of Wavell's first counter-attack, codenamed Operation BREVITY, which took place a week later. However, despite 'this excellent intelligence',[21] BREVITY faltered, eloquent proof that 'Enigma would be more valuable about what it said about order of battle and supply than for tactical battle intelligence – the British inferiority in field intelligence was as marked before and during the battle as it had been during the retreat'.[22] Now that the veil of official secrecy has been

lifted on Britain's wartime cryptographic achievements, and the existence of the signal CX/JQ 914 has been revealed, it is clear that
Churchill's explanation of a spy who had disclosed details of Rommel's
handicaps was actually a semi-transparent attempt to conceal the true
source: ULTRA. Obviously, when Churchill wrote his memoirs, and he
was unable to reveal Bletchley Park's invaluable contribution to the
desert war, he had to find a vaguely plausible reason for his caustic
telegram to Wavell of 5 May. Given what we now know, Craig's *raison
d'être* simply evaporates. After all, with unimpeded direct access to the
motherlode, why risk the human factor?

It should also be noted that, given the true context of Churchill's
remark about a spy in close touch with Rommel's headquarters, he could
not have been referring to Robert Craig, because, according to Vacha,
von Warnke was not captured until early May, a few days after the specific moment when Churchill was crediting the existence of a well-placed
agent in the enemy camp. Indeed, Vacha says Craig did not infiltrate
Rommel's headquarters until a month or so later, in early June 1941.
Therefore, whoever Churchill was referring to in his memoirs, if to
anyone at all, it could not have been Craig.

But might it have been another spy, perhaps elsewhere in the structure of the German High Command? One cautious qualification for this
explanation of Churchill's remark, though not directly relevant to North
Africa, must be the strange case of Baron von Weizenbeck, who was
General von Rundstedt's Chief of Staff throughout much of the war. Not
only had he sent his two Jewish stepchildren to live in England after hostilities broke out, but they were not subject to any of the usual
restrictions that were applied to most German Jews classified as enemy
aliens. Indeed, at the end of the war he was promptly appointed ICI's representative in Munich, a lucrative post that indicates more than a degree
of official approval for him from the occupying powers.[23]

That the Germans became convinced that there was a traitor in the
General Staff who was betraying their secrets is a classic example of a
phenomenon known as recognitive dissonance, the refusal to accept a
proposition even when presented with the supporting evidence. Thus
there was a preference to believe that local members of the French resistance were responsible for disclosing the departure times of U-boats
leaving their protected pens, long after it should have become obvious
that the integrity of their communications had been compromised. Even
when overwhelming proof of the Enigma system's insecurity had been

released in Britain, three decades after the end of the war, there was still a marked reluctance in some quarters to admit that such a breakthrough really could have been possible. Nevertheless, Rommel was himself very suspicious that his communications had been compromised, particularly after the loss of a wealth of cryptographic material from the 15th Panzer Division during Operation CRUSADER, the British offensive of November 1941. Continuously outmanoeuvred by his opponents, Rommel complained to Berlin that he believed the Allies were reading some of his Enigma traffic. The proposition was rejected without discussion.

Leaving aside the principle of whether the very few people alleged to have been privy to Craig's operation would have sanctioned the infiltration of an agent into Rommel's HQ, with all its attendant high risks, when they were already receiving a constant flow of utterly reliable intelligence from a proven source, there remain a few doubts about the practicalities of such an operation. Would a mere three weeks of observation have been sufficient for even a skilled imitator to adopt all the mannerisms of an individual previously unknown to him? Or anyway develop enough of a passing resemblance to fool his German brother officers, even if they had known him for only ten days? And what happened to the real von Warnke? According to Vacha, Craig raised this issue with Colonel Brinton:

> 'You've got to kill him, I suppose?' I asked wearily.
> 'If you want the sordid truth, yes. But forget it,' he snapped. 'It's not your business.'[24]

Assuming for a moment that it was policy to murder individual prisoners of war to further sensitive operations, and no similar case has ever been disclosed, one is bound to wonder whether SOE was the organisation most likely to mastermind such a project, or whether operations which were solely orientated towards intelligence-gathering were not the responsibility of quite another military branch, the Secret Intelligence Service, which, in Cairo, masqueraded as the Inter-Services Liaison Department (ISLD). In fact, there was a clear-cut and well-established convention, designed to avoid wasteful duplication and potentially hazardous overlapping, that the recruitment and handling of agents for purely intelligence objectives was to be undertaken by ISLD, leaving sabotage, paramilitary activities and unconventional warfare to SOE.

Leaving aside the niceties of the ISLD/SOE rivalries in the Middle East, which were especially bitter, no survivor of either organisation can recall any scheme of the kind described by Vacha.

Of course it could be argued, as indeed Vacha has, that the circle of those allowed to know about Craig was so tiny that no word of it has ever leaked out. Yet that line of defence is negated by an analysis of the technical support required to sustain the operation over a period of nearly two years. In terms of communications, it is clear that Craig was in radio contact with the Allies. He is mentioned as having transmitted in Morse on at least three occasions, using 'a complicated five-letter block transposition code',[25] and his preliminary briefing from Brinton was explicit on this topic:

> Since you'll be on Rommel's ops staff, you'll quite often be on the move, probably in a scout car. Like ours, they're fitted with short-wave transmitters. You'll send your messages from one of those. It's easy enough to switch the wavelength to use the one I'll give you – 6.93 metres. Alternate to 6.99 metres. You know the drill. Your call sign is GTZ. Preface all your calls with that and end as per normal R/T procedure. Also remember your security . . . check, your deliberate mistake somewhere in your transmission so that we know it's you by the position of the error. If you are discovered you could be forced to continue to send fake messages or they could send them themselves. If you send on their instructions and don't make the mistake, we'll know you've been blown and can act accordingly, see? . . . Try to get a message over at least once every ten days, even if you've nothing else to report. . . . You're Agent 43, your call sign is GTZ and your code name is Karl. Those are your sole means of identification.[26]

Without a regular radio schedule, British operators would have had to maintain a special watch for Craig's messages on short wave, which was clearly impossible in the circumstances of this operation because dozens of men and women, working in shifts, would have had to monitor Craig's two preassigned wavelengths. Furthermore, specific instructions would have had to be issued to them all so as to ensure that all signals with the GTZ call sign were routed to the appropriate recipient, who, presumably, was the ubiquitous Colonel Brinton. Indeed, the number of people involved in Craig's operation must have been even greater than the staff devoted to the receipt and transmission of clandestine wireless, for there is also the role of the mysterious Otto Rahmer to consider.

Rahmer is the agent in Bielefeld who was to be a key figure in Craig's operation. As Colonel Brinton had explained, he 'is one of our human post-boxes. All the information you get is to be duplicated to him and you'll use the Double Playfair, Grille, and one-time pad codes I'm giving you.'[27] As well as communicating by these complicated codes through the regular postal service, even in peacetime an uncertain method of conveying data swiftly, this procedure appears to have been a grotesque breach of security, with all military mail being subject to routine censorship. Quite what the censors were supposed to have made of the coded five-letter groups in what purported to be an innocuous letter is unclear, but evidently Brinton was satisfied their appearance would not attract unwanted attention to either correspondent. In addition to this being a two-way traffic, with Rahmer writing letters to Craig (which presumably meant he had been allowed into the increasingly large circle of people in the know), Rahmer is also alleged to have maintained a radio link to the War Office in London. On the assumption that Rahmer was in place prior to Craig's infiltration, and he survived after Craig's return to the British lines in February 1943, Rahmer had the distinction of being the only wireless agent in Germany to survive undetected. If so, his existence goes undocumented in any of the intelligence material declassified since the end of the war.

One must also question whether Craig could really have transmitted so many illicit messages to the British lines with such ease. During the course of the North African campaign, it became clear that Rommel's tactical signals intelligence organisation was vastly superior to its British counterpart. 'The Germans were reading the British field codes and cyphers,'[28] admits the official historian, and Rommel's 621st Signals Battalion was permanently located close to his headquarters, where a specialist unit, the *Fernemeldeaufklärung* Company, maintained a highly efficient surveillance of the airwaves. Indeed, this signals unit was far superior at monitoring tactical wireless traffic than any Allied equivalent. The proposition that a German staff officer could occasionally slip away unescorted from the compound in an armoured car to transmit lengthy signals to the enemy undetected is, to put it mildly, somewhat fanciful.

Apart from Brinton's remarkable confidence that von Warnke, despite his capture and, ostensibly, the weeks he had spent in enemy hands, would be posted back to Rommel's HQ, this passage seems to display a rather casual approach to security with Craig being told matters about himself, such as his agent number, which could be of no possible use to him but might aid the enemy if he were forced to disclose it under pressure. Furthermore, Craig was despatched with some very compromising espionage paraphernalia, not the least of which was a codebook that declared itself to be exactly what it was, with no attempt having been made to disguise the unambiguous English title on the cover. Strangely, Craig retained this highly damaging item even after it had landed him in trouble with Hildegarde, who was suspicious of it and accused him of treachery; and he had been obliged to shoot Oberst Reimann, who had spotted it after it had accidentally fallen out of his pocket.

The codebook was not the only potentially compromising item Craig had carried on his mission. Before his departure, Brinton had briefed him on Wavell's intention to launch his counter-offensive, Operation BATTLEAXE, on 15 June 1942. To allow anyone with a knowledge of future plans to stray accidentally into a combat zone is an unusual occurrence, but to despatch an agent deliberately into enemy territory equipped with specific information about an imminent attack is an astonishing breach of security, particularly when, in this scenario, there was no real reason for it to be imparted to Craig. For Brinton's purpose, which was to emphasise the need for him to report on Rommel's tank strengths quickly, it would have been enough to have demanded answers to a questionnaire by a stated deadline, rather than spell out the strategic significance of the need for the intelligence. In any event, Brinton's assertion that 'our intelligence is a little scanty at the moment and not too reliable'[29] was rather wide of the mark. In reality, the ULTRA material relating to BATTLEAXE was, in strategic terms, very comprehensive. The Enigma key used by Rommel to communicate with his subordinates, codenamed PHOENIX, had been broken in November 1941 and had allowed the codebreakers to read, retrospectively, Rommel's instructions to his commanders in the field. Unfortunately, these texts were not available for BATTLEAXE, which turned into a disaster, not just for the troops involved, but for Field Marshal Wavell himself. On 21 June 1942, six days after BATTLEAXE had begun, Churchill sacked him, appointing General Sir Claude Auchinleck to his command. While Vacha claims that Craig succeeded in supplying 'full knowledge of the German strength, particularly in tanks, and exactly where they were,'[30] in time for the offensive, the truth is, in the opinion of the official historian, that the British 'failed to detect Rommel's success in bringing forward in good time a large part of his reserve armour' because 'neither air reconnaissance nor any other source had betrayed the movement forward of the enemy tanks'.

> British field intelligence was weak both before and during the battle. Before the counter-attack began, it was known that Rommel was strengthening his defences; air reconnaissance had found no signs that he had retrieved any important reinforcements during the past month. . . . But the evidence about the number and disposition of Rommel's tanks was unsatisfactory and the Army was again complaining that air reconnaissance and PR were inadequate. How inadequate – and how defective – were all other sources of intelligence . . . was revealed when the fighting began. The British forces had counted on meeting 100 German tanks. They were met by more than twice that number, Rommel having once again brought up practically all his reserves from the Tobruk area at the right time without revealing their movement.[31]

This conclusion, that 'at a tactical level intelligence was, indeed, virtually non-existent', amounts to an emphatic contradiction of Vacha's proposition that Craig's information had played a key role in BATTLEAXE's success. In reality, the reverse was the case, for the offensive had proved a catastrophe as a result of faulty intelligence. Indeed, if the bogus 'von Warnke' had really been responsible for the fiasco, his controllers might reasonably have decided that he had been detected and had come under enemy control.

In addition to the doubts already expressed, there are some further flaws in Craig's tale. For him to have been granted a fortnight's leave starting on 16 July 1941, to be spent in Berlin, would have been truly exceptional. Following his victory in BATTLEAXE, Rommel had been promoted to *Panzer General* and was busy planning his next campaign, a wildly over-ambitious thrust through Egypt to Iraq. This period also coincided with a time of extreme difficulty for his supplies, with an escalating loss of Axis shipping in the Mediterranean. Between July and November, forty-eight cargo ships were sunk by the Allies, and Rommel's lines of supply were fully stretched. With air transport at such a premium, it seems odd that 'von Warnke' should have been allowed to take up valuable space for what was a purely recreational purpose. Certainly Vacha gives no explanation as to why 'von Warnke', who had, after all, only arrived in Libya in April and had been active for just a fortnight before his capture early in May, had been allowed a spell of home leave.

Upon his return to the desert at the end of his leave in July 1941, the author reports that Craig went straight to Rommel's headquarters at Sidi Rezegh, which is odd because this site was then still the centre of an intense tank battle, being captured by the 7th Armoured Brigade and then recaptured by the 21st Panzer Division. Rommel's headquarters during this period was actually much further to the west, at his *Panzergruppe*, located at El Adem.

Given the multitude of inconsistencies and improbabilities in Vacha's story, and his strange misrepresentation of BATTLEAXE as a model of good tactical intelligence, one is bound to conclude that Robert Craig's remarkable story properly belongs on the fiction shelves. But that is not quite the end of his story. In 1975, Vacha published a novel, *Phantoms over Potsdam*, in which the principal character is a foreign correspondent based in Bonn named Robert Craig. Curiously, Craig is described as having worked for SOE during the war and having retired from SIS only eight years earlier. His plot involves an approach from his former employers, who seek his help to destroy what is perceived in London as an untimely attempt to unite the two Germanies. With Craig's reluctant support the scheme is ruthlessly scotched. Quite how much Vacha's second book is based on fact only he can tell . . . and he isn't.

8

Tony Duke: The Spy in Berlin

'Leaving out impersonal facts, such as explanations of his code or the organisation of British or Russian Intelligence in Germany, he told me of the people he knew.'[1]

What is the origin of the story about a British spy in Berlin, perhaps even the one referred to by Robert Vacha? One explanation is to be found in *Slipstream*, the story of a young Briton, Tony Duke, as told by his sister, Madelaine Duke. She had first mentioned him in *Top Secret Mission*,[2] in which the authoress described how, immediately after the war, she had joined the Allied Control Commission in Vienna to search for her brother, whom she had last seen fleetingly in Paris in July 1939. In the sequel, published in 1955, Madelaine claimed that, far from being a Nazi sympathiser who had stayed willingly in Germany during the war to broadcast anti-British propaganda over the radio, her multi-lingual brother had been a spy employed by British Intelligence, having been recruited by Bill Keir, an expatriate teacher at the Berlitz languages school in Berlin. So that there should be no doubt about *Slipstream*'s credentials as a work of non-fiction, apart from the names of some of the characters, the book contained a short foreword written by Colonel A. P. Scotland OBE, the former British military intelligence officer and author of *The London Cage*, who had established his own formidable reputation by interrogating enemy prisoners of war in London.[3] Scotland had observed that in Berlin during the war 'there were always plenty who could obtain and pass on information but how to dispatch it to its ultimate destination was not so simple'.[4] Evidently Scotland believed that Tony

Duke had managed to overcome the obvious difficulties of communicating with London from the heart of the Reich, and had even made the slightly improbable assertion that, 'until the bombing of Berlin forced Hitler and Bormann to organise the people of the country and towns into mass security squads, there was practically no security and agents and information moved as freely as it did in Holland and Belgium in the First World War'.[5]

After Keir's arrest and execution in November 1939, Tony took over his transmitter, which had been hidden with a friend, the Baron Brandolf, at his villa in the Wannsee area, and installed it in his studio overlooking the Kurfürstendamm, 'an excellent place for the wireless. Any broadcast from there would be hard to trace.'[6] Despite the risk, Tony had 'packed the wireless into his rucksack'[7] and carried the set into the city. According to Madelaine, 'Up to Keir's arrest, he had collected technical information; while Bill had dealt with military and political matters.'[8] Later, in 1940, Tony had buried the radio and instead conveyed his messages to London in coded messages concealed in the texts of his regular broadcasts.

> Co-ordinating the news or propaganda the Germans expected
> him to broadcast with the intelligence information he wished to
> pass on to Britain, at the same time, proved the most unpre-
> dictable and capricious task he had ever taken upon himself.
> While the subjects chosen by the Germans ranged from book
> reviews to stories of 'women and children brutally murdered by
> British troops in Africa', the material Tony had to inject into those
> harangues pointed to subjects as diverse as the spring plans of
> the German High Command and the RAF damage sustained by
> Krupp's factories at Essen. The code Bill Keir had taught him
> depended on an elaborate system of wording, a clever juxtaposi-
> tion of syllables, stresses and pauses.[9]

In August 1941, one of Tony's contacts introduced him to a Soviet intelligence officer named Solakov, and through him he arranged to send coded messages in German radio programmes broadcast in Russian. Solakov was later shot dead, but Tony continued to insert illicit messages into his broadcasts until the fall of Berlin. Arrested by the Russians in his apartment, Tony was sent to a succession of camps until he escaped from one in Hungary and made his way to Vienna, where he was found by his sister. After his death in a motor accident in Italy in 1948, Madelaine says that she decided to write his story, but by her own admission she knew very little of what had really happened to him:

> Tony very seldom talked about himself but, in the case of his life in Berlin, he made an exception; probably because he wanted to compensate me for all the waiting and uncertainty of the war years. He did so generously. Leaving out impersonal facts, such as explanations of his code or the organisation of British and Russian Intelligence in Germany, he told me of the people he knew, how they affected him, and how they reacted to the physical and moral deprivation of war.[10]

Thus, Tony had omitted to divulge to Madelaine exactly how he had maintained contact with London during the war, which leaves the claim that he had inserted coded messages bearing secret intelligence into radio broadcasts looking a trifle thin. Indeed, in the one passage in which Madelaine describes her brother signalling London on Keir's clandestine transmitter, she makes it clear that he used a speech channel. 'Towards the end of March Tony was able to broadcast details of General Fromm's plans for Norway':

> 'The 7th Airborne Division and the 22nd Division to be used in Norway,' he announced in code. 'There's been a switch. . . . A regiment of the 1st Mountain Division for Norway; also two Divisions of the 7th Wave.' Tony paused to listen. Nothing. 'And a motorised brigade. Over and Out,' he concluded, with a strange feeling of relief.[11]

Tony's relief had been shortlived, for moments later he had been interrupted by a woman who had demanded, 'Do you know you were talking to yourself?'[12] From this episode one can deduce that Madelaine believed her brother had been in voice contact with London, a technical impossibility over such a distance with the equipment then available to Tony, which had been small enough to fit in his rucksack for the journey from Wannsee into Berlin.

So is there any evidence at all that Tony had done anything, ever, for British Intelligence? When this question was put to the author, now Mrs Alex McFarlane, in 1982, she had replied from her home in

Hurstpierpoint in Sussex that a former diplomat, the late Sir Clifford Heathcote-Smith, had confirmed the existence of 'Bill Keir' to her before his death and had corroborated what Tony had told her. Sir Clifford had served in Naval Intelligence during the Great War and, after long service as a consul in the Levant, had retired as Consul General in Alexandria in 1943. His connection with Tony presumably had stemmed from his work as the British representative in Italy on the Inter-Governmental Committee on Refugees at the end of the war, but this could not be ascertained. Whether this gentleman was in any position to confirm Tony's sister's tale seems unlikely, but there is certainly no other evidence to support her account.

The reality is that there were no British agents left in Germany in 1939, and the only contact maintained with Berlin after the outbreak of hostilities had been through the medium of neutral embassies. Later in the war, there was a limited, one-way traffic with Allied prisoners of war who communicated with SIS via a prearranged code concealed in prisoner-of-war correspondence arranged by the Red Cross. Could Tony Duke have employed a similar system? Such a proposition is quite impractical, as Colonel Scotland ought to have recognised, considering that whereas prisoners of war were free to compose their own apparently innocuous letters home, Duke had been obliged to work with scripts prepared by officials of the Nazi Ministry of Propaganda. Therefore, one is bound to infer that even if Tony Duke really had tried to spy in Berlin, he never possessed the means to communicate with London, a conclusion that rather undermines *Slipstream*'s *raison d'être*.

One unsolved conundrum is why Colonel Scotland contributed what might be interpreted as an endorsement to *Slipstream*. The most obvious connection between the authors is that they shared the same London publishers, Evans Brothers. Scotland's *The London Cage* was released two years after *Slipstream*, but it was on the same 1957 list as Madelaine Duke's *No Passport*, the biography of Jan Felix, a Polish refugee who became an SOE officer after a series of remarkable adventures. Both books were controversial, but for different reasons. Scotland's memoirs charted his career from a young Scot who emigrated to the Cape Colony just after the Boer War, and subsequently joined the local militia in German South-West Africa, to his return to Europe to serve as an intelligence officer in France. Accordingly, he had served in both the German and British armies, a distinction which was to achieve headline news when he gave evidence during the war crimes trial of Field Marshal

Albert Kesselring in Venice in February 1946. During his testimony, his expertise on the subject of the Wehrmacht was challenged, leading to an exchange in which Scotland had confirmed details of his past service for the Kaiser. Naturally the disclosure created a sensation, but more than a decade was to pass before Scotland released his book, an event that prompted some criticism from the War Office and obliged him to insert an unusual disclaimer stating that 'the War Office does not in any way vouch for the accuracy of the facts and does not necessarily accept any opinions expressed in this book'.

At the end of the Great War, Scotland had returned to South Africa and had later worked in Argentina. In 1933, he had been posted to London and during his retirement had visited Germany on several occasions. Upon the outbreak of war, he had volunteered his services to the War Office and, because of his fluency in languages, was appointed an interrogator of enemy prisoners at the London District Cage, a large private mansion in Kensington Gardens. At the end of the war, he commanded a War Crimes Investigation Unit, which conducted numerous enquiries that formed the basis of his memoirs. He eventually retired in 1948.

It is likely that his connection with Madelaine Duke came about through Evans Brothers, for there is also a link to be found between them and Bruce Marshall, the author who wrote a short preface for Madelaine Duke's first book, *Top Secret Mission*. Marshall had served as an intelligence officer in SOE's RF Section for two years and had later worked with Madelaine in the Allied Control Commission in Vienna. The author of several books, Marshall had spent twenty years in France before the war, and in 1952 had completed *The White Rabbit*, the biography of SOE's RF Section agent, Wing-Commander Forrest Yeo-Thomas, for Evans Brothers. By contributing a preface, Marshall effectively endorsed Madelaine's first book, but it raises the question of why he did not do the same three years later when she turned her attention to Jan Felix, who allegedly had not only served in SOE too, but had operated as an agent for one of SOE's French sections. Of course there may have been any number of reasons why Marshall did not participate in *No Passport*, but one possibility is that Jan Felix was not quite what he seemed.

According to Madelaine Duke, Jan Felix was a veteran of the Spanish Civil War, who had fought with the Republicans. He had later settled in Belgium, but on the outbreak of war had fled to France, only to be

arrested at Limoges and interned at a detention camp in Perpignan. In
March 1941, he escaped across the Pyrenees to Barcelona, but was
arrested again and sent to the notorious Miranda de Ebro prison, where
he languished until his release in Madrid in June 1943. He finally arrived
in England as a refugee from Lisbon in November 1943 and had been
detained briefly at 'the Patriotic School in Kensington'[13] before his
recruitment into SOE. He had been talent-spotted for the organisation by
a certain Major Spencer, supposedly SOE's representative at the British
Embassy in Lisbon, who confirmed the details to Madelaine after the
war. By May 1944, Felix had been flown to Gibraltar with two companions on what seemed to be a rather vague mission to replace an agent in
Paris named Stanislaus with whom SOE had lost contact five months earlier. When he reached the French town of Tarbes, Felix described his
mission to a contact named Troy and listed his principal objective as finding Stanislaus, who had been part of Troy's network:

> If I do find him I'll establish an organisation of my own. I'm to
> build up a route for passing parcels and people to you; it'll be a
> line extending from Belgium to Paris, and from Paris to Tarbes.
> Besides, I must find suitable spots where the RAF can drop arms
> for the Maquis, and possible landing-grounds.[14]

The group had been passed up an escape line from Spain supervised by
Troy, and had caught a train to Paris in Lyon. Felix had carried a wireless set and papers which 'stated that he was a member of the German
Army, an ordinance inspector,' and these were scrutinised during a
search when the train 'was stopped on the demarkation-line by order of
the Gestapo'.[15]

Felix had been accompanied on this dangerous journey by 'Grant,
who looked as English as he was,' and their French guide, Hilaire.[16]
Their route took them from Gibraltar by boat to Algeciras, then Seville,
Madrid and Barcelona to the Pyrenean village of La Ainsa, where they
were challenged by the police and forced to return to Barcelona. From
Madelaine's account, it is clear that none was physically fit, and the journey proved an ordeal for Felix:

> The gastric ulcer had made him ill before he was due to leave
> England, and a medical officer had told him that he should be in
> hospital. His commanding officer had only reluctantly given Jan

Quentin Reynolds, a war correspondent of great distinction. Reynolds was duped by a Canadian Walter Mitty, who persuaded him that he was The Spy Who Wouldn't Talk.

THE FOREIGN SERVICE
OF THE
UNITED STATES OF AMERICA   MAY 2, 1945

REPORT ON CONDESA GLORIA RUBIO DE FURSTENBERG
AMERICAN EMBASSY

Subject was born GLORIA RUBIO, Veracruz, Mexico, August 27, 1913.

Subject left Mexico at age of 16 for United States. Spent two years in Hollywood. At 18 subject went to England. At 19 married a Dutchman called FRANK _____. At 21 met COUNT FRANZ EGON GRAF VON FURSTENBERG: subject divorced her Dutch husban, Furstenberg divorced his American wife and the couple married in London. (Ex-American wife of Furstenberg is now living in New York under name of Countess Fursten-berg.)

Subject lived in Germany with husband until Jan. 1943 when she left for Spain. Husband fought on Russian front at beginning of War and later was recalled to Berlin (Address: CAPT. FRANZ EGON VON FURSTEN-BER, army number 12960).

In Spain subject lived with her two children, boy age 5 and girl age 8, at Palace Hotel in Madrid.

Subject is not actually considered suspect although known to have had various German connections in the German Embassy in Madrid, (HANS VON STUDNITZ, German agent in the S.D.). While living in Germany subject was very friendly with PEPE MAKAL, then the Spanish Ambassador to Germany. Also subject has been friendly with GENERAL AGUILAR, Mex-ican Minister in Lisbon. She has probably used her influence with AGUILAR and with a mexican relative called MORAN, aide to the Mexican Ambassador in Paris to obtain her French visa which she received about a month ago.

On April 26th, 1945 subject left Madrid with two children and nurse for Irun (Address: GLORIA RUBIO, HOTEL TERMINUS, IRUN) where she will rent a home for the children for the summer months. Subject will then ppoceed alone to Paris; she has her papers arranged to leave Irun for Paris May 12th. In Paris she will immediately contact her friend AHKMED KAHKRY, son of Egyptian minister to France and Spain. Her plans are to obtain divorce from FURSTENBERG in France and to marry PRINCE FAHKRY. Subject has Mexican passport in name of GLORIA RUBIO, Nr. 8/469, issued by Mexican Consulade in Lisbon.

FAHKRY is 5'6", slight, light brown hair, distinguished appearance, wears glasses, 24 yrs but looks older.
GLORIA RUBIO (which is name she will use constantly in France) is 5'9", thin, age 32, black hair, fair complexion, distinguished appear-ance, extremely well-dressed.

The original OSS report written by Aline, Countess of Romanones, when she was a cipher clerk in Madrid with the codename *Butch*. Her subsequent autobiographies gave an entirely different picture of a refugee, Gloria von Furstenberg, whom she falsely accused of being a Nazi collaborator and Himmler's mistress.

Johnny Nicholas, the mysterious black OSS agent who is alleged to have parachuted into France and worked undercover in Paris in 1943. But did he ever exist? The evidence is slim.

The postcard Johnny Nicholas is alleged to have sent from the concentration camp Buchenwald to his brother in Paris, one of the few items to confirm that such a person really was held by the Nazis. But was he a spy?

A comparison between MGM's film *School for Danger*, released after the war, and the photos in *A Man Called Intrepid* prove that the picture below came from the movie and not from a secret wartime archive, as claimed by the author, William Stevenson.

Sir William Stephenson. Despite an impressive career, Sir William collaborated on a fictional version of his intelligence experiences, most of which had been inexpertly borrowed from other authors.

John Cottell lecturing at Wichita State University in 1992, holding what he claimed to be his wartime parachute suit.

The true story
of 'Jay Bee' —
the only woman
in Churchill's
Secret Circle.

CYANIDE IN MY SHOE

by Josephine Butler

The dustjacket of one of Josephine Butler's books, *Cyanide in My Shoe*. Although a fully qualified medical practitioner, Dr Butler fabricated dozens of secret missions into enemy-occupied territory and published two books describing her adventures.

Roxane Pitt in 1957, publicising her book *The Courage of Fear*. But was she really a secret agent? The two versions of her memoirs give entirely contradictory accounts of her clandestine missions in France and Italy.

A respected historian, Leonard Mosley invented a bogus Nazi spy, codenamed *The Druid*, to link separate incidents mentioned in other books.

The X Troop: a group photo which was taken in May 1943, when *Nimrod* could not have been included, as the historian James Leasor claimed.

permission to take up his assignment, after he had signed a declaration that he was going abroad on his own responsibility, and against medical advice.[17]

Felix's epic journey across Spain and France had been assisted by Troy, who 'was an extremely successful British agent in southern France' and who reportedly

> had built up an efficient escape-route for Allied personnel across the Haute Pyrenees into Spain. His intelligence network extended all the way to Gibraltar in the south, and Lisbon to the west. Apart from shepherding airmen and escaping British prisoners of war out of enemy territory he was constantly supplying the War Office with military information, and his knowledge of the Germans' activities in Vichy France had always been amazingly reliable.[18]

Troy joined Felix for the next stage of his journey, from Tarbes to Avignon, as did his assistant, Simone, and they arrived safely in Paris, having eluded the German controls en route. Soon after his arrival in Paris, Felix identified himself to 'a couple whose address he had been given in London', a certain Monsieur Coiffin and his wife Toni.[19] With their help he traced Stanislaus through a woman described as his secretary, but he then heard that the missing agent had been arrested for carrying forged papers. Felix tried to help Stanislaus by stealing new documents and stamps from a German headquarters, and otherwise busied himself 'arranging a dropping-ground for the RAF on the Evereux route'.[20] He also fell out with Grant, who had taken to alcohol and nightclubs, and had been placed under guard in a safehouse.

On 18 August, Felix left Paris for Belgium on a motorcycle and was liberated there by the Allies in September. When asked to prove his bona fides by the British officer to whom he had reported, Felix explained that he had been trained 'near Fort William, then Altringham for parachute training, London for code and wireless instruction, the Vineyard, Bournemouth for fieldcraft'.[21] Satisfied with his credentials, Felix returned to London for debriefing and later worked for the War Office History Department in some unspecified capacity. At some point he encountered Madelaine and the result was *No Passport*, which purported to be his biography.

Upon closer examination, *No Passport* can be seen to contain numerous clues which at first blush suggest that the book is a hoax. Quite apart from the central improbability of a previously unknown foreigner being recruited into SOE, given a commission, trained as a wireless operator and parachutist, only to be sent to Paris by the longest possible overland route, all in the space of six months, there are numerous difficulties with Madelaine's narrative. The travel data appears to make no sense, particularly when one considers that the demarcation line between the Occupied Zone and Vichy had been made redundant in November 1942, when the entire country had been occupied. It therefore was not in existence, as Felix had stated, in May 1944.

Felix's purported employment by SOE is also suspect. There was no 'Mr Spencer' working for SOE at the British Embassy in Lisbon in 1943, where the long-serving local representative was L. H. Motimore, who operated under his own name. The details of Felix's SOE training are also somewhat flawed. This is particularly significant because Felix allegedly had offered this information to prove his authenticity. Certainly hundreds of SOE personnel underwent initial training in Inverness-shire at a collection of establishments located near Fort William, but the detail about parachute training at 'Altringham' is slightly wrong. In fact, SOE's parachute course was conducted at Altrincham in Cheshire, on a site which is now Manchester airport. As for 'the Vineyard, Bournemouth', again Duke was not quite right. The only SOE special training school close to that name was The Vineyards, designated STS 35, which was an F Section facility near Brockenhurst in Hampshire, not near Bournemouth, which, of course, is in Dorset. Finally, no wireless training was given to SOE trainees in London. SOE's Signals Section ran three radio courses, but none took place in the capital. Thus, when Felix allegedly reeled off his SOE background in Brussels in order to persuade a British intelligence officer of his credentials, his errors could have been expected to ensure his immediate arrest as an obvious impostor.

Felix's tale cannot be verified by reference to other individuals named in the text. As has been noted, 'Major Spencer' was not in Lisbon. The other SOE officers named, such as Captain Burnes and his assistant Martine, are equally untraceable, although Felix is mentioned as having married Martine after the war. As for Felix's acquaintances in France, at least one can be traced: Troy, who had created such an impressive intelligence *réseau* and escape line centred on Tarbes but extending into

Spain, is Edouard Troy, whom Madelaine described as 'a well-groomed young man' and whose photograph had been shown to Felix in London.

Finally, there is the matter of identities. Felix claims that he was equipped with false papers showing him to be in the German army, an astonishingly dangerous risk as SOE invariably gave its personnel civilian documents because to have placed an agent in a position where he would be the subject of the enemy's military discipline would have ensured immediate execution if discovered. This also raises the question of how he came to be selected for the mission in the first place, considering that he was in poor health and had been told that he spoke 'French with a foreign accent'.[22] Indeed, his German was not much better, for at one moment he was told that he had 'got a foreign accent in German as well'.[23]

Despite the many points of dubious detail in Madelaine Duke's account, her tale is indeed largely true. Although Jan Felix never existed, his story does in fact coincide with that of Hans Felix Jeschke, a German who later became naturalised and changed his name to 'John Hilton'.[24] According to SOE's archives, Jeschke, who had been born to German parents in Leipzig, was a Socialist seaman who had found himself in trouble with the authorities in several countries because of his political activities. He was imprisoned briefly in Hamburg in 1935 and had fought with the Republicans in Barcelona the following year. He had volunteered for the Belgian army in 1940 and had been interned in France before escaping to Portugal, where he was expelled, ending up with a false Canadian identity at the Miranda de Ebro camp in Spain. He finally escaped to Lisbon in September 1943 and, two months later, was recruited by SIS for a mission to either Belgium or Austria. He arrived in England in December 1943, having travelled via Gibraltar, and was interviewed at the London Reception Centre by a Lieutenant A. Walters, who completed a lengthy report on 30 December 1943. He was commissioned with the rank of 2nd Lieutenant at the end of January 1944 and enrolled by SOE's DF Section in preparation for a mission to develop an escape line from Belgium to France. He left for Gibraltar by air on 12 June 1944 accompanied by a Belgian radio operator, Sergeant Quinaux, codenamed *Goffin*. In the field he was known as *Juanito*, and he teamed up with Edouard Troy in Tarbes late in June in time to accompany him by train to Paris via Toulouse.

Jeschke's assignment in Paris was to establish contact with Stanislaus at Jean Coiffin's home in the Boulevard de Beauséjour, and to build a new escape line of safehouses for the RAF crew sheltering under their protection. This Jeschke accomplished, making his headquarters at a hotel in the rue Petron, despite the unsatisfactory behaviour of Stanislaus, who had spent large sums of SOE's money and made too many dubious contacts. Resentful of Jeschke's arrival, Stanislaus subsequently disappeared, forcing the network to reorganise at very short notice.

By August 1944, Jeschke had identified several dropping zones around Paris for SOE, established three radio sets in Clichy, and recruited a Belgian named Jadoul, who held a position as a potato distributor which allowed him considerable freedom to travel. He also cultivated a printer in the Boulevard Haussmann who specialised in forging German documents. With his help, and using a motorcycle with stolen German plates, he extended his circuit to Lille and Ghent. He was in Brussels when the city was liberated in September, and identified himself to Major Paul Boggis-Rolphe of SOE, Airey Neave of MI9 and a Major Wolfe, but was unable to explain where his headquarters in London was, or to what section he was attached. When SOE was eventually contacted, Jeschke was ordered to return to London, where he was debriefed on 18 September 1944 and recommended for a Mention in Despatches. According to his personal file, he remained on SOE's strength until 9 July 1945.

Although Madelaine Duke's version of Jeschke's experiences reproduced in *No Passport* was somewhat garbled, there can be little doubt that her Jan Felix is the same as Hans Jeschke, and however improbable his tale, it is supported by the declassified documents released by the Foreign Office in 1994.

9

The Paladin

'Churchill's paladin – that was something to be proud of and if it was all you had left it was enough.'[1]

Christopher Creighton is the *nom de guerre* of the hero of Brian Garfield's story, *The Paladin*, an account of the exploits of a young man who became Churchill's private spy while still a schoolboy. The rather odd title refers to any one of the Twelve Peers of Charlemagne's court, whose name has come to designate any knight errant or champion. Garfield, who wrote the novel *Death Wish* which was subsequently made into a movie directed by Michael Winner, is an experienced author who has dozens of titles of fiction and non-fiction to his credit. He insists that Creighton is a real person, averring that 'perhaps only Christopher can say how closely and at what points the narrative coincides with the truth'.[2]

According to *The Paladin*, Creighton was eleven years old when he first met Churchill, in June 1935, while playing in the grounds of Chartwell Manor, Churchill's country home near Westerham in Kent. Creighton's parents had divorced and a family friend known to him as 'Uncle John' had arranged for his mother and her three children to rent a cottage on the Chartwell estate. His father, who never makes an appearance, is described as 'an important surgeon' with a home in Harley Street, who had once won an Olympic gold medal in a track event.[3] He had also spent two years attending a school in Germany, where he struck up a friendship with Joachim von Ribbentrop.

It was Uncle John who provided the connection between the boy's family and the Churchills. At different times during the Great War he had served in the same mess with the boy's father who had been an RFC pilot, and with Churchill who after leaving the war cabinet had served at the front with a combat regiment; Uncle John had become Mr Churchill's aide and they had remained friends ever since.[4]

In April 1940, while still attending an unnamed public school, Creighton was summoned to London by Uncle John and met by 'Colonel John Metcalf', who wore the insignia of the Intelligence Corps on his uniform. Metcalf escorted the boy to the Admiralty, where he was assigned a secret mission by Churchill, then the First Lord.[5] He was to obtain an invitation from his schoolfriend Prince Paul to stay with the Belgian royal family at their château near Antwerp during the imminent holidays, and to discover 'the dispositions of the Belgian army and to report anything else you consider of import'.[6] The mission was necessary because, according to the briefing given by Churchill, 'no British military officer now remains on Belgian soil'.[7]

Creighton duly carried out his assignment in Belgium with the aid of a pair of British agents 'posing as a honeymoon couple on a camping trip', who were equipped with 'a bulky B-Mark-II shortwave set'.[8] While staying with his friend Prince Paul, he learned that his father's old friend von Ribbentrop, who 'had come to the house several times in 1936 and 1937',[9] was in contact with some Belgian officers who 'were planning a traitorous Belgian surrender'.[10] Creighton confided this news to Prince Paul (who was subsequently killed with one of his sisters when the aircraft carrying him to England was shot down by a Messerschmitt) and managed to alert the British Expeditionary Force to the plot by warning Colonel Metcalf, who had been seconded to Lord Gort's staff in France.

Upon his return to England via Dunkirk, Creighton went back to school briefly, before being summoned for a second time to see Churchill, who was by now Prime Minister. The occasion was the loss of British agents, 'nine men . . . four women',[11] in Eire, where they had been investigating the existence of a secret U-boat refuelling facility on the coast of Donegal. On the pretext of staying with another schoolfriend, Creighton travelled to Ireland and discovered a German base near Lough Swilly. In doing so, he killed a sentry, but managed to escape across the border to Londonderry, where the authorities were informed of the existence of two camouflaged enemy submarines, both with full crews undergoing replenishment.

It is at this stage that Creighton, who 'had just turned sixteen', was posted to 'Number Two RAF Initial Training Wing' somewhere in the Fens with the identity of 'Peter Hamilton, nineteen years old'.[12] Apparently, 'files and records had been slipped into numerous archives to support the existence' of this new name. Creighton's unorthodox training required him to participate in the execution of six Germans, two enemy aliens from an internment camp on the Isle of Man and four prisoners of war. 'All six of them come from the condemned cells,' explained a training officer.[13] They included a spy named Kriesler, who passed himself off as a Swedish businessman based in Oxford Street and who had murdered his English wife and their two daughters; a Nazi diamond dealer named Beck, who shot a Jewish family in Bristol; two SS corporals, who had participated in a massacre in Belgium; and two junior naval ratings, who murdered the crew of a ditched Blenheim bomber. All six, who had been sentenced to death, allegedly were knifed by Creighton and his fellow trainees.

Following this ghoulish initiation, Creighton was sent to the Loire in occupied France on his apprenticeship, a mission to free a tortured girl from an enemy prison camp. The assignment was a success and upon his return the young man, aged 'seventeen this past birthday', was despatched on 4 December 1941 to 'a bomber station in Cornwall',[14] where he was flown by a Liberator aircraft to Canada and then on to San Diego, California. His task, which required him to parachute into the Pacific where he was to rendezvous with a Dutch submarine, was to masquerade as 'an expert in warheads and explosives'.[15] He inserted a timing mechanism into each of the submarine's torpedoes while pretending that he was improving the weapons with a magnetic device. In reality, his purpose was to blow up the vessel and 'the fifty-six officers and men aboard',[16] having been dropped off first in Fiji, where the same Liberator bomber was to collect him from Suva.

Creighton's circuitous return journey took him to Perth, Mombasa and Cairo, and then on 12 December to Southampton by Berwick flying boat from Alexandria. However, he experienced some pangs of conscience about the number of loyal Dutchmen he had murdered. It was then that 'Uncle John', codenamed *Owl*, had imparted the motive for the ruthless sabotage. At 0532 on 2 December 1941, the submarine had spotted a large Japanese carrier force steaming towards Hawaii. 'Those unfortunate Dutch sailors saw something they shouldn't have seen. Their destruction was a matter of policy.'[17] A calculated decision had been made to stop a warning from being relayed to the Americans.

Our best analysis was that they'd get highly indignant and call in the Japanese ambassador and demand to know what a Japanese battle fleet was doing in those waters. It would have forewarned Tojo and of course they'd have cancelled the attack and withdrawn the fleet. America might still have been tottering along the fence of neutrality when Hitler marched into London. The sentiment of the American people was firmly against war until last Sunday. This attack, or something like it, was the only thing that could do the job for us.[18]

This was not only Uncle John's view. Churchill is quoted as confirming that he had gained the impression in America that President Roosevelt was anticipating a surprise attack:

I came away from Washington with the distinct feeling he'd known it was coming and he'd kept his mouth primly shut and allowed it to come. . . . It seems his cipher people had been working terribly hard. They'd broken the Japanese purple diplomatic code – several weeks before the attack I believe. Clever rascals. Whether the President knew the exact time and place of the attack is open to conjecture and I'm sure he'll never give anyone the satisfaction of full knowledge – his distaste for disclosure is notorious – but I believe he knew an attack was coming and, more, I believe he welcomed it.[19]

This interesting proposition was followed by a series of murders, all carried out in London by Creighton, of those who had handled the fateful warning message from the Dutch submarine. 'Lieutenant Randall died without a word under the wheels of a tube train and Lieutenant Colin Cosgrove RNR, his neck broken by one blow,'[20] was found dead in a bomb-damaged house. The third victim, a Wren second officer named Ann Colquhoun, died on her way home from a single blow to the head in an alleyway close to Oxford Street. Temporarily filled with remorse, Creighton got drunk in a pub and attacked three policemen, but, following his mother's intervention, he was released from jail without a formal charge.

Satisfied of the necessity to kill these three wholly innocent officers, Creighton was ready for his next assignment: deliberately to betray the Allied intention to mount a raid on Dieppe. 'You're talking of plotting the premeditated betrayal and sacrifice of our own loyal soldiers!' protested Colonel Metcalf when he was informed of the scheme, but Churchill, who allegedly was under pressure to open a second front in 1942 from President Roosevelt's chief adviser, Harry Hopkins, and Generals Eisenhower, Clark and Marshall, saw some advantage in demonstrating 'to the Americans the impracticability of storming the French coast'.[21] He also thought that it might be a useful experiment to launch an assault under 'the worst possible conditions, so that we may test ourselves against the best the enemy can put up against us in a major assault'.[22]

It was this somewhat strange logic that led Creighton to Dublin, where he presented himself to an Abwehr officer, Rudolf Breucher of the German Legation, as a rather junior Royal Navy coding clerk attached to the Signals Distributing Office of Lord Mountbatten's Combined Operations headquarters. His 'Peter Hamilton' identity was dropped, and Breucher, an SS officer named Kinski and three other Germans who met Creighton in a wood just outside the Irish capital appeared to accept his story of holding the rank of Leading Coder. He was flown to Berlin on 14 August, via Lisbon and Switzerland, and introduced to Admiral Canaris, to whom he imparted the scheduled date of the Allied assault on Dieppe, five days hence. He remained in the Abwehr's hands long enough to witness the raid from a bunker overlooking Dieppe, accompanied by Canaris, and to collect £10,000 in counterfeit notes as the price for his treachery. This performance was intended to authenticate Creighton as a reliable source for the Abwehr. Not long after his return journey to London, he was instructed to use his new status to deceive his German controllers. Accordingly, on 7 November 1942, he made his way to a second rendezvous with Breucher in Dublin, fixed by a prearranged signal on an innocuous-looking postcard, and informed him that an Allied invasion of North Africa was to begin the following morning, with amphibious landings at Tobruk, Casablanca and Tripoli. The real targets, however, were to be Algiers, Oran and the north Moroccan coast.

Having 'only just turned eighteen',[23] Creighton's next assignment was almost as momentous as his clandestine involvement in the raid on

Dieppe: the assassination of Admiral Darlan in Algiers. Reverting to the guise of Peter Hamilton, he flew to Blida from Gibraltar with instructions from Uncle John to help Fernand Bonnier de la Chapelle shoot the troublesome Frenchman. As Uncle John had explained,

> If Darlan was murdered by an Englishman the repercussions would thunder round the world. . . . The assassin must be French. To that extent we and the Free French are agreed. Nevertheless the young man they have chosen is an emotional chap, I'm told, competent but perhaps not likely to remain cool under stress. Quite bluntly, I do not trust a hot-blooded young zealot to bring it off properly – and if it's botched it will put us all at risk. You are to see he doesn't botch it.[24]

However, at the vital moment, when Bonnier and Creighton confronted Darlan in his office on Christmas Eve 1942, Bonnier's nerve failed and Creighton fired the fatal shot – a dum-dum bullet – into the Admiral's stomach. Creighton then leapt from a window and made his escape while Bonnier was taken into custody, tried by summary court-martial and executed on Boxing Day.

Early in the New Year of 1943, Creighton's wish to become a more orthodox naval officer was granted and, after a training course at HMS Lochailort in Scotland, he was posted to the Combined Operations Pilotage Party, a specialist group gathered to reconnoitre and clear underwater obstacles from beaches in anticipation of the invasion. Creighton undertook one COPP mission, on which he killed a German sentry, but five days before his tour of operational duty was due to end he was recalled to Whitehall for an interview with the Prime Minister, his seventh recorded encounter with Churchill since the war had begun. The subject was D-Day. Churchill explained that 'the date is tentatively scheduled for the beginning of June. About six weeks from now,' before giving a more detailed account of the exact beaches in Normandy that were to be hit, and the deception campaign that had been prepared to cover the planned offensive. In closing he observed:

> 'I've told you the general outlines of the actual plan and I trust you will keep it to yourself. Now I intend to tell you what you're to tell the Germans. You're to help persuade them that our real target for the invasion is the Pas de Calais. Patton attacking from Dover.'[25]

Creighton's new task was to re-establish contact with the Abwehr in Dublin and then sell them the secrets of D-Day for a quarter of a million pounds. Equipped with a cyanide capsule concealed under a false tooth, Creighton returned to Dublin, where, unexpectedly, he was seized by Rudolf Breucher and taken by U-boat to France for interrogation. Creighton endured appalling torture at the hands of the Gestapo in the SS headquarters in Cherbourg and was eventually driven to attempt suicide, but although he succeeded in releasing the poison, it failed to work. Thereafter, unable to resist any longer, he succumbed to his tormentors and, on 4 June, gave a comprehensive account of his work as a British agent since 1940. In doing so he confirmed that D-Day was to be 6 June and would take place in Normandy. However, soon after delivering his confession, he was freed from his prison by Heinz Gruber, a Gestapo officer who had been born in England of German parents, and who was an undercover British agent.

Naturally Creighton was dismayed at having cracked under torture, but Gruber reassured him that this was all part of a fiendishly machiavellian plan. He explained that his German colleagues

> believe Churchill and your controller put on an elaborate charade
> for your benefit – the maps, the plans, Normandy, 'Utah',
> 'Omaha', the lot. A deception designed to mislead *you*. Follow
> me? They know you're a British agent, a professional because
> nobody issues suicide capsules to amateurs, and they know the
> controllers don't tell agents anything the agents don't need to
> know, so they believe you were told about this Normandy plan so
> it would be tortured out of you.[26]

Reassured that he had not let the side down, Creighton made good his escape from captivity, but Gruber was gunned down in an ambush. Undeterred, Creighton took a twenty-five-foot fishing boat out into the Channel, signalled a patrolling British submarine, HMS *Seahorse*, and was restored to England to be thanked personally by the Prime Minister.

If even partially true, Creighton's exploits must add up to one of the most astonishing stories of the war: U-boats in Ireland, sabotage in the Pacific, betrayal at Dieppe, assassination in Algiers, duplicity in Dublin and numerous other assorted adventures. It might well be asked which remarkable organisation sponsored all this activity, and there are several indications that for part of the time Creighton worked under the auspices of SOE. When Churchill authorised the creation of SOE in June 1940, he did so with the famous instruction to Dr Hugh Dalton to 'set Europe ablaze'. This exact order is mentioned in a conversation reported by Garfield between Churchill and 'Uncle John': 'You've ordered my section to set Europe ablaze. A fine phrase Prime Minister, but I've got to be able to feed my people and get them across the water before they can set any fires.'[27]

This would seem to suggest that Uncle John's section was identical to SOE, and this is supported by other evidence. After his first operation in occupied France, to a circuit run by a certain Rollo in the Loire in 1941, Uncle John, who is mentioned as working from 'the SOE office, Room 60 upstairs in the Annexe,'[28] justified Creighton's premature recall with the remark: 'Anybody in the SOE can do the job you've been doing.'[29] Creighton is also described as 'thinking like an SOE agent again' while escaping from his SS cell, and there is a brief reference to Creighton having 'been in Cherbourg . . . two years ago on Resistance jobs',[30] which, in the context, would suggest at least one other mission into occupied France. Certainly Garfield mentions Creighton undergoing 'training and exercise and SOE in France'.[31] He also states that Creighton was no stranger to escapes from German prisons: 'he'd done four different jobs in three different camps, breaking people out'.[32] However, a search of SOE's meticulously kept records of operations in France has failed to trace a single reference to anyone operating in the way described by Garfield.

It is also clear from the text that Creighton's principal sponsor was a private organisation run by Churchill. Colonel Metcalf, for example, says, 'our little detachment is rather secret. . . . In fact it's so secret it doesn't even have a formal name,' which leads Uncle John to explain:

We're known here and there as 'The Section'. We're amateurs – gifted amateurs but amateurs none the less. Our paymaster was His Majesty the King – the budget used to come out of his pocket, you see, rather than from government allocations. We are now on the official budget but I think we may regret that in the long term. We've avoided bureaucracy up to now. We've functioned as a private little team and we've had to report to no one except the King and Mr Churchill. They tell us now that we're going to have to co-ordinate our activities with the formal intelligence services and I suppose they're right, if only to prevent us from blundering into one another's operations, but I suspect that as long as the war lasts there will still be a need for a section that can function privately without the knowledge of the staff or the Cabinet.[33]

While superficially attractive and perhaps even plausible to the uninitiated, the problems of running dozens of different, unco-ordinated covert operations are truly horrendous. Quite apart from the dangers of overlap and duplication, there is the continuous hazard of inadvertent disclosure. But what is particularly puzzling about 'The Section' is that none of the other organisations, with which it is purported to have liaised, has ever come across it.

There are two clues in the text to buildings in London that allegedly accommodated 'The Section'. One is a large block, Northways at Swiss Cottage, which supposedly concealed an office behind the front of an authentic Admiralty unit. Uncle John is referred to as having 'a two-room suite of offices there in the unmarked naval intelligence section behind Admiral Submarines'.[34] Such a proposition is difficult to verify, but the other site is rather more specific and can be verified as one of SOE's many premises in the Marylebone district of London: 'the MO/D Sub-Section office in Dorset Square – the old offices of Bertram Mills Circus and now the headquarters of the Section'.[35] The designation MO/D is authentic and was the precursor to SOE's Free French section known as 'RF' for République Française, to distinguish it from SOE's two principal French sections (assigned respectively 'F' and 'DF'). All SOE's sections and personnel were labelled by a complex but comprehensive system of initials, which, to the *cognoscenti*, instantly identified the role and status of an individual and the particular component to which he (or she) belonged. Thus 'MO/D' was the original designation for a sub-section of SOE's Operations Directorate headed by 'M', who was Colin Gubbins. The attractive property on the corner of Dorset Square was acquired by SOE for MO/D in late 1940 from Bertram Mills Circus. However, according to Cyril Mills, a former MI5 officer who arranged for the transfer of his offices at 1 Dorset Square to SOE in May 1941, no unit of the kind described by Garfield operated there, and none of the many SOE personnel who worked in MO/D (which was later retitled RF) recalls Churchill's private intelligence service being based in the building, which is a relatively small townhouse.

Garfield's account, as described in *The Paladin*, is further undermined by a second book, *The Khrushchev Objective*,[36] this time written by

Creighton himself with Noel Hynd. Published in 1988, it revealed that Creighton had narrowly prevented the assassination of Nikita Khrushchev while on a state visit to England in April 1956. Once again using the formula of fact written as fiction, the authors averred that 'the broad base of this story is true',[37] declaring that Lord Mountbatten had insisted the disclosure could not be made for twenty-five years, and only after his death. When Mountbatten was murdered by Irish republican terrorists in 1981, Creighton was freed from his undertaking. He described how he had been recalled to active service with Section M by Mountbatten to thwart a plot hatched by White Russians seeking to take revenge for the death of the Czar and his family. It is a tale of murder and mayhem across England and France, with some memorably improbable scenes, including one in which Sir Winston Churchill complains about the Berlin Wall (five years before it was built) and Khrushchev rails against the U-2 aircraft . . . before it has even flown. However, the heart of the story is Creighton's involvement with Commander Lionel Crabb, the diver who disappeared under the Soviet cruiser *Ordzhonikidze* in Portsmouth Harbour during Khrushchev's visit. Creighton claims to have killed Crabb while the latter was removing a limpet mine from the warship's hull, a version of events contradicted by those who employed the veteran frogman to undertake an underwater survey of the ship's sonar equipment. In particular, the former SIS station commander, Nicholas Elliott, has given a detailed account of the episode so embellished by Creighton, casting considerable doubt on the rest of the author's extravagant exploits.

Creighton's third book, *OpJB*,[38] written with Milton Shulman and Duff Hart-Davis, was published in 1996 and deals with events after Creighton's return to England in June 1944, to a limited degree overlapping with some of the episodes mentioned in *The Paladin*. Therefore, it can be taken as an illuminating measure of the original version's authenticity. The organisation for which he worked was known as Section M, which was headed by the late Sir Desmond Morton, who, it should be noted, had died shortly before *The Paladin* was released. However, although there is no further direct mention of SOE, the author twice states that he had been trained under General Donovan at 'Camp X at Oshawa on the north shore of Canada's Lake Ontario'.[39] Only referred to as 'Camp X' in the highly unreliable *A Man Called Intrepid* (see Chapter 6), this establishment was actually known as Special Training School 103, and as such was part of SOE's Directorate of Training, which implies a further link between Creighton and SOE.

On the issue of which version should be believed, Creighton avers:

the story remains as scrupulously accurate as memory can
recall. The facts come mainly from what I saw and knew as a 'first
witness' and also from official reports that were either written to
me or to which I had access, and finally from information freely
circulated in the command secret circle of M Section.[40]

In the original manuscript of *OpJB*, which was entitled *Operation
James Bond*, Creighton reveals rather more about his own background,
some of which contradicts Garfield's account. Creighton says that he was
educated at St John's Beaumont and Ampleforth College in Yorkshire,
before entering the Royal Naval College at Dartmouth and receiving a
commission. His parents are named as 'Sir Jack and Lady (Marguerite)
Creighton'[41] and 'Uncle John' is revealed as Desmond Morton. He apparently joined the navy 'at fifteen and a half', but the surname Creighton
was one that had been assigned to him as a cover when he first joined
the navy. The question of identities is at the heart of the Creighton
conundrum because, as Garfield had stated, 'Creighton is not his real
name'.[42] Creighton confirms 'for reasons of operational security, some
naval officers in the M Section used one or more *noms de guerre*. I had
three,' and explains how it was the navy's convention to add non-existent
names to the *Navy List* as an investment for the future and to provide a
useful pool of false identities from which to draw should the need arise:

. . . cover has always been part of my life – as this story will
reveal. Cover is one of the key weapons of intelligence work,
especially in irregular sections such as mine; and with cover go
deceit, murder, betrayal, disloyalty, amorality, and the total renun-
ciation of God, and of anything touching on decency or
friendship.[43]

Supposedly the system of creating bogus identities had begun 'During
the First World War, [when] Admiral Sir Reginald "Blinker" Hall, the
DNI [Director of Naval Intelligence], had devised a simple but effective
practice of entering on the Navy List names of officers who did not
exist.'[44] Whilst it is impossible to rule out completely such a prescient
arrangement, there are difficulties of a bureaucratic kind relating to the
navy's establishment size which militate against the manipulation of

entries in the *Navy List*, a document treated akin to a Bible within the Admiralty. If Hall did institute this scheme, there is no evidence that anyone other than Creighton was its beneficiary.

In the original manuscript of *OpJB*, Creighton elaborated on his family background:

> In 1919 at the end of World War One after service in the Royal
> Flying Corps, my father had gone to Christ's College Cambridge
> to read medicine. At the same college, sponsored by the Royal
> Navy, was the nineteen year old Sub Lieutenant Lord Louis
> Mountbatten. The two men became fast friends and this had
> extended to two other undergraduates, the Prince of Wales and
> the Duke of York, later Kings Edward VIII and George VI, and both
> cousins of Lord Louis. All three royals had enthusiastically sup-
> ported my father's gold medal quest in a field event at Antwerp
> the following year.
>
> In 1909 my father, then aged thirteen, had been sent for a year
> to a special school in Berlin before going on to Westminster
> School for his main education. At this Berlin school he had met
> and become friendly with Joachim von Ribbentrop. In 1936, when
> Ribbentrop was the Nazi Ambassador to the Court of St James,
> my father performed a minor operation on his old friend. I met
> Ribbentrop many times in my father's Harley Street house and he
> took me on many trips to the Zoo, the theatre and soccer
> matches.[45]

This second, more elaborate account does not match the earlier version given by Brian Garfield, in respect of the time his father spent in
Germany (two years in the first version, one in the second) or how often
he had met von Ribbentrop (just 'twice' in the first, but on 'many' occasions in the second). Nor does it match Ribbentrop's own account of
his schooldays in Metz, not Berlin. As for the final version of *OpJB*, the
passage concerning his father's encounter with Ribbentrop is quite different, with the references to Berlin omitted:

> Before the First World War my father was sent to school at the
> Lyceum in Metz for a year, to learn German, and Ribbentrop was
> a fellow pupil there. It may be that the two boys were drawn
> together by their proficiency on the violin.[46]

These discrepancies are relatively trivial when compared to the other aspects of Creighton's tale which tend to undermine his credibility. Take, for example, his first adventure in Belgium. His story revolved around his friendship at school with King Leopold's son Prince Paul, who was tragically killed before his eyes in May 1940 when a Luftwaffe fighter shot his unarmed plane out of the sky as it took off for England. Creighton gives two slightly different versions of the story, with Admiral Sir Roger Keyes assigning him his secret mission in the second version, which omitted the involvement of the two British agents pretending to be campers, but instead had Creighton using a semaphore system to communicate secrets from King Leopold's château. 'These signals were received and read by two Wren Signal Code and Cypher Officers who then transmitted them to Bletchley by short-wave radio.'[47]

The principal flaw with Creighton's Belgian episode is that King Leopold had three children, Baudouin, Albert and Josephine-Charlotte, but no son who might have been Creighton's contemporary. Nor did any of the Belgian royal family receive an education at Ampleforth. Leopold's only daughter, whose brother is now King Albert of the Belgians, is married to the Grand Duke of Luxembourg, and she is emphatic that Creighton's tale is sheer fiction. She had no brother named Paul and there was no aircrash of the kind described by Garfield in *The Paladin*. As for the two British agents who were camped near to the Belgian royal family's château, and acted as Creighton's link to London, they simply disappeared in *The Paladin*, but in the original manuscript of *OpJB* the agents were 'two young ladies . . . pretending to be ardent Girl Guide campers',[48] who were later both killed. According to John Bygott, an SIS officer who was attached to Colonel Calthrop's SIS station in Brussels at this time, no such incident occurred, and no British espionage of the kind described was required in Belgium because of the close liaison maintained between his service and his Belgian counterparts.

There is also a serious structural problem with the other episodes recounted by Creighton. In *Operation James Bond*, he retells his adventure in Donegal but adds that as well as discovering the enemy's covert submarine base, he subsequently returned to the scene by submarine with a force of Royal Marine commandos and destroyed it, sinking two U-boats in the process: 'I guided in a Combined Operations attack on the German submarine base in Donegal, an episode in which I killed for the first time, murdering four men, three with my bare hands.'[49] Quite apart from the fact that there is no record whatever of any British commando operation of this kind, or the deployment of any British submarine on such a mission, and the difficulty in Eire of concealing the loss of the eighty Irish soldiers mentioned in the author's original manuscript, there is considerable doubt about the simultaneous destruction of two U-boats in October 1940. Meticulous records have been kept of the voyage of each U-boat and, according to the distinguished naval historian Jurgen Rohwer, who has spent many years studying the Kriegsmarine archives, no such loss was ever sustained in the period between the sinking of Leutnant Kuehl's *U-57*, rammed by a Norwegian freighter in the Baltic in September, and the loss in the Atlantic of Leutnant Willfried Prellberg's *U-31* on 2 November in a surface engagement with the destroyer HMS *Antelope*. During the period of June to December 1940, only one U-boat is unaccounted for: Leutnant von Kloth's *U-102*, which disappeared in the North Sea in August, presumed to have been the victim of a mine.

The idea that a clandestine fuel depot for U-boats had been established in Eire was, admittedly, one that had preoccupied the British Admiralty for a short period in 1939. What is rather less well-known are the measures taken by the Naval Intelligence Division to determine the truth of the rumours. Sidney Cotton, SIS's Australian pilot who had undertaken most of the pioneering pre-war aerial reconnaissance flights, had been commissioned to overfly the suspect territory so as to identify any secret Nazi base. As he later recalled, 'We did in fact photograph the entire Irish coast in the course of the next few weeks, proving beyond doubt that no refuelling facilities existed there.'[50]

In correspondence, Creighton has alleged that all the relevant German naval records had been recovered from Tambach by Desmond Morton and Ian Fleming, and doctored on Churchill's orders in June 1945 to conceal references to the refuelling facility in Donegal. While it is impossible to disprove such a claim, no evidence to support it has been produced. Garfield's characterisation of Anglo-Irish relations in October 1940 as those of deep mutual hostility is also insupportable. In reality, the Irish Director of Military Intelligence, Colonel Liam Archer, was in close contact with his British counterpart, Colonel Dudley Clarke, and a clandestine coast-watching service had been set up to monitor any enemy activity in neutral waters.

Similar structural problems are encountered with Creighton's next episode, his participation in the sinking of an unnamed Dutch submarine which had accidentally stumbled across the Japanese fleet steaming towards Pearl Harbor and reported the sighting in a signal to London. Whereas it might be argued that the Allies had the motive and opportunity to seize and perhaps alter the Kriegsmarine's official record of U-boat losses in 1945, there can be no possible reason for the Dutch authorities to conceal the loss of a Royal Netherlands Navy 'S-K' submarine in the Pacific on or around 8 December 1941. But, dismissing the other peripheral problems associated with this incident, let us examine exactly what is alleged to have taken place. The original text of the critical message that apparently condemned the submarine to Creighton's sabotage has not survived, partly because Creighton murdered the British personnel who saw it. He also removed the relevant page from the submarine's log, but fortunately Garfield has reproduced it:

SIGHTED FLEET 0535 DEC 2 . . . INTERMITTENT SIGHTINGS UNTIL 0750 FLEET ZIGZAGGING MEAN COURSE 135o (T) SPEED APPROX 16 KNOTS. SIGHTED 6 AIRCRAFT CARRIERS 2 BATTLESHIPS 3 CRUISERS 6 DESTROYERS. IF PRESENT SPEED AND COURSE MAINTAINED DESTINATION OAHU ETA 0600 DEC 7. 0800 SURFACED TO RECHARGE BATTERIES. SENT SIGNAL CLASS 1 CIPHER TOP SECRET IMMEDIATE C-IN-C EASTERN FLEET REPEATED ADMIRALTY EYES COMMANDER IN CHIEF & FIRST SEA LORD ONLY.[51]

If one assumes that this entry formed the basis of the submarine commander's fateful message, it is distinctly odd because, for a start, it does not disclose his estimated current position. Without that significant data, the Admiralty would have no method of double-checking his calculation regarding the enemy's intended destination. The calculation required would place the huge Japanese force 1,888 nautical miles away from Oahu on the reciprocal bearing of 235 degrees. At such a distance it is extraordinary that a submariner, ostensibly watching seventeen ships in zig-zag formation (although in reality there were twenty) at an uneven speed, for a period of slightly over two hours, could deduce the information reportedly detailed in the log. Indeed, considering that the carrier-borne aircraft (and not the ships of the battle group itself) launched their attack on Pearl Harbor in Oahu at 0753 hours on 7 December, it would seem that the Dutchman was blessed with uncanny foresight, apparently compensating automatically for the last 200-mile leg of the journey being undertaken by aircraft flying at relatively high speed, his calculations having been wrong only by a factor of *seven minutes*. Perhaps even more incredible was his choice of Oahu from among all the hundreds of islands in the Hawaiian chain, which stretch for over 1,000 miles across the Tropic of Cancer, from Kure to the big island of Hawaii itself. From a distance of nearly 2,000 miles, on a bearing of 135 degrees, one might have expected one of the many other islands, most notably Laysan, Necker, Nihoa or Kauai, to be the fleet's first landfall, rather than Oahu.

It is illuminating to compare the data contained in the submarine's signal with the actual position of the Japanese ships on 2 December. In fact, the Japanese task force sailed from Kuril's Tankan Bay, north of Japan, on 26 November 1941 and, after a pause to refuel five days later on 4 December, proceeded directly to the location designated as the aircraft launch site. The distance from Tankan Bay to Pearl Harbor is 3,150 miles and, at what what we now know from the Japanese to have been an average speed of eighteen knots, this meant that the fleet covered rather more than 400 miles a day. On this basis, it had already travelled 2,400 miles to the south-east when reportedly spotted by the submarine, and had a distance of only 750 miles to complete, which contradicts the calculation of 1,888 miles supposedly made by the Dutch submarine commander.

Researching the loss of Dutch submarines in the Pacific only adds to the puzzle. When Holland joined the war in 1940, the Royal Netherlands Navy possessed just twenty-seven submarines, none of which bore the prefix 'S-K'. All the 'K' or 'colonial' long-range submarines deployed with the East Indies Squadron had been redesignated 'O' in 1937. Of the total of fourteen in the Pacific, only three were lost in 1941: the O-16 was mined in the East Indies; the 0-20 was scuttled, having been damaged by Japanese depth charges; and the 0-17 was hit by a Japanese mine. When challenged on the question of exactly which submarine he had sabotaged, Creighton identified the K XVII (0-17), perhaps not realising that this craft had been seen on the surface on 14 December, a week after he had supposedly sunk it. In fact, on that date the 0-17 exchanged lamp signals with the 0-12. Indeed, the son of the 0-17's commander traced his father's wreck in 1982 in the South China Sea, off the east coast of Malaysia, and has confirmed after an underwater inspection that it had been sunk by a mine, not an internal explosion.

Perhaps wisely, considering the Dutch Government's denial that any Royal Netherlands Navy submarine was lost in the Pacific on 7 December 1941, Creighton decided against including this particular episode in his second book, mentioning only in the original manuscript that in early December 1941 he had found himself 'in the Pacific and in Singapore'. This latter detail had been omitted from his earlier itinerary, and it is not possible to include it on his originally stated route of Perth–Mombasa–Cairo in the time available, his departure from Fiji on 8 December and his delayed stopover in Cairo four days later. The omission may be connected with the vast distances alleged to have been travelled in such a very short period of time by a slow submarine. The fateful signal places the submarine somewhere 1,888 nautical miles north-west of Oahu early on 2 December. Five days later, it was within the Liberator's range of San Diego, to pick Creighton out of the sea, and by midday the following morning it had reached Fiji. However, the distance from Hawaii to Fiji is 3,198 miles, so that even if the submarine had taken a heading for Fiji immediately after it had spotted the Japanese warships on 2 December, and proceeded on the surface at full speed all the way, it could not have accomplished the journey inside of three weeks. Even the most modern submarines in 1941 could do no better than seven knots submerged and twelve on the surface. Thus, the chronology presented by Garfield for Creighton's adventure in the Pacific makes it rather difficult to believe. As for the murders Creighton confesses to in London, no record of them survive; nor is there any reference to the personnel named in the relevant editions of the *Navy List*.

The question of whether Britain, or for that matter the United States, had advance knowledge of Japan's plan to attack Pearl Harbor is one that historians have argued over for many years. As Churchill is rightly reported as explaining to Uncle John, the US Office of Naval Intelligence (ONI) had indeed solved the PURPLE cipher machine, used for high-grade diplomatic cables by the Japanese, but the Commission of Enquiry set up to investigate the circumstances of Roosevelt's 'day of infamy' eventually concluded that there was nothing in the PURPLE messages decrypted before or after 7 December 1941 to indicate that the US Pacific Fleet's anchorage was to have been a target. However, the same could not be said of the Imperial Japanese Navy's J-19 code: several transmitted messages, intercepted *before* the attack but deciphered *afterwards*, contained strong clues to Japanese intentions. Unfortunately, these vital signals had been overlooked because the decryption of the J-19 traffic had been designated a low priority. Paradoxically, the Americans had found it much easier to read the PURPLE texts, but the ONI's very limited cryptographic resources had been concentrated on the more sophisticated machine cipher, which turned out subsequently to contain nothing of relevance to the surprise raid. Accordingly, it took about a fortnight for J-19 messages to be intercepted, decrypted, translated and distributed, and it was only some considerable period of time *after* the eighteen American ships in Pearl Harbor had been sunk or damaged that the crucial J-19 texts, which suggested that installations on Oahu had received special attention from the Japanese, were circulated. Thus Churchill's surmise that the President 'knew an attack was coming' because 'they'd broken the Japanese Purple diplomatic code' was incorrect.[52] As to whether, if the Admiralty had truly divined the Japanese plot, Churchill (who was himself half American) would have concealed the news from Roosevelt, is up to the reader to decide. Similarly, as there is no evidence to support Creighton's confession to the murder of three British signals staffers, that too must be left to the reader's judgment.

We now come to one of the central themes of *The Paladin*: the calculated betrayal of Operation JUBILEE, the Dieppe raid which took place on 19 August 1942 and cost the Allies 3,623 casualties. In his original version, Creighton claimed to have contacted the Abwehr at the German Legation in Dublin one evening in August 1942, and to have met five of its representatives in a wood the following morning where he offered to disclose details of an imminent raid on the French coast. He describes delivering a message to 'Number 52 Northumberland Road',[53] whereas the Legation was in fact at number 58. He had been detained for three nights in a house 'some miles south-west of Dublin'[54] and had then been flown to Berlin in a civilian aircraft. There, on 14 August, he had told Admiral Canaris of an amphibious landing planned for Dieppe on 19 August and together they had witnessed the carnage on the beaches as the Allied troops were slaughtered. Based on this chronology Creighton (for he had abandoned his 'Lieutenant Peter Hamilton RN' guise on this occasion) had been absent from London between at least 11 August and 20 August, even though he had originally told his German contacts that he was 'due back in London in a week's time'[55] and had been assured he would be.

In *OpJB*, Creighton gives a slightly different version, saying that his initial approach to the German Legation had been as 'Leading Seaman John Davis' and had taken place in April 1942 (not August). A brief visit to Berlin had then followed, via U-boat from Cork, and he had made a *second* trip 'late in July'.[56] Thus, there is a clear contradiction between the two accounts given by Creighton of the same episode, but is it enough to undermine the credibility of the central issue, that Operation JUBILEE was compromised deliberately? This issue has been the subject of intense study by military historians because of the scale of the Allied losses sustained. Certainly the raid was not wholly unexpected, in the sense that the Channel port of St Nazaire had been raided as recently as 28/29 March. Operation CHARIOT, which had destroyed the port's lock gates, had prompted the German High Command to suggest that the experience should have 'put all soldiers on their mettle' and to state: 'The Führer has information from abroad to the effect that the British and Americans are planning a great surprise. He sees two possibilities: either a landing or the use of new massed bombers.'[57]

The month after the St Nazaire raid was marked by dozens of rumours about further Allied operations of a similar type, and on 19 May the commander of Dieppe's garrison, Major-General Conrad Haase, wrote in his diary that 'a British landing operation under the command of Vice Admiral Mountbatten is being planned'.[58] Five days later, he noted that the German Foreign Office had predicted an imminent British assault on the west coast of Jutland. Both these entries indicate a heightened degree of German awareness of the possibility of an enemy raid ... four months before Creighton alleges that he approached the Abwehr. In *The Paladin*, the exact date of his initial approach in Dublin is somewhat vague, but the chronology suggests a date in mid-August, and, in any event, Churchill is reported to have suggested the scheme 'in the July heat'.[59]

The origin of many of these rumours may have been Operation RUTTER, another commando raid on Dieppe planned for the end of June 1942, but postponed until 7 July because of bad weather and then cancelled. Thus, Dieppe had been a target for Allied attack some months before JUBILEE had been launched, an obvious threat to security. Haase recorded that information from secret agents suggested that large-scale landings could be expected 'around 20 June' near The Hague, La Rochelle and 'possibly at Le Tréport', the latter of the three locations being of special significance to him as it fell within the 302nd Division's forty-five-mile stretch of coastline. Early in June 1942, Haase issued a directive which was rather more specific:

> According to reliable sources the British intend the installation of a Second Front in Belgium and France prior to June 22. This is confirmed by other reports which indicate that preparations for an invasion are being carried out in England at high pressure.[60]

Poor weather prevented the original plan, Operation RUTTER, from being executed, but the delay gave the Germans more opportunities to launch aerial reconnaissance missions over the assembly areas around the Isle of Wight. On 23 June, for example, von Rundstedt's staff reported an armada gathering in the Solent, and drew a connection between this naval activity and the recent arrest of twelve resistance saboteurs, members of SOE's AUTOGIRO *réseau*, then in a state of collapse. According to the German interrogation reports, the network had been planning to disrupt railway lines to the Channel ports and 'these incidents can be linked to indicate a planned British landing operation'.[61]

Hitler was also convinced that an amphibious assault was likely and, on 29 June, directed that the coastal defences be strengthened: '. . . large-scale Anglo-American landing must be reckoned with, which will have as its object the creation of a Second Front, this being required from the enemy's point of view for political reasons, both internal and external.'[62] This was followed by von Rundstedt's own general alert, issued on 7 July, which marked what he believed to be the beginning of the 'most favourable period for enemy landings' between 10 and 24 July. On the eve of this warning, Hitler issued a further directive calling attention to air reconnaissance reports of concentrations of enemy landing craft in the Channel:

> The areas particularly threatened are, in the first place, the
> Channel coast . . . between Dieppe and Le Havre, and Normandy,
> since these sectors can be reached by enemy planes and also
> because they lie within range of a large portion of the ferrying
> vessels.[63]

When at the end of July no attack materialised, General Haase reduced the state of readiness of his troops and started a series of exercises at regimental and divisional level. However, towards the middle of the month von Rundstedt announced a second 'Threatening Danger' alert for a ten-day period from 10 August, based on his conclusion that the 'lunar and tidal conditions are such in this time-span that they could be favourable for an Allied landing'.[64]

Despite all this German sensitivity, von Rundstedt himself was never very confident that Dieppe would be singled out for a raid. On 7 July, he announced to his staff that ' due to the small capacity of its port, it is not the type of harbour the Allies are likely to choose as an invasion base'.[65]

Thus, although the Germans can be said to have expected some surprise attack in the second half of August, they had no foreknowledge of even the broad target area, and had actually discounted the town of Dieppe itself.

In fact, there is no evidence that JUBILEE was even placed in jeopardy unintentionally. A major security investigation after the Dieppe disaster concluded that 'though the raid had not been compromised, there had been defects and indiscretions during the planning of it'.[66] Naturally, that raises the question of whether there is any indication that the Germans had acquired advance warning of the raid. A study of documents seized from the 571 Infantry Regiment, which provided two battalions to garrison the town, shows that a general alert was issued on 10 August along the entire French coastline, but Dieppe was not identified as the target, and no specific date for the attack was mentioned. Indeed, the records show that General Haase, the garrison commander, only sounded the alarm at 0500 on the morning of 19 August, one and a half hours after the Allied fleet had been engaged by three E-boats that had encountered them by accident in mid-Channel while escorting a group of coastal steamers. Thus, although the German defenders ought to have been warned by around 0400, they remained in their beds undisturbed for a further hour.

The inescapable conclusion that the Wehrmacht was taken completely unawares by Operation JUBILEE is the verdict reached by Terence Robertson in his *Dieppe: The Shame and the Glory*, in which he concluded: 'The Dieppe raid was not betrayed, nor was security broken.'[67] Professor Campbell of McMaster University, who has made a study of the captured enemy papers, reinforced this view, as did Sir Harry Hinsley, the official historian of British Intelligence, who noted in 1979 that 'the raid achieved tactical as well as strategic surprise'.[68] Thus, it would seem that Creighton's tale, with its flawed chronology, is open to doubt to the extent that, if he really did possess advance knowledge of the raid, either he did not convey it to the Abwehr or, if he did, he was disbelieved. That then leaves the curious matter of his method of approach to the enemy, via the Legation in Dublin.

Anglo-Irish liaison in the security and intelligence fields remains a sensitive topic even today, fifty years after the end of the war, because of the continuing campaign of terrorism conducted in Eire and Ulster by the Provisional IRA. Historians delving into the degree of co-operation exercised between Britain and the neutral republic, and the exact nature of the measures taken jointly to render the German diplomatic staff in Dublin impotent, are met with a distinct lack of official help. However, Colonel Dan Bryan, who headed the Irish intelligence service G-2 during 1942, did concede that not only did he and his principal assistant, Dr Richard Hayes, maintain a close relationship with Cecil Liddell, then in charge of MI5's Irish sub-section known as B1(g), but that he had also kept all the German nationals in Eire under constant surveillance. The German Minister in Dublin since 1937 was Dr Edouard Hempel, a member of the regular diplomatic corps with a doctorate in law, who had gone to scrupulous lengths to preserve the status and integrity of his mission. In 1945, President de Valera wrote of him: 'During the whole of the war, Dr Hempel's conduct was irreproachable. He was always friendly and invariably correct.'[69] Whilst it is true that he eventually joined the Nazi Party midway through the war, he did so only because all members of the German Foreign Service were ordered to enrol. Nor were there any intelligence personnel on his staff, which consisted of two junior envoys, an SS major and two secretaries. The SS officer, Major Henning Thomsen, was only a member of the Reiter SS, a largely cere-monial mounted unit used frequently as a refuge for those who saw a career advantage in Nazi membership but were unwilling to make a full commitment. Certainly his behaviour in Eire during the war did not pre-vent him from rising to ambassador rank in the Federal Republic's post-war foreign service. The Legation's original cable communications with Berlin were via a teleprinter landline, which happened to be routed through London, so after the outbreak of hostilities they were switched to Washington DC, where the German Embassy there relayed the texts by wireless back to Berlin. After Germany declared war on the United States in December 1941, this channel closed. The Legation's radio had been used for broadcasting weather reports, but the Irish authorities put a stop to this, after British protests, in September 1941. Hempel eventu-ally surrendered his transmitter to the custody of a Dublin bank at the end of 1943, and it is now known that virtually all his telegrams were decrypted throughout the war. There were no illicit flights to and from the Continent, and the Embassy's short-wave radio traffic was inter-cepted and decrypted on a regular basis. Accordingly, it is inconceivable that Creighton's lengthy relationship with the Abwehr could have remained unknown to MI5, and members of Cecil Liddell's staff are emphatic that no such contact ever took place. It is perhaps worth noting that based on a study of Abwehr records captured at the end of the war, and the interrogation of enemy personnel, the Security Service satisfied itself that every German agent infiltrated into Eire had been identified and neutralised by G-2. However, when Brian Garfield wrote *The Paladin* in 1980, the extent of Cecil Liddell's achievement was still classified and therefore unknown to the public, with the first disclosures on the subject being made in 1981 by Colonel Dan Bryan, who supplied much of the information contained in *MI5: British Security Service Operations 1909–45*.[70]

On the basis that there is no collateral evidence for Creighton's claims relating to Dieppe, or to his assertion that he 'became not only the Abwehr's and Gestapo's most trusted agent, but to the delight of Morton, the M Section's first successful double agent',[71] his hyperbole should be dismissed. However, it is still worth taking a brief look at the remaining operations in which he says he participated, namely the murder of Admiral Darlan and the deception cover plan for D-Day.

Darlan's assassination, and the speed with which military justice was exacted upon the young Frenchman convicted of the crime, remains a matter of controversy to this day. Curiously, Creighton does not refer to this episode in *OpJB*.

According to Creighton in *The Paladin*, he was abducted in Dublin while negotiating the sale of D-Day secrets and taken to Cherbourg, where he endured appalling torture at the hands of the SS. He gives no date for his arrival in Eire, but, by working backwards from the day of his escape, which is declared to be 4 June 1944, one can calculate roughly when he was seized, on the second of two meetings with the Germans in a wood outside the Irish capital, one forty-eight hours after the first. He had been taken in a van to the coast and put aboard a fishing boat at night before being transferred to a U-boat for the cross-Channel journey to France. There he was driven a short distance to a prison, where he remained drugged and hideously tortured for an undefined period, which included at least one twelve-hour stretch of sleep, before his exfiltration on 4 June. Based on this chronology, Creighton's subsequent assertion in the original manuscript, *Operation James Bond*, that on 1 June he had 'returned to Germany by one of the well-tried routes and managed to sell the D-Day cover secrets to the SS for £1,000,000, which was deposited in a Swiss bank account', and had then been maltreated in 'the grim prison in Cherbourg', appears impossible. Once again, there is a significant discrepancy between the two versions, which suggests that perhaps one or both accounts are incorrect. Indeed, in *OpJB* Creighton offered a third version, in which he had arrived in Dublin on 20 May and, two days later, was facing Field Marshal Rommel 'in the castle of the Duke of Rochefoucauld'[72] in an attempt to dupe the enemy about the exact location of the imminent invasion.

Whilst it is certainly the case that the enemy was deceived by a sophisticated deception scheme for diverting the High Command's attention away from Normandy, there is no evidence to suggest that individual agents played any role in the plan. Professor M. R. D. Foot says that 'no use was made of SOE's work in France for any purposes of deception',[73] and Professor Sir Michael Howard has reached the same conclusion. Nevertheless, the theme of ruthless British case officers deliberately despatching agents briefed with faulty information into the hands of the enemy remains a popular one with fiction writers. A recent example of the genre was Larry Collins's *Fall From Grace*,[74] which, as a novelty, suggested that a woman agent had been the innocent victim of such manipulation. Another significant flaw in Creighton's original version of his escape from France is the fortuitous way he succeeded in signalling and boarding a British submarine, HMS *Seahorse*, in June 1944. According to the Royal Navy, His Majesty's Submarine *Seahorse* was sunk in the Heligoland Bight by German minesweepers on 7 January 1940.

Despite the references in *OpJB* to the events previously described in *The Paladin*, the main story in the book concerns a secret plan to extract Hitler's deputy, Martin Bormann, from the ruins of Berlin in 1945 and resettle him in England under a new identity, in exchange for access to the huge foreign currency reserves salted away by senior Nazis in Swiss banks. The operation had apparently been the brainchild of Ian Fleming, and had been executed by Creighton and his 'new C sub-section' of M Section,[75] which was based at HMS *Birdham*, a Royal Navy and Royal Marine commando training establishment. Here Creighton supervised the training of a group of 'German Freedom Fighters', who also 'underwent further covert training with No. 10 Commando – the Allied Commando'.[76]

The assignment required Creighton, who adopted the identity of 'the disaffected trainee pilot John Davis',[77] to re-establish contact with the Germans in Dublin, which he accomplished on 23 January 1945. A brief meeting followed, at which a representative of Ribbentrop invited Creighton to Germany. The arrangements were subsequently confirmed and, on 8 February, Fleming and Creighton flew from Croydon to Lisbon on a Portuguese aircraft, staying overnight before completing their journey to Basle and then Zurich in a Swiss plane. Finally, on 13 February, they crossed into Germany and stayed as Ribbentrop's guests in a villa outside Weinheim, near Heidelberg. For the next week Creighton and Fleming negotiated with Ribbentrop, and then made the three-day journey home to Hampshire, arriving at HMS *Birdham* on 18 March. The outcome of the secret rendezvous in Germany was the decision to mount a clandestine airborne raid on Berlin with the intention of exfiltrating Ribbentrop and Martin Bormann from the ruins of the Third Reich. The main party, which was mostly Jewish, would comprise

> ten men and ten women of the GFF, the German Freedom
> Fighters, five of them natives of the city. With them would go
> twenty Royal Marine Commandos some of them Special Boat
> Service and some mine disposal specialists, as well as ten opera-
> tional Wrens and Naval Commandos from the M Section itself –
> in all about fifty men and women with twenty kyaks and allied
> equipment.[78]

Their task was to be made easier by an advance party of four other agents, who 'were already in Berlin near the Grosser Muggelsee'.[79] Led by Captain Hanna Fierstein (twenty-six years old with 'a degree in philosophy from the Sorbonne'),[80] the team was flown to its target on 8 March. Two days later, Creighton and Fleming flew to Zurich via Madrid on papers identifying them as Foreign Office couriers, changed into SS uniforms at Vorarlberg in Austria and were then transported by the Luftwaffe the rest of the way to Templehof via Nuremberg and Zwickau. In Berlin, they met Bormann in a bunker under the Foreign Ministry building and he confirmed the proposal first made by Ribbentrop: that in return for a safe passage to England, he would hand over the vast treasures accumulated overseas by the Nazis. His main condition was that a dead body, matching his own, would have to be left in his place as a decoy so that his sudden disappearance went unremarked. Having agreed the terms, Creighton and Fleming returned to HMS *Birdham* on 18 March 1945.

In preparation for the execution of the main plan, 'another hundred men and women, including mine-disposal experts from HMS *Vernon*,'[81] were dropped to the Grosse Muggelsee. As for the provision of a suitable body, a German prisoner was flown from his prisoner-of-war camp in

Canada to London, where his appearance was changed by a certain Mr A. B. Aldred, a Mayfair dentist, and Archibald McIndoe, the pioneering plastic surgeon from the Queen Victoria Hospital, East Grinstead. Working from medical charts and X-rays supplied by Bormann, the prisoner, Otto Gunther, was transformed into Bormann's double. All this took a little over a fortnight. In the meantime, the force waiting outside Berlin was strengthened: 'The twenty-eight men and women detailed to go in as the command group included Bloem, nine of his paratroopers, ten Royal Marine Commandos and SBS.'[82]

The operation finally got under way on 22 April, when Creighton, Fleming, Bormann's double and twenty-five others flew from Tempsford in a Wellington from 161 Squadron to Brunswick, a staging-post just behind the front line. After an overnight stay, the team flew on to Berlin and landed safely in the Muggelsee lake, where they were met by the advance party and accommodated in a pair of safehouses. Two days later, Creighton and Fleming, both wearing SS uniforms, were ushered in to meet Ribbentrop in his office, where he announced that he had found an alternative escape route, but Bormann would proceed with the agreed plan. During the five days that followed, Creighton and Fleming hid in Bormann's bunker with Otto Gunther and the raid's American commander, Barbara W. Brabenov, waiting for an opportune moment to emerge and make their escape by kayak along the rivers and canals that criss-cross Berlin. On 1 May, the group made their way to the banks of the River Spee, with Creighton shooting the hapless Gunther en route and leaving his body to be identified as Bormann's. The remaining four then met up with their commando escort and paddled in kayaks to the Muggelsee, where a Lysander aircraft evacuated Fleming to England. The rest of the party continued northwards to the River Elbe and, on 11 May, after a journey of ten days across Russian-occupied territory aided by forged Soviet credentials, the mission was received by Desmond Morton, who was waiting on the bank of the River Havel. Bormann was promptly removed to England and 'housed in the comparative luxury of a secure wing at Birdham'.[83] Archie McIndoe was called in to alter his appearance and, once transformed, he was established in a house in Highgate under a new identity with two German girls playing the role of his daughters. Soon afterwards, his rehabilitation complete, Bormann was apparently 'adopted' by a British couple and lived with them, running a riding school in a quiet village in the country, until his death of a heart attack on 19 April 1956.

Creighton states that Bormann's latter history was only recounted to him quite recently. After his return to *Birdham* in May 1944, he was assigned to a new operation, codenamed ANDREW, which abducted useful Nazis from Europe and provided them with new identities in return for their co-operation. Among those who allegedly received this treatment was the rocket scientist Wernher von Braun, who was accommodated temporarily at HMS *Birdham*.

Creighton alleges that since 1945 there has been a comprehensive cover-up to rid the official records of any references to Operation JAMES BOND or related matters. Accordingly, the statement that no documentary material supports Creighton's story is rejected by the author as self-evident:

> The 'shred, doctor and forge' unit had almost completed its task of expunging every trace of Operation James Bond from the face of the earth (except with its own records, of course). Churchill's original order to Morton had left no room for manoeuvre: not the slightest hint of the operation must ever leak out, the Prime Minister had decreed. The manipulation of records had to be carried out in such a manner as to make it seem impossible that any such operation could have been mounted.[84]

This explanation, a massive conspiracy of breathtaking proportions, is the reason for the total absence of any corroboration for any aspect of the story. Only a handful of people knew it in full, Creighton claimed in his original manuscript: 'Fleming was very satisfied to note that other than the King, Churchill, Morton, Eisenhower and Donovan, only four people in their operation knew that the pick-up targets were Bormann and Ribbentrop. They were Fleming, Susan Kemp, Barbara Brabenov and myself.'[85] Of these, six are dead, no record exists of any US naval officer named Barbara W. Brabenov, and although the former senior Wren 'Susan Kemp' is supposedly willing to authenticate Creighton's story, she has neither come forward nor revealed her true identity. Neither MI5 nor MI6 was indoctrinated into the plan. Fleming had apparently made the condition that 'only the officers directly involved in the operation need know anything about it – and this firmly excluded MI5 and MI6'.[86] What is truly astonishing is that anyone could believe that an operation on such a scale, involving the infiltration of hundreds of British, American and German personnel into enemy territory, could have been organised in total secrecy and its integrity preserved for fifty years. Whereas it might be possible to be persuaded that a well-known operation, the details of which were in the public domain, actually had a hidden objective, this is not the case here, where the proposition is that the entire undertaking, together with the deployment of parachutists from planes, and the exfiltration of commandos by amphibious aircraft from a lake in Berlin, remains classified to this day. Considering that such a triumph, of supporting more than three hundred men and women in Berlin for a period in excess of two weeks, would represent one of the major Allied achievements of the war, it is difficult to know why knowledge of it should have been denied. The relative success of such an operation should be compared to the failure of SOE's German Section to mount a single successful operation, and of SIS's total lack of human sources inside the Third Reich.

On the basis that no surviving archival data is to be trusted, so therefore there is only futility in demonstrating repeatedly that there are no records of any participation by named units or personnel in a particular scheme, there are only two remaining methods of analysing the story: a study of the peripheral items mentioned in the text to determine whether they provide collateral support for the main narrative, and an investigation of the personalities involved. Most of the latter, of course, are untraceable by conventional means.

The two key figures, apart from Creighton himself who will be examined later, are Desmond Morton and Ian Fleming. Morton is revealed as the 'Uncle John' character who dominated *The Paladin*, and he died in 1971. From 1930 he ran the Industrial Intelligence Centre in London, a quasi-official branch of SIS, which also acted as a conduit for information to Churchill, for whom he acted as a personal assistant during Churchill's term as Prime Minister. It can only be noted that Morton's alleged involvement with Creighton was only revealed after Morton's death, when he was hardly in a position to refute it. As a lifelong bachelor, he has no surviving family to comment one way or the other.

As for Ian Fleming, who died in 1965, his family insist that he played no part in any operations in Germany between January and May 1945. For example, on 20 March 1945 Creighton says that he and Fleming were summoned to SHAEF at Rheims to be briefed by the Allied Supreme Commander, General Eisenhower. However, on this date Fleming was in Jamaica negotiating the purchase of his famous property at Port Maria in St Mary known as 'Goldeneye'. Creighton counters this with the assertion that Fleming's visit to the Caribbean was a clever cover constructed by Sir William Stephenson, the man 'known as 'Intrepid' or the 'Quiet Canadian'.[87]

What might be termed the peripheral aspects of the book, or the sub-plots, are worthy of some attention. Two in particular are of special interest. The first deals with the unexpected appearance of two wartime MI5 officers, Anthony Blunt and Roger Hollis, who have now acquired some notoriety. They are mentioned as having attended a training course at HMS *Birdham* and as having been involved on the fringe of the main operation, apparently having used it as a vehicle to enter Germany in April 1945. According to Creighton, both men were assigned to his command in March 1945 and were due to travel to Germany with an escort of twenty soldiers with the main force, and then to peel off to recover for the royal family some of the Duke of Windsor's embarrassing correspondence from the Schloss Kronberg, near Frankfurt. 'Blunt and Hollis had been assigned the job of finding the letters and getting them out.'[88] When they first met, Creighton recalled that Blunt

> wore the uniform of the Army Field Police and said he was attached to MI5. The second was Roger Hollis, wearing battle-dress and the insignia of a captain in the Army Intelligence Corps: slightly older than his colleague, he was described as a career officer in MI5.[89]

Certainly this episode is entirely fictitious, for Hollis, a stooped, wheezing tubercular who was then recovering from a recurring bout of the illness, never had a military rank and never wore a uniform in his life. Although Blunt was nominally in the Intelligence Corps during his wartime service in MI5, he only wore civilian clothes after June 1940. As for his mission to Germany in 1945, it was to the Duke of Brunswick, not to the Schloss Kronberg, and its purpose was to snatch some art treasures away to England before they were plundered by the Red Army. At no time did the mission take Blunt behind enemy lines, and Hollis played no part in it whatsoever.

Creighton himself has assiduously attempted to preserve his true identity and he says with apparent candour in *OpJB* that the 'shred, doctor and forge' unit of the M Section had been falsifying the record:

> blackening that name with a criminal record which showed

various petty offences dating from 1940. . . . I had become an ardent disciple of the Fascist leader Oswald Mosley, and an avid supporter of Germany against England.[90]

These crimes apparently relate to his original, authentic identity, which, he freely concedes, and Garfield confirms, is not 'Christopher Creighton'; nor is it 'Lieutenant Peter Hamilton' or the third adopted persona, the traitor 'John Davis'. Quite why he should have gone through this elaborate charade to conceal John R. Davies, the name under which he now lives with Greta, his wife, and his son Christopher, in a basement flat in Rosecroft Avenue, north London, is unclear, although it may have been an attempt to make the task of peeling away the skins of deception more difficult. The only clue to his father's identity in *The Paladin* is the fleeting reference to his success in the 1920 Olympics at Antwerp. Only six Britons won a gold medal in track events that year and John Creyghton Ainsworth-Davis won a gold in a relay event. Although he never received a knighthood, he was educated at Christ's College, Cambridge, and did subsequently qualify as a doctor in 1923 at St Bartholomew's Hospital, later becoming a distinguished urologist. He also died on 4 January 1976, which neatly fits with Garfield's description of him, and the brief account of his military service in the Great War, with the Royal Flying Corps, is also true. However, whilst most of the details regarding John C. Ainsworth-Davis are authentic, very little of the material concerning his son is genuine.

Certainly there is no logical thread running through his decision for the Dieppe operation to switch from 'Peter Hamilton', an officer whose rank had allegedly been nurtured over a long period (although no trace survives in the relevant *Navy Lists*), back to 'Christopher Creighton', who in *The Paladin* is described as a Leading Coder. There is further confusion when, in *OpJB*, Creighton claims to have used the name 'John Davis' to deceive the Abwehr during this same episode.

The reality is that John Davies has little of the background he claimed for himself as 'Christopher Creighton'. John Davies was born John Ainsworth-Davis and was educated at Ampleforth. According to his stepmother Irene, who now lives in Devon, John was a troubled boy who ran away from his school and joined the navy. He failed to achieve a commission, despite his father's pleas to Lord Mountbatten, who was his patient, and he later worked on the stage using the name John Ainsworth, once appearing in a play with Laurence Olivier. He has lost contact with his sisters, Jennifer and Mary, and since leaving the acting profession he has supported himself as a pianist.

Considering that none of Christopher Creighton's fanciful claims stand up to prolonged analysis, how were respectable publishers on both sides of the Atlantic taken in? According to Brian Garfield, who still believes Creighton's tales, his New York publishers employed William Stevenson to investigate and authenticate *The Paladin*. He did so, allegedly, by consulting Sir William Stephenson, who acknowledged having heard of the boy spy's exploits. In a letter written from Bermuda dated 16 November 1976, addressed to his New York publisher, Stevenson who knew Creighton as 'Peter Hamilton' and hoped to co-author his story, stated:

> Our mutual friend who calls himself 'Peter Hamilton' is authentic.
> However, there are problems with regard to the declassification
> of certain material. I have read the relevant documents, kept here
> in absolutely secure circumstances, and the information they
> contain is labeled PRIVILEGED. This does not prevent 'Hamilton'
> from giving his own version.

This also seems to have been enough for James Wright, Macmillan's resident expert in London, who was himself employed at Bletchley Park during the war. With backing from Stevenson and Wright, *The Paladin* was published. As for *OpJB*, this was eventually published in September 1996 with support from Milton Shulman. However, when word spread that Creighton's claims had failed to stand up to scrutiny, he made a feeble attempt to elude those seeking to research his background. While filming an interview in Berlin, Ainsworth-Davis tried to fake his own disappearance, leaving his hotel room in a state of disorder to suggest to journalists that he had been abducted. In reality, he had slipped away unseen, checked into another hotel and shaved off his beard. Much to his embarrassment, he was traced by his camera crew, who used the simple expedient of checking the telephone calls made from his room the previous day. One call had been to another hotel to make a reservation under yet another name, and this is where he was discovered, and his surprise was recorded on video tape. Since this episode, he really has dropped from sight.

10

The Year of the Rat

Mladin Zarubica may well have got his amazing tale 'straight from the horse's mouth'.[1]

A Californian businessman of Yugoslav extraction, Mladin Zarubica states that he has merely written an account of a story that he believes to be true. His proposition was that sometime early in March 1944, an Allied agent was dropped into Denmark near Copenhagen and, with the help of a local resistance group, set up a roadblock with the intention of capturing a specific, but unnamed, Wehrmacht general. The intended target landed at the Luftwaffe airfield at Kastrup on a flight from Madrid and, within minutes of his arrival, was snatched from his staff car. The impostor, identified by Zarubica only as 'Abraham B' and accompanied by two other agents masquerading as a chauffeur and an aide, continued the general's journey into Copenhagen. The original general was described as a 'member of Hitler's inner circle, a man so capable that only the most important missions were turned over to him. He was completely trusted by Hitler and, as his private envoy, answered to no one but the Führer.'[2]

After the contents of the general's attaché case had been examined and passed to another Allied agent posing as a German officer, the impostor conferred with a Wehrmacht staff colonel, who informed him that there was no new information regarding the imminent Allied invasion of Europe. The following day the substitute general and his companions flew from Kastrup to Stockholm, where he resumed a love affair with a German countess, 'one of the most beautiful women in Europe',[3] who also happened to be an Abwehr agent. She had first met the general 'at a hospital benefit in Berlin in 1934'[4] and since then had married a wealthy American, who had been killed in a motor accident. In March 1944, the widow had 'maintained a luxurious apartment and a handsome farm retreat'[5] in Sweden, and the general and the countess spent eight days together 'under the most intense surveillance by Allied agents'.[6] Satisfied that his lover had not detected the substitution, he flew to Madrid to meet one of his contacts, a German spy based in London who 'had long since defected to the Allies'.[7] The agent supposedly 'had gained access to classified material of extreme secrecy and importance',[8] and this was handed over to the impostor. Codenamed OVERLORD, the documents proved to be the complete Allied plans for D-Day. These were driven by the general and his two companions to Biarritz, where he was reunited briefly with the countess. The next day they continued their journey to Paris, where the general held a meeting with the Military Governor of France, General Karl Heinrich von Stuelpnagel.

Having persuaded von Stuelpnagel of the authenticity of the Allied plans, the impostor drove to Château La Roche-Guyon, the headquarters of the Commander-in-Chief, and presented them to Field Marshal von Rundstedt. In them, 'June 10, 1944, was set as D-Day for the first diversionary attacks to the south and west if the weather permitted. Also dependent on the weather, the main attack at Calais was to follow within nine days.'[9] Clearly impressed, von Rundstedt kept a photograph of the plan and sent the original to Berlin for onward transmission to Berchtesgaden. According to the author, 'Hitler had optimistically accepted the Allied document the moment it had been revealed to him', and it had been designated 'Project 669'.[10] The impostor then stayed at the Château to dine with Field Marshal Rommel and the next morning returned to his apartment in Paris, where, a few days later, he was joined by the countess. Together they travelled to the countess's other home, a villa some miles east of Paris between Lagny and Crécy-en-Brie, where contact with the French underground was re-established. Here the general remained, having married the countess, until 21 June, when he was smuggled out of the house in a coffin and collected from a field near Coulommiers by an Allied plane. The operation was judged to have been a complete success, although the countess was later sentenced to death in Munich and executed for her part in the 20 July plot to assassinate Hitler.

According to Zarubica, the story of this elaborate hoax had been given to him by 'Carlo', an Austrian hunting guide, immediately after the war, although he had delayed until 1965 before publishing his account of it, *The Year of the Rat*. At that time the author, who had served in the US navy in the Pacific theatre, had become the owner of a successful construction business in Los Angeles. Whilst he admitted to 'filling in small gaps of time and conjuring words that were never spoken',[11] the remainder, he asserted, was a faithful version of what Carlo had told him some twenty years earlier: 'I have failed to discover any single discrepancy between what he told me then, including the historical details of "The Hoax", and the facts as they were described by the most reliable reporters later.'[12]

Zarubica's opinion was supported by Ralph Ingersoll, a former US army intelligence officer supposedly with first-hand experience of wartime deception operations in Europe with the US 12th Army Group, and the author of *Top Secret*, a highly critical study of the Normandy landings. Although he confirmed that he could testify to the success of the cover-plans prepared to deceive the enemy, the former lieutenant-colonel declared that 'the talented Carlo took liberties'[13] in some aspects of his story, but nevertheless he found the main theme entirely plausible:

> It is not that the idea of using a look-alike agent to impersonate a top-flight German general is farfetched. It isn't, at all. In fact, I am certain that if the British planners came across such a coincidence of spit and image, they would have used it – and most likely in the exact way described; i.e., by doing away with the real general and having a whack at substituting their own man – even though, as Abraham B. obviously was, he would most likely be an amateur. He would have to be specially, and laboriously, trained for the part. All this is better than plausible.[14]

Thus, Ingersoll acknowledged that in his professional judgment, and although he had no personal knowledge of the operation, Carlo's 'hoax *could* have happened'.

Ingersoll's conclusion is surprising because, despite the abduction of Major General Karl-Heinrich Kreipe by SOE in Crete in April 1944, and the impersonation of General Bernard Montgomery in May 1944, there is no known example of an Allied agent being substituted for a general. As an illustration of how such operations were prone to accident, Kreipe had not been SOE's original target. The original objective had been General Muller, but, unknown to SOE's planners, he had been replaced by Kreipe. In the other example, designated Operation COPPERHEAD, Montgomery had been impersonated by a look-alike, Lieutenant Clifton James of the Royal Army Pay Corps, in an attempt to persuade the enemy that Monty had been posted to Gibraltar to command the invasion of southern Europe from the Mediterranean. Both stories have received wide circulation and are well documented. W. Stanley Moss, one of the SOE officers who participated in the operation in Crete, relived the adventure in *Ill Met by Moonlight*.[15] The details of COPPER-HEAD were first revealed by Captain M. E. Clifton James in 1954, in *I Was Monty's Double*,[16] and his version was confirmed by Stephen Watts, one of the MI5 officers who had supervised the project, in *Moonlight on a Lake in Bond Street* in 1961.[17]

Whereas in the first case an enemy general had been captured, and in the second a British general had been impersonated, elements of both had never been combined. Indeed, Kreipe survived his experience and was eventually repatriated from his prisoner-of-war camp in Canada. There is, however, no record of any German staff officer being captured in Denmark in March 1944, in the circumstances described by Zarubica. Nor, surprisingly, can any other detail of the operation be authenticated from official files.

Ralph Ingersoll had been emphatic that 'the men who conceived and directed the implementation of the Overlord Cover Plan were capable of engineering such an audacious hoax as that which Mladin Zarubica describes',[18] but the reality is that no such scheme ever played a part in FORTITUDE, the complex deception campaign devised to mislead the enemy, which has now been declassified and published in full. Thus, Zarubica's tale is exposed as rather more of a hoax than he ever suggested. However, one is left wondering about the role of Ralph Ingersoll. Why did he lend his name, and thereby put his reputation at risk, by collaborating with Zarubica?

Ingersoll had written four books about the war when *Top Secret* was published in 1946.[19] As soon as it was released to become the number two bestseller of the year in the United States, the author was condemned by the critics, led by Charles H. Taylor, then Professor of Modern History at Harvard, for his heavy anti-British bias and, in particular, for the venom he aimed at Field Marshal Montgomery, whom he accused unjustly of having lost the battle for Caen. While purporting to offer a detailed analysis of D-Day, Ingersoll had made numerous slips, not the least of which was his error in naming von Kluge instead of von Rundstedt as German commander of the armies in the West. Taylor concluded that 'it would be hard to find a more basic or total misconception of main operations' than Ingersoll's, and Arthur M. Schlesinger Jnr denounced the author as 'a confused and adolescent political thinker' for his pro-Soviet attitudes.[20]

For all his alleged experience in the field, *Top Secret* was eloquent testimony to the author's lack of knowledge of the complex deception campaign to conceal D-Day. It is especially significant because it allows the reader to assess Ingersoll's credentials as a reliable authority capable of endorsing the work of other authors researching in the same area, such as Zarubica. The best example occurs in relation to FUSAG, the non-existent First United States Army Group, the military formation which had been created in the fertile minds of the deception planners and whose sole purpose was to exaggerate the Allied order of battle. FUSAG was a paper unit designed to dupe the enemy, and was a key component of the FORTITUDE cover plan. However, it is clear from *Top Secret* that Ingersoll was not let in on that particular scheme, which clearly fooled him as well as the Wehrmacht. Not realising that FUSAG was entirely notional, he described it as the 'loneliest of the American headquarters'. 'Poor forgotten FUSAG' had allegedly 'languished forlorn and unnoticed in Bryanston Square', close to where Ingersoll had been billeted.

> FUSAG was hardly in existence a month before the mention of its name in London was as good for a laugh as a mention of the Brooklyn Dodgers in a Manhattan revue – for FUSAG had no troops, no mission and, as far as anyone could see, no future. Since most of the jokes came from British headquarters that had an interest in discouraging the establishment of an American rival, this was understandable. But the officers in FUSAG certainly did their best to give them material. In London the principal contribution they made to the war effort was an excellent mess. The headquarters was a curious institution, a mixture of veteran planners brought belatedly from Africa and fresh recruits just in from America. The latter set the atmosphere. They fussed over thousands of unnecessary details and the high point in their career came when they met the problem of how to toughen themselves for the coming life in the field.[21]

Ingersoll completes his description of FUSAG with a graphic eye-witness account of how the headquarters' building sustained a direct hit from an incendiary bomb:

> Poor FUSAG. The unkindest cut of all was to come in March when the Luftwaffe made its last attempt to burn London down. Where would they have to unload their fire-bombs, one night, but smack on FUSAG's roof.
>
> On all the neighbouring roofs there were the fire watchers of London's famed air warden service – who promptly put out their incendiaries. But those that lit on FUSAG's attics found no watchers. The British had, of course, withdrawn their civilians and FUSAG had not gotten around to taking its own air raid precautions. So the incendiaries burned down the headquarters' post office, some of the personnel records and the office of the headquarters commandant and some other odds and ends.[22]

Whilst hugely amusing, particularly Ingersoll's account of a picnic held by FUSAG in Bryanston Square, the tale must have been fabricated in its entirety. FUSAG was only a few sheets of paper locked in a safe in Norfolk House and certainly never physically occupied a building in Bryanston Square, or anywhere else. It had no staff, no personnel to throw lunch parties, and no troops to prepare for the imminent assault. As for the claim that it had received a direct hit in March 1944, one can only gasp at the author's imagination. FUSAG did not even materialise on paper until 30 March 1944, when the scheme was adopted and the 21st Army Group agreed to co-operate with the cover plan.

Clearly Ingersoll had been given no clue that FUSAG was an imaginary organisation and this omission tends to undermine his status as an authority on D-Day deceptions. Accordingly, *Top Secret* casts an interesting, though not very flattering, light on Zarubica's previously untold version of how D-Day was accomplished.

11

Codename Badger

'I was told again and again that it was necessary to blot out all traces of my past – marriage, military record, everything – so that if a hostile power ever tried to check up on me, they would run up against a stone wall.'[1]

In March 1985, Lieutenant-Colonel John Cottell MVO OBE MC addressed an audience in Lexington, Kentucky, at one of some three hundred lectures he had delivered across the United States in recent years. He told how, in 1942, aged seventeen, he had volunteered for the army and found himself working for SOE. He joined SOE's Dutch Section and undertook several missions into occupied Europe before being captured, tortured and imprisoned at Buchenwald. After the war, Cottell's adventures in the intelligence world continued and, in 1957, he was arrested by the KGB in East Germany and subsequently released in exchange for a Soviet spy convicted of espionage in England.

Cottell's astonishing career, backed up by some memorabilia and testaments to his rank and service with SOE, attracted the attention of a *Reader's Digest* writer named Arthur Gordon, an author of fifteen books who also lived in Savannah, Georgia, where Cottell had made his home. Together they collaborated on an autobiography entitled *Codename Badger*, the cryptonym assigned to Cottell for his first secret mission.[2]

According to *Codename Badger*, Cottell was born on 4 December 1924 in Lincolnshire and educated at Stamford, a small private boarding-school in Leicestershire. In 1943, he was commissioned into the Royal Army Service Corps with the rank of first lieutenant and, after a series of interviews at Lansdowne House, Berkeley Square, and a lunch with

Colonel Claude Dansey, was transferred to SOE. Dansey explained that he worked for another secret organisation, known as 'Z', and Cottell was to report to him as well as his superiors in SOE. After six weeks' training at Lansdowne House, followed by a spell with SOE's French Section at Wanborough Manor, he was flown to Canada for a course in clandestine warfare at Camp X, on the shores of Lake Ontario. In December 1942, Cottell was back in England, based at another SOE training school at Beaulieu in Hampshire, where he passed an unusual initiative test: a convicted murderer from Dartmoor Prison had been released in the local woods and told that if he succeeded in killing Cottell he would be granted his freedom. Cottell graduated by cutting his throat.

Having passed the test at Beaulieu, Cottell learned to parachute at RAF Ringway, outside Manchester, and in March 1943 he was received by the Prime Minister, who told him that at the next full moon, on 21 March, he would be parachuted into Holland to deliver 'a memorised coded message'[3] to a leader of the Dutch resistance in Gelderland. Undeterred by his inability to speak any Dutch, or by the capsule of cyanide which was inserted under a hollow molar in his upper jaw, Cottell drove to Sandy, near Bedford, for a flight to the Netherlands. 'The Lysanders, painted black, were single-engined aircraft with open cockpits,' recalled Cottell.[4] 'They were designed to carry only the pilot and one passenger. My pilot was a squadron leader whose name, I'm quite sure, was Hugh Verity.'[5] Cottell parachuted safely to the ground, where he was met by a reception committee and escorted to a safehouse near Arnhem, where he met the resistance leader and delivered Churchill's message.

The plan had been for Cottell to return straight to England, but he was told that it

was going to be difficult if not impossible to get me back to England. Nazi patrol boats had closed the Channel ports. Escape by Lysander was too risky: German Intelligence seemed to know the plans of SOE in advance. Drops of arms and ammunition constantly fell into Nazi hands. Many agents were being picked up and made to transmit radio messages back to Britain at gunpoint. Even when they included prearranged distress signals to indicate that the message was being sent under duress, the signals were ignored, or perhaps suppressed by some traitor within SOE itself.[6]

Although dismayed by this news, Cottell stayed in Holland and participated in several sabotage operations organised by the local resistance. While on his way to his third target, he was arrested by the Germans, but managed to escape from a truck while in transit between a prison in Scheveningen and the Gestapo headquarters in Arnhem. As a wanted man in Holland, with his photograph on display in railway stations, Cottell felt obliged to begin his journey back to England, bearing a coded message from the Dutch resistance about the degree of Nazi penetration within the organisation's ranks. He travelled to Brussels and there made contact with the COMET escape line, which conveyed him through Paris to Bordeaux and then over the Spanish frontier. The instruction he gave to COMET's members en route resulted in him being awarded 'the French and Belgian Croix de Guerre for these relatively minor contributions'.[7]

Soon after his arrival in Spain in late January 1944, Cottell was arrested by the Spanish police near Irun, together with some Allied airmen also making their way to neutral territory, and incarcerated at the Miranda de Ebro camp. After a few days in custody, he was freed by a British diplomat, a major in the British Embassy in Madrid, who supplied him with papers identifying him as an Irish labourer. He was 'driven at night, with great secrecy and stealth, to Lisbon', and a few days later was flown to England to be

debriefed at the Royal Victoria Patriotic School [RVPS] in London. At this debriefing Brigadier Colin Gubbins, who was head of SOE, presided. I passed along the coded message I had brought all the way from Holland. It was received in noncommittal silence. I got the impression that my interrogators thought they had better sources of information. Or perhaps they didn't want to hear too much about traitors at work within SOE.[8]

Released from the RVPS, Cottell was sent 'for training with the airborne troops at Thames [sic] Park near Oxford' and, at the end of June 1944, went on a mission to France with four other members of SOE. 'To this day I don't know what the exact purpose was, we were told nothing in advance,'[9] says Cottell, who anyway injured his ankles upon landing on a farm roof, and had to abandon the mission and be evacuated. He was taken by rowing boat to a trawler, which held a rendezvous with a British submarine and carried him to the coast of Kent. There he paddled ashore near Deal and was met by Seymour Bingham, the head of SOE's Dutch Section, who gave him dinner in a local pub.

In September 1944, Cottell was flown to Arnhem in a glider with the 1st Airborne Division on Operation MARKET GARDEN. His first task was to make contact with another SOE agent in Oosterbeek named Ian Elliott and then to liaise between the resistance groups and the troops, taking care not to engage the enemy directly himself. In the event, Elliott was killed in a burst of machine-gun fire and Cottell took part in the ambush of a German staff car that contained Major General Kussin, the Feldkommandant of Arnhem. 'I was not able to report my part in this episode until months later. Eventually, in 1947, I was awarded the Military Cross (MC Special List) by King George for my role in killing the German General.'[10] The delay was caused in part by a mortar barrage which left Cottell wounded, and by German captivity. Unfortunately, an alert Gestapo officer had recognised Cottell as the British agent code-named *Badger* and he was removed from the St Elizabeth Hospital in Arnhem to the SS headquarters for interrogation. He endured maltreatment and mock executions for five days, and it became clear to Cottell that the Germans had built up an extensive understanding of SOE's activities: 'The knowledge the Gestapo had of British Intelligence and all that went on at Baker Street was incredible; I knew someone must be supplying it from within.'[11]

Sometime at the end of October 1944, Cottell was taken by train to Buchenwald, where he was to remain until April 1945 when the camp was liberated by the Americans. When he revealed himself to be an SOE officer, he was initially disbelieved because, according to Baker Street, 'Captain John Cottell had died by firing squad in Holland the previous year'.[12] However, when he eventually established his identity, he was flown to a hospital in London and was then moved to 'St Andrew's Hospital in Northampton, which had a military wing for service officers who had broken down under strain'.[13] During his recovery, Cottell came to realise that before his first mission to Holland he had deliberately been supplied with bogus intelligence by the Prime Minister, with the intention that it would be conveyed convincingly to the enemy, and that the suicide capsule he had kept in his false tooth had probably been quite harmless: 'my suspicions that I had been given false information by Churchill were growing. In any case the conviction that I had been betrayed and used by my own people spread like a shadow over my already shadowed mind.'[14] Dansey did not deny this when challenged by

Cottell, and over luncheon with Churchill at 10 Downing Street the Prime Minister confirmed that he 'had sent me to occupied Holland, hoping that I would break under torture and reveal false information to the enemy'. Churchill was unrepentant, explaining that 'it was a calculated assessment. . . . You had not come up to the standard in some of your training, and so you were singled out along with certain others in a plan to deceive German Intelligence and save many lives.'[15] Cottell accepted the Prime Minister's apology for his ruthless treatment.

Soon afterwards, Cottell learned that his wife, Marianne de Roubaix, had been killed the previous year, 'very soon' after the birth of her son in November 1944, while on her third mission for SOE into occupied Europe. According to Cottell, he had met Marianne, who had worked as a telephonist at the Belgian Embassy in London, soon after joining SOE and had started an affair with her when he discovered that she too had been posted to Wanborough Manor for training with F Section. Colin Gubbins had broken the news of her death to Cottell, explaining that his son had gone to live with Marianne's parents in Belgium. Later, during the summer of 1945, Cottell had been assigned to Northumberland House, sorting 'photographs of displaced persons or refugees or inmates of concentration camps to see if by any chance I could identify any of them from my experiences on the Continent'.[16] One picture, of a young naked woman seated on the edge of a grave at Ravensbrück, he recognised as his wife, and this traumatic discovery led him on a search across Europe to find those responsible for her death.

Cottell hitched a ride to Paris with Squadron Leader Giles from RAF Wittering and, with the help of the Sûreté, tried to trace Marianne's movements after her arrest. 'As a British Army major in uniform I was able to move about quite freely,'[17] and he travelled to Switzerland and Holland on a quest for information. He obtained a first-hand account of Marianne's ordeal in Ravensbrück from a former fellow inmate, Cornelia ten Boom, in Haarlem, and later an SS prisoner at the Santé prison in Paris identified two of her executioners. Early in May 1946, Cottell found one of them, an SS corporal in Lüchow, and shot both him and his German wife.

During the months that followed, Cottell was variously posted to the detention centre run by Colonel Scotland in Kensington Palace Gardens, which was known as the London Cage, where he participated in the court-martial of eight Nazis accused of war crimes who were subsequently hanged at Pentonville, and to Holland, where he assisted Oreste

Pinto to investigate the case of a notorious double agent. He was also seconded to the Palestine Police 'as an expert on guerrilla warfare',[18] but this assignment was to be brief because Cottell 'began to show signs of an emotional breakdown'.[19]

Cottell says that on 20 January 1947 he was decorated with the Military Cross by King George vi at Buckingham Palace, together with Odette Churchill and Field Marshal Sir Archibald Wavell. He then went to work first as a clerk in the construction department of a Butlin's holiday camp and then as a dishwasher at a Lyons Corner House. However, throughout this period Cottell remained in touch with British Intelligence and he eventually received a summons to a Jacobean mansion in Sussex, where he underwent an intensive training course. He was 'programmed to give false testimony in case the inquiry regarding Dutch Section ever became a reality'[20] and was taught guerrilla warfare in the surrounding woods. This was in preparation for a secret mission to Poland to recover two Nazi prisoners, who were also being sought by the Soviets. Cottell was taken by a Danish gunboat to Ustka in the Baltic, where he received the men and escorted them to Groningen. Despite an incident near Lübeck, when the Soviets ambushed their two jeeps, Cottell succeeded in moving his prisoners to Celle and thence to the Hook of Holland for a voyage by tank landing-craft across the Channel to Tilbury. 'About a year later',[21] Cottell was visiting the headquarters of the new post-war German intelligence service at Pullach, near Munich, and recognised a senior intelligence officer there as one of his prisoners.

Soon after this adventure, Cottell was hospitalised again because he 'could not think rationally for any sustained period of time'.[22] He then found a job as a photographer first in Nottingham and then with the Butlin's holiday camp organisation. Simultaneously he was operating 'mainly as a courier to various establishments'[23] for British Intelligence. Another job, in an Electrolux factory in Luton, was also cover for 'additional indoctrination, some weapons, combat retraining and intensive schooling in foreign languages'.[24] His subsequent move to Torquay was prompted by the need for 'secret courier work' in the Plymouth area. 'I was ordered to keep an eye on Soviet shipping, and to report conversations I overheard that might have some bearing on the activities of the enemy. Most of the time I was merely a messenger, carrying microfilm.'[25]

'Late in September 1956',[26] Cottell was arrested for stealing coins from a telephone kiosk and sentenced to six months' imprisonment, but he did not stay long at Exeter Gaol. In fact, the entire scheme was an elaborate deception, and Cottell was whisked up to London to meet Maurice Oldfield, later to become SIS's Chief, 'whom I had known at the Home Office'.[27] There he was briefed on his mission: to enter Hungary from Austria and receive a microfilm from two men in Budapest. Equipped with a false passport, he was flown to Vienna and then, after further briefings, driven across the border. He was still in Budapest on 23 October, when Russian tanks entered the city to crush the growing anti-Communist dissent, and only escaped to Vienna later in November. After a flight to Prestwick, Cottell was driven to London for debriefing and then was placed in an open prison near Newton Abbot to complete the remainder of his sentence.

After his release in January 1957, Cottell was warned that his identity had become known to the Soviets and his life might be in danger. As a precaution, he went to Ireland with a bodyguard and narrowly escaped an assassination attempt in a Dublin hotel. They moved out into the country, only to be ambushed again, Cottell's minder receiving a fatal bullet wound. After being patched up in the Royal Victoria Hospital in Belfast, Cottell was flown to London for a new assignment, this time in East Germany. His mission, together with another British businessman posing as a representative selling precision instruments, was to travel to Dresden from Holland and deliver a special briefcase to a third agent. The pair arrived safely in Dresden from Eindhoven, but were attacked while walking to their hotel. The case was seized and they were arrested by the police moments later. Both underwent an interrogation, but were released at the West German border. In retrospect, Cottell wondered 'whether the case had contained false or misleading information designed to confuse the Soviets'.[28]

No sooner had Cottell recovered from this ordeal than he was sent back to Dresden to deliver another microfilm, this time with papers identifying him as Neil McDonald Smith from New Zealand. However, the day after his arrival, he was arrested in the street, charged with espionage and sentenced to ten years' imprisonment, eight of which were to be served at the Vladimir prison camp outside Moscow, after two years of solitary confinement. However, Cottell got no further than the Lubyanka, where he was interrogated for eleven months before being flown to Berlin to participate in a swap for an unnamed Soviet spy. At the exchange, Cottell was welcomed by Maurice Oldfield and a period of rehabilitation was arranged at a hospital in London. Once recovered,

Cottell learned that he had been betrayed by a senior MI6 officer, who was being held under guard in a Ministry of Defence compound at Lulworth Cove, Dorset. Nine months after his release in Berlin, 'in the late summer of 1958',[29] Cottell broke into the Ministry of Defence establishment and murdered the traitor.

By 1960, Cottell was working in London, having been trained at a school for the blind in order to pretend to be blind. He recalled that he spent his time 'sometimes as a courier abroad, sometimes in the city itself . . . listening for moles or subversives at various levels of London society'.[30] It was during this period in his career that a second attempt was made on his life. Several KGB agents masquerading as tourists tried to trap him in Dartmouth, but one was killed and two others, both Hungarians, were imprisoned and then deported. In 1966, there was a similar incident with the KGB using an English and a Hungarian agent to try and break into Cottell's home, on the Dorset–Hampshire border. Both were shot dead, and news of the affair was suppressed by the police.

Cottell's final assignment, to Northern Ireland, he says, 'was part of what is an ongoing operation'[31] and, therefore, he is inhibited in his account of it, apart from saying that he once flew back to London to brief Prime Minister Edward Heath. Soon afterwards he was summoned to a disciplinary hearing at the Foreign Office and charged with lobbying for changes in the Official Secrets Act. This offence led to his dismissal and to his exile.

This short summary of Cottell's remarkable career does little justice to the account of it he gave to Arthur Gordon in which he disclosed that Marianne de Roubaix's son, named Peter, who had once survived an attempt on his life by the KGB, had studied engineering at Heidelberg University but had died, aged twenty, of leukaemia. Cottell had also been assigned counter-subversion duties and, on one occasion, was responsible for spying on the Communist wife of an army major. Despite several rows with his superiors and a conviction for shoplifting at Harrods, Cottell insists that on his final mission to Northern Ireland he wore his 'British colonel's uniform'.[32]

Cottell's collaboration with Arthur Gordon, *Codename Badger*, was scheduled for publication in New York in 1990 by William Morrow & Co., but while it was still in galley proofs the publishers abandoned the whole project. They were faced with a dilemma: should they continue to support Cottell, who had warned them that pressure might be brought to bear on them to prevent the book's release, or should they persevere and risk ridicule for backing a Walter Mitty? Much of Cottell's story had proved difficult to verify, but he himself had warned the publishers candidly that he had already been the victim of smears, and that the authorities had taken elaborate measures to alter official records and remove traces of Cottell's activities. The extent of the deception was considerable as he recognised when he acknowledged that 'even my birth certificate, on record in Somerset House, was changed, making me two years younger than I actually was'.[33] Certainly the birth certificate of John Harry Landown Cottell, which is John E. Cottell's true name, gives his date of birth as 4 December 1925 in Lincoln, and identifies his father as a civil servant in the Ministry of Health living at 24 Burns Gardens. However, in his book Cottell says that he was born on 4 December 1924 and his family home was 'a big, rambling farmhouse'[34] near the ruins of Royal Bolingbroke Castle in Lincolnshire. Thus, before his narrative has hardly begun two basic conflicts emerge: what is Cottell's true name, and what is his age? Strangely, John E. Cottell says that he was 'still only seventeen' during 'the last days of 1942',[35] when he joined the army, which conforms with John H. L. Cottell's age, as he turned seventeen on 4 December 1942. He claims that the switch in dates, which only took a year off his true age (and therefore did not make him 'two years younger'), was intended to make it 'theoretically incapable of [his] having been in the service at certain times'.[36]

The service referred to was Special Operations Executive, the organisation for which Cottell undertook his first mission to Holland, but the chronology suggested by Cottell is confusing. He is vague about specific dates, but there are clues in the text as to where he was, and when. For example, we know that he was still at school 'in the last days of 1942',[37] when the headmaster suggested he leave. He then tried to join the Royal Navy, but 'after a few weeks' his application was turned down. Next he tried the Royal Army Service Corps, only to suffer rejection because he was 'not officer material'.[38] He did subsequently enlist in the RASC, and he says that he received his commission on the second attempt, which presumably was sometime in 1943. He recalls signing the Official Secrets Act upon his transfer to SOE, when he 'was only eighteen years old',[39] which would suggest that the event took place (on the basis of Cottell's claimed birthdate in 1924) between December 1942 and December 1943. This is confirmed by one of his superiors, years later, who mentions that Cottell had 'joined up back in 1943'.[40] His training in Canada must also have taken place during this period for he mentions that upon his return, 'near Christmas, I was sent to yet another SOE facility, this one at Beaulieu',[41] which would place his subsequent interview with the Prime Minister on 'a cool March morning' in 1944.[42]

Cottell says his mission to Holland started on 21 March, but he omits the exact year, and this is where the main problem arises. In recording his subsequent adventures, he says that he was dropped from a Lysander and was obliged to remain in enemy-occupied territory until 'late in January'[43] the following year, when he crossed into Spain, which, if he had spent ten months on the Continent, would make the year of his arrival in Spain 1945. This makes a nonsense of Cottell's other adventures which supposedly occurred during the same period, such as his spell 'training with the airborne troops at Thames [*sic*] Park' in 'the summer of 1944', and his 'mission into German-held France', which took place 'not long after D-Day, near the end of June'.[44]

This bizarre contradiction means that Cottell's first mission must have started in March 1943, which is supported by a brief reference to his Belgian wife and the 'strange, intense, and wonderful life we lived together in wartime London in the spring of 1943'.[45] This in turn implies that his lengthy training in Canada, Wanborough Manor and Beaulieu must have happened in 1942, when he was still a schoolboy. No other explanation accounts for the missing year in Cottell's purported chronology. In any event, Cottell's statement that the alteration in his birth record was intended to disqualify him from having served in SOE is clearly untenable. Being born in December 1924 or 1925 would still have made him seventeen (or eighteen) in December 1942, which would not necessarily have excluded him from military service. Indeed, the youngest recipient of the George Medal was a wartime sailor, Tommy Brown, who was only sixteen when he received his decoration in 1942.

A simpler solution to the conundrum of the missing (or concertinaed) year might be to check the date of Cottell's commission as he is emphatic that he had been 'given a commission – first lieutenant – in the Royal Army Service Corps, assigned to SOE',[46] when he joined SOE's French Section. Unfortunately, the only Cottell to appear in the *Army List* at any time during the war is his younger brother, Anthony J. E., who was commissioned into the RASC in April 1944. Accordingly, it would appear that by calling himself John E. Cottell, John H. L. Cottell has attempted to claim the rank properly attributed to his younger brother, Anthony J. E. Cottell.

Cottell's claimed service in SOE is not substantiated by any of the organisation's archives. The codename *Badger* was used, but by a Belgian agent, Raymond André Holvert. According to Gervase Cowell, the SOE Adviser at the Foreign Office, Cottell 'was never a member of SOE . . . nor was he a member of the Dutch Section of SOE'.[47]

Cottell, of course, anticipated such a denial and had already explained that the authorities were determined to discredit him, but one is bound to wonder about their motives. What was it about his conduct or the information he possessed that supposedly led them to take such extraordinary steps to alter records and conceal his clandestine career: 'to obliterate all traces of my war activities'?[48] Cottell himself gives two reasons. One, which carries little weight, is connected with his attempts to reform the Official Secrets Acts. This laudable ambition has been shared by uncounted thousands of others from all walks of life, and lobbying for a democratic change to legislation has always been regarded as entirely acceptable behaviour. It is difficult to imagine the circumstances in which someone would be singled out as a target for smears and worse for simply campaigning to amend the widely discredited Section II of the Official Secrets Act. If Cottell had really studied the Act, as he suggests, he ought to have known that it did not date 'back to 1911, when it was designed to deal with the Irish terrorists'.[49] In fact, the OSA was first passed in 1888 to prevent the leakage of official documents, and was amended in 1911 to deal with what was believed to be an outbreak of German espionage. Neither piece of legislation had any relevance to Fenian terrorists. Cottell also asserts that the Act made it 'impossible for individual citizens or investigative reporters, or even members of Parliament to reveal, say, the degree of infiltration into the SOE achieved by the Nazis during the war, or similar successes by the Soviets in the years that followed',[50] a claim unsupported by recent history, which shows numerous examples of MPs taking an interest in security issues, quite apart from the Government's decision to publish a series of official histories covering various aspects of SOE's wartime activities, some of them specifically dealing with the issue of enemy penetration.

The second reason deployed is only slightly more credible. Cottell alleges that as a member of SOE's Dutch Section, he became aware of sensitive information that the authorities preferred not to disclose. But what exactly was this? He hints that the Dutch Section harboured a traitor in its London headquarters, a familiar theme that we shall return to in subsequent chapters, but he seems to have heard this originally from a Dutch resistance leader in Holland immediately after his arrival in

March 1943. Clearly, therefore, others were aware of the gravity of the situation and it was not exclusively Cottell's conclusion. This was the opinion he reported to Colin Gubbins and his fellow debriefers upon his return ten months later, for he remarks that 'they didn't want to hear too much about traitors at work within SOE':

> ... it was thought I had too much information about the tragic loss of so many agents in Holland and the success of Nazi counterintelligence in anticipating our moves. Therefore I was a distinct threat to those who had something to hide. Some of these people argued that I should be eliminated and thus silenced altogether. Others felt that I might be helpful in constructing a defense, using false testimony, in case of an intensive investigation, which at that point seemed likely.[51]

So what was it that SOE and subsequently MI6 had been so anxious to suppress? The implication is that sheer incompetence combined with treachery in high places to decimate the agents flown to Holland, and it is Cottell's proposition that there was no searching enquiry into N Section's conduct. In reality, there were several enquiries, including one by the Dutch Parliamentary Commission, which concluded that there had been no traitor at work in London. If Cottell had come across any firm evidence to the contrary, he gives no sign of it in *Codename Badger*.

Cottell's claimed service with SOE has been denied by the relevant authorities. Enquiries were originally initiated in 1968, when a fellow member of the Special Forces Club queried some of his claims and had him thrown out. The English Speaking Union withdrew an invitation to address one of their meetings in 1979 after learning that Cottell was a phoney, and his publishers, William Morrow & Co., were dismayed to hear from the Central Chancery of the Order of Knighthoods at St James's Palace that Cottell had no entitlement to any award of the Order of the British Empire or the Royal Victorian Order. Nor did the Ministry of Defence have any record of Cottell's Military Cross, nor Buckingham Palace any recollection of his investiture on 28 January 1947. This adds a certain irony to Cottell's statement that 'in Britain to claim a high decoration that has not in fact been awarded is the worst kind of deception and dishonour imaginable'.[52] Enquiries in Paris and Brussels have also failed to find any trace of Cottell's claimed award of the French and Belgian Croix de Guerre.

Even supposing that Cottell had indeed been the victim of a massive conspiracy, it is difficult to understand why the authorities would have gone to such lengths to discredit him. Not only would his own records have had to have been faked, but those of several others connected to him allegedly were also tampered with. For example, there is no trace of any woman answering Marianne de Roubaix's description ever working for F Section, let alone undertaking two missions into occupied France, or being caught during a third into Belgium in late 1944. Even if she had been despatched, as alleged, to Belgium 'very soon' after the birth of her son in November, it is difficult to imagine what her mission had been, considering that Brussels was liberated in September and the rest of the country was in Allied hands by December 1944. In fact, records show that no woman agent ever made three missions into occupied territory, and none was despatched to Belgium in late 1944. Furthermore, very detailed enquiries were made at the end of hostilities to establish the fate of every missing F Section woman agent, but none of the resulting dossiers matches Cottell's account of Marianne's capture and subsequent fate. Nor is there any clue as to why the authorities should have removed all trace of her, especially as she was so well-known and so highly rated. According to Cottell, she was 'a clandestine radio operator' and had 'impressed our instructors greatly. . . . Everyone admired her.'[53] Cottell describes her as 'a year older than I', which would presumably have made her twenty in 1943. She was 'five-foot-nine, and slim, with slender capable hands and a complexion made dusky by years under the fierce Congo sun'.[54] She was also 'courageous, steadfast, calculating and tough, a crack shot with both pistol and rifle'.[55] With such attributes one is bound to wonder how knowledge of her exploits could have been suppressed. Her parents apparently survived the war, as did her younger brother, although her elder sister disappeared during the occupation.

Marianne also happens to be the key to the chronological contradiction centring on whether Cottell's first mission took place in March 1943 or March 1944, because it is said to have happened while they were both training and before Cottell's departure to Camp X in Canada. Cottell describes their marriage 'in the Church of St Paul's before an elderly priest with no witnesses except my best man and Marianne's parents',[56] but asserts that the authorities erased all his records, 'including my marriage. Later I was to find that all records of our wedding in St Paul's Church in Knightsbridge and all references to Marianne as a member of SOE had disappeared.'[57] Indeed, in addition to the absence of any SOE record of her, there is no trace of any person with her name in the First Aid Nursing Yeomanry (FANY). Twenty-three FANY officers went to France, of whom only six were caught and executed, and Odette Hallowes, another FANY who survived Ravensbrück, has denied that Marianne de Roubaix was incarcerated there. Perhaps even odder is that as well as making Marianne effectively disappear, the authorities did the same for Cottell's son Peter, who was allegedly born in November 1944 and who reportedly died in June 1964. 'They had even changed Peter's middle name on his birth certificate in Somerset House so that his paternity could not be traced to me,' says Cottell.[58] Whilst it is perfectly clear from the text that Peter's birth took place in November 1944, between Marianne's second and third mission, this event adds a further mystery to Cottell's story, for he states that in June 1964 Peter 'was just twenty years old'.[59] But if he had really been born in November 1944, he would have been nineteen, not twenty. So did Cottell not know how old his only son was when he died, or was his original account of his birth in 1944 incorrect? If the latter was the case, and Peter was born in November 1943, there are further implications because that would in turn suggest that Cottell had joined SOE and met Marianne by February 1943, the probable date of Peter's conception, but this scenario is also contradicted by Cottell's deeply flawed chronology.

If Cottell really did work for SOE, why was he chosen in the first place? He did not appear to have any special assets or qualities for his role as an undercover agent, as he himself admits: 'I was just a truck driver in the regular Army. I didn't know why I had been selected. No one told me that losses among agents were so high that SOE was being forced to recruit inexperienced youngsters like myself.'[60] According to SOE's records, the youngest agent ever sent into the field by F Section was Tony Brooks, who was dropped into France in June 1942, soon after his twentieth birthday. He had been recruited eight months earlier, when he was nineteen, and as well as speaking perfect French (having been brought up in Francophone Switzerland), he had already proved himself a resourceful operator by working for an escape organisation in Marseilles. Cottell, however, could speak neither French nor Dutch, yet, improbably, was given a week's crash course in Dutch just before his departure. The contrast between Brooks and Cottell could not be starker.

A detailed analysis of Cottell's supposed adventures with SOE reveal them to be entirely fictitious. Camp X, the training school which Cottell says he attended 'on the Oshewa [sic] river'[61] in Canada has received widespread publicity in North America because it was used by so many American and Canadian agent candidates. However, although it was staffed by British personnel, none of the trainees was British, so Cottell could not have undergone a course there. Similarly, returning SOE agents were excluded from the routine refugee screening process at the Royal Victoria Patriotic School in Wandsworth, which makes a nonsense of his claim to have been debriefed there in 1944. Equally puzzling is Cottell's claim that he was not briefed for his second mission to Europe, which he says took place soon after D-Day: 'To this day I don't know what the exact purpose was; we were told nothing in advance.'[62] Nor does his description of a Lysander aircraft as having an open cockpit make sense, a detail he would surely not have got wrong if he had truly flown in the plane.

Cottell's purported post-war career in the intelligence field is as difficult to confirm as his wartime exploits. The first episode of significance that can be checked is his second mission to Dresden, which resulted in his imprisonment in the Soviet Union. 'The Communists ran investigations trying to associate me with the British Secret Service. They were unable to do so, and my cover as a harmless businessman was preserved,' says Cottell.[63] The date of this adventure is a little obscure, but Cottell was refreshingly precise about the length of time he was in Soviet custody, saying that he was kept 'a prisoner of the Communists for exactly eleven months, two weeks and four days'.[64] He also refers to an event in 'the late summer of 1958. Nine months had passed since my release from Lubyanka',[65] which would place the alleged spy-swap in the previous November or December. This also conforms with his passing remark that he had been in his 'thirty-third year',[66] which expired on 4 December 1957. Accordingly, one can reasonably deduce that Cottell was exchanged for an unnamed Soviet spy in about November 1957 and that his detention in Dresden had occurred in about December 1956, although no similar arrest was reported in the British papers.

The other problem with this scenario is that there was no Soviet spy in any British jail at any time in 1957. The sole Briton convicted of offences under the Official Secrets Acts, John Clarence, was a harmless eccentric and conman, who often claimed to be the Duke of Clarence and who had been sentenced to five years in December 1954. A veteran member of the Communist Party of Great Britain, as well as a diagnosed schizophrenic, Clarence had tried to sell a list of anti-aircraft sites in Northumberland to the Soviet Consulate in London. His scheduled release from prison was imminent in November 1957, but he certainly was not exchanged for any British agent in Berlin.

The sad truth is that John Cottell is a deluded Walter Mitty, who has weaved a preposterous tale around his rather pathetic life. Of his claims that can be checked, his imprisonment in September 1956 for the theft of money from a telephone kiosk in Devon can be verified. He was arrested on 3 August (not 'late September') and was convicted on three charges of theft and attempted theft. He was sentenced to six months' imprisonment on each charge, to run concurrently. This may seem a harsh sentence for the trifling amount involved, which was sixpence, but the magistrates heard that Cottell had a number of previous convictions and, therefore, he was by no means a first offender.

It might well be asked how it was possible for Cottell to dupe so many people and give his account such an air of authenticity even if it did contain a number of awkward contradictions. Certainly many of the episodes and personalities mentioned in the text are real characters drawn from intelligence literature. Colin Gubbins, Maurice Oldfield and Claude Dansey are all well-known figures whose names have often appeared in print, and all are dead. The few references to each are unremarkable and, with the exception of an erroneous remark about Oldfield having once worked in the Home Office, accurate. Other *personae*, such as 'General Pavel Ludoplater, Chief of the Soviet Foreign Espionage Service', are either entirely fictional, or perhaps a mistake for General Pavel Sudoplatov, who did indeed hold such a position.

A few of the individuals mentioned, particularly Colonel Scotland and Oreste Pinto, have written their own accounts of their wartime activities, and this tends to suggest that Cottell had a limited access to books of the genre and that he relied heavily upon them as sources. It is probably significant that all three played central roles in books published in the 1950s, and much of Cottell's account dovetails with the data already published, although there remains an element of exaggeration. For example, Cottell says that in the summer of 1946 he was assigned to the interrogation centre in Kensington Palace Gardens which Colonel A. P. Scotland wrote about in his 1957 autobiography *The London Cage*. The facility certainly existed, as did Scotland, but the latter was emphatically not 'an extraordinary man who during the war had been a major general on Hitler's staff'.[67] In fact, Scotland had served in the German Colonial

Army in South Africa in 1904, long before the First World War, and therefore had the unusual distinction of having been commissioned in both
armies, but he had not 'served in the German Army' and simultaneously
'been a major in British Intelligence, supplying invaluable information to
our side'.[68] As for the court-martial presided over by Colonel R. H. A.
Kellie, and in which Cottell says he participated, that of 'the eight
German soldiers who had callously killed a German sergeant major on
the day peace was declared',[69] no record of it exists. Five Nazi prisoners
of war were convicted of murdering a suspected enemy stool-pigeon at
Cromie prisoner-of-war camp in December 1944 and were executed in
October 1945, a year earlier than in Cottell's version. Considering that
his account fails to give the correct dates or number of defendants, it
seems unlikely that Cottell played any part in the court-martial at all, or
that he actually sat on the board itself with the rank of major. According
to Cottell, the German had been killed simply because he had been overheard to say 'that he was glad the war was over and wanted only to get
back to his wife'.[70] In reality, Feldwebel Rosterg died at the height of the
Ardennes offensive, when the war was far from over, because his com-
rades rightly suspected that he had betrayed an escape plot from a
prisoner-of-war camp at Devizes. Wolfgang Rosterg, who was certainly
not the 'fanatical and dangerous'[71] Nazi whom Cottell had portrayed,
had admitted his duplicity to his fellow prisoners and had been beaten
and then hanged in a washroom. Indeed, Colonel Scotland had referred
to Rosterg as 'a comparatively liberal-minded anti-Nazi',[72] and the incident had been the cause of some embarrassment to Scotland, for he
had authorised Rosterg's transfer from Devizes to the camp at Cromie,
which accommodated only hardened Nazis. Only five ringleaders of
those involved in his murder had been charged with the offence, and all
had been found guilty.

Scotland's book, which gave a brief description of the court-martial,
did achieve some notoriety at the time of its publication, because the
author had not sought the permission of the War Office to write it, and
clearly Cottell relied upon it to add some authenticity to his account.
Alas, when Scotland's official reports were released to the Public
Records Office, they demonstrated his tendency to exaggerate. As for
his references to Andrée de Jongh, who supposedly helped his escape
from Belgium in 1941, Cottell can be seen to have relied upon Airey
Neave's biography, *Little Cyclone*, published in 1954.[73]

As well as being a wartime interrogator of Dutch escapees, Oreste

Pinto was the author of several books about espionage, including *Friend or Foe?*, *Spycatcher* and *The Boys' Book of Secret Agents*.[74] None are regarded as useful sources for historians, and his misplaced trust in unreliable secondary sources may have helped undermine a tale that otherwise might have been believed. Whatever the truth of Cottell's sources, they certainly failed to give his story any credence.

Cottell himself now lives in Oakland, California, having moved from Fairfield, Connecticut, and he frequently fulfils lucrative engagements in the United States booked by the Keedick Lecture Bureau. Still calling himself Colonel Cottell MVO MBE MC, he insists that the British Government has spent vast sums 'to intimidate, smear, obliterate my credentials and generally to bring me to my knees'.

12

Churchill's Secret Agent

'This is not a work of fiction, or even near fiction.'[1]

The publishing world was intrigued when, in March 1982, the respected Devon publishers David & Charles announced a sensational scoop: the imminent release of the memoirs of a woman secret agent who had been run personally by Winston Churchill. According to the publicity material heralding the book's release, Dr Josephine Butler was a respected physician specialising in the treatment of cancer, who had been a member of an organisation known as 'The Secret Circle', a dozen agents who had worked personally for the Prime Minister. However, almost as soon as the news of *Churchill's Secret Agent* had broken, there was a further announcement: Messrs David & Charles had decided to scrap the entire project. By way of explanation, a spokesman for the company stated that the board had abandoned 'one of the most unusual personal stories of the Second World War' because 'Dr Butler refused to answer some questions about her personal life'.[2]

Whilst Dr Butler's reluctance to reveal her maiden name or give the date of her marriage may have deterred David & Charles, it did not have the same effect on all publishers. A year after the controversy, another firm, Methuen, brought out her book, which, it was alleged with typical hyperbole, was the story of a woman who had been 'flown more than fifty times into enemy territory'.[3]

In fact, Josephine Butler's claims are not quite as extravagant as her publisher would have people believe, but they did cause some dismay among the *cognoscenti*. Professor M. R. D. Foot scorned the existence of the Secret Circle and Hugh Verity, who flew twenty-nine Lysander missions to France, dismissed her account as 'complete nonsense'.[4]

According to Dr Butler, she had been educated at a convent in Bruges, which had been evacuated to Menton during the First World War. This had given her French as a first language. Later, she had attended the Sorbonne in Paris, where she had 'qualified as a Doctor of Medicine with a degree in Sociology'.[5] In 1932, she had married a man (presumably named Butler) who was related by marriage to her first cousin Florence, a woman who was two years younger but who in appearance was virtually her double. The explanation for this was that their mothers had been twin sisters, and when Josephine married Florence's second husband's cousin, they both acquired the same surname. Florence's nickname had always been Jo, so, when in February 1942 Josephine was asked to undertake work of a very secret nature, her cousin obligingly impersonated her. Thus, her own family never came to suspect that Josephine was not working in the Ministry of Economic Warfare, but actually was undertaking clandestine missions in occupied France.

This extraordinary state of affairs came about, according to Dr Butler, because of a sequence of events which had occurred after she had left the private clinic in Paris where she had worked since qualifying. In 1938, she had returned to London and, when war was declared, she joined FANY, not as a doctor but as a driver. She was to recall that 'as a member of FANY I drove many VIPs, among them Sir Stafford Cripps. He was a member of the War Cabinet and liked a silent driver.'[6] Although intending to put her medical background to good use, she was prevented from doing so by her transfer to the Ministry of Economic Warfare (MEW). It was here that she was talent-spotted by a mysterious officer who saw her at work in the MEW building in Berkeley Square. There she was placed in the Theatre Intelligence Service and

was to translate the secret reports coming in from France, and to pick out items from these and file them; also to go through photographs and pictures and to establish whether they were true or false. Most of the reports were in dialect, but I found them quite easy to translate as I knew several of the French dialects. Most of the officers connected with this section were Engineers, and I

learned that we were working on plans for the invasion of
Europe. Security was very tight.[7]

Dr Butler's first interview with the Prime Minister at the Cabinet War
Room under Storey's Gate, arranged by his secretary George Rance,
reportedly took place one evening 'towards the end of 1942'.[8] Alone with
Churchill, she was indoctrinated into 'his Secret Circle which only had
twelve members',[9] and informed that henceforth she was to be known by
the codename *Jay Bee*, her initials. Later, she was to learn that this band
of conspirators had existed prior to September 1939 and 'at least two of
them continued to help during the war, in the Secret Circle. These were
Professor Lindemann and Group Captain Tor Andersom, the latter on
retirement Air Vice Marshall [*sic*].'[10]

During the course of this first encounter with Churchill, Dr Butler
was introduced (but not by name) to a man who subsequently was only
referred to as 'the Major'. Rather later, when Josephine describes dining
with 'the Major' at Claridges in 1945, she remarks that she had 'never
seen him since and I still do not know his name'.[11] He was to supervise
most of her secret missions, but, as Churchill had explained, elaborate
preparations had been made already to conceal her involvement in
undercover work:

> All records of your association with FANY have been removed.
> You will live for the time being in a flat in Sloane Street. This
> means a complete break with friends and family, they must not
> under any circumstances know of your work. Just say you are on
> special work at MEW requiring a change of address. Your social
> life will be nil. If you are asked out you can make excuses – or
> your cousin will impersonate you. Oh yes, we know all about your
> double. The Major will see her and brief her.[12]

Having accepted these unusual arrangements, Dr Butler was
instructed by the Prime Minister in the need for secrecy. 'Few people, he
explained, knew of the existence of the Circle, and the fewer the better.'[13]
Dr Butler underwent a period of intensive training in the martial arts by
'a Japanese expert' and then went to Lincolnshire, where she was taught
'how to drop out of a moving plane at four feet from the ground. . . . The
plane was a Lysander.'[14]

Having completed her rather unconventional training, Dr Butler was summoned back to the Prime Minister in July and he elaborated on the purpose of 'The Secret Circle'. It had been set up because 'he did not trust others to keep him informed'.[15] However, it was not until a third meeting, in March 1942, that he outlined the objective of what was to be her first mission to occupied France. 'He wanted to know the attitude of the French to the Germans' and 'he was especially anxious for first-hand information about Paris'.[16] No final instructions were produced until 'early in September', when, during a fourth and then a fifth interview, Churchill told the Major that he wanted 'her to go to France next month', where she was 'to obtain a true picture of conditions there'.[17]

With these rather vague directions, Dr Butler was supplied with forged papers identifying her as a schoolteacher named Yvonne Millescamp and flown by Lysander from RAF Tempsford to a field outside Tours. She says that she walked into the city, caught a train to Paris and made contact with the owner of a café in the Avenue de la Grande-Armée. She also reintroduced herself to Jacques, the Communist concierge at her old apartment building in the Île St Louis, and stayed there for an undefined period before returning to England by plane from Tours. She was debriefed the next day by the Major and 'the following evening we were at Storey's Gate, and I went over all my experiences and impressions again for the Prime Minister. He was delighted with my report and asked a lot of questions.'[18]

Two days after this sixth meeting with Churchill, Dr Butler was despatched on another mission, this time to Normandy. Her contacts 'lived near Évreux' and she 'had only two days to visit certain places'[19] before she made her rendezvous with a Lysander. A third assignment followed 'at the end of November', when she 'went to Paris again to see Jacques and try to form some Maquis groups'. She also discussed the idea of setting up an escape route from Paris, across the country to the Pyrenees, for VIPs. It was to be based on a chain of schools and 'was ready by 1943, but it was rarely used as far as I know'.[20]

By December 1942, Dr Butler was back in Paris on her fourth mission, which was to include a visit to Clermont-Ferrand, where she recruited a group of nineteen Communists to work in the resistance. 'Four of these men were trained in Morse and codes and they became my contacts. They were my "special group". When I arrived in France they were always there to meet me, and they saved my life on many occasions,'[21] she recalled. At the conclusion of this visit, Dr Butler submitted a report about the activities of the German counter-intelligence authorities, and in particular about Hugo Bleicher, who was especially feared by the *résistants* in Paris: 'The power there was in the hands of Sergeant Bleicher, despised by the Military and hated by everyone else. . . . He believed in torture and some terrible stories were told.'[22] Dr Butler had been warned of Bleicher by Jacques during her first mission, but by her fourth she had acquired more information about him and his organisation. 'Admiral Canaris was officially in charge, but he did not appear very often. It was Sergeant Bleicher, the hated one, who seemed to have limitless power.'[23] This was reported to the Prime Minister 'early in January 1943', and soon afterwards she was given her next task:

> [I was] to go to Paris again. I was to look out for a certain man, a German and a member of the Abwehr, who held a very high position and was known to dislike Himmler. There had also been rumours that he did not approve of Hitler's methods. The Major showed me a photograph and said this man liked 'good living'. He liked a pink champagne each morning at eleven o'clock when possible; and he liked women, especially French and Italian women. All I had to find out was whether he was in Paris. The best places to look for him would be the smarter hotels and cafés.[24]

Once again Dr Butler was flown by Lysander to Tours and 'fell out of the plane four feet from the ground'.[25] She travelled the rest of the way to Paris by train and started a search of the capital's fashionable restaurants. 'On the third day' she sat in a café on the Champs-Élysées and spotted a man in civilian clothes:

> . . . he was the very man I was looking for. I had been shown a photograph, but I had not been told his identity. However, as soon as I saw him in the flesh I knew that my suspicions were confirmed – it was Admiral Canaris whom I had seen before the war in both Berlin and Munich.[26]

Before Dr Butler could convey the news of her discovery to London, she was arrested by the Gestapo and endured two days' imprisonment at their headquarters in the Avenue Kléber. Her offence had been to protest when two Gestapo officers in the café had killed an old man who had been begging for cigarette ends. Upon her release Dr Butler took a train to Tours and, en route, she was surprised to see the Major, 'who came in and sat down opposite me'.[27] Evidently he too was undertaking a secret mission, for 'he wore an armband and had a Railway Inspector's badge on his jacket'. They gave no sign of recognition to each other. After Dr Butler had alighted at Tours, she made her way to a nearby rendezvous, where she was collected by a Lysander and flown to Tempsford. 'Two days later the Major arrived, looking every inch a British Major and not in the least like a French Railway Inspector.'[28]

In view of her ordeal Dr Butler was given some leave, which she spent in Bournemouth. At the end of March 1943, she was escorted to her eighth interview with the Prime Minister. Her new assignment concerned canal traffic in France, particularly barges laden with German ammunition, and she 'was to find out as much as possible about their movements'.[29] This was Dr Butler's sixth mission and it took her to Lyon where she learned that German mobile radio detection equipment was being operated from inside vehicles disguised as ambulances. As a result of her discovery, 'one saboteur group took positive action, and some of these phoney ambulances were blown up'.[30] Apparently, some of the river traffic had also been disrupted, particularly cargo 'on its way to Italy'.

On her seventh mission, Dr Butler became Josephine Maisonnave and toured the area around Lyon spotting, during a picnic on the banks of the Saône, a new miniature German submarine. When she 'confirmed the existence of the underwater craft', Churchill considered the information 'very valuable' and declared that 'the pens must be found and destroyed!'[31]

At the beginning of June 1943, Dr Butler undertook her eighth mission and stayed in the Lyon area supervising various sabotage groups. The next month she was despatched to Normandy to familiarise herself with 'Caen and Bayeux and the surrounding district'.[32] Her next assignment, later in the autumn, was to be more substantial:

> I had a message for Admiral Canaris and had to take back his reply. The message was from Churchill and resulted in the Admiral helping the Allies in every way he could. I now understood why I had been asked to find out if he was in Paris. . . . The Admiral was to arrange with one of our country's Service Intelligence Officers to get Hitler out of Germany.[33]

Although Dr Butler gives no details of her 'Top Secret' assignment in Clermont-Ferrand, where presumably she met Canaris, she later travelled to Limoges to take part in the abduction of 'a member of an important French family who was reputed to be a Nazi sympathiser and working with the Germans'.[34] For unknown reasons his seizure would 'greatly assist our war effort', but when the moment arrived to kidnap him, he was found to have been shot dead, together with his German mistress. 'We never discovered who had committed the murders or why,' she recalls, adding that she was back in London within thirty hours.[35]

Two further meetings with Churchill followed, at which he expressed his concern about the cement being used to build the Atlantic Wall, mentioning a particular expert that had been identified as a key figure in the construction of the defences along the Channel.

It was believed by his firm, one of the largest in the world, that he was dead, but there was some evidence that he was alive and working for the Germans. The man was English, but he had been naturalised French after his marriage to a Parisian. His parents had also lived in France. His father had died, but his mother lived in Paris.[36]

Churchill wanted Dr Butler to trace this individual, and she had used a contact in Lyon to relay a message to Jacques, her concierge. 'Within four days we had the information we wanted. Jacques had traced the man but not his wife or mother. He was very much alive and living in Lyon.'[37] By chance his address was a hotel known to Dr Butler, and when she disclosed this to Churchill (at their twelfth meeting), he asked her to fly to Lyon to reconnoitre the building, which also happened to accommodate a contingent of Gestapo officers. This she did, three days later (on mission number eleven). Upon her return, a plan was prepared for the abduction and exfiltration of the cement expert. The scheme, decided with Churchill present, was for Professor Lindemann to concoct 'a very pungent smelling chemical in capsule form',[38] which would be dropped into the hotel's drains. The Gestapo would no doubt call in the plumbers, and Dr Butler's men would take the opportunity to penetrate the heavily guarded building and find out exactly where in the hotel the valuable technician was located. Apparently, this is exactly what transpired, and his room was discovered on the second floor of the hotel.

In October, Dr Butler flew to Lyon on her thirteenth mission, the 'most dangerous assignment I had yet undertaken'.[39] Indeed, it was so hazardous that Churchill insisted that she 'should wear a light uniform under my civilian dress'. She succeeded in checking into the hotel, but when she approached the cement expert she was suspicious of him, and two of her companions immediately rendered him unconscious. He was then carried from his room's balcony to a waiting car and driven to a rendezvous with a Lysander. Bound hand and foot, he was tied 'securely into the seat beside the pilot'[40] and flown to Tempsford while Dr Butler started a long walk to Pau in the foothills of the Pyrenees, a distance of 300 miles, which she covered in fourteen days. With the help of an unsuspecting Wehrmacht general who gave her a lift in his car as far as Tarbes, she made her circuitous way to Lyon, and from there was picked up by a Lysander. Later, Churchill was to assure Dr Butler that the 'successful capture of the cement expert in the autumn had contributed to the Liberation plans'.[41]

Quite when Dr Butler returned from France on this her thirteenth mission is difficult to determine because, although her long journey between Limoges and Tarbes happened under 'a beautiful, clear October night',[42] she must have been back in London by the end of the month because Churchill was due 'to leave the country on various missions in early November and we would not see him again until December'.[43] In the Prime Minister's absence, the Major despatched her to Paris 'to obtain a true picture from someone actually in the city', because there were reports 'that many Resistance workers were being arrested'.[44] She was flown to Évreux and from there went to the French capital to hear at first hand of the round-ups then being conducted by the Gestapo. After three days, she had 'got a lot of information from Jacques about the feelings of the people of Paris' and flew back to London with a report for the Major.[45]

In February 1944, Dr Butler was back in France, touring Normandy, but the mission was a short one, followed soon afterwards by another to Paris, her fifteenth to occupied territory. 'The Prime Minister wanted on the spot information', so she consulted with 'Jacques' Communist Maquis friends' and also encountered a famous SOE figure, Forrest Yeo-Thomas.[46] Upon her return, she was debriefed by Churchill and was given enough clues as to the date of the impending invasion to deduce 'that D-Day was likely to be in late May or early June'. A week after this interview, the Major informed her that 'the date of D-Day had been decided, and I would know soon. He wanted me to return to Normandy',[47] which constituted her sixteenth mission and was to last seven days. It took her to Falaise, where she passed on instructions to a Portuguese friend of the Major's, and to Caen, where she engaged the local military governor in conversation in a café.

Dr Butler's seventeenth mission, on 16 May 1944, was to be momentous, not just because her Lysander pilot was killed on his way home to Tempsford after dropping her off, or that it was to be her last secret mission, but because of the vital information she carried. She 'knew the plans for the beaches, Omaha and Utah for the Americans, Juno, Sword and Gold for the British, Canadians and Allies'.[48] Whether it was wise for her to be told these details before her departure will be discussed later, but between 16 May and 'the end of August', when she returned to England in a Hudson bomber from Tarbes, Dr Butler says that she was operating under schoolteacher cover in Normandy. She saw Churchill for the last time in May 1945, and he made her promise that, if eventually she chose to write her memoirs, she stick to the truth.

> You will have to wait at least twenty years before you can say anything about your work with the Circle. I shall probably be dead by then so shall not have to answer any awkward questions. Be careful when you write not to mention names or individual buildings, just towns and areas. . . . Others will undoubtedly write books. They will write fiction and non-fiction and near fiction – I ask only one thing Jay Bee, let yours be truthful.[49]

In response, Dr Butler gave the following solemn undertaking: 'I promised that, if ever I did write my book, I would write only the truth, and this I have now done to the best of my ability. This is not a work of fiction, or even near fiction. It is a true account of the years I spent as a member of the Secret Circle.'[50] The only question remaining is the extent to which Dr Butler has remained faithful to her pledge.

Historians wasted no time in querying the accuracy of Dr Butler's memory, especially in regard to the number of missions she undertook in France, and the fifteen separate meetings she says that she attended with the Prime Minister. No record survives of even a single appointment for her with Churchill between February 1942 and May 1945. Whether she could have carried out even a fraction of her secret assignments is also open to considerable doubt and ought to be put into context. The highest number of missions recorded by an SOE agent was seven, and only a mere handful went more than twice. Thus, her claimed total of seventeen is quite extraordinary; indeed, even half that figure would have been quite unique. What makes insiders so sceptical is that she says all these operations were conducted by Lysander aircraft, yet there is no trace of her in the RAF's copious records kept by 138 Squadron and 161 Squadron, the units at Tempsford responsible for clandestine air movements. To have drawn the same pilot more than twice would also have been exceptional, and considering that Lysander landings and pick-ups were restricted to the nights of the first and last quarters of the moon, those of her claimed departure dates which can be identified do not coincide with them. The necessity to restrict flights to the period around the full moon resulted in the RAF's clandestine units becoming known as the moon squadrons.

This latter point is an important one. 138 Squadron operated almost exclusively for SOE, an organisation that Dr Butler did not belong to, and flew converted Whitley, Halifax, Wellington and Hudson bombers, but no Lysanders, from Tempsford. 161 Squadron, which shared the field at Tempsford, handled flights for various other clandestine bodies. Altogether only two Lysander aircraft were lost over France, one with the pilot lost, shot down outward bound in 1942, the other in 1944 destroyed on the ground. No Lysander was lost on 16 May 1944.

Dr Butler asserts that she maintained a separate radio link direct to the Prime Minister: 'Churchill's personal radio code was via Kent and changed every few weeks, only the few who used it knew of its existence. The Bletchley Code Breakers never got on to it.'[51] She explains: 'We seldom used radio in case the Bletchley Code Breakers became too clever and picked up our messages. The Secret Circle was unknown to anyone outside it and must remain so.'[52] Alas, the secret of this strange organisation, if it ever existed outside Dr Butler's imagination, will never be revealed, for she died at her home at Thornton Dale in North Yorkshire on 14 June 1992, after a long illness.

Shortly before her death, in December 1991, Dr Butler released a second version of her memoirs, entitled *Cyanide in My Shoe*,[53] which repeated her claim to have dropped into enemy territory more than fifty times. In the book, she described having met Winston Churchill on seventeen separate occasions, and having landed in France on a similar number of missions. What makes the book remarkable is that, although it does not refer to *Churchill's Secret Agent*, it is an exact duplicate. Indeed, the only difference between the two books is in the biographical data on the dustjacket. Whereas on the first version Dr Butler is described as having kept 'a silence of 35 years',[54] the second edition mentions 'a silence of 40 years',[55] leaving the suspicion that perhaps the author had not mentioned her earlier effort to her second publisher.

None of Josephine Butler's claims can be verified from external sources, and none of the events she chronicles coincide with any recorded clandestine operations. Those identified as having been indoctrinated in the Secret Circle, such as Professor Lindemann, had died years earlier and records of even the most basic data, such as her medical qualifications, have proved elusive. Several of those named in her autobiography, such as Forrest Yeo-Thomas and Hugo Bleicher, had achieved considerable fame during the 1960s, and both had been the subject of books. Details apparently drawn from these secondary sources appear authentic, but the moment her account strays into technical areas, particularly in relation to Lysander aircraft, it becomes obvious that an element of invention has crept into the narrative. However, the fact that the author managed to publish the same book twice is itself testimony to her enterprise, if not to her imagination.

13

Lady Clarke Looked Right

'In 1941 Elizabeth Denham, only twenty-one years old, began
to lead a double life.'[1]

Dr Butler's curious story is in some respects reminiscent of Elizabeth
Gibbs's tale entitled *I Looked Right*. Published by Doubleday in 1956, the
purported memoirs of Elizabeth Gibbs, using the pseudonym Denham,
alleged that aged twenty-one she had been a participant in the flotilla of
small boats that had rescued the British Expeditionary Force from
Dunkirk. Her own boat, which she had sailed from the Hamble to Dover
to assist in the evacuation, had been sunk in mid-Channel, but she and
her companion, a RNVR officer, had been rescued by a destroyer.
Undaunted, they had found another launch and made a second crossing
to pick up a group of soldiers, whom they returned to England without
further incident, although upon their arrival they were briefly detained
by the police.

   This episode had brought her to the notice of an unidentified intelligence service, which sent her to occupied France in June 1940 on a
mission to collect Allied stragglers. Her partner was an unnamed agent
referred to as Jon, a former journalist who had worked in Spain during
the Civil War and had been known to Elizabeth 'in France some years
before'.[2] After a minimum of training, in which the topics of 'maps, codes,
wireless, signals and finally wardrobe' were dealt with 'at half hour intervals'[3] during a single morning, Elizabeth was driven past Salisbury to a
naval base. There she joined 'a very small ship'[4] for an overnight voyage

to the Gironde, where she and Jon were dropped in the marshes 'at first light, nicely timed to avoid other river traffic',[5] equipped with a wireless receiver. Their purpose was to gather up British stragglers and then return to the same spot forty-eight hours later to be picked up. Together they hitched a ride into Bordelais, where they encountered plenty of soldiers whom they escorted to the rendezvous point. A 'small destroyer'[6] took a group off the beach the first night and then returned again the following evening for the remainder.

This was to be the first of numerous missions, of which eight are described by her in rather vague terms. Few dates or locations are given, but her story is quite remarkable. According to her version of events, at the outbreak of war she had joined some uniformed organisation based in London which was not part of the military forces. On impulse she had accompanied a friend to Dunkirk, and this episode had resulted in her recruitment by a mysterious colonel and in her introduction to Jonathan, who was to be her partner on secret missions to the Bordeaux area for the following three years. Her second trip, made soon afterwards 'to see how the land lay and what contacts I could make in that region',[7] was on a requisitioned steam yacht; on the return journey, her trawler was met at a rendezvous in the Channel by a motor torpedo boat. On subsequent missions, when she visited Paris and Marseilles, she was exfiltrated either by submarine or aircraft.

Justifiably, Elizabeth's memoirs were described by her publishers as 'the true hair-raising adventures of an English girl in occupied France – one of the untold epics of World War II'.[8] What made them particularly special was the fact that Elizabeth appears to have pursued her clandestine activities without alerting her principal employers of her dual role. For example, at the conclusion of her first assignment she had returned to London and, having changed into her uniform, had resumed her duties:

I sneaked into my office and my secretary gave me a good idea of my unpopularity in the department in going on leave at such a time. She then gave me a list of my lectures and meetings during the day. When I got up on the platform and started a singularly dreary lecture on administration, the last few days seemed so unreal that, had I not been so sleepy, I should have thought I had dreamed it all.[9]

Elizabeth's second mission occurred 'soon afterwards'. Her task was to return to the Gironde in 'a steam yacht belonging to a man with advanced ideas of decor'.[10] She was dropped near a village on the Biarritz to Bordeaux railway line. She caught a train to Bordeaux and thence took a bus to a château 'about a hundred miles from Bordeaux'[11] owned by a count and his wife, an American from Arkansas. There Elizabeth found two airmen who had taken refuge, and she arranged for them to be returned to England. She re-established contact with Jon, who obtained agreement from London over his radio for the airmen and a group of other soldiers to be met offshore by a naval vessel. An obliging trawler skipper in Bordeaux collected Elizabeth and the men from the harbour and transferred them on to a Royal Navy MTB near to Guernsey. Elizabeth stayed in London just long enough to deliver a lecture at her office on the subject of security; then she was swiftly on her way back across the Channel to a sandy beach south of Bordeaux, where a friend, an elderly French princess, owned a villa. Despite Elizabeth's admission that her 'knowledge of wireless was nil',[12] she learned how to master the radio and to arrange a rendezvous for a further group of soldiers. Once again, she escorted them to the coast and accompanied them back to England.

Elizabeth's fourth mission followed a period of 'instruction in high explosives and their uses',[13] when she also 'was to learn something of radio and ciphering'.[14] She and Jon were flown 'from an airfield fairly near London'[15] to a field in France, where they were welcomed by a local resistance leader named René. Although Elizabeth does not identify the aircraft used, the pilot is reported as saying that 'he could take a dozen'[16] on the return flight, and apparently did so.

On this particular mission, Elizabeth travelled to Marseilles by train because a report had been received of some airmen stranded on the Riviera, five of whom proved to be injured. She contacted London on the radio she had carried across France and organised a pick-up off the beach. A fast smuggler's speedboat was used, but a firefight developed as the launch headed out to the Mediterranean. Shots were returned 'with a small gun near the bows'[17] and, 'several days later',[18] the damaged boat reached England.

In retrospect, it is odd that these five wounded airmen were not taken to Gibraltar, but instead completed the voyage all the way back to England. Perhaps it is not surprising that, following their ordeal, 'there were ambulances standing on the quay to take the airmen to hospital'.[19]

Within a few days Elizabeth was back in action. 'From an agent in

Germany it was known that there had recently been an organized break from a prison camp. The men were still at large and there were hopes of them being routed into France.'[20] Accordingly, Elizabeth was dropped from a boat near 'the mouth of the Gironde'[21] to find Jon, and together they spent an unquantified time collecting together evaders for despatch by air to London, and preparing an ambush on an enemy convoy carrying a cargo of bombs to a local airfield. However, during the attack Jon injured his shoulder and the pair were later evacuated by submarine. Thereafter Elizabeth made numerous trips to France: 'throughout the long, bleak winters and cheerless summers of '41, '42, '43 I went over at intervals to Jon – or Raoul – with explosives, supplies, money to help bring back any of our men they had collected.'[22]

These operations, which included a visit to Paris, were largely uneventful, but in June 1943 Elizabeth was arrested and tortured by the Germans, who broke all the fingers of both her hands before she escaped in a daring rescue mounted by the *maquis*. Jon, her principal contact in the resistance, was later shot by the Gestapo, and the American lady who gave her shelter was also to die, so no corroboration of Elizabeth's claims is available from anyone mentioned in the text. Nor, curiously, is there anything else to confirm her story, but there are some odd clues to indicate that the whole tale is a fiction. By her own admission she believed her grasp of the language was so 'atrocious' that 'any Frenchman who heard my French would know me to be English',[23] and in anything 'more than a routine check my accent would give me away', but apparently this disadvantage did not disqualify her from secret work.

Also, doubts about whether Jon ever existed are not unreasonable. According to Elizabeth, he was drunk when they met, just hours before their first assignment together, for which she had received only a minimal preparation lasting a couple of hours. Despite his insobriety, he appears to have accomplished more than any other British agent. As Elizabeth eloquently put it,

Except for short intervals for training, he remained in France for most of the war, a trial of endurance and courage that can only be fully appreciated by those who have spent time in an occupied territory in wartime. There is always the sure knowledge that one slip and you are for it – not a quick death, but questioning by extortion, transportation to a labour camp, or a lingering ghastly death. All those who aid you will be involved in your fate and there is ever-present the nerve-shattering fear that your every action is incriminating not only yourself but others with you. Inaction is worst, because to rest in one place is to invite betrayal; anyone, everyone, is your potential enemy, and when you are caught, as you surely will be sooner or later, no one will dare help you. And so the utter loneliness closes in on you, and you trust no one, not even yourself in the end. When self-confidence is gone, the end is near and sure. To such men should go the highest praise, but they rarely even get recognition. Every time I went to France I would find Jon a little more taut, a little more tired, and increasingly distrustful.[24]

Since there must be some doubt about the author's veracity, a little research reveals that Constance Elizabeth Gibbs was first married to John S. Langton, an engineer who joined the Grenadier Guards, but, following a motorcycle accident, spent much of the war training tank crews at Bovingdon in Wiltshire. In 1947, Elizabeth left her husband for Humphrey Clarke, who succeeded to a baronetcy upon the death of his father two years later. For Sir Humphrey, who had worked at the British Embassy in Washington DC during the war, this was his third marriage, but it only lasted until 1953, when they divorced. Three years later, his ex-wife wrote her book, which was serialised in the *Daily Express*. In *I Looked Right*, Elizabeth mentioned her family only briefly. Initially she said that her husband 'was with his regiment training in the north of England',[25] and also spoke of her brother, with whom she had enjoyed cycling. However, Elizabeth Gibbs's brother Henry had been killed in a car accident before the war, and her husband had been in Pirbright at the time she described him variously as having been in the north and on leave. In later years, Elizabeth lived at Poulton, Gloucestershire, becoming a respected County Councillor, and when she died in June 1991 her family was still somewhat embarrassed by the success achieved by her book. What made it so memorable was the single incident of her arrest: having stepped off a kerb into a busy street in occupied France, she looked in the wrong direction for approaching traffic. Her mistake had been spotted by a German, or so she claimed, and the consequence had been a painful interrogation. This episode so caught the public's imagination that it was widely accepted as genuine, so much so that the head of SOE's F Section, Maurice Buckmaster, embroidered the tale and repeated it in his war memoirs, *They Fought Alone*.[26] However, as her closest relatives knew, she never set foot abroad during the entire war, but out of loyalty they remained silent and thereby allowed *I Looked Right* to go unchallenged. The book caused considerable awkwardness within her family, especially for her two sons, but the author's use of a *nom de plume* ensured that few realised that Elizabeth Denham was actually Lady Clarke, fomerly married to the fifth baronet. As for her readership, none questioned the authenticity of her astonishing adventures.

14

With My Little Eye

'The events described in this book are all true.'[1]

Edward Edlmann's astonishing career as a secret agent, revealed in his memoirs published in 1961, rivals anything written previously, even by his competitors in these pages. Born in Florence in 1893, he was exceptionally well qualified to become a spy because, by the time he had left the Bromsgrove School, Eastbourne, he was completely fluent in Italian and German as well as English. According to his own story, his adventures in the field of espionage had started on the Western Front during the Great War, where he fought as a subaltern with the Lincolnshire Regiment. He had been badly gassed with phosgene during the bloody conflict at Hill 65 and was sent back to England to recover. When he returned, early in 1918, it was ostensibly as an intelligence officer attached to the 2nd Canadian Division, but he recalls that this was really a cover for his work at

> a secret HQ far removed from, and entirely unconnected with, any acknowledged military formation. Here I shed all identity of my former self. I was no longer a lieutenant in the British Army. I became a German private of the 163 Reserve Infantry Regiment.[2]

In his new guise as Gefreiter Schultz Edlmann, he was deployed in the

vicinity of Vimy Ridge, north of Arras, and ordered to infiltrate the
German trenches.

> The practice was for the agent to hover on the outskirts of the
> raiding party, watch his opportunity to slip through unnoticed in
> the general upheaval and make his way as quickly as possible
> towards the hinterland, after which the rest was up to him. The
> fact that by this process a number of lives were almost invariably
> lost weighed nothing with the sponsors of the action, nor did the
> participants realize for what purpose they were being jeopar-
> dised.[3]

The objective of Edlmann's first mission was Vouvroy, a railway station six miles behind enemy lines, where during the two and half days of
the mission's duration, he moved up and down the rear echelon units,
noting their positions and strength before slipping back across No Man's
Land at the appointed time and place. Despite the detailed order-of-battle
intelligence Edlmann had succeeded in accumulating, which was swiftly
conveyed to the appropriate quarter and his Chief,

> The proper quarter, however, as events proved only too well,
> chose to disregard it in great part, as they did similar news sup-
> plied by others, with the result that when 21 March came, and
> with it the greatest enemy attack, the only part of the front they
> had not thought worth while to safeguard adequately was the
> very one which the German General Staff had selected for their
> incursion.[4]

Undaunted by the failure of his superiors to evaluate his information
properly, Edlmann next adopted the identity of 'Hauptmann von
Mertens',[5] an engineers officer in the area of Villers-Brettoneux, east of
Amiens. Here, on 25 July 1918, he made his way through the wire to
spend two days surveying the enemy's strongpoints. This mission was
completed without incident and contributed to the success of the Allied
attack on 8 August, which by nightfall on the same day had advanced ten
miles into enemy territory 'with hardly any casualties . . . an incredible
feat in this war of trenches'.[6]

After one further episode behind enemy lines in October 1918, which
Edlmann says 'can hardly be classed as the real thing as, by that time,

the whole of the German front was so disorganised that utter confusion prevailed, and chaos was everywhere',[7] he remained in Germany, based in Cologne and Bonn, as an intelligence officer, and then as the British representative to the Inter-Allied Plebiscite Commission's railway branch in Kattowitz. The Commission was dismantled at the end of July 1922 and Edlmann was restored to civilian life, but in 1938, as a member of the Intelligence Reserve, he was invited to attend a series of lectures at the War Office in London. According to Edlmann's entry in the *Army List*, this led him to be called to the colours on 28 August 1939 with a commission that had been granted first on 26 June 1920. It is at this point that a degree of doubt enters into his narrative.

In *With My Little Eye*, the author recalls being assigned a counter-intelligence post in France by the military intelligence authorities, with responsibility for counter-espionage throughout the Cherbourg peninsula. However, just before sailing to take up the post, he had been interviewed by a tall, mysterious naval officer at an address near the Charing Cross Road: 'I never learnt his name and I believe that Canaris, the head of the German Intelligence, never knew it either.'[8] Edlmann had volunteered for any specialist work that might require his skill at languages, and his offer was to be taken up two months later, in November, when he was recalled to London to undertake a secret mission. He was to travel to The Hague, where he was to be met by a British agent named Price whom he had once known as a football player. Price supplied him with two sets of German papers to facilitate his journey into enemy territory, which was planned to last a fortnight. One identified him as 'the Kaufmann Adolf Schultz, travelling between Holland and the Rhineland on Government business', the other as 'a major attached to the Western HQ General Staff and ordered that every facility be accorded me in the way of transport, accommodation, etc. This was properly signed and stamped by the Head of the Intelligence Service, Western Front.'[9] Armed with these impressive credentials Edlmann began his peregrinations, which took him first to a *gasthaus* near Cleves to learn of local troop movements, and then to München-Gladbach and Cologne. It was here that, by coincidence, he learned that Hitler was to address a Party meeting at the Dreesen Hotel in Godesberg; posing as the well-established Nazi Adolf Schultz, he attended it. He then continued his tour to Mainz, Wiesbaden and Frankfurt. It was back in Cologne, en route to his rendezvous with Price at the Dutch frontier, that Edlmann heard of a prisoner in

Klingelputz prison charged with espionage. He suspected that this was actually 'one of our most valuable men, an officer of no little distinction in a by no means undistinguished regiment. His long absence and silence had distressed and disturbed our people at home for weeks.'[10] With the help of a disgruntled former head warder, Edlmann forged the prisoner's release papers and, wearing the uniform of an Obersturm-führer, presented them to the prison governor, who promptly turned the spy over into Edlmann's custody. The pair then caught a train to München-Gladbach and from there were driven in an official car to the border post at Cleves to meet Price.

Edlmann's report to his Chief in London was based on his observations of 'the present dispositions of all the regiments and divisions in Western Germany, their approximate strengths and locations':

> 'From the German dispositions,' I went on, 'it looks very much as though the attack will come through Belgium and Holland, but this time it will be reinforced by overwhelming air power. I saw no signs of air activity, but I heard a great deal of the contem-plated air attacks on, so far, neutral countries. It seems to be of general knowledge and expectation and one must reckon on Holland and Belgium being overrun in a matter of days.'[11]

Having completed his prescient report, Edlmann returned to his reg-ular duties in Cherbourg, only to be recalled again in March 1940. On this occasion, he was to be assigned an even more dangerous mission: to receive a secret document from an anti-Nazi dissident working in the Wehrmacht GHQ in Frankfurt. Edlmann was to be 'dropped by heli-copter outside Cologne in the area of Lindenthal'[12] by a pilot who happened to be a well-known boxer, and collected on the 14th of the month. The journey to Frankfurt completed by rail, Edlmann entered the headquarters building with the aid of 'the pass issued to staff officers'[13] and received the classified papers from the disaffected clerk. On his return journey, Edlmann dined at the officers' mess in Cologne, mas-querading as a staff colonel, and arrived at the agreed rendezvous the following day in time to be whisked 'hedge-hopping all the way' to some-where 'presumably in the Sedan area'[14] prior to a flight to London. The only hitch in the operation had been when a waiter in the officers' mess, who had once worked for Edlmann during the occupation as an inform-ant, recognised him but had not denounced him. 'A month later we heard from a reliable source that Paul, the waiter, was no more. Shot for treachery and double crossing.'[15]

Once again Edlmann returned to Cherbourg, but was evacuated on 18 June. During the months that followed, he underwent a training course in 'German and Italian at the Interrogation Centre at Matlock'[16] and in mid-November joined the SS *Orontes* at Glasgow for a voyage round the Cape to Mahdi, the location of the Combined Services Detailed Interrogation Centre outside Cairo. Here Edlmann used his skills of impersonation to extract information from a certain Italian general named Calvo by sharing a cell with him disguised as an officer in an Italian artillery regiment. The ploy apparently worked, and Calvo 'aired his views at great length on current military strategy and aims and their future course'.[17]

Some weeks after this coup, Edlmann was posted to Crete, but almost as soon as he arrived he was evacuated to Alexandria on board HMS *Orion*. His next adventure was with the Long Range Desert Group, which he accompanied on a raid to 'a mixed German and Italian HQ at Derna'.[18] Disguised as 'Major Ferrari from Benghazi', Edlmann succeeded in bluffing his way into Derna, 'but the big disappointment of the evening was that our principal and, indeed, our only quarry, Rommel, was not among those present, as we had confidently been led to believe he would be'.[19] Edlmann's next posting was to Abyssinia, where he commanded a prisoner-of-war camp for nine months; this was followed by two months in Madagascar with the Occupied Enemy Territories Administration before he moved to Nairobi and finally Sidi Bish, near Alexandria.

It was during this second tour of duty in Egypt that Edlmann was approached to participate in another secret mission, this time to Italy. The planning of the operation was to be slightly haphazard, with the stated objective being to discover 'whether Hitler intends to evacuate the country and concentrate on the defence of his own frontier, or reinforce his army in Italy and fight it out there. And this information had got to be absolutely accurate and reliable, and obtained with the least possible delay.'[20] Despite the apparent urgency of the situation Edlmann was told that he would 'be free to come and go in your own good time' and that it would be up to him 'to find out all you can'.[21] Apart from a list of contacts provided in Valletta by a mysterious Maltese, Edlmann's mission was largely planned by him. He was dropped by a British submarine on the beach near Varazze, west of Genoa, in the uniform of 'Colonel Bruno Francesco Canavese, a colonel on the General Staff', with an agreed rendezvous in the same place exactly three weeks later.[22]

After a successful landfall, Edlmann's mission took him to Varazze and Genoa before he made contact with a glamorous marchesa in Florence, who arranged for a secret document of exactly the kind he had been seeking to be smuggled out of the local German headquarters, copied and replaced. His helper, by coincidence, was an anti-Nazi major whom he had previously known in peacetime in Kattowitz. Having copied the crucial paper in longhand and having narrowly evaded Colonel Stamm, head of the local Gestapo, Edlmann returned to Varazze in time to meet the submarine and, in a dramatic hail of bullets, made good his escape to Malta. There he joined a flight to Cairo and, three weeks later, in mid-December 1943, was back at the Intelligence Corps' headquarters near Rotherham for reassignment to an Italian prisoner-of-war camp at Happenden in Lanarkshire, and then in March 1944 to another camp, Lodge Moor, near Sheffield.

While still at Lodge Moor, Edlmann was summoned to London and briefed on a new mission, this time to reconnoitre an underground factory between Bielefeld and Hanover which was suspected of manufacturing 'V1s and V2s'. His task was to infiltrate the site in the guise of a slave labourer and report on what he could see. Although fluent in German and Italian, Edlmann's French was, he admitted, 'rotten',[23] but none the less he was supplied with two identity cards, one in the name of a Frenchman from Arras, to be used once inside the camp, and the second in the name of Franz Reichert, a German railway employee. Accompanied by another, unnamed agent, Edlmann crossed the North Sea in a submarine from the Firth of Forth and landed undetected on the Dutch coast near Groningen.

Edlmann had no difficulty in reaching Bielefeld by train, via Rheine and Osnabrück, and made contact with a certain Herr Schneider, whose name had been given to him as a reliable person 'who would supply all my wants'.[24] This Schneider did, by introducing Edlmann to a foreman at the forced labour camp named Choquet, who obligingly agreed to sneak him into the factory and allow him to discover a vital component for the V-2 rockets being assembled there which turned it into 'a new multiple super rocket'.[25]

'With this new development,' a well-informed German explained to Edlmann, 'the situation will have completely altered. For every one missile previously fired, we shall now be able to send over a hundred.'[26]

Having discovered the secret of the underground factory, and learned the route taken by the trucks carrying the vital parts in crates to the final assembly point outside the Ruhr, Edlmann made his way back to the Dutch coast and was met by the submarine that had delivered him a fortnight earlier. The return journey across the North Sea to Scotland was uneventful, and Edlmann reported to his Chief in London. Welcoming his report the Chief confirmed that

> there is news from two other quarters which seems to dovetail in with yours. I think we may act on this now, though it would have been better to have known precisely what those crates contained. It will give the Air Force the opportunity to show what it can do in the way of precision bombing, and more or less disrupt that particular line of supply.[27]

Edlmann's return to Lodge Moor was to prove temporary, for in the 'late autumn of 1944'[28] he was given his final assignment: another mission to Germany, this time to buy a Soviet policy document 'drawn up at the highest level, probably by Stalin himself, laying down the course of military operations to be followed in the immediate future, and another one dealing with post-war political aims and ambitions'.[29] This vital paper had fallen into the hands of Karl Becker, a 'waiter employed in a third-rate restaurant in Beuel',[30] and, as Edlmann was familiar with this industrial suburb of Bonn, he had been given the task of parachuting into Germany to complete the transaction. A couple of days' parachute practice at an RAF station in Wiltshire followed, and then Edlmann, dressed as a German medical NCO, was dropped from a bomber during a large-scale raid on the Ruhr valley. He landed between Wesseling and Mehlem, and was able to mingle with a search party out looking for an enemy parachutist. Having befriended one of the searchers, from the nearby village of Poppelsdorf, he spent the night as his houseguest and obtained a lift to Bonn on a cart the next morning. Becker was found without difficulty and the purchase completed quickly. Just as Edlmann was contemplating the part of his mission which had been unplanned, namely his return to the Allied lines, he suddenly encountered the same British agent whom he had freed from prison in Cologne nearly five years earlier. He explained that he was also on a secret mission and had adopted the guise of 'a sort of super staff colonel with a roving commission, and have been for months past! They've accepted me at my face value, chiefly because of my arrogance and rudeness, and I'm supposed to be quite a character to steer clear of.'[31] Dinner and dancing at the Dreesen Hotel in Godesberg followed, and then the pair made their way in a Mercedes staff car requisitioned in Aachen to the front, where they slipped across No Man's Land and found some American soldiers to surrender to. After a night at the local Divisional HQ, they were driven to Brussels and handed over to the British, who arranged for them to be flown to 'the same RAF station in Wiltshire from which I had flown such a short time previously'.[32]

The conclusion of this final mission did not mark the end of Edlmann's adventures, for he was to experience a very narrow escape when an attempt was made on his life while on leave in London from Lodge Moor: he was pushed from behind by an unseen assassin while waiting for a tube train at Piccadilly Circus underground station. Edlmann was propelled into the path of an oncoming train and very nearly killed. However, the incident was observed by a police officer, who promptly arrested the individual responsible. He had 'been following him for days as being a suspected person', and it subsequently turned out that the man, though found to be carrying genuine RAF identification papers, was 'a German who has lived here most of his life'.[33]

That the Germans should try to attack selected British agents in England was not, apparently, entirely unexpected. Upon his return from his first mission to Germany in 1944, Edlmann's Chief had warned him of

recent indications that some sort of enemy organization exists with the primary object of eliminating members of our particular branch. Within the past fortnight there have been attempts on the lives of two of my people, and though both failed, luckily, there is no reason to suppose that they will not be repeated.[34]

In Edlmann's case, a trial was conducted and 'this misguided person had duly paid the penalty for his misdemeanours . . . unanimously it was decided that he had lived long enough, and so he ceased to be'.[35]

Lest there be any doubt that this remarkable tale is authentic, Edlmann states in his preface: 'For obvious reasons the names of certain characters have been deliberately changed but the events described in this book are all true.'[36] However, as we shall see, there is ample reason to doubt the author's veracity, and to question whether any of the operations in which he claims to have participated ever really happened. Concentrating on the events he described in the Second World War, where the declassified intelligence records are rather easier to double-check than those from the First, it must be assumed that the organisation for which he undertook so many clandestine missions is SIS. Certainly, the description Edlmann gives of the Chief, as a greying, blue-eyed, possibly retired, naval officer,[37] would appear to fit Admiral Hugh Sinclair, who was indeed Chief of SIS in November 1939, but only for four days because he died on 4 November 1939 and was succeeded by Stewart Menzies, a regular army officer then aged forty-nine, who had been deputising for Sinclair for the past twelve months during the latter's long battle with cancer.

Edlmann's first mission to Germany, via Holland, and his decision to help another British agent escape from prison in Cologne is remarkable because this operation is alleged to have been undertaken at a moment when SIS's networks based in the Netherlands were in turmoil. On 9 November 1939, Captain Sigismund Payne Best and Major Richard Stevens, both key SIS officers in Holland, were kidnapped by the Sicherheitsdienst while attending a rendezvous at the German frontier with a man purporting to be a disaffected Luftwaffe general. This embarrassing affair became known as the Venlo incident, after the name of the border town where the abduction occurred. Not only did the episode leave two well-informed SIS officers in German hands, where they were to remain until their release in 1945, but it led to the death of a Dutch liaison officer, who was on the scene to ensure that the British encountered no bureaucratic obstacles while travelling so close to the frontier. Lieutenant Dirk Klop died of wounds after being shot by the Germans as they raced back to German territory with their two prisoners. The entire episode received little publicity at the time because both the British and the Dutch were anxious not to jeopardise the captives unnecessarily. *The Times*, for example, reported only 'an armed clash between German officials and Dutchmen', omitting all reference to British involvement. Clearly the fiasco was a culmination of a well-orchestrated plan and demonstrated that SIS's activities in the Netherlands must have been compromised for a long time. The SIS station, based in the British Passport Control Office in The Hague, was thrown into chaos and confusion reigned at SIS's headquarters in London. Yet this is precisely the moment that Edlmann claims he was sent to The Hague en route to Germany for a mission that was to last a fortnight. In The Hague, he was

met by 'Price, a competent footballer, and the last person I would have
suspected of having been co-opted for this sort of thing',[38] who was able
in a matter of hours to produce German documentation for the two identities Edlmann wished to adopt on his assignment. He asserted
confidently that 'if a signature or stamp, relevant to any particular document, was ever changed, the change and its substitutions were available
for issue on our side within twenty-four hours'.[39] Despite obtaining all the
necessary papers, Edlmann had to wait until he reached Cleves before
he could acquire 'the necessary military garments' that conformed to his
documents.[40]

The Venlo incident heightened tension right along the border and
was used for propaganda purposes by the Nazis to link the British to the
assassination attempt made on Hitler's life in the Burgerbraukellar in
Munich the previous evening, 8 November. A bomb had detonated
wrecking the beer cellar, but Hitler had escaped unharmed, determined
to blame the British Secret Service.

Frustratingly, the author is somewhat vague about the exact chronology of events. The recall from Cherbourg for his initial interview with
his Chief is mentioned as 'about November '39',[41] but he does not elaborate on how long it took him to travel to Holland and the duration of his
stay there in 'some second-class hotel'.[42] Accordingly, it is impossible to
pinpoint the exact date of his entry into Germany, but if it took place
prior to 9 November, his optimism would be understandable. If so, however, the real purpose of his mission, which is described as determining
the number of German divisions deployed along the Western Front,
would appear to be redundant, bearing in mind that SIS thought that it
already enjoyed good sources in the area and anticipated the imminent
recruitment of a Luftwaffe general. With the prospect of such an impressive asset, why risk sending an undercover agent to Cleves and
München-Gladbach?

If, on the other hand, Edlmann's mission occurred after the fateful
date of 9 November, SIS's behaviour is even more inexplicable. To have
risked sending a British agent across the frontier not so very far from
Venlo, on a tour of agents in the locality, must have been incredibly foolhardy at that very sensitive time. The first was 'the proprietor of the
local Gasthaus', who helped him obtain a car and the uniform of a
Wehrmacht staff major. 'He was also able to confirm certain troop locations in his immediate area and other items of local military interest'.[43]
His second contact, 'near München-Gladbach, was more fruitful' and

disclosed 'the approximate location of three divisions, none of them of any military renown, but [I] obtained a reasonably accurate idea of their strength and dispositions'.[44] Edlmann also relied on what he termed 'commercial contacts' in Cologne and describes meeting contacts in 'Remagen, Coblenz, Mainz and Wiesbaden' and finally Frankfurt.[45] The existence of such a network of informants working for SIS in these cities in 1939 is entirely unsupported by any evidence that has since come to light.

Edlmann's purported encounter with Hitler at the Dreesen Hotel in Godesberg is also puzzling. To have contemplated attending such a gathering, equipped as he was with a 'perfectly genuine SS badge',[46] would have been dangerous in the extreme for, if caught and revealed, his exposure as a British agent would have lent weight to the Nazi Government's bogus attempts to establish SIS's complicity in the Munich plot. Thus, what Edlmann describes blithely as a minor event during his mission might in fact have had repercussions on an international scale. Much the same could be said for his daring rescue of the British agent from Klingelputz prison and his successful exfiltration to a British consulate in Holland. This second mission to Germany, undertaken in March 1940, is odd because Edlmann says that he was transported across the frontier by helicopter. Whilst it is true the German Fl-282 Kolibri, built by Anton Flettner, went into military service in that year, and the French had achieved some success with the Bregeut-Doand Gyroplane and Henrich Focke's four-seater Fa-233, none was available to the RAF. In fact, the first experimental helicopter, the VS-300, flew a year earlier, but moved in every direction except forwards. Igor Sikorsky's prototype is generally regarded as the first successful example of the machine, but it did not overcome all its problems until 1941, a year after Edlmann says that he was delivered to a spot near Cologne, and then collected again . . . *at night*. When Edlmann's story first appeared and was serialised in the *Sunday Despatch* in April 1961, numerous aeronautical enthusiasts complained that there were no helicopters in service with the RAF and, therefore, the whole story must be untrue. However, when Edlmann retorted that the machine he had described as a helicopter was technically an autogiro, the Air Ministry confirmed that there were several autogiros operated by the RAF and that two were 'on detachment' in France in March 1940.

Edlmann died in Lisbon in August 1971, since when his military record has become available. It seems to contradict many of his assertions, particularly in respect of his adventures in Italy. During the very periods he claimed to have been undertaking secret missions in enemy territory, the British Army says that he was guarding prisoner-of-war camps. Which version is correct? The odds are against Edlmann.

Edlmann and Robert Vacha are the only authors to have described the role of the impostor. As we have seen, both published tales that defy belief.

15

The Courage of Fear

'How different becoming a spy had been from what I had imagined!'[1]

Roxane Pitt was, according to her publishers, 'one of the principal woman agents of World War II'.[2] Her story, and her background, are really quite unusual.

According to Roxane Pitt's war memoirs, published in April 1957 and entitled *The Courage of Fear*, she was the younger daughter of a union between a certain Angus Pitt, a direct descendant of Prime Minister William Pitt, and the daughter of a Spanish nobleman, the Marquis of Mendoza. Pitt and the Marquis had met in dramatic circumstances in May 1908, when the younger man prevented an accident as the Marquis was being driven along The Mall in a landau. In gratitude, the Spaniard invited Pitt home to 13 Curzon Street and later employed him as his assistant in his international trading company. His first post was in Egypt, where he met and married one of the Marquis's daughters.

Roxane and her sister Juana, who was a year older, were born in Aden, but were brought up at the Mendoza home in Heliopolis. However, during the Great War Angus returned to England to serve in the army and his wife left him for a French officer named Bedun. Roxane and her sister were sent to a convent in South Harrow, where they remained until the summer of 1925, when they were moved to a school in Zug, Switzerland. Later, Roxane attended Wycombe Abbey and read Law at Lady Margaret Hall, Oxford. While still at university, or possibly soon afterwards, she met and married a businessman from Birmingham named Lionel Chester, who 'belonged to a titled family'.[3] Their marriage, which was conducted at Caxton Hall followed by a reception at Claridges, lasted only a few days for Roxane abandoned her husband during their honeymoon in Normandy and fled to England to obtain an annulment. Sometime afterwards, but probably in May 1932, she moved to Paris and was introduced to Madame Scarlatti, who ran 'a School of Diction in the Rue Bonaparte'.[4] There she was taught to become an actress and, after six months' tuition, was cast in a small part in Molière's *Les Précieuses ridicules* at the Comédie-Française in December 1932. However, she was unable to fulfil the engagement because her sister Juana, who had married the Italian commercial attaché in Aden, Roberto Volpe, was experiencing difficulty with her pregnancy in Milan.

Soon after the birth of her niece, Anna Christel, in mid-1933, Roxane and Juana moved to their mother's villa at Cap d'Ail in the South of France. There Roxane had an affair with an Italian, Julio Constanza. His family in Rome disapproved of the match so Roxane returned to England and buried herself 'in the dusty archives of Oxford'.[5] Following the death of her father in September 1937, she stayed with her mother at Cap d'Ail and married Bill Carstairs, who described himself as the director of a shipping company based in Mombasa. However, this second marriage was even shorter than her first, for Carstairs turned out to be a bigamist and sailed from Marseilles for Africa alone.

Roxane's introduction to intelligence occurred during the first week of the Nazi occupation of Paris in June 1940, when she sought help from Madame Scarlatti. Roxane believed herself to be at risk from the Germans because she held a British passport and because her mother, the daughter of the Marquis, was Jewish. Both her mother and her sister Juana are believed to have subsequently perished at Ravensbrück, so her fears were well founded. Madame Scarlatti agreed to help her former pupil and introduced Roxane to 'Monsieur Beaulieu', who was actually Alwyn Temple, a dealer in precious gems and a friend of Roxane's father, whom she had met in Marseilles.[6] On that occasion Temple had investigated the background of her absconding husband, Bill Carstairs. Now he was the brains behind an organisation helping Allied servicemen escape German captivity.

Roxane adopted the identity of Madame Scarlatti's niece Jacqueline Jaures and worked as a dancer at the *Folies Bergère*. She also sang and danced in hospitals for the Red Cross, appeared at the Comédie-

Française and had a part in Rameau's *Les Indes galantes* at the Opera House. Many of those involved in these productions were members of Beaulieu's network and Roxane mentions her certainty 'that many of the masked figures who did no dancing were escaped prisoners and British airmen'.[7] As well as acting as an escort for evading Allied servicemen and as a courier, Roxane was entrusted with extracting sensitive information from enemy officers. She flirted with Field Marshal von Weitzleben for clues to a German invasion of Spain and duped a staff colonel, who was persuaded to be indiscreet to a room of prostitutes masquerading as schoolchildren. One of her more regular duties was to attend

> a rendezvous in a square by the Bois de Boulogne. Between midday and twelve-thirty I would sit on one of the benches pretending to be a love-sick girl absorbed in writing a *billet-doux*. Presently someone would come and sit beside me. It might be a man or a woman, but it would always be somebody different, a stranger whom I had never seen before.[8]

At midday on Christmas Eve 1942, Roxane changed identities again and, armed with Juana's Italian passport, was driven to Italy in a German staff car, accompanied by Alwyn Temple, who wore the uniform of Hauptmann Franz Schumann. They completed the journey from Paris to Milan at dawn the following day and, after a short rest, Roxane proceeded to impersonate her elder sister by presenting herself at Juana's home in the Piazza Costello. Juana's husband Roberto was apparently in Russia fighting with an Italian division and her niece, Anna Christel, accepted her aunt as her mother without demur, as did Roberto's sister, Pia, and Anna's governess, Magda. So too did Juana's friends, whom Roxane met at the first night of *Rigoletto* at La Scala. Roxane continued with the impersonation during a mission to San Marino, where she was reunited briefly with Julio Constanza, and later when she pretended to be a journalist operating in Rome. Shortly before the Salerno landings, she was despatched to the coast under the cover of 'an accredited archaeologist on research work'[9] and undertook a clandestine survey of the fortifications and gun emplacements in the area. Having successfully completed this assignment, Roxane was instructed by another British agent, Monsignor Resca, the senior Vatican librarian, to go straight to Sicily. Hitching a lift in an Italian military aircraft, Roxane established contact with a lighthouse keeper in the coastal hamlet of Villa Asmunda who was equipped with a radio, and she remained on the island until the Allied invasion. As soon as she saw British troops, she declared herself to an officer and was escorted to the nearest headquarters, where she was confronted by her ex-husband, Bill Carstairs.

After being debriefed by Major Erskine of the SIB, the Special Investigation Branch of the Corps of Military Police, she was issued with a military police uniform and sent as an interpreter to discover from Sicilian farmers the location of mines laid by the enemy. She also participated in the interrogation of captured Blackshirts before exchanging her police uniform for an 'officer's uniform with the ENSA [Entertainments National Service Association] flash'.[10] As well as running a hostel for visiting theatrical stars who were entertaining the troops, Roxane helped question Italian prostitutes in Catania and worked as an assistant to Major Clements, a senior British liaison officer supervising local political matters. After the tip of the mainland was liberated in September 1943, Roxane and her ENSA unit were moved to Bari. She was then transferred to a parachute course run by Special Force No. 1 in anticipation of a secret mission to Yugoslavia.

At the completion of her course, Roxane was flown to Foggia and then dropped in the Apennines at dawn with four companions, but she lost contact with them on landing. The following day the area was overrun by Canadian troops and Roxane returned to Bari. In June, she moved on to Rome and continued her work for SIB until her arrival in Florence, just as it was liberated, to open an ENSA cinema.

In October 1944, Roxane undertook her second parachute mission and was dropped alone from a Lysander aircraft into the countryside near Forlimpopoli. Her assignment was to link up with a local partisan leader and discover whether he was willing to participate in the capture of Forli, the local town and Mussolini's birthplace. Roxane completed her mission successfully and made her way back to the Allied lines, where she was met by Polish troops. Upon her return, she was put to work tracing looted art treasures and switched from her ENSA cover to that of a military journalist. In reality, she was rounding up German and Italian saboteurs dropped behind Allied lines around Ancona. Roxane eventually ended the Italian campaign in Genoa and, in September 1945, was flown to Northolt, where she was met by a Foreign Office official.

Roxane concludes her remarkable story with a brief account of her post-war activities. She worked as a journalist in Hamburg and

Düsseldorf, and then reported from Abyssinia. In 1949, she met Julio Constanza again, in Genoa while en route from Australia to England, and married him. However, when the Italian press discovered the nature of her wartime work, her life in Rome became unbearable and she returned to London, leaving Julio on his own to practise law.

Roxane's first autobiography, *The Courage of Fear*, carried a foreword by Sir Robert Bruce Lockhart, the former diplomat and wartime Director-General of the Political Warfare Executive. He described her story as having been told 'with pleasing modesty and yet great frankness',[11] and appeared to confirm that she had operated exactly as she had claimed, 'by helping British prisoners-of-war to escape and by supplying information to the British Secret Service regarding the dispositions and intentions of the German and Italian armies'.[12] The book, he says, 'bears the stamp of truth on every page'.[13] Rather less specific was an endorsement from Colonel John A. Balfour OBE, who was quoted as stating:

> During the Sicilian and Italian Campaigns I had the good fortune
> to meet the authoress and I well remember this courageous lady.
> In the North of Italy she was posted to my command and her
> knowledge of the country and the working of the Italian mind
> was invaluable to me.[14]

Close attention to the works of Bruce Lockhart and Balfour reveal that neither has certified that, to his personal knowledge, she undertook any of the missions described in her account. Bruce Lockhart was primarily preoccupied with wartime propaganda, while Balfour has limited his comments to acknowledging having met her in Sicily and having worked with her in northern Italy. Curiously, Balfour does not appear in the text of the book, so the reader cannot judge in what circumstances they encountered each other while she was under his command. Another curiosity regarding *The Courage of Fear* concerns the acknowledgments contained in the Author's Note. She thanks Gerald Langston Day, who evidently ghosted the manuscript, and mentions Alain Romans as having assisted in the book's preparation. Romans, of course, was the subject of Barry Wynne's story, *The Empty Coffin*, which is described in Chapter 3, and is himself the subject of considerable doubt as to the veracity of his war experiences. Two others she consulted are instantly recognisable, although both are dead, and it is unclear from the text quite what contribution they made: Sir John Nott-Bower was Commissioner of the Metropolitan Police until 1958, and Naomi Jacob was the celebrated actress and novelist who for many years lived in Italy until her death in August 1964. She is quoted by the publishers as having described Roxane as 'the bravest woman I ever met'.

As Roxane herself admitted, 'truth is sometimes stranger than fiction',[15] and certainly her tale is an odd one. Even the most basic biographical details of her background seem hard to corroborate. Take her name, for example. If her paternal grandmother had been related to Pitt the Elder, as she stated, it seems unlikely that she could have inherited that surname. Usually English families take the husband's surname, and we know only that her paternal grandfather, Angus Pitt's father, had been 'a gentleman of Slav extraction' and 'a friend of Garibaldi'.[16] The possibility that Pitt was not her true name may go some way to explain why there is no record of her at Lady Margaret Hall, Oxford, and no trace of her ever having graduated from Oxford University. According to Lady Margaret Hall's comprehensive register, the only person named Pitt to have been a member was Alethea, whose maiden name was Dew and who matriculated in 1932. Obviously, this was not Roxane. The publisher's statement that their author had also graduated from the University of Milan also seems odd, bearing in mind that, if her book is to be believed, she spent no appreciable amount of time in Italy before the war, except on vacation. Nor are the doubts limited to her claimed academic achievements. There is, for example, no trace of a marriage in England between Lionel Chester and Roxane Pitt between 1927 and 1934. Nor, for that matter, is there any death certificate registered in the name of her father, Angus Pitt, in 1937, the year he supposedly died. Regrettably these difficulties cannot be cleared up by Roxane's family, for few members survived the war. Her father succumbed to cancer of the throat in September 1937; her mother and sister Juana allegedly perished at Ravensbrück; her brother-in-law, Roberto Volpe, died in Russia; her half-brother Leslie 'volunteered to fight with the Polish Brigade and was killed while still a boy';[17] and her stepfather, Monsieur Bedun, was killed in a car accident in 1939. According to Roxane's account, only three children survived the war: a half-sister, Rhesy Bedun, her younger brother Xavier, and Roxane's orphaned niece, Anna Christel Volpe. Unfortunately, none would have been old enough to corroborate Roxane's version of events.

Accepting for a moment that the author has, for personal reasons, concealed her family origins, one could examine some of the other personalities that emerge from *The Courage of Fear*. One of the key figures has to be Alwyn Temple, the old friend of Angus Pitt who helped Roxane following her disastrous marriage to Bill Carstairs in 1938. He was then a dealer in precious gems at 3 Place Marceau in Marseilles. She described him as 'a very tall distinguished-looking Englishman of about fifty', who boasted offices in London, Paris and Bombay. Two years later, he had adopted the identity of Monsieur Beaulieu, a theatrical producer operating from Madame Scarlatti's school in the rue Bonaparte. Roxane learned that he was 'in radio communication with London', but

> Who he was I don't know even now, but I think he must have
> been someone high up in the British Secret Service, and that he
> had been spying long before war broke out. His transformation
> from a jewel merchant to a theatrical manager showed how easily
> he could change his identity.[18]

As well as assisting evaders, Temple was 'spying or forming resistance groups in other parts of France' and 'more than twice he was picked up by night and flown to London'.[19] The proposition that his organisation was engaged in resistance work is confirmed by Roxane, who recalls that 'An extremely dangerous task which the men in our network had to carry out was to collect ammunition which had been looted from German dumps or brought in after it had been dropped from a British aircraft.'[20]

The clear implication of this statement is that Temple was operating for SOE, which was the only unit supplying weapons to *réseaux* in occupied France. Yet his involvement with evading prisoners of war implies a link with MI9, the entirely separate body which managed the escape lines. Overlaps between the two organisations were avoided so as to preserve security, and neither was authorised to collect intelligence which was the sole and jealously guarded responsibility of SIS (MI6). Yet Roxane remembers that Temple was also 'gathering military intelligence from the Germans'.[21] In addition to fomenting resistance, helping evaders and collecting information, Temple was also able to don a Wehrmacht uniform and be driven across Europe, from Paris to Milan, in record time.

Roxane's knowledge of Temple's activities in Paris started in June 1940 and ended in December 1942, when she moved to Italy. This means that Temple was active during a period of thirty months when SOE and MI9 were struggling to develop, and SIS had virtually no assets whatever in the occupied zone. From the standpoint of British Intelligence, the position inside Paris was even bleaker. In fact, according to British records, the first parachute drop of weapons to France was not made until 13 June 1942, and on that occasion two containers were delivered to an SOE *réseau* east of Limoges. Altogether the RAF made ninety-three successful flights to France for SOE during 1942 and delivered a total of twenty-three tons of *matériel*, some of which was landed, the remainder dropped. However, none of these sorties was made to any network conforming to Roxane's description of that headed by Alwyn Temple. Indeed, there is nobody in SOE who matches him, and neither SOE nor SIS was in radio contact with such an individual during 1941 or 1942.

It is highly unlikely that Alwyn Temple ever existed, but if he did, he was unknown to any branch of British Intelligence. His cover name, Monsieur Beaulieu, is also slightly curious, for coincidentally Beaulieu in Hampshire was the location of a concentration of SOE's special training schools. The Germans learned about Beaulieu's existence from captured agents who had undergone training there, in the grounds of Lord Montagu's estate near Brockenhurst, but they were puzzled by the French name. They were unsure whether the agents had not meant the small town on the south coast of France, not England, and remained fascinated by the conundrum. Thus, 'Beaulieu' was probably the name least likely to have been assigned by SOE to one of its agents. In consideration of SOE's rather late entry into the clandestine war, for it was only created by the War Cabinet in July 1940, by which time Temple was apparently already well-established in Paris, it is more probable that, if he was not entirely imaginary, he operated for SIS, but no trace of him survives.

Leaving the mysterious Alwyn Temple aside for a moment, one has to consider the evidence Roxane herself provides about her adventures. Her only independent method of communicating with London, once Temple had escorted her to Milan, was via a contact in the Vatican library and, surprisingly, a wireless receiver. There is only one reference in *The Courage of Fear* to this instrument, and Roxane never explains who supplied it or when she was trained as a radio operator. In the single passage relating to her wireless, she reflects on an incident that supposedly occurred sometime in 1943, just as she moved from Milan to Rome:

I had picked up on my radio set a shortwave message for

'Jacqueline' from someone describing himself as 'Paul' speaking from a French torpedo boat. He said that Tunis Harbour was packed with submarines and that he would be in Rome in two days' time when he would ring me at 6.45 a.m. He never did. Perhaps he was a counter-espionage agent or a German spy; perhaps he was killed before he could get to Italy. If the first were the case it was disturbing for it meant that the Germans had not forgotten 'Jacqueline' and had trailed me to Rome.[22]

This episode is bizarre, not least because Allied agents operating in Europe did not use short-wave voice channels to communicate with each other. The universally adopted methods were Morse signals or very short-range voice transmissions to aircraft circling overhead. A voice channel from a boat would have been technically impossible on short-wave in 1941, and there must be some doubt about any purported message using a name in a broadcast that was bound to be monitored by the enemy, and thereby compromise an individual's operational identity. 'Jacqueline', after all, was not a codename, but an authentic identity she had been assigned by Alwyn Temple, complete with genuine documentation.

That Roxane had become known to the Axis counter-espionage apparatus is hardly surprising. She had broken every rule in the tradecraft handbook by holding a high-risk, regular rendezvous at the same location in Paris, meeting new contacts who, she says, were entirely unknown to her. This hazardous behaviour would have made her extremely vulnerable, not just to a determined attempt at penetration by the Germans, but even to the most casual, routine surveillance. Although Roxane may not have recognised the dangers at the time, she does admit that while in Sicily she received a parcel bomb in the mail. Whether an agent who had acquired sufficient notoriety to merit such treatment would have been sent into the field again is not an issue that had to be addressed in any other case, for Roxane was the only Allied agent to be a target in this fashion. In any event, whatever the deliberations behind the scenes, she says that she undertook three further missions behind enemy lines, all by parachute.

The first mission, according to *The Courage of Fear*, was a parachute drop to partisans in the Apennines. She had been trained for the drop by Special Force No. 1, which sounds not unlike No. 1 Special Force, the principal SOE unit infiltrating liaison personnel into enemy-occupied territory. However, there was no parachute training school at Bari, where Roxane says that she was taught on a special course in anticipation of being sent to Yugoslavia. In reality, these courses were conducted at two sites, in Palestine and in Egypt. Bari was an operational airfield without training facilities. Preparation apart, Roxane's first mission failed, partly because she lost contact with her companions, but mainly due to the proximity of the front line. On the day after her arrival, Canadian troops liberated the area, which suggests that her mission had been the victim of very poor co-operation. However, her second jump, in October 1944, could not have taken place in the way described. She recalls being 'hurled downwards from the Lysander which had flown me to this spot deep in the enemy lines',[23] but it was not possible to parachute from a Lysander aircraft. In short, her version of the second mission simply could not be true, and there must be strong reservations about the veracity of the first.

Roxane's third mission took place 'early in 1945',[24] when she was dropped from a Douglas bomber between Trento and Bolzano, equipped with documents identifying her as 'Magda Weiner', a black marketeer from Milan. Her objective was to locate works of art looted by Marshal Goering, and by establishing contact with a local family whose daughter worked in Trento's museum she was able to trace a cache of stolen art treasures hidden in nearby caves. Having completed her task, she was collected at night by an aircraft and flown back over the Allied lines.

With so much of Roxane's story undermined by technical detail, one is left wondering whether she had any connection whatever with any of the organisations that operated in enemy territory. Curiously, the only body she directly identifies is SIB. As soon as she declared herself to British troops in Sicily, she was placed under the command of 'Major Ferrier of the S.I.b.'.[25] Roxane had already introduced the SIB in another context, when describing the function of the Italian military intelligence service, SIM. She said that SIM 'corresponds more or less to the British S.I.b., or MI5 in the field'.[26] In reality, of course, SIB conducts criminal investigations within the army and has only a limited field security role, which primarily is the responsibility of the field security sections of the Intelligence Corps. Similarly, it is the field security wing of the Intelligence Corps which acts as the executive arm of the Security Service, MI5, in the field. The Italian *Servizio Informazioni Militari* (SIM), on the other hand, was actually far closer in structure and role to Britain's SIS (or MI6), an organisation Roxane never mentions. Thus,

Roxane seems to have had some difficulty in grasping the division of responsibility for Allied security and intelligence matters. Whilst it may be true, as she said, that SIB 'is a master card that can trump any suit' in an internal military investigation, perhaps into fraud or black-market activity, it was not a clandestine body or a 'mysterious agency'.[27]

Roxane's flawed memoir, *The Courage of Fear*, was followed in 1975 by a further autobiography, *Operation Double Life*, which gave a rather different account of her experiences and, according to her publishers, covered the period she 'served with MI5 and MI6 in North Africa, Sicily, Italy and Germany'.[28] Indeed, far from clearing up the discrepancies that had emerged from her first book, the second merely compounded the problems.

The first batch of difficulties concern her family and her background. There is no mention of the Marquis of Mendoza and her mother is described as being half French. As for Roxane's education, she abandons Wycombe Abbey and in its place refers to the Milan Lyceum and a convent in Milan; she then obtains a degree in Classics at the university there, before reading Roman Law at Lady Margaret Hall, Oxford, 'for a few terms, just to please my father, but with no intention of becoming a lawyer'.[29] Although having originally said that her father had died in England in 1937, she now asserts that he died in Bombay on 1 September 1939. Indeed, his background is also somewhat altered. The version that he was the son of a union between 'a gentleman of Slav extraction' and a descendant of William Pitt is rejected in favour of a Scot in the British Colonial Service, who marries in Zanzibar the daughter of 'a French Nobleman of Spanish origin whose wife, a Russian beauty, was the acclaimed hostess of the Colony'.[30]

Roxane confirms that her mother, who is named as Wanda, perished aged 'forty-two in a gas chamber' in Ravensbrück, but there were no gas chambers at Ravensbrück. She also gives an entirely different account of what happened to her sister, who, in *The Courage of Fear*, had also died in the same concentration camp, having been arrested by the Germans in June 1940. Yet in *Operation Double Life* she says of her sister:

> I still don't know what happened to her, now at so many years distance, no one has been able to find out how she disappeared.
> Then, at the end of 1942, all I knew was that she had not returned home from her errand. That was the time lots of people disappeared, simply vanished and were never heard of since. But my

sister was a beautiful girl of twenty, she had a husband and a daughter.[31]

Of her brother Leslie, whom Roxane previously had described as having been 'killed while still a boy' serving with the Polish Brigade, she reveals, without elaboration, that he is alive: 'My brother Leslie had accepted a job in Texas, something to do with oil and plastics.'[32]

Of her own first marriage, Roxane ignores Lionel Chester, the man from the titled family in Birmingham whom she met on a cross-Channel steamer and married at Caxton Hall. In his stead we are introduced to James Alec, whom she married at the Quay Street registry office in Manchester, aged eighteen, while she was still a student at Oxford. The honeymoon was spent at a resort fifty miles from Manchester and, like the first version, had ended in disaster and an annulment a few months later. There are sufficient similarities between the two versions of Roxane's first marriage to deduce that she is describing the same events. However, the truly extraordinary revelation contained right at the end of *Operation Double Life* is that she bore her first husband a daughter after the annulment. 'The war tore us apart, but my child was safe in Scotland,' she recalls.[33]

Roxane asserts that she was twenty when, in July 1939, she was offered an academic post in Rome. There she met Roberto Salviati, whom she subsequently married in London after the war, possibly in 1950.[34] Considering the similarities with Julio Constanza, one may be forgiven for assuming that Roxane has simply changed the name of this particular character. The marriage, her second, was ruined by disclosures made in the Italian press about her wartime activities and this resulted in a miscarriage three days after the ceremony. On the advice of the British Embassy in Rome, she flew back to London. Much later, in 1963, she was to meet David while teaching Classics at a girls' public school in Ascot; later, they married. This third marriage also failed. However, the important issue is Roxane Pitt's real age. If she was truly twenty in 1939, the entire chronology of *The Courage of Fear* is demonstrably bogus, for in that account, which omits any references to a daughter or a later miscarriage, she was born before the First World War. Certainly she could not have been born in 1919, for she had originally recollected that 'It was in 1919 that Grandma took Juana and me to London with her. Arriving at Victoria we were met by Father who had been on military service . . . we were so tired by our journey that after supper [we] went quickly to bed without giving Maman another thought.'[35] Considering that by this time Roxane had spent four years in Aden and had been brought up by her grandmother in Heliopolis, the contradiction is considerable.

As regards Roxane's experiences during the war, they also conflict sharply with what she had said eighteen years earlier. For example, during her period in Paris she describes some of her exploits with the resistance, and recalls 'that a Lysander was going to drop weapons in a certain area'.[36] She helped to save seven British aircrew from a plane that had crashed in the forest of Vincennes, and had 'to try and find out where the factories of the infernal V1 and V2 were hidden, where the launch pads were and how we could destroy them. This we did by every possible means, regardless of danger and loss of lives.'[37] After her arrival in Milan, Roxane had adopted the identity of her elder sister Juana and had pretended to her niece that she was her mother. In the later version Roxane excludes the child, saying that she had been put 'in the care of her paternal grandmother, safely in Switzerland'.[38]

The sequence of events after Roxane's appearance in Rome is also radically different from the account which appeared in *The Courage of Fear*. In the later version, she had enrolled as a nurse and had been flown to Agrigento in Sicily by a pilot she had met in Paris: 'Jacques had been one of the men we had whisked through Spain. He had escaped from a POW camp in Germany and had found his way to Paris. How was he now in Rome? No way of asking.'[39]

There are also some changes to be found in the account Roxane gives of her three parachute missions in Italy. The first operation, she says, was

> when Captain Good of Special Investigation suggested that I
> should go with him to Campobasso on the Apennines. We were
> dropped there by an aircraft from Foggia and found that not only
> had the Germans vacated the town, but the Canadians had
> already moved through.[40]

From the context of the original, it is evident that the mission from Foggia had taken place before June 1944, when she had moved on to Rome. On that occasion, she had been accompanied by four companions and the area had been overrun the 'next day' following their arrival.[41] This is clearly at odds with the second story. There is also a discrepancy in the two accounts she gives of her second drop. In the original, she went to Forli to liaise with local partisans, but in the later version she is 'smuggled into Monza'.[42] The third operation, near to Trento, is omitted entirely from *Operation Double Life*.

The questions that immediately arise regarding Roxane's claims concerning her activities during the war centre on her period in Paris between 1940 and 1942. For example, her reference to weapons being dropped from a Lysander is puzzling. The Westland Lysander was a light monoplane with just enough room for four passengers in an emergency. Accordingly, it was unsuited to carrying heavy freight and the configuration of its wings prevented it from being used in parachute drops. As Professor Foot has observed, 'stores larger than a suitcase were not handled'.[43] Thus, Roxane's suggestion that a Lysander was used for this purpose is doubly wrong.

There are similar technical and chronological flaws in Roxane's remark about her preoccupation with V-weapons. At that time very little was known about either the V-1 or the V-2, which were then still in an experimental stage. Certainly there were no launching pads to be found and destroyed in France at the time she alleges, for the first reports of V-1 launch sites filtered from the Abbéville area at the end of October 1943. The first aerial reconnaissance pictures of six German secret weapon locations in a ten-mile radius of Abbéville reached the central photographic interpretation unit at RAF Medmenham during the first week of November 1943, eleven months after Roxane had left France. Obviously, she could have played no role whatever, as she claimed, in the detection and destruction of these sites.

In her second autobiography, she makes just a single remark concerning Alwyn Temple, the key figure in *The Courage of Fear*. She says: 'I can't reveal the Master's name nor am I sure about it; he changed his name and personality so often I could not keep track. But just to make things easy let me call him Mr Temple.'[44] This seems odd because, although she concedes that 'he had assured me that he had been a friend of my father's',[45] she appears to have forgotten that her father had given her the introduction to him in the first place.

A further mystery surrounds Roxane's relationship with Alain Romans, whose help Roxane had acknowledged in *The Courage of Fear*, without actually mentioning him in the text. However, in *Operation Double Life*, she describes the circumstances of their encounter, which is important as it sheds light on the central atrocity upon which Barry

Wynne's *The Empty Coffin* is based. In that version, it was alleged that Romans had been dropped into France in 1941 by SOE on a secret mission, and that all six participants had been caught by the Gestapo and shot. Miraculously, Romans had succeeded in cheating death. Roxane refers to this episode, but recounts an entirely different story, of six Jews who

> were found hiding in a cellar. The Germans lined them up against the wall in the very street where they were captured and shot them. A few bystanders were asked to bury them, in the ditch, by the Seine. One of the impoverished diggers came to report to Philippe de Vomécourt that the men were not all dead, one or perhaps two seemed alive and should be dug out quickly. We saved one: he was Alain Roman [*sic*], the composer, whose escape he himself narrated in his book. . . .[46]

Although Roxane's account gives no indication of the date at which this remarkable incident occurred, there can be little doubt that it is supposed to be the same one recounted by Barry Wynne, although the latter had not mentioned Philippe de Vomécourt's involvement. Indeed, de Vomécourt himself, who was one of three key SOE agents, had neglected to mention it in his 1959 autobiography, *Army of Amateurs*.[47] Furthermore, Wynne's tale took place not on the Seine, as alleged by Roxane, but in Brittany, and in his book the 'unfortunate creatures' were SOE agents.[48] Could this be one of those most unusual of phenomena, one fake being taken in by another, and developing an even more elaborate scenario?

If *The Courage of Fear* seemed strangely full of inconsistencies, improbabilities and contradictions, Roxane's second book makes the task of sorting fact from fiction quite impossible. Her convenient excuse is that 'the mysterious ways of the Intelligence Service are kept secret by the very fact that one is not allowed to ask when and where', so the reader is still left with conundrum after conundrum. As Roxane says in *Operation Double Life* (admittedly in another context), 'I have not solved that puzzle. It's practically impossible to get a straight answer from the men in MI5 or MI6.'[49]

16

The Druid

'The more plausible an experienced espionage agent's story sounds, the more suspiciously it should be regarded.'[1]

Subtitled *The Nazi Spy Who Double-Crossed the Double-Cross System*, Leonard Mosley's biography of the Sicherheitsdienst super-spy, allegedly codenamed *The Druid*, caused a sensation in 1981. Until the author disclosed the existence of this hitherto unsuspected agent, conventional wisdom had assumed that all the German networks in Britain had been arrested and successfully manipulated by the Security Service, MI5.

The first person outside the intelligence community really to study the subject of wartime German espionage was Ladislas Farago, a former US Naval Intelligence officer of Hungarian extraction, who stumbled across microfilm records of the Abwehr's secret files in the National Archives in Washington. He discovered that dozens of steel cases that had been left untouched since 1946 contained an extraordinarily comprehensive account of the operations conducted by several of the Abwehr's satellites. Of special interest was the Hamburg Abstelle, which, in line with the organisation's policy of delegating geographical targets to sub-units in each of the German military districts, had been granted decentralised responsibility for espionage in Britain and America. Farago was enchanted by his discovery, especially when he studied the films and realised that they represented proof of espionage on a previously unacknowledged scale. Some of the individual cases of espionage referred to were familiar to him as they had received publicity during the war when the British and American authorities announced the arrest of a particular spy-ring. However, Farago's treasure-trove placed the official statements in their proper perspective and gave a more detailed picture of the preparations made by the Germans for each mission. But what really astonished the researcher was the very large number of spies deployed by Hamburg to Britain and America, far more than Scotland Yard or the FBI had ever previously admitted. Not surprisingly, Farago interpreted the obvious discrepancy between the number of spies caught and those with apparently active files at headquarters in Hamburg as an indication that the Abwehr had been far more successful than anyone had ever contemplated, and that dozens of enemy agents had been free to operate without interference.

This sensational conclusion was the substance of the original version of Farago's book *The Game of the Foxes*,[2] which, at a very late stage, the author discovered was fatally flawed. His proposition that the Hamburg Abstelle had masterminded a massive, hitherto undiscovered espionage offensive against the Allies, was to be directly contradicted by Sir John Masterman, the former Chairman of the Twenty Committee, a secret body created in January 1941 which co-ordinated the work of British (and American) agencies with an interest in the phenomena of double agents. Shortly before publication of *The Game of the Foxes*, Farago was tipped off to the undisclosed fact that, whilst dozens of Hamburg's spies had indeed been active throughout the war, virtually all of them had come under the control of the two British intelligence organisations, MI5 and SIS. Far from being ignorant of the scale of German espionage, the entire effort had been turned against the Abwehr, for the greater part of the networks had been run directly from London.

Fortunately for Farago, he received word of Masterman's intention to reveal how, during the war, MI5 '*actively ran and controlled the German espionage system*'[3] in Britain and was able to rewrite large portions of his own book to take account of the insider's astonishing admission. This was a lucky break for Farago because, for example, he had intended to announce that the Abwehr agent numbered V-3725 had been free to transmit more than a thousand wireless messages between his arrival in Britain in September 1940 and the end of the war. However, having read Masterman's case history of the double agent codenamed *Tate*, it was plainly evident that Wulf Schmidt had been arrested and turned within a few days of his arrival, and that every one of his wireless transmissions had been made under the close supervision of his MI5 handlers, who had also carefully constructed the texts of all his secret messages. If, at the last moment, Farago had not been alerted to this sensitive secret, he might have been gravely embarrassed.

There was never any doubt about the validity of Masterman's story, which was authenticated not just by Professor Norman Holmes Pearson of Yale University, who was known to have worked alongside Masterman in MI5's wartime headquarters, but also by the struggle that the Oxford don had experienced in obtaining permission to publish. When the book was eventually released in 1972, it was published with the express consent of Prime Minister Edward Heath and the Foreign Secretary Sir Alec Douglas-Home (who had both been taught by Masterman); by agreement, half the royalties were to go to the Crown. The Government had originally opposed publication on the grounds of the continuing need for secrecy about wartime intelligence operations, but Masterman forced the reluctant co-operation of the authorities by threatening to circulate an unexpurgated edition in the USA. His trump card had been his unauthorised retention, in September 1945, of a book which he had been commissioned to write for the archives about his committee's work. This typescript was what was to be declassified and thus become his seminal study on the phenomenon of the double agent, each copy bearing a Crown copyright imprint.

In his book, *The Double Cross System of the War of 1939–45*, Masterman explained how each Abwehr agent had come under MI5's control, and described the system of interlocking networks created by the Germans that had been intended to lend their sources greater security. Before each agent arrived, he was invariably briefed with an emergency address where he could get help, and some assignments involved a check on the credentials of a previously established spy. This arrangement was supposed to provide Berlin with continuous confirmation, through random checks, that the Abwehr's agents were still at liberty and operating independently, and gave their men the security of a local contact if something went wrong with their mission. While this sounded a sensible procedure on paper, in practice it enabled MI5 to scoop up each arrival and supervise the appropriate signals to reassure the German controllers that all was well. It also gave the Security Service's case officers a method of ensuring that their own activities had remained undiscovered by the enemy. Thus, *Tate*'s imminent infiltration had been compromised by his friend Goesta Caroli, who was captured in early September 1940 and who had been promised that his life, and that of Wulf Schmidt, would be spared if he co-operated with his British captors. Codenamed *Summer*, Caroli was paid by an MI5 double agent of long standing, known as *Snow*. When Schmidt was interrogated, he admitted that he had been given an emergency contact, the address of a pianist in Al Lever's dance-band named Bernie, who, though of British parentage, had been brought up and educated in Germany. In fact, Bernie had volunteered to work for MI5 earlier in the war and had been allocated the codename *Rainbow*, so Schmidt's confession neatly served to confirm to the British authorities that Bernie's duplicity had gone unnoticed by the Abwehr. Bernie's apparent continued freedom indicated to the Germans that Schmidt was himself still at liberty, and in due course yet another spy, Karel Richter, was despatched to England in May 1941 for the purpose of supplying Schmidt with money and a new crystal for his wireless set. Richter's other assignment was to confirm Schmidt's continuing independence, but he too was intercepted by the police before he could endanger anyone.

In addition to the security offered by the German preference for interlocking spy-rings, instead of running their agents in a cellular system of carefully isolated compartments, MI5 also enjoyed a further advantage, which, at the time of Masterman's disclosures in 1972, was considered too sensitive to mention in any detail. Occasionally the author referred obliquely to unspecified 'secret sources' which had somehow given an insight into the enemy's intentions, and it was not until Group Captain Fred Winterbotham's revelations two years later regarding ULTRA that it emerged that the Radio Security Service (RSS) had enjoyed access to many of the Abwehr's clandestine communications. Winterbotham himself gave no direct acknowledgment of what the RSS had accomplished in the cryptographic field, but the fact that so many of the enemy's Enigma keys had been solved itself suggested an explanation for Masterman's discreet remarks about 'secret sources'. So, as well as monitoring the day-to-day work of their double agents, evidently MI5 had also tapped into the enemy's wireless circuits and had read the Abwehr's assessment of the performance of each agent. This proved to be a hugely important inside track for it allowed MI5 to adjust its handling of a particular agent so as to coincide with the wishes and expectations of his (or her) Abwehr controllers. In other words, the Security Service could not only check on the standing of each double agent by monitoring others in the network, but it could also alter the behaviour of each to ensure the maximum satisfaction for all parties concerned, not the least of these being the Abwehr.

This, then, was the context in which Leonard Mosley announced that although the Abwehr had been duped by MI5's control over its wartime sources, the rival Nazi security agency, the Sicherheitsdienst, had been immune to the deception and had operated an agent in Britain entirely independently. Indeed, the Security Service itself had scarcely believed its luck when it had belatedly realised that its impressive stable of double agents appeared to represent the sum total of the enemy's intelligence efforts in Britain.

Mosley, whose career as a respected author and foreign correspondent dated back to before the war when he had served as a *Sunday Times* journalist in Berlin, said that he had first received hints that such a spy had existed when researching his book on Johan Eppler entitled *The Cat and the Mice*, which was published in 1960.[4] Eppler was an Abwehr agent who had been arrested in Egypt in 1942 and had been turned, albeit reluctantly, into a double agent by the British security authorities. Mosley claimed to have first met Eppler in Cairo while working under the control of MI5's local branch, Security Intelligence Middle East (SIME). According to Mosley, Eppler had been approached by Ernst Kaltenbrunner of the Sicherheitsdienst because the SS 'had become increasingly dissatisfied with the intelligence it was receiving from the principal Nazi espionage service, the Abwehr, and had decided to put its own agent in place, not only to send back information but also to check on the quality of the work done by the rival organisation'[5] in England. Eppler had turned down the offer to become a spy in London and instead had opted for a mission in North Africa, heeding Kaltenbrunner's warning not to discuss his suggestion with the Abwehr. Indeed, the SD officer had later confirmed to him that another candidate had been selected for the assignment and had been despatched successfully to England:

Eppler never did tell the Abwehr that the SS had sent a rival spy to England. But later, when being debriefed in Cairo by the SIS, he mentioned it to his British interrogators. That was in 1942. Undoubtedly they passed on this fascinating item of information to London. Neither Eppler nor I knew anything about the Double Cross System at that time, but the SIS was well aware that all Abwehr agents in England had already been captured and 'turned'. Eppler's information must have given them their first warning that an independent spy was still running loose in Britain, even though he could give them no information at that time as to who and where he was.[6]

After the war, Mosley tracked Eppler to his bookshop in the Saarland to collaborate on the story of his espionage adventures and, in doing so, again raised the topic of German espionage in Britain. On this occasion, Eppler had apparently made an interesting disclosure. Soon after the German surrender, Eppler had been repatriated and had accidentally been placed in a camp reserved for hardened Nazis. Here he had been cross-examined by two British intelligence officers, who had demanded to know more about his conversations with Kaltenbrunner, 'and in particular, more details about the SD spy who had been sent to Britain by him. Who was he? Where did he come from? What was his background?'

Rather grudgingly, the interrogators let slip the fact that there were rumors an SS agent had somehow managed to infiltrate into Britain during the war and succeeded in operating without being detected. Moreover, Eppler gained the impression that he had contrived to vanish in the confusion created by the end of the war, and that the British had lost track of him. Captured senior SS officers were being stubborn and uncooperative, and the records had been burned.[7]

Considering that he had already co-operated with SIME, Eppler had been anxious to find new accommodation and, having insisted to his two interrogators that he knew nothing of the agent recruited by Kaltenbrunner, had sent a plea to a British intelligence officer named 'Captain N. Elliot', who had not only handled his case in Cairo, but conveniently had recently been transferred to field security duties in Hamburg. In his message, Eppler had threatened to reveal his role in Cairo and 'tell about DRUID'. This had been sufficient to secure his release from captivity 'within a few days . . . with a clean bill of health'.[8]

Prompted by this rather remarkable turn of events, Mosley had researched the possibility that the SD had sent a spy codenamed *The Druid* to England, and apparently found some evidence in the Allied interrogation records of two suspected war criminals, SS Standarten-führer Walter Huppenkothen and Kriminal Inspektor Hugo Hoffmann.

Huppenkothen had been prosecuted at Munich in January 1951, and again at Augsburg in October 1955, and had subsequently served a total of ten years' imprisonment. According to Mosley, Huppenkothen and Hoffmann had been very suspicious of the Abwehr's performance in England and had advocated sending a trusted SS agent there to report independently. And although 'neither Huppenkothen nor Hoffmann made any mention of the agent the SS eventually dispatched to England',[9] there were three references in some reports compiled by Kaltenbrunner in 1944 to what he had termed 'our information from England'.[10] This, Mosley asserts, is *prima facie* evidence of the existence of a hitherto undiscovered spy: 'It seems that Huppenkothen, Hoffmann, and Kaltenbrunner took the most rigorous steps to see that all references to their agent were either destroyed or expunged from what SS records were left behind.'[11]

In other words, the only documentary corroboration Mosley could find for Eppler's tale lay in three rather vague allusions to 'information from England', and one further ambiguous item culled from the records of another war crimes prosecution, that of Kriminalkommissar Franz Sonderregger. Together with Huppenkothen, this unsavoury individual had participated in the Gestapo's investigation of three Abwehr officers who had been suspected of making contact with the British. During their interrogation, he had repeatedly threatened them with information that, he claimed, had come from a Welsh source in London. The transcripts of these interrogations, of Josef Muller, Hans von Dohnanyi and Dietrich Bonhoffer, had been used by the public prosecutor in Lüneburg at Sonderregger's trial, although Mosley noticed that the intriguing references to Huppenkothen's 'special source of information in England', and in particular 'our Welsh comrade',[12] had mysteriously but significantly been omitted from the documents presented in court.

These were the rather obscure hints that had encouraged Mosley to pursue the identity of the unknown SD spy, and the author says that he received assistance from two unexpected sources. The first were apparently victims of 'a panic purge'[13] conducted inside the British intelligence community following the defections of Guy Burgess and Donald Maclean, followed by H. A. R. (Kim) Philby, and culminating in the arrest of George Blake. Exactly when this purge was supposed to have occurred is unclear, for Burgess and Maclean defected in 1951, and by the time Philby defected in 1963 Blake had already been arrested and convicted.

Whatever the exact timing, the author claims that some of his information relating to *The Druid* came from disaffected members of the British
intelligence community, who were 'thrown out of the service', but

> were completely innocent of any involvement and were therefore
> considerably aggrieved at the abrupt termination of their careers.
> Others found to have been involved, directly or peripherally, with
> the Soviet KGB were given the choice of being tried for treason
> or of continuing their lives as double agents – this time against
> rather than for the Russians.[14]

This is strong meat indeed, for 'it was from these elements, their lips
loosened by the unexpected turn of events, that details began to emerge
of the British side of the wartime espionage story, from which came
clues to the background and activities of the Druid'.[15] In plain English,
this means that Mosley says that he was told about *The Druid* by people
who had been thrown out of SIS for being suspected, correctly or incorrectly, of treachery.

His second unexpected source was a previously unpublished manuscript written by one of MI5's wartime double agents, the Welshman
named Arthur Owens:

> After the war he tried to write an account of his checkered career
> as not just a double but as a triple spy, but could never get per-
> mission to publish it. But extracts have been seen by some of his
> ex-colleagues, and they have found them more than surprising.
> They certainly add some startling new facets to the story of the
> Double Cross System.[16]

To his credit, Mosley makes it clear from the beginning that his
material has been constructed over a number of years. He says candidly: 'I make no apology for recreating some of the incidents,
reconstructing and rejigging others, and reproducing conversations to
which I could hardly have been privy. I can say no more than they are
based on memories and recollections.'[17] He cautions the reader to be
wary 'about the motives of professional people' and warns that all the
codenames and characters are authentic 'with four exceptions and I have
concealed their identity for personal reasons'.[18]

The essence of Mosley's story is that the Sicherheitsdienst did indeed recruit a spy who operated in London and successfully evaded MI5. His true name was Gwyn Evans, a fervent Welsh Nationalist, who had been born in 1915 to a Welsh father and German mother in Gaiman, Patagonia. Educated at a British prep school in Buenos Aires, he had been a member of the Wesleyan chapel choir of Bryn Crwn which had won a prize in the Gaiman Eisteddfod in 1928, and the following summer he had sung at the international competition held annually at Caernarvon Castle in Wales. In 1932, he spent a month on a German training ship, which called in at Bahia Blanca, and subsequently he joined the Nazi Party with his mother. In 1937, his mother took him to Germany, where he enrolled at the University of Berlin to study languages, literature and the violin. He could speak German, Spanish, Welsh and English fluently, and this facility with languages may have brought him to the attention of the SD. In any event, Huppenkothen and Hoffmann had already voiced their doubts about the integrity of the Abwehr's operations in England and had advised Kaltenbrunner to ascertain whether its information was genuine. 'There is only one way to find out. We need a trustworthy agent of our own – in England. Sent over there unknown to the Abwehr, to discover the truth for us.'[19]

Exactly how Evans was recruited is unknown for Mosley's account jumps from Evans's academic life to that of a secret agent, parachuting into the Welsh hills overlooking Cardigan Bay on the night of 10 May 1941. He was apparently flown in a 'Junkers courier plane'[20] from an airfield near Cherbourg and dropped not far from Swansea while hundreds of Luftwaffe bombers created a diversion elsewhere, allowing another German agent, Captain Heinz Richter, to land 'in the flat marshlands of Lincolnshire'.[21] Richter suffered the misfortune of being swiftly arrested 'by British security police',[22] but Evans was luckier and transmitted a safe-arrival signal before making his way to 16 Kidwelly Street in Swansea, where he contacted Arthur Owens.

Arthur Owens was MI5's double agent, who, according to Mosley, succeeded in duping his Security Service case officers by acting as Evans's principal contact. His motive for helping *The Druid* was his love for Trudy Korner, 'a tall, Nordic, leggy blonde with an angelic face and a sympathetic voice', who 'was ostensibly a member of the secretarial pool at the German embassy in Grosvenor Square, but had been a member of the SS since she was seventeen years old'.[23] Owens had confided in her that he was already working for both the Abwehr and MI5, and she had duly reported this. Owens wanted to marry Trudy and on a visit to Hamburg in August 1939 had been told by the Reich Security Agency (RHSA) that his future with her would depend on his willingness to co-operate with the SD: 'Owens learned that henceforth he would be not a double spy but a triple one. He would continue to serve the British and the Abwehr, but he would report on both of them to the RHSA.'[24]

This arrangement, though made under duress, apparently suited Owens, who travelled to Lisbon to confirm his compliance and meet Trudy. Obligingly, she had been posted as a secretary in the German Embassy, and during the forty-eight hours he was in Portugal Owens established contact with his new Abwehr controller, Paul von Fidrmuc, and delivered information about British airfields and aircraft production'.[25] Upon his return to London, Owens continued to play a complicated double game serving both the Germans and MI5, but when he encountered Evans he gave no hint of his divided allegiance, but neither apparently did he report the arrival of Evans to his Security Service case officer.

Having established himself with rented rooms in Praed Street, Paddington, and having found a job with the Council for the Encouragement of Music and the Arts (CEMA), Evans embarked upon his mission as a spy operating independently. As a member of CEMA, he attended a concert given for troops of the Canadian 2nd Division near Ryde in the Isle of Wight; there he had learned from a French Canadian lieutenant of an imminent seaborne assault on the coast of France. When Evans transmitted his first message back to his Lisbon controller, Paul von Fidrmuc, 'late in May, 1942',[26] he revealed that the Allies intended to launch a raid on Dieppe on Midsummer's Day, codenamed Operation RUTTER. When the attack failed to materialise as predicted, Evans was informed by his earlier French Canadian source of the postponement, and duly relayed the information to Portugal in good time, three days before the operation. As the author commented unequivocally, 'It was quite obvious from the start that the Wehrmacht knew they were coming, and had made all the necessary preparations. It was the Druid's first success.'[27]

It was also through Evans's connection with CEMA that he met Tommy Harris, an art dealer and MI5 case officer. Harris invited Evans to a party at his sumptuous home in Chesterfield Gardens, where he was introduced to some of Harris's friends, among them Guy Burgess, Kim Philby and a Spanish newspaper correspondent, Luis Calvo. When he accidentally overheard Harris and Calvo compiling the text of a signal for the Abwehr, Evans 'sent a message to his control in Lisbon asking for discreet enquiries to be made in Madrid and Berlin about the background and proclivities' of the journalist. His reply

> came back from Hugo Hoffman [*sic*] himself. It informed him that Calvo was the most successful agent the Abwehr had ever infiltrated into enemy territory, his achievements so invaluable that a campaign was being mounted in Berlin to have the Führer thank him personally – if he survived, of course.[28]

Having been informed that Calvo was the Abwehr's star agent codenamed *Arabel*, Evans was incredulous and deeply suspicious. However, before he could report his doubts to Lisbon, he was himself the subject of an investigation conducted by his new acquaintance, Kim Philby. Evans's contact in Portugal, Paul von Fidrmuc, was himself playing a double game and had admitted to Philby that he had an active sub-agent in London. To identify the spy, Philby obtained the release from prison of another Abwehr agent, Vera von Schallburg, who had been caught and convicted of espionage in 1940. During her interrogation, she had reported to another SIS officer, Denzil Roberts, that she had met a mysterious Welshman while training, and Roberts divulged this information to Philby, who arranged for the beautiful Norwegian to befriend Evans in the hope that she would recognise him and extract a confession from him. Evans, however, was too shrewd for Vera and checked her bona fides with Owens. When Owens informed him that Vera had been thoroughly compromised, Evans held one last rendezvous with her and then vanished. His disappearance was linked to his discovery that *Arabel* was really a double agent working for the British. But when Evans reported *Arabel*'s treachery to von Fidrmuc, his message was ignored, leading him to deduce, correctly, that he had also been deceived by his own controller. Vera too dropped from sight, leading Mosley to speculate that

> the only certain thing is that since June 2, 1944, when she turned up at King's Cross station for her meeting with the Druid, Vera de Schallberg [*sic*] has never been seen again. Was the Druid responsible for her disappearance? Well perhaps. But not quite in the way one might imagine. For there are strong rumours –

which again no official source will confirm or deny – that after
Vera came back from her trip to Scotland with the Druid, she was
picked up and interrogated. As a result of those interviews, so
the story goes, she was arrested and subsequently charged and
tried for espionage in time of war. And hanged.[29]

Finally, Mosley concludes his story with further speculation which
'some of the former members of the Double Cross System helped him
piece'[30] together: quite simply that Philby, with the support of Owens,
traced Evans and recruited him as a KGB agent!

The proposition that there was a Sicherheitsdienst agent operating
independently in Britain is an interesting one and raises two questions:
what is the quality of the external evidence cited for his existence, and
how good were Mosley's sources?

The answer to the first, in terms of chronological fact, is not encour-
aging. According to the author, Evans was dropped into Wales on 10 May
1941, the same night that 'Heinz Richter landed in the flat marshlands of
Lincolnshire'.[31] However, Karel Richter is the only Abwehr agent who
matches Mosley's description, and he was parachuted into a Hertford-
shire field four days later, on 14 May 1941. So what about Arthur Owens,
the MI5 double agent who received Evans in May 1941 and was able to
advise him about Vera de Schallburg's unreliability in June 1944?
According to the official account, Owens was taken into custody in
September 1939 in Wandsworth and, apart from a brief spell at liberty in
1940, remained in prison at Dartmoor from March 1941 until the end of
hostilities. Similarly Kim Philby was not 'the liaison officer between MI5
and MI6'[32] at the time he is introduced into Mosley's narrative. Indeed,
Philby did not even join MI6 until September 1941, and when he did he
never held the post described.

If it is difficult to confirm *The Druid*'s existence from the text, what
about the principal achievement credited to the spy: warning the
Germans of an imminent attack on Dieppe three days before it took
place? Certainly the original plan, codenamed RUTTER, had been abandoned in July and then reinstated in August as Operation JUBILEE, as
has been described in Chapter 9. But is there, as Mosley asserts, evidence 'that the Wehrmacht knew they were coming'?[33] This is an issue
that has been analysed at some length by historians, who are almost
unanimous that the enemy had not been forewarned, but that the element of surprise had been lost when the Allied armada unexpectedly

encountered a small convoy of five German ships in the Channel escorted by three fast gunboats. The three submarine chasers, the *4011* and the *1404*, led by the *1411*, had been engaged by the much larger Allied fleet, and an alert had been transmitted to shore where a radar-based report from the Pourville *Freya* station had already been disregarded by the High Command.

Because the Dieppe raid took such an appalling toll of Canadian troops who were trapped in a crossfire on the beaches, with 3,623 casualties, some of those who escaped were convinced that the only explanation for the catastrophe lay in treachery. As Terence Robertson remarked in *Dieppe: The Shame and the Glory*, 'the sense of betrayal shared by this minority had nothing to support it'.[34] Nevertheless, the fear of treachery has been exploited by others, including Christopher Creighton, but none has produced any convincing evidence. Indeed, as has already been seen, enemy documents captured during the raid indicate that no special alert had been received by the Wehrmacht and that the local garrison had not been strengthened recently, and definitely not in the three days prior to 19 August. As James Leasor, who has made an exhaustive study of the raid for his *Green Beach*, concluded: 'The Germans had no prior warning of Jubilee; Canadian and British security had not been breached.'[35]

If *The Druid* existed, and he really did give the enemy advance warning of JUBILEE, no trace of that warning survives, and such evidence as there is – both from Field Marshal von Rundstedt's headquarters and from documents recovered from the two battalions of the 571st Infantry Regiment that comprised the Dieppe garrison – tends to militate against the possibility. So what then of *The Druid*'s other really significant accomplishment, his timely identification of Luis Calvo as the Abwehr agent codenamed *Arabel*, also known to MI5 as the double agent *Garbo*? This is a particularly interesting proposition because Mosley could hardly have been more wrong. His central thesis is that *The Druid* accidentally overheard Luis Calvo plotting with Tommy Harris at the latter's home in Chesterfield Gardens in 1944 and, upon checking with his controller in Lisbon, was informed that the journalist was *Arabel*. He was thus able to alert the enemy to *Arabel*'s duplicity, although his signal was deliberately ignored because of Paul von Fidrmuc's treachery.

At the time Mosley wrote *The Druid*, he had every reason to believe that Calvo was *Arabel*, for he had been identified as such, albeit incorrectly, by Richard Deacon in *The British Connection* as early as 1979.[36] Calvo was the London correspondent of the Madrid daily *ABC*, but his

Spanish nationality and his presence in London during most of the war was all that he shared with *Garbo*, whose true identity was not to emerge until 1984, three years after the publication of *The Druid*. Calvo was as surprised as anyone by Deacon's mistake, but he did little to correct the author because the offending book had been withdrawn by the publishers after libel proceedings had been brought by someone else. The main difficulty about Deacon's, and Mosley's, identification of Calvo as *Arabel/Garbo* was that the journalist was never at liberty in London in 1944 to visit Tommy Harris at his home, or anyone else. From the moment of his arrival in Britain in February 1943, until his deportation in August 1945, he was kept a prisoner in MI5's interrogation centre at Camp 020 on Ham Common. This means that the entire section of *The Druid*, in which Mosley describes dozens of verbatim conversations and wireless signals connecting *Arabel* and Calvo, must have been fabricated. Indeed, in June 1984 the real *Garbo* emerged from Caracas, Venezuela, where he had lived since the end of the war, and revealed his true identity as that of Juan Pujol. He later gave a detailed account of his activities as MI5's star double agent in his memoirs, *GARBO*, and for anyone with any lingering doubts, his credentials were confirmed in Volume v of the official history of *British Intelligence in the Second World War*, released in 1990.[37]

This critical error, Mosley's identification of *Garbo*, combined with his baseless assertion that the Dieppe raid had been betrayed, renders *The Druid* valueless as a work of non-fiction, but one is bound to wonder why, and how, a biographer of Mosley's reputation should perpetrate a hoax. As to his motives, they are difficult to fathom, and as the author died at his home on Captiva Island, Florida, in June 1992, they cannot be challenged. His methodology, however, is a textbook example of mixing verifiable fact with plausible sounding fabrication. This is well illustrated by the references to Paul Fidrmuc, the German spy codenamed *Ostro*, whom Mosley asserts was Evans's controller, and the man whom Philby visited in Lisbon, recruited and turned into a double agent in 1943. Paul Fidrmuc was indeed *Ostro*, but his true story was rather different to the one presented by Mosley, who relies on a single sentence in Dusko Popov's memoirs, *Spy CounterSpy*, for a wholly fanciful account of a trip to Lisbon allegedly made by Philby to investigate *Ostro*.

Paul Fidrmuc was indeed a Sudeten German living in Lisbon, who earned money by manufacturing reports and claims for expenses from notional sub-agents. In some respects his experience is similar to Juan

Pujol's, who also began his intelligence career by inventing messages purporting to come from England. However, while Pujol approached the British and was enrolled as the double agent *Garbo* in April 1942, *Ostro* remained undetected by the British authorities until the autumn of 1943. Once identified from Abwehr decrypts, various suggestions were made to eliminate him, but, as Masterman recorded, 'they did not succeed. Consequently *Ostro* continued to operate and cause us anxiety till the end of the war.' So if Masterman had confirmed in 1972 that *Ostro* had never come under British control, how did Mosley get the idea that the imaginative spy had been recruited by Philby? The answer is to be found only in *Spy CounterSpy*, where the wartime double agent Dusko Popov says that 'MI6 got on the case immediately, sending Kim Philby to Lisbon to work on the case. By our combined efforts we soon knew more than the Abwehr about Fidrmuc.'[38]

Mosley's trust in Popov was misplaced, for although the double agent did alert his MI5 handlers to the existence of *Ostro*, and was given the false impression by them that this was valuable news, the reality was that all of *Ostro*'s communications with the Abwehr had been intercepted and decrypted from the beginning. When Popov volunteered information about von Fidrmuc in November 1943, having been handed it by his Abwehr contact who was anxious to defect, it was ancient history to the Security Service, although, for security reasons, it was obviously preferable to prevent Popov, who had not been indoctrinated into the secret of MI5's access to the Abwehr's signals, from learning the truth. Indeed, even at the time of the publication of his autobiography in 1974, Popov had no idea that Bletchley Park had been decrypting much of the Abwehr's wireless traffic. He had read Masterman's book, *The Double Cross System* . . ., which had been published two years earlier, but he had not yet read Fred Winterbotham's *The Ultra Secret*, which appeared in 1974, just before his own account. Not surprisingly, he had failed to grasp the very few veiled hints made by Masterman to the astonishing Allied success in the signals intelligence field and, therefore, had every reason to believe that MI5 had been tipped off to *Ostro*'s existence by him.

In fact, Philby did not go to Lisbon in November 1943, or at any other time during the war; nor did he have control over SIS's operations in the region. This common misconception has led countless authors to exaggerate Philby's wartime role in the Iberian peninsula, which was really that of a traffic analyst engaged in the detailed study of enemy signals. Philby supervised Section v's counter-intelligence teams, which scrutinised every Abwehr decrypt relating to Spain and Portugal (and later North Africa and Italy). Each geographical area was the responsibility of a separate sub-division of Section v, which was itself to be the largest in SIS, employing 1,000 intelligence personnel. Philby's post was one that required his continuous presence at Section v's offices, first at St Albans and then in Ryder Street, until his appointment to another branch late in 1944. It was unnecessary for him to travel abroad, and Section v's sensitive business was conducted in the field by specially indoctrinated officers attached by Section v to each SIS station overseas. In Madrid, Section v's representative was Kenneth Benton, an experienced SIS officer who was attached to the Embassy under diplomatic cover. In Lisbon, it was Ralph Jarvis, a merchant banker based at the British Repatriation Office. Thus, the investigation of *Ostro* was conducted in Portugal by Jarvis.

Popov never met Philby and never even knew of his existence until the spy achieved notoriety in 1968 through press publicity and the publication of his autobiography, *My Silent War*,[39] in which, incidentally, he mentions only two overseas trips during the war, to France and Italy early in 1945, and later in the summer to Germany and Greece. Nor does Philby refer in it to *Ostro*, so what prompted Popov to insert the single, unfounded sentence about Philby leading an investigation in Lisbon? Popov died in August 1981 so he cannot tell us, but he also died just before the release of *The Druid*, so he was never in a position to correct Mosley, even if he had been inclined to do so. Mosley seized on Popov's gratuitous and unsubstantiated assertion, and exploited this flimsy evidence to justify the proposition that Philby had not just met Fidrmuc, but had actually recruited him. Not surprisingly, while Mosley often quoted Masterman, he appears to have overlooked the latter's emphatic statement that *Ostro* never fell under Allied control. To have done so, of course, would have removed a key component of *The Druid*.

That Mosley intended *The Druid* to be taken as a work of non-fiction is undoubted. He cautions the reader in his introduction only to make allowances for some of the scenes in which he had presented conversations which he could not have witnessed. Nevertheless, he vouches for the book' s provenance, claiming that it comes from intelligence sources which are

based on memories and recollections. A word of warning about that: as I write later on in this narrative about the motives of

professional intelligence people, which are you to believe? Are
some of them deliberately deceiving you for their own dark purposes? But all the codenames (both Nazi and SIS) used in this
narrative are the actual ones by which the agents involved were
known during World War ii. So are all the names of the characters – with four exceptions and I have concealed their identity for
personal reasons.[40]

Thus, Mosley alleges that his story has come from insiders, even if
their memory might be slightly faulty. This is important because his
book makes several quite extravagant claims. For example, he asserted
that 'at least two and probably four MI5 officers working inside the
Double Cross System and manipulating captured Abwehr agents were
also working for the KGB'.[41] This is quite an allegation, and is emphasised by another statement concerning British personnel 'found to have
been involved, directly or peripherally, with the Soviet KGB'.[42] These
people, according to Mosley, 'were given the choice of being tried for
treason or of continuing their lives as double agents – this time against
rather than for the Russians. Indications of the identity of some of these
individuals will be found in the narrative that follows.'[43] Thus, the author
has not only suggested that at least two MI5 officers were traitors, but
that his book contained clues to their identities. Not surprisingly, this
engaged the attention of the surviving wartime case officers, and succeeded in enraging them to the extent that four of them wrote a letter of
protest to the British publishers, Eyre Methuen. The four were Colonel
T. A. Robertson, the former head of MI5's B1(a) section which handled
the Abwehr double agents, and three of his subordinates: Cyril Mills,
Christopher Harmer and William Luke. Of these, only Robertson had
been identified and quoted in *The Druid*, and he vehemently denied ever
having been in contact with Mosley, or having participated in any conversation of the kind reported by the author. So if Robertson had not
supplied Mosley's material, who had? An analysis of the British
Intelligence personalities mentioned in *The Druid*, in order of their
appearance in the text, makes an interesting exercise.

The first, already referred to, is 'Nicholas Elliot',[44] the person Mosley
described as 'an SIS officer with the same last name who had acted as
one of Eppler's contacts during the war',[45] and who had allegedly
secured Eppler's release from detention in Germany after the war. This
must surely be Nicholas Elliott, a former senior SIS officer who served

in the Middle East during the war and was briefly in Cairo, although he was never one of Eppler's case officers. Nor was Elliott 'case officer for another persuasive double agent, Tricycle (Dusko Popov)',[46] nor was he in Germany after the war, although he was assigned to the SIS station in Berne and Vienna in the immediate post-war era. Curiously, he did work, briefly, for Colonel Robertson's section in MI5 in 1940 before he was transferred to Istanbul for SIS.

The next officer to be mentioned by Mosley is Kim Philby, whose help he had sought while compiling a biography of the Dulles family. Although Philby plays a key role in *The Druid*, it is very doubtful that their correspondence covered any substantive issues as virtually all Mosley's observations concerning Philby, who 'had control of the SIS Iberian sector',[47] and MI5, which he erroneously describes as 'the internal wing of SIS',[48] are flawed.

An SIS officer given equal prominence to Philby in *The Druid* is 'Denzil Roberts', who Mosley says 'was a veteran of the counterintelligence business'[49] and who had been involved in the Venlo fiasco in November 1940. This is a positive clue to the true identity of Roberts, for when Sigismund Payne Best and Richard Stevens were abducted from Holland by the Sicherheitsdienst, one of their staff was Rodney Dennys. Mosley describes 'Roberts, who had been delivering dispatches and had gone along for the ride,'[50] as having been on the scene when the SIS men were seized on Dutch territory and hauled across the frontier into Germany. Now although Dennys never went to Venlo, he was in The Hague on that fateful morning, and he also served in the Middle East, as referred to by the author. Accordingly, given the similarity in the sound of the two names, it is probable that Mosley intended to conceal Roberts's true identity. But why should he have done so, for there is nothing in the text that is remotely pejorative of Dennys? Certainly Dennys has no answer, for although he has confirmed that he knew Mosley before the war, and had seen him very occasionally since, he never gave the author permission to quote him in the terms attributed to Denzil Roberts. Dennys acknowledges that he is 'Denzil Roberts' and this admission indirectly identifies another of Mosley's characters with a false name. Denzil Roberts is mentioned as having a 'girlfriend and colleague, Ann Kirby',[51] and since Rodney Dennys courted and married Elizabeth Greene, who was indeed an SIS colleague, there remain only two other British intelligence personnel whose true identities can be seen to have been disguised.

Five other British intelligence officers are mentioned in the text. The first is John Newcob, the Oxford mathematician 'who liaised between the XX Committee and GCCS [the Government Code and Cipher School] at Bletchley Park'.[52] As there was never any 'John Newcob' in MI5 or GCCS during the war, this presumably is a reference to Herbert Hart, the MI5 officer and future Professor of Jurisprudence at Oxford, who headed B1(b), the Security Service section responsible for the analysis of enemy decrypts from Bletchley. His appearance in the text is very innocuous and no conclusions can be drawn from it. Cecil Gladhill, 'the SIS station chief in Lisbon',[53] however, is a rather different case. The reference to Gladhill must be to Cecil Gledhill, who did indeed fulfil the post described by Mosley. However, the author's mistaken spelling of his surname, on several occasions, serves to confirm that one of Mosley's sources had been, not Gledhill himself, but Dusko Popov, or at least his memoirs: Mosley had made the same spelling error that had occurred repeatedly in Popov's autobiography, *Spy CounterSpy*.[54]

The other three MI5 officers to be identified by name by Mosley were Sir John Masterman (whom the author described as 'retired and living in Oxford',[55] when he had died four years earlier, in June 1977); Tomas Harris, *Garbo*'s case officer, who had been killed in a car accident in January 1964; and Anthony Blunt, one of Herbert Hart's colleagues in B1(b), who had been exposed publicly as a Soviet spy in November 1979. On the assumption that Blunt was one of the traitors Mosley had in mind, in that he qualifies by virtue of his status as a wartime MI5 officer and his (limited) knowledge of the double-cross operations conducted by B1(b), there remains at least one, and possibly as many as three others, involved with the KGB. This was the inference that infuriated Robertson, Luke (who had been Popov's case officer), Mills (who had first handled *Garbo*) and Harmer. Who among their wartime colleagues was Mosley accusing? It was a question he never answered.

The most likely explanation is that Mosley invented Evans *The Druid*, and that there never was any such person. Most of the book can be traced to three published sources: Ladislas Farago's *The Game of the Foxes*; Masterman's *The Double Cross System in the War of 1939–45* and Popov's *Spy CounterSpy*.

17

The Unknown Warrior

'Fiction, after all, is only a distorting mirror for truth, and often a dull and cloudy mirror.'[1]

Subtitled '*The true story of the spy who ensured the success of the Normandy invasion*', James Leasor's account of a mission undertaken by Stefan Rosenberg to France in May 1944 was published in 1981 as *The Unknown Warrior*. According to the author, who had been attracted to the story following the success of *Green Beach*, in which he had documented the authentic exploits of Jack Nissenthall at Pourville,[2] Stefan Rosenberg was an Austrian of Jewish extraction who had been brought to England by his parents just before the First World War as a baby of only a few weeks. When war broke out, his parents returned to Germany, but Stefan, stricken with diphtheria, remained in the Arnold Street, Salford, home of their landlord, a certain Mr Rigby. After the war, when the Rigbys' eldest child perished of influenza, the Rosenbergs were informed in error that Stefan had died. In fact, the Rigbys had given Stefan their son's identity and, thereafter, he had been brought up as Stephen Rigby.

In 1938, Stefan travelled to Vienna to be reunited with his real parents. Soon after the plebiscite, his father moved to Switzerland, but died in Geneva. His widow then moved to Montreal to stay permanently with a cousin, while Stefan returned to England and found work in a wireless factory in Hendon. At the outbreak of war, Stefan was detained on the Isle of Man as an enemy alien, and was then shipped across the Atlantic to the Sherbrooke internment camp in Canada, where, late in 1940, he accepted an invitation extended by an official visitor, Sir Alexander Paterson, to return to England and join the Pioneer Corps. As HM Commissioner of Prisons, Paterson had been appointed by the Home Secretary to inspect conditions in the Canadian internment camps, which accommodated so many of Britain's enemy aliens; he also appears to have acted as an unofficial recruiter for those willing to fight the Nazis.

As the Pioneer Corps usually undertook a rather unglamorous non-combatant role – for example, Stefan had to dig ditches and latrines in Bideford, and clear bomb damage in Liverpool – he volunteered for a transfer to a new commando troop which would see action. Having been accepted, he was invited to apply for an even more dangerous assignment, and during an initial interview in an office overlooking St James's Park, an unnamed major described his task: to persuade the enemy 'that we will land in the Pas de Calais. Other landings, if any, will simply be for diversionary purposes.'

> You are required to proceed to France by parachute or light aircraft, ostensibly as someone involved with the French Resistance. You will be supplied with papers as a French citizen and you will also carry other more secret documents which will back up what you have to tell the Germans.[3]

The scheme explained to Stefan at this preliminary meeting by the officer, identified only as a former history don at Cambridge, was remarkably bold. He was to masquerade as an Abwehr agent recruited in England by one of MI5's double agents:

> Over the past four years we have captured a number of German agents who landed in this country, and they are working for us and not the Abwehr. Their German masters, of course, do not know this and trust them implicitly. . . . These agents will corroborate your story, of course. And remember that many in the German High Command already believe implicitly what you will have come to tell them. Your presence – with other measures that we will undertake here to substantiate your information – will reinforce their belief and should bring the doubters into line.[4]

Having had his credentials established and confirmed by an Abwehr double agent, Stefan was to insinuate himself into SOE, be dropped into France and be ready to contact the Germans within twenty-four hours of his arrival, identifying himself as *Nimrod*.

Having duped the enemy, Stefan was to wait for the invasion and then to 'get out of their sight as quickly and discreetly as you can'.[5] Undaunted by his assignment, Stefan underwent training 'for several days, the maximum time to spare in view of the urgency of his assignment,'[6] at one of SOE's special schools at Beaulieu in Hampshire, and acquired the identity of Stéphane Dubillier in anticipation of his acceptance into the French resistance as a wireless expert. After a further briefing by 'Captain Angus' at the Polygon Hotel in Southampton, he was taken to a military base in Portsmouth, where he was given authentic French clothes and the usual suicide pill, and put under hypnosis so that he would recall his cover story under interrogation. Stefan was then driven to a house in Kent to meet Ricard, a French agent who had undertaken several missions into France, and with whom he was to travel. Having been introduced as a wireless expert equipped with an apparatus to boost the signal strength of resistance transmitters, Stefan accompanied Ricard to an airfield outside Chichester, where a Lysander pilot was under instructions 'to land two agents in Northern France and bring one out'. The decorated RAF flight lieutenant gave the two agents their pre-flight briefing, reminding them that their parachutes were under their seats, and then installed them in the tiny aircraft.

The plane took off at eleven o'clock and flew for just over two hours to somewhere 'south of Bayeux'[7] by the light of the full moon. It landed in a field, where they were received by three of Ricard's friends, André, Jules and André's brother Louis, who lived in a farmhouse nearby. While Stefan went to stay with Louis, the other three spent the night at another house, where they were discovered early the following morning by a German patrol searching for the spy codenamed *Nimrod*. André was shot dead, and Ricard and Jules were captured, so Louis arranged for Stefan to be moved. However, the pair soon encountered another German patrol. When asked whether he was *Nimrod*, Stefan acknowledged that he was, to the fury of his companion who believed him to be a traitor; as Louis drew his pistol, he was promptly shot dead. Stefan was escorted to a nearby château, the headquarters of the local garrison, where he demanded to see an intelligence officer from Army Group B; he was then driven the same afternoon by Captain Arngross, who explained that he had been expecting *Nimrod* 'for days', to La Roche Guyon, now occupied by Field Marshal Rommel.

At Rommel's impressive headquarters, Stefan was interrogated by Colonel Ritter, who had apparently worked in London in the military attaché's office before the war, and his Abwehr counterpart, Herr Mannheim. Having confirmed his background and details of his recruitment by another German spy named Hans Weber, Stefan extracted a small oilskin pouch from inside the lining of his sleeve. It contained 'half-a-dozen negatives, the size of postage stamps',[8] which upon examination proved to be a classified movement order for the 4th Canadian Armoured Division, Aldershot, and a directive issued by the Royal Electrical and Mechanical Engineers to the Canadians on the subject of waterproofing tanks. The third was a memorandum from the Chief Medical Officer about sea-sickness tablets, addressed to the US Third Army in East Anglia. The others included photographs of

> tanks in Suffolk; petrol bowsers in east Kent; landing craft in
> Essex creeks and river mouths; maps of the Pas de Calais printed
> on silk squares like scarves; lists of steep gradients, narrow
> bridges, the tonnage they could bear, sharp corners that could
> prove difficult for an armoured column to navigate; known
> German defensive positions around Calais and the units
> involved.[9]

Stefan claimed that he had photographed this impressive haul after he had removed a staff officer's briefcase from a locked cupboard at SOE's headquarters in Baker Street, mentioning that the other material had been taken from desks in the building. Apparently satisfied with Stefan's authenticity, the following morning Ritter introduced him to Rommel, a meeting that the Field Marshal insisted should not appear in his official War Diary. The spy then gave Rommel a comprehensive briefing on the deployment of Allied units in southern England. This further success led to him being flown with Captain Arngross to Berchtesgaden, where he again met Mannheim and was required to undergo a further interrogation at the hands of two Wehrmacht colonels. Having completed this cross-examination, he was escorted to the Berghof for an audience with Hitler at which he repeated his tale about an imminent Allied landing in the Pas de Calais and a preliminary diversionary landing elsewhere. Also present at this interview was Field Marshal Wilhelm Keitel of the

High Command, who asked about the target area of the deceptive operations, and his chief of operations, Colonel-General Alfred Jodl, who confirmed that Stefan's information coincided with what was known from other reliable intelligence sources. However, after the interview had been concluded, and Stefan had been dismissed, Hitler announced that he disbelieved the spy, whom he denounced as a triple-cross deception, asserting that his arrival with vital information was too fortuitous to be true and that the Allies had already made the calculation that he would be rejected. Accordingly, he concluded,

> Nimrod is totally expendable, a messenger written off by the
> enemy the moment he left England. But his message remains.
> We will therefore reinforce our defences in the Calais area to the
> limit of our powers. For that is where the main Allied force will
> land – as I have for long steadfastly believed it would.[10]

Thus, having persuaded Hitler's rather twisted logic that Calais was indeed the Allies' true target for the invasion, Stefan was flown to Paris and then returned to La Roche Guyon by staff car. Once again accommodated in the castle, he was awake early the following morning, 4 June, to witness Rommel leaving for Paris by road to attend an important strategy conference. Stefan was informed that he was also to go to Paris, on Wednesday, 7 June, but the night before, while visiting a local brothel with his escort, the obliging Captain Arngross, he escaped, attempting to kill Mannheim as he did so but sustaining a bullet wound in his arm.

Despite his injury, Stefan made his way on foot to Mantes, but after a fracas with the Sicherheitsdienst in the railway station and some adventures with the resistance, he crossed the German lines and surrendered to British troops in Bayeux, identifying himself as from Ten Commando. Repatriated through Newhaven, he was brought to London to be thanked personally by Colonel Ronald Wingate, who explained that what he had accomplished would prevent him from undertaking any further military service. Instead, he was to have plastic surgery to alter his appearance, and then start a new life with a new identity in Canada. As Wingate explained,

> When we thought that our agents on the continent faced the risk
> of being recognised, because they had lived there before the war

or for any other reason, they sometimes had plastic surgery to change their appearance as a precaution before they went back.

Stefan's surgery took place in the London Clinic, and 'in the third week of July' the stitches were removed. 'No one would recognise him now, he thought, for he could scarcely recognise himself.' He remained in the Clinic until he joined the *Queen Mary* at Southampton a few days later for a voyage across the Atlantic to New York.[11]

The outline of this remarkable story was apparently told to the author James Leasor by Sir Leslie Hollis, the wartime military secretary to the War Cabinet, 'more than twenty years' before the publication of *The Unknown Warrior*. Hollis 'had described in the broadest terms how a volunteer of German–Jewish extraction, serving under a British name in the Commandos, had helped deceive the Germans before the Normandy landings in 1944',[12] but, curiously, Leasor had not referred to the episode in *War at the Top*, his account of General Hollis's wartime experiences, which was published in 1959.[13] A distinguished military historian with fifteen works of non-fiction to his credit, and the author of several novels under the pen-name Andrew MacAllan, Leasor subsequently moved to Wiltshire and coincidentally met Hollis's colleague, Sir Ronald Wingate, who had 'recalled in some detail this particular episode'.[14] Thus, the account that had originated with Hollis, and had died with him in August 1963, had been confirmed by another senior former War Cabinet official, Wingate, who had died in August 1978. Intrigued by what he had learned from Hollis and Wingate, Leasor had pursued further research of the unit, designated 10 (Inter-Allied) Commando, but had discovered that the Public Record Office would not allow its papers 'to be released for public view until 2042',[15] so, undaunted, he had enlisted the help of Lord Mountbatten, who 'introduced me to Sir Michael Cary, then Permanent Under-Secretary at the Ministry of Defence, and permission was granted for me to examine and make use of any relevant documents'. Sir Michael, who was appointed in 1974, died while still in office in March 1976, so when Leasor's book was eventually released, in 1981, those who had given him the greatest assistance were all dead.

While acknowledging that 'because of the secret nature of the operation and the need to preserve the anonymity of some of the participants even today, certain personalities and incidents have been disguised', the author insisted that 'it is a true adventure story of such secrecy that it can only now be told'. He added that, 'in the spirit of secrecy that shielded the activities of X-Troop, I have changed some names and para-phrased certain incidents in this book'.[16] Thus, the reader is assured that the essential core of Stefan's story is indeed true, but upon closer exam-ination, as we shall see, some doubts emerge.

Certainly there was a military unit designated Ten (Inter-Allied) Commando, which was created on 2 July 1942 under the command of Lieutenant-Colonel Dudley Lister. Ten Commando consisted of a French (No. 1) Troop and a Dutch Troop (No. 2), later to be augmented by Belgian (No. 4), Norwegian (No. 5), Polish (No. 6) and Yugoslav (No. 7) Troops. Bryan Hilton-Jones, a fluent French and German linguist who was to be killed in a car accident in Spain after the war, was appointed X Troop's commanding officer. He was assisted by his sergeant, George Lanyi, a Hungarian-born, Oxford-educated journalist. Initially, the rest of the Troop were in the main Sudeten Czechs, who had volunteered for active service from the 77 and 87 Alien Companies of the Pioneer Corps, and had adopted English surnames. Later, they were joined at their base in Aberdovey in October by a collection of German and Austrian anti-Nazis, who had been screened by MI5. By April 1943, X Troop boasted a strength of eighty men, and over the next eighteen months numerous X Troop members were detached to participate in military operations. For example, five went on the ill-fated Dieppe raid in August 1942, but only two returned. According to 10 Commando's War Diary, deposited at the Public Record Office, X Troop saw plenty of action in Italy, Belgium, Holland and Germany after D-Day.

However, we are primarily concerned with Stefan's adventure, and what occurred just before the invasion. In this respect, the records are far from comprehensive, but they show for instance that Corporals Bentley and Miles were posted to the Small Scale Raiding Force in December 1942, and probably assisted in Operation HUCKABACK, a raid on the Channel Island of Hern, on 27 February 1943. Several others were detached for missions that were aborted, sometimes at the last minute, so much of X Troop's activities was limited to training in Wales and Scotland. Corporal John Wilmers (formerly Johan Wilmersdoerffer of Munich, then a Cambridge undergraduate and later an Appeal Judge in the Channel Islands) dropped into France on Operation FORFAR/ITEM in September 1943 and landed near St Valéry-en-Caux for an overnight reconnaissance before making a rendezvous with an MTB on the coast. Similarly, X Troop's Russian member, Corporal Jones, acted as signaller on HARDTACK 11, a beach survey of the coast near

Gravelines undertaken on 23 December 1943 from Dover. TARBRUSH 10, mounted in May 1944, was led by Lieutenant George Lane (formerly George Lanyi) to look for new types of enemy mines off Onival, but ended with his capture and that of his Royal Engineers officer, Lieutenant Roy Wooldridge.

Clearly many of X Troop's personnel fitted the general description of the unit given by James Leasor, but it is Lanyi's experience on TAR-BRUSH 10, for which he was awarded the Military Cross, that coincides with *The Unknown Warrior*. After his capture on 18 May, Lanyi stuck to his cover identity of the Welshman George Lane, but he and Wooldridge were taken to La Roche Guyon, where they met Field Marshal Rommel. After a short interview, they were driven to Fresnes prison in Paris for further interrogation and ended the war in prisoner-of-war camps.

So did Leasor base Stefan's story on what had befallen Lanyi? Evidently not, for when Stefan was interviewed by Rommel in Leasor's account, the Field Marshal reportedly had remarked that he had met two Commando officers in the same room 'less than a week ago', and that one of them was named George Lane. Accordingly, one must dismiss the notion that George Lanyi might have been *Nimrod*, but there remains the rather odd overlap between Stefan's mission and Lanyi's. Leasor is somewhat vague about the precise date Stefan embarked on his operation, but, by working backwards from the moment Stefan saw Rommel leave La Roche Guyon, early on the morning of Sunday, 4 June 1944, one can suppose that he had arrived in Paris from Berchtesgaden the previous day, which places his interview with Hitler on about Friday, 2 June. Just how long he spent in Germany, and how many nights he spent at La Roche Guyon immediately after his capture, or whether he spent any time in Paris before his flight to Berchtesgaden, are unknown, but there is a clue in Rommel's reported remark that he had interviewed George Lanyi and Roy Wooldridge 'less than a week ago'.[17] Since the records of TARBRUSH 10 are clear that these two officers were captured early in the morning of 18 May, and were interviewed by Rommel several days later, one can use Rommel's comment, and the knowledge that Stefan spent one night in the care of the resistance, to put Stefan's exploits into a time window between 25 and 28 May 1944.

Having established roughly when Stefan is supposed to have dropped into the Cabourg–Bayeux area of Normandy, one can examine the rest of the timetable, and immediately at least one unsatisfactory feature stands out. This concerns the warnings transmitted to the Abwehr in advance of

Nimrod's arrival. According to Leasor, the MI5 double agent Hans Weber had provided *Nimrod* with his credentials and had sent messages about his expected mission to Cabourg throughout the early part of May 1944. On 17 May, the enemy responded with a demand to know where *Nimrod* was planning to land, and evidently this information was supplied because Leasor reproduces the text of 'an urgent message that had originated from the senior Intelligence officer in the headquarters of the 7th Army',[18] which, for the ten days prior to Stefan's arrival, had been the basis of Captain Arngross's nightly patrols: 'IMPERATIVE CAPTURE DISCREETLY AND UNHARMED ENEMY AGENT NIMROD DUE ARRIVE AREA CABOURG–BAYEUX STOP INFORM SENDER IMMEDIATELY WHEN APPREHENDED.'[19] Thus Arngross, then the acting intelligence officer of the 1st Battalion, Artillery Regiment, 352nd Division, recently moved to the coast from St Lô, had been alerted to *Nimrod*'s existence in mid-May and had taken the appropriate action: 'For the past ten days, Captain Arngross had received repeated enquiries . . . asking whether any enemy parachutists had landed in his area. Had any clandestine landings of small enemy aircraft been reported?'[20]

Nor was Captain Arngross alone in his search for enemy infiltrators along that part of the coast. Leasor describes how other Wehrmacht units had been deployed in the search for *Nimrod*:

> Every night, each regiment in the area sent out special recon-
> naissance patrols to cover the most likely landing places. Some
> patrols went on foot, others by bicycle. They might have heard an
> engine coming down the sky, or seen a glimmer of light at the
> edge of a wood, but by the time the soldiers reached the area and
> forced their way through prickly hedges, there was no one left
> for them to see, nothing to find. Each morning Arngross received
> the same reply: Nothing to report.[21]

Now, this version of events is particularly strange because, during this very period, Cabourg was the subject of intense Allied attention, one of the results of which had been the capture of George Lanyi and Roy Wooldridge. Even if TARBRUSH 10 had been an isolated episode, it would surely have qualified as a significant incident in Captain Arngross's all-too-quiet existence, and the capture of two commando officers must have been an event of some celebration among the occupiers locally. However, Lanyi's mission had been part of a series of reconnaissance missions concentrated on the same stretch of French coastline during this period of moon darkness. Codenamed HILTFORCE, the first raids took place on 15/16 May, but went undetected by the enemy. However, the following night a German patrol exchanged fire with TARBRUSH 8 at Quend Plage before the British team withdrew. As for TARBRUSH 10, the capture of the two officers the next morning was but one part of it. Earlier, the two NCOs had been discovered by the enemy and a fierce firefight had ensued, complete with starshells that had illuminated the men on the beach and their MTB lying offshore. Sergeant Bluff and Corporal King RM had been engaged by accurate fire from two German patrols for nearly two hours until they managed to escape by boat, to be picked up further down the coast by the MTB. Accordingly, there was plenty of excitement for Captain Arngross to record on 16 May, yet, according to Leasor, he was completely unaware of what had happened in his sector at the very time he was supposed to have exercised special vigilance.

A further unsatisfactory aspect to the story is that, bearing in mind that a total of eight commando raids were planned for the vicinity of Cabourg in the second half of May, it is astonishing that *Nimrod*'s British controllers should have wanted to send their spy into an area of such intense enemy activity; on the other hand, it is hard to believe that Combined Operations would contemplate launching so many missions into the one stretch of Normandy coastline where the enemy had deliberately been tipped off to expect an intruder. Indeed, considering that the invasion was scheduled for 5 June (but was postponed twenty-four hours because of inclement weather), it is scarcely credible that anyone would have authorised MI5 to let Hans Weber use his radio to warn the Abwehr of an imminent British clandestine operation in Normandy.

The crucial role allegedly played by MI5 in Stefan's story deserves scrutiny, and the central figure of Hans Weber also requires examination. Certainly James Leasor had acquired some knowledge of MI5's double-cross operations, and by the time of publication of *The Unknown Warrior* in 1981 much had been published on the topic, both by Sir John Masterman and Ladislas Farago. However, some of Leasor's details are a little shaky, as can be seen from this passage in which he relates the basis of the work of the Twenty Committee:

Since 1939 more than 100 German agents had been captured on arrival in Britain by parachute or from U-boats and given the choice of full collaboration with the British or summary trial and execution.[22]

In reality, of course, only a fraction of this exaggerated number of enemy agents had been captured, with just six having arrived by parachute. Of these six Josef Jakobs and Karel Richter had been executed in 1941; the other four, *Gander, Summer, Tate* and *Zigzag*, had become double agents, but only Wulf Schmidt (*Tate*) had been threatened with death. As for agents arriving by U-boat, there was not a single case at any time during the war, which leads us to Hans Heinrich Weber, the spy who had been invited to join the double-cross system 'soon after his capture on arrival on the east coast of Scotland from a U-boat'[23] in 1940.

Weber's background is recounted by Leasor in some detail. Having fought in Flanders, where he had won the Iron Cross, he had moved to a house in Upper Belvedere, Manchester, and had given private piano lessons, using the false surname of Werner.[24] By an extraordinary coincidence, Werner had taught the young Stefan Rosenberg music and German, had later sponsored his university education at Imperial College, London, and had also attempted to recruit him as a spy. After Stefan had graduated in electrical engineering, he had found a job making radio equipment at a factory in north London, and at this point, early in 1938, Weber had reintroduced himself as an official attached to the German Embassy and had invited Stefan to supply details of the British Army '38' radio receiver. Stefan had rejected the offer, but had not reported Weber to the police.

Thereafter Weber must have returned to Germany, for he had been captured in Scotland in 1940 'within hours of his arrival',[25] and had accepted an offer to become a double agent. According to Leasor, Weber's arrival by U-boat had been betrayed by another spy, codenamed *Snow* by MI5, for 'his German controller informed *Snow* where and when other agents would land in Britain. They were all duly intercepted, "turned" or executed. Sometimes *The Times* carried a brief notice of their deaths.'[26]

This part of the story is unsustainable, for the *Snow* case is well-documented, and he did not identify any arrivals to the Security Service. His true name was Arthur Owens and, as related earlier, he was detained at Dartmoor in 1941. Although he had a peripheral connection with *Tate*, to whom he once supplied some cash by post, he operated independently from the other agents sent over by boat or plane in 1940, and was never in a position to alert his MI5 handlers to the imminent appearance of other spies. Certainly it is true that nine German spies arrived in Britain in 1940, of whom three were caught within hours of their arrival by seaplane at Buckie in Scotland. Robert Petter and Karl Drücke were executed in June 1941, and their companion, Vera de Cottani-Chalbur, served a term of imprisonment. Of the others, *Gander*, *Summer* and *Tate* accepted invitations to become double-cross agents, while four others, Jose Waldberg, Carl Meier, Charles van den Kieboom and Sjoerd Pons, landed from a fishing boat in Kent in September 1940. Of the latter four, only Pons escaped execution, having been acquitted by an Old Bailey jury. Thus, one is left to speculate about Hans Weber, whose description does not even remotely fit any of the other German spies. Indeed, very few other details about him ring true.

In Leasor's account, Weber had been given a new identity, that of Robert Frazer, and he had been accommodated at a house in Finchley Park Road with his MI5 case officer, who masqueraded as his nephew, and a Royal Signals wireless operator, 'who had copied his style of sending – his "wrist" as signallers called the way of tapping the key'[27] – and was on the air 'four nights a week to a receiving station in Hamburg'. The MI5 case officer is unnamed, but since all the Security Service personnel who served in B1(a), the sub-section which handled double agents, are known, this is quite odd. In any event, none fits the profile of Weber's 'nephew', not least because Leasor mentions that the case officer habitually wore his uniform in London, whereas MI5 officers invariably wore civilian clothes. Nor did they move in with their agents, as there were never more than seven handlers on Major T. A. Robertson's staff, and most dealt with more than one agent simultaneously. Leasor also asserts that Weber 'was never allowed to tap the Morse key himself'[28] and his transmissions 'were all sent by a Royal Signals operator',[29] which again was an unusual departure from MI5's procedure of using their own personnel to operate the enemy's equipment. Certainly there was never any need for the Security Service to call in the Royal Signals, and there is no other instance of this happening.

Finally, one comes to the fundamental flaw at the heart of *The Unknown Warrior*. Quite apart from the considerable doubts that emerge regarding Stefan, Weber and the other individuals involved, one has to question the central proposition that in May 1944 the Allies were on the point of desperation. Leasor describes the period thus: in 'a desperate last minute attempt to convince Hitler, possibly against his commanders' views, a volunteer was sought to fly to France, carrying what would seem unarguable evidence that the main landings were to take place around Calais',[30] but the evidence is that in May the Allies had good reason to be confident about the efficacy of FORTITUDE, the principal deception plan to cover the invasion. Indeed, ULTRA had provided the Supreme Commander with a magnificent window through which he could monitor the impact of FORTITUDE's various interlocking components, and analysis of the Abwehr's intercepts allowed MI5 to gauge the enemy's reaction to each item of intelligence supplied by the main participants, who were *Garbo* (Juan Pujol), *Brutus* (Roman Garby-Czerniawski), *Bronx* (Elvira Chaudoir) and *Tate* (Wulf Schmidt). Quite simply, there was room for neither *Nimrod* nor Hans Weber, and absolutely no need.

Put in the baldest terms, *The Unknown Warrior* is a story about an enemy alien who is considered sufficiently dangerous to be interned at the outbreak of war, is allowed to join Ten Commando, and is then selected for a clandestine mission into enemy territory with the specific purpose of imparting deceptive information to the Nazis. En route, of course, he has been indoctrinated into the success MI5 has achieved with the double-cross system and is given the true location of the invasion. And all this to someone who had strong connections with German Intelligence before the war, and failed to report it.

At first blush the tale beggars belief, but close study of the chronology of events reveals some disturbing lapses, one of which centres on Stefan's internment. According to Leasor's account, Stefan had been arrested by two Special Branch officers at his flat in Hendon on the outbreak of war, and had been accommodated at Alexandra Palace before moving to the Isle of Man. Then, 'early the following year', he had 'travelled to Halifax in the hold of the SS *Duchess of York* with 5,000 other young Germans, ironically listed in the manifest as "friendly enemy aliens"'.[31] Once installed at Sherbrooke, Stefan had settled into the harsh existence of a detainee, but 'during the spring of 1940, the internees started a university in the camp'. Then the news arrived that Paris had fallen. Thus, from Leasor's account it is quite clear that Stefan was interned in the Isle of Man in 1939, and was in Canada when Paris fell in May 1940. The problem with this version is that general internment of enemy aliens in Britain did not commence until the end of June 1940, soon after Italy had joined the war. By the end of July, 23,000 Austrian and German aliens had been detained.

Of the 71,553 enemy aliens registered in September 1939, only 572 were assessed as 'Category A', which required their immediate detention. Most were given their complete freedom as 'Category C', while

6,890 were considered 'Category B' and were the subject of some mildly inconvenient restrictions, such as not being allowed to own a car or bicycle. It was only when the Nazis advanced towards the English Channel that Category B males between the ages of sixteen and sixty, who had been in Britain for less than five years, were required to report for internment. Clearly, as Stefan had been interned in 1939, he must have been placed in Category A, which would have been very unusual. Indeed, the majority of Category A internees were not arrested by Special Branch officers, but simply requested to report to their local police station. Accordingly, Stefan's experience, if faithfully reported by Leasor, would have been extremely unusual, of the kind reserved for suspects of the most hardened variety. According to the official statistics,[32] the police nominated eighteen people, all known to be members of the IRA, for internment, and MI5 produced a list of just twenty-two espionage suspects, of whom William Joyce and two others were considered 'unreservedly Nazi'. Nor was the internment process arbitrary. Every case was individually assessed by a tribunal led by a County Court judge or a King's Counsel. If Stefan had been sent to Canada as an enemy alien, it could only have been as a result of a monumental blunder, and one that he would certainly have been aware of, especially if he had been accused of espionage or membership of the IRA. Strangely, Leasor makes no reference to any error, or to any appeal made by Stefan to the Internment Tribunal. Indeed, none of the other details concerning Stefan's internment withstand any scrutiny. He could not have been interned on the Isle of Man in 1939, since the first camp, for women and children only, was not established at Port Erin until the end of May 1940, and he could not have been processed at a temporary camp at Alexandra Palace in September 1939 because none existed. As for Stefan's voyage on the SS *Duchess of York*, which supposedly carried him with 5,000 Germans to Canada early in 1940, the reality is that the Canadian Pacific steamship did not sail until 21 June 1940, and no internees were sent to Canada prior to this date. Nor could Stefan have been at Sherbrooke in May 1940, for the camp did not open until October.

Even on the assumption that there was some confusion over Stefan's internment, one is bound to be cautious over his alleged role as *Nimrod*. Putting aside for a moment the obvious curiosity any observer would reasonably express over precisely why Stefan of all people had been selected, at the very last moment, for such a crucial mission, it is difficult to ascertain for whom he was working. Certainly Ten Commando personnel were detached routinely to other units and one, Captain Guido Zembsche-Schreve, transferred to SOE's French Section and was dropped into France in July 1943. So which organisation recruited Stefan and despatched him on his mission? Again there is plenty of room for doubt, for according to Leasor's account it must have been SOE. Stefan underwent training, albeit very briefly, at one of SOE's special schools on the Beaulieu estate, an event that effectively rules out the other principal contender, the SIS. However, the way Stefan was moved to a hotel in Southampton and then a military base outside Portsmouth, before driving to Kent to meet Ricard, his French travelling companion, was highly unusual. If he was to fly across the Channel from 'an airfield outside Chichester',[33] why was Ricard in Kent, and why was it necessary to drive halfway across southern England to be introduced to Ricard, only to return to Chichester? Leasor does not identify the airfield from which the Lysander flew, but one can suppose that it was RAF Tangmere, a large fighter base close to Chichester from which Lysanders from 419 Flight operated. Not only would it have been unusual for an agent to have been accommodated so far from the airfield, and there is no record of SOE maintaining any facilities in Kent, but there is an aura of unreality about the entire episode, accentuated by the ludicrous advice allegedly given by the Lysander pilot, that 'there's a parachute under your seat'.[34] In fact, Westland Lysanders did not carry parachutes for passengers.

If one accepts the proposition that SOE was indeed the mystery clandestine organisation responsible for sending Stefan and Ricard into France, one has to ask why SOE was participating in a deception scheme. SOE's role was strictly limited to fomenting resistance in the occupied territories and deception was no part of its brief, a demarcation fiercely defended by SIS and Whitehall. The very idea of briefing an agent on the intricacies of the double-cross system, and the plan for the invasion, and then exposing him to the enemy, would have sent a chill down the spine of even the most irresponsible intelligence officer.

So did *Nimrod* ever exist? The odds against it seem high. There is no record of any such deception scheme and, as we have seen, there was no requirement for one. Nor is there any trace of these events in German archives or memoirs. Rommel's Army Group B headquarters at the Château La Roche Guyon was purposely kept quite small, around a dozen officers, and there was no Colonel Ritter on his staff, or a Herr Mannheim of the Abwehr. Rommel's senior intelligence officer was Colonel Anton Staubwasser, of whom there is no mention in *The*

Unknown Warrior. Therefore, there must be doubts about all of Leasor's other principal characters. Certainly every one of the references to Stefan Rosenberg and Hans Weber is erroneous in some respect, even down to the only documentary evidence Leasor offers, which is a group photograph of X Troop, the caption identifying it as having been 'taken during training in North Wales, 1942. One of these men is *Nimrod*.' Curiously, the identical picture appears in Ian Dear's history of *Ten Commando 1942–45*[35] with the correct location and date, 'Eastbourne, May 1943'. Quite obviously, since *Nimrod* had been detached on his intelligence assignment, he could not have been available to appear in X Troop's group photo.

When *The Unknown Warrior* was released, X Troop's survivors were baffled by the mysterious Stefan Rosenberg, alias Stephen Rigby, for none could recall such a person in Ten Commando. Indeed, George Lane MC recalls being interviewed by James Leasor before publication, but he made no mention of *Nimrod* and was more interested in X Troop's activities. One is therefore left wondering quite how James Leasor learned of *Nimrod*'s extraordinarily improbable tale. If he was told it by Leslie Hollis and Ronald Wingate, and neither man was in a position to explain in 1980, both men must have been deluded. Quite why the author did not discover this for himself as his digging progressed, one can only speculate, but doubtless he had spotted the treatment his *Green Beach* had received at the hands of William Stephenson (see Chapter 6), which ought to have cautioned him as to the hazards of relying on imagination to fill research gaps.

Conclusion

What leads ostensibly respectable people to fabricate stories about wartime exploits? Why should a biographer of the status of Leonard Mosley decide, towards the end of his career, to perpetrate a fraud? On the basis that a hoaxer is someone who misrepresents facts and then cheerfully admits to the scam when challenged, Mosley falls into a different category, for when offered an opportunity to admit that his book was fiction, he merely conceded that he might have been misled 'by people with motives which I don't fully understand'.[1]

Mosley had acquired a world-wide reputation when, on 6 June 1944, he parachuted into occupied France with the first wave of D-Day invaders. Armed with nothing more than a portable typewriter, his reports from Caen made front-page news across the globe. Later, he achieved further acclaim with his studies of Orde Wingate, Lord Curzon, Charles Lindbergh, Sir Archibald McIndoe and Hermann Goering. So what possessed him to jeopardise all the respect he had earned by manufacturing a tale like *The Druid*? One might just as easily ask why Lady Clarke deceived everyone except her immediate family with her extraordinary story of rescuing Allied airmen from the Continent, or why George DuPre hoodwinked Quentin Reynolds and *Life*.

The compulsion that led Edward Edlmann, Josephine Butler and George Milkomane to indulge their fantasies so publicly is not such a rare phenomenon. John Cottell is still on the lucrative lecture circuit in the United States, thrilling audiences with breathtaking disclosures of gallantry in the battlefield and personal privation while under interrogation at the hands of the KGB. Nor is it insignificant convicted thieves who behave in this way. In 1987, Miles Jackson-Lipkin QC, a well-regarded and popular High Court judge in Hong Kong, resigned from the bench when the *South China Morning Post* revealed that the eminent lawyer's tales of wartime exploits were as phoney as his entitlement to the medals he proudly displayed on ceremonial occasions. Educated at Harrow and Oxford, the judge had written two books, *The Beaufort Legitimation* and *The Scales of Justice*, and in 1986 had been elected a Freeman of the City of London. Everyone is entitled to have their own private dreams, and Jackson-Lipkin paid a high price for his, but there is a world of difference between mild exaggeration behind closed doors and the egregious folly of publicly flaunting, or peddling, wares that are suspect.

Quite apart from the embarrassment and disgrace of exposure, there is a further more insidious consequence to the deception. This is eloquently illustrated by the frequency with which some of these books, now revealed to be untrue, are quoted by the unsuspecting as respectable sources. Whilst *A Man Called Intrepid* has been widely discredited for containing historical inexactitudes, hitherto the scale of the inaccuracy has never been documented and the errors have been generously ascribed to poor scholarship rather than fabrication. Similarly, the way in which *The Courage of Fear* has been accepted as factually accurate by some eminently respectable but naïve figures, and the way *I Looked Right* is still quoted and requoted as an authentic account of wartime operations, demonstrates the danger. Unless challenged, Mladin Zarubica's tale, or Madelaine Duke's talent for invention, may become accepted as what they purport to be: authentic accounts of wartime undercover work. And as those with first-hand experience of these matters succumb to old age, there are fewer left to ask the right questions, or to know where to look in the appropriate archives.

Given that Aline Romanones and Roxane Pitt are guilty of no more than failing to rein in their relatively harmless imaginations, what is one to make of those other, professional authors who have misled their readers? Clearly Quentin Reynolds was an innocent dupe, and Barry Wynne might likely be the same, even if he does appear to have been deceived twice. But what about the Canadian writer William Stevenson, who can hardly not have known that the photographs in *A Man Called Intrepid* were as bogus as a high proportion of his text. Was he an innocent victim of his subject, Sir William Stephenson, or a plagiarist on a grand scale? On every journalist who communicates to the public there is a responsibility to make at least the most obvious checks on the veracity of his or her sources. If Sir William claimed that the brave Norwegian saboteurs who dropped on to the Hardanger Plateau in 1942 to destroy the Vermork hydro-electric complex had been trained by his organisation in Canada, why did the author fail to telephone Knut Haukelid, who had survived the operation and only died, highly decorated, in April 1994? He had given a first-hand account of his experience in *Skis against the Atom*,[2] but he was never consulted before the credit was seized for *Intrepid*. Admittedly none of the assassins who killed Reinhard Heydrich lived to give their version of events, but to produce a variant so radically different from previously published accounts surely requires an explanation and some additional care. However, when one examines Stevenson's treatment of Noor Inayat Khan, the number of excuses diminish. Sir William's purported connections with the beautiful SOE agent were non-existent, and it is obvious from the text that her story has been reconstituted from published sources. This cannot be a case of a loyal Boswell faithfully recording his master's recollections, but that of a willing and undiscriminating collaborator in as gross a case of literary misrepresentation as one is likely to find.

The competition for such an unsavoury accolade is considerable and is continuing. In 1985, a Texan journalist, Roger A. Ready, published *Operation Killer Mouse*, an account of the exploits of an OSS agent named by him as 'Colonel Devlin Morgan', who allegedly led a team of assassins across North Africa and France on a series of missions to liquidate dozens of senior Nazis. Devlin apparently survived two years of ruthless butchery behind enemy lines before being captured by the Gestapo in April 1944. In reality, 'Devlin's' adventures, although claimed to be 'based on true and accurate exploits',[3] were really founded on the imagination of Gene Gassaway, a Walter Mitty figure who had duped Ready and who had never served with OSS or killed anyone. Gassaway, who died in 1989, insisted to the end that he was still under the CIA's control and that official records had been sanitised to remove all references to him. Ready, who lives in Richardson, Texas, apparently never questioned his tales.

Undoubtedly some of those responsible for manufacturing these literary fabrications believe their tales to be true. A case in point must be that of an eminent and respected doctor, Albert Haas, who wrote *The Doctor and the Damned* in 1984.[4] From his retirement home in New York City, he recalled his harrowing experiences in a series of Nazi concentration camps and gave a detailed account of his activities as an intelligence agent in the South of France before his capture in 1943. Although he may well have undergone the privations at Dachau, Flossenberg, Auschwitz and Mauthausen he documented so realistically, there can be no doubt that the portion of his autobiography detailing his training in Britain, and the numerous operations he claims to have participated in, are entirely bogus.

A Hungarian Jew by origin, Haas was apparently born Haasz. When the war broke out, he was studying in Antwerp, having read medicine at a medical school in Budapest. As a dual national, with French citizenship through his mother, he was called up for military service in the medical corps, but after the French surrender he worked as a general practitioner in Arles, where his regiment had been demobilised.

Haas says that his recruitment into the French resistance took place at the end of 1940 through the Marseilles representative of the BCRA (the Gaullist intelligence service), Colonel Louis Deronne. Thereafter, he and his Belgian wife Sonja were based in Mandelieu, working at a local refugee camp for Spanish republicans and at the Hôpital Mixe in Cannes, as well as assisting a physician at La Napoule. His resistance cell, known as the Groupe Surcouf ('named for a submarine commander from Toulon'),[5] was 'part of the much larger Reseau Marco Polo',[6] and sometime in the summer of 1941 he and his wife received a coded signal over the BBC which ordered them to England for training. One night they were picked up off Cap d'Antibes by a submarine whose 'commander was . . . a Frenchman' and taken on a journey lasting 'several days' to the English coast. They landed 'about 120 miles from London' and were driven to a private home in Soho, before receiving a briefing given in a darkened room in 'an official building in Whitehall' by a senior figure in the BCRA, General Paul Guivante de Saint-Gaste.[7] Then they went on an intensive course 'at the Resistance training center in London'.[8]

> We began with jujitsu and the art of sabotage, including the use of plastic explosives. Our espionage teachers taught us to decipher architectural plans and to read upside down. They trained us in the arts of observation, they taught us how to steal, and they drilled us in responding coolly to unexpected dangers.[9]

The course lasted for four weeks and included a visit 'to an airfield in Sussex to learn parachute jumping. Our very last task was to memorize the codes that would enable us to decipher our orders from the cryptic messages of the BBC evening broadcasts.'[10] Having completed their training, the couple 'were sent back to France by air and parachuted down near Grenoble'.[11]

Upon their return, Haas and his wife 'were given a variety of missions to carry out' and 'were called back to England a few more times'[12] to attend briefings. During the following eighteen months, he went 'on two different missions'[13] by parachute to Austria, was dropped into Belgium and participated in a 'series of parachute jumps'[14] in the Vercors. His last visit to England took place in November 1942, when he was picked up by plane and flown to London to receive a new assignment, to penetrate the Nazi labour system, the Todt Organisation. However, the following year Haas and his wife were arrested in Nice on suspicion of espionage. This brought his adventures to an abrupt halt and marked the start of his odyssey through the Reich's most notorious concentration camps.

Despite having experienced torture at the hands of the Gestapo, and being moved across France, Germany, Poland and Austria as he was transferred from one death camp to another, Haas survived the war and lived to be reunited with his wife, who had also endured the Holocaust and had escaped from Auschwitz, ending up in Russian hands. However, his version of events must be open to doubt, and in particular the proposition that the BCRA masterminded at the very least seven separate operations (the exfiltration from Antibes, followed by the parachute drop to Grenoble, two into Austria, one into Belgium, a 'series' into the Vercors and a final return trip to London by air from Nice) for a single husband-and-wife team in a period of eighteen months, from mid-1941, is quite remarkable, if not untenable. The author is sketchy on detail, but such an achievement would be worthy of considerable public recognition. However, it seems improbable that any of these missions really happened. As to precisely when they occurred, one can only be guided by the clues provided by Haas. He alleges that their last mission into the Vercors took place when Sonja was three months pregnant, and since he mentions elsewhere that their son François was born in October 1942, it is safe to calculate that the missions happened between the summer of 1941, when they were despatched from England, and April 1942. As for the exact number of missions packed into this short period, it seems likely that a total of seven is a conservative estimate, for although the author only describes a single journey made by submarine, he does state that he and his wife had made 'submarine trips' in the plural, implying that there had been others. But whatever the exact number of missions, upon further scrutiny of the author's story, the doubts multiply, and some are fundamental to Haas's credibility. For example, Haas alleges that, under the control of the BCRA, he worked in isolation from the British services, and indeed asserts that he was warned about 'the British-directed French Resistance units that were also being formed': 'We were told that their real purpose was to feed false information to the Germans, and that their members were unwitting pawns in the process. We had to stay clear of them or we would endanger our own lives.'[15]

Haas is emphatic that the agency which gave him this warning, and which recruited him for clandestine activities, was the BCRA, and he describes Colonel Deronne's introductory remarks 'at the end of 1940': 'The network was going to be coordinated from London by the Bureau Central de Renseignements et d'Action.'[16] The fundamental problem with this scenario is that the BCRA did not exist in 1940 or 1941, and was not created until the late summer of 1942, when Haas says he had been operational for eighteen months. Thus, whatever organisation Haas thought he was working for in 1941, it could not have been the BCRA. So could it have been some other French secret service? Perhaps, but given the fact that the French did not possess independent air or sea transport facilities in 1941, and relied wholly on SIS for their communications, either via wireless links or through the BBC's broadcasts, it is difficult to imagine which organisation sent Haas and his wife on seven missions to France, Austria and Belgium in 1941/42. Certainly the name of the official identified as having briefed the author in London, General Paul Guivante de Saint-Gaste, is an elusive character. Haas says the General met them in Whitehall, whereas de Gaulle's headquarters were located some distance away, at 11 Carlton Gardens, and the Free French intelligence service in 1941 was accommodated in Duke Street in St James's, even further from Whitehall. As for the General himself, Haas recalls that he met him in Mauthausen and asserted that the General and his aide, Captain Jean Veit, 'had both returned to France on an assignment' in the autumn of 1943, and had been denounced to the Germans and arrested.[17]

At the heart of this particular aspect of Haas's story is the claim that a very senior Free French intelligence officer was sent to France in

1943, accompanied by another staff officer, and that they were both arrested, imprisoned at Flossenberg and yet survived the war. Despite an extensive search for anyone or any episode even vaguely matching this set of events, absolutely none can be found, leaving the researcher to conclude that the General and his aide must be figments of the imagination.

The awkward fact that the BCRA did not exist in 1940 is not the only obstacle to believing Haas's version of his recruitment. He is uncharacteristically specific in his description of the key role played by the BBC's transmissions and recalled how he had been briefed in 'the middle of March 1941' on the particular phrase which would signal his summons to a prearranged rendezvous:

> In two weeks we had to start listening to the BBC broadcasts regularly. Our orders would be broadcast the night before we were supposed to meet our unknown comrades. We would be identified by our codenames. I was *oiseau* ('bird'). Sonja was *canard enchaîné* ('chained duck'). We listened nightly until we heard the phrase '*oiseaux est pret à voler avec le canard enchaîné* ('the bird is ready to fly with the chained duck'). This was the signal that we would be contacted at 1.00 p.m. the next afternoon at a preselected café in Cannes.[18]

According to Haas, this broadcast was simply one of dozens, and he mentions a further signal, broadcast the very next evening, which was monitored by another *résistant*, Lieutenant Konrad. After they had 'turned on our radio and found the frequency', they had begun 'to listen to the Free French broadcast over the BBC'. This time the text 'was his coded order to leave from Cap d'Antibes the next morning on a submarine to England'.[19] After Konrad's exfiltration, Haas says, 'Sonja and I began listening to the BBC's broadcasts. Each night we listened excitedly and there was still no code message for us.' However, 'after a seemingly endless series of frustrating broadcasts, the introductory bars of Beethoven's Fifth Symphony were finally followed by: "*L'oiseau est pret à voler avec le canard enchaîné.*" Tomorrow was our big day.'[20]

Such a momentous event is not forgotten, particularly because Haas and his wife had been monitoring the BBC news from 'the middle of March 1941'[21] until their encounter with the submarine off Antibes in the summer. Three months of anxious waiting is a long time, and not a trivial matter that one would fail to remember, yet the uncomfortable fact is that the BBC did not broadcast any coded messages during this period. In fact, the first personal messages transmitted on behalf of the clandestine networks in France were not broadcast until October 1941, long after Haas and his wife say they had completed their mission to England for training and had returned home. Thus, the author's memory, that while in London he had been taught 'to memorize the codes that would enable us to decipher our orders from the cryptic messages of the BBC evening broadcasts', must be erroneous.[22]

Haas recalls that while in London he was interviewed by 'General Paul Guivante de Saint-Gaste, chief of the Reseau Marco Polo' to which the 'local unit Surcouf belongs',[23] but there is no record of either this individual, who may of course have adopted a *nom de guerre*, or of the network. However, the 'Groupe Surcouf' cannot have been 'named for a submarine commander in Toulon who had already become a martyr in the struggle against the Germans',[24] and it is most unlikely that any clandestine organisation would have chosen Surcouf as its name. The reason is that the *Surcouf* was a submarine, not a person, and in 1940 it was the largest submarine ever built, notorious for its two eight-inch guns and its aircraft hangar on the deck. It was also an embarrassing absurdity, a sort of French naval white elephant, because it could not submerge. Far from having enjoyed a glorious history, the *Surcouf*'s entire crew had been interned at Devonport in July 1940 because it had supported the Pétain regime. The *Surcouf* disappeared in the Caribbean in February 1942, lost with all hands, but certainly not the victim of any martyrdom, and its ignoble story is so well known that it is astonishing that Haas did not know it. In fact, considering the *Surcouf*'s associations, which included an exchange of fire between the French officers and British ratings in Devonport, resulting in some deaths, it is remarkable that anyone would have contemplated using the name *Surcouf* in a Free French context thereafter. Whatever else the *Surcouf* was, it most definitely did not represent a symbol of France's heroic struggle against the Nazis.

Apart from the inherent difficulty of Haas's recruitment into a BCRA circuit in 1941, the story of his voyage to England raises more problems. There was a French submarine operating for the clandestine service in the Mediterranean in the summer of 1941, but the *Casabianca* was based at Gibraltar, and there was no Royal Navy submarine commanded by a Frenchman at any time during the war. As for the claim that the entire journey had been completed submerged, it must have been an exceptional episode. Most exfiltrations from the Riviera ended in Gibraltar, where passengers completed their journey by air, and it is difficult to understand the need for such a very long journey to be undertaken, or the requirement to remain submerged for the entire voyage, which would have made its duration much longer than the 'several days' mentioned by the author.[25]

Having reached England, Haas alleges that he and his wife were lodged in Soho at the home of an English couple, 'who didn't speak French or German',[26] but supplied them with a pair of Free French uniforms. An interview followed in 'an official building in Whitehall'[27] with Paul Guivante, and thereafter they underwent four weeks of intensive training in London, apparently leaving the capital only to learn to parachute in Sussex. Once again, the author's version of events fails to account for the absence of any sabotage training schools in London, or of any parachute facilities in Sussex, which was a combat zone regularly overflown by enemy fighters. Accordingly, all parachute training was concentrated in the Midlands, near Manchester, and the lack of suitable sites in London for sabotage training meant that these activities were restricted to certain isolated locations well away from the conurbations. The author's idea that 'the use of plastic explosives' was demonstrated in central London is really quite fanciful.[28]

Having concluded their training, Sonja and Albert allegedly were parachuted back into France near Grenoble, where 'a member of our local group was waiting to drive us to Nice',[29] which is a strange itinerary to have chosen when virtually every other infiltration into the South of France opted for a route via Gibraltar or North Africa. Haas offers no explanation for this eccentricity, but, more significantly, the RAF flew no clandestine missions to the Grenoble area between June and September 1941. Indeed, no record exists of any flight for Haas or his wife to Austria or Belgium either, and no weapons were delivered to the Vercors region during the period described.

Haas's claim to have jumped into Belgium is a curious one. Official records show that a total of 250 agents were despatched to Belgium during the war, of whom 190 survived the experience, but none match Haas and his wife. Similarly, operations into Austria were controlled by SOE and, apart from one disastrous attempt in April 1942, in which both the RAF aircraft and the (Soviet-supplied) agent perished, no missions were launched until September 1944. Thus, the author's two purported assignments cannot have been undertaken under the auspices of the British authorities, and there was no other way for them to have occurred.

As well as dropping into other countries and supervising consign-ments of arms to the Vercors, Haas mentions that he invented 'a successful charade to transport wounded Allied pilots to freedom'.[30] This involved a German ambulance, borrowed from his hospital in Nice, and carrying 'the pilots to Chambéry, near the Swiss border,' where arrange-ments were in place to 'smuggle them across the border into Switzerland'. The patients were accompanied by a friend 'dressed in the distinctive blue-and-white-striped German nurse's uniform',[31] which implies that these activities occurred during the German occupation, which, of course, did not extend to southern France until November 1942. This seems particularly odd, because by then there was already a well-established, highly sophisticated escape route for evading aircrew along the coast into Spain. Certainly Switzerland offered no 'freedom' to Allied pilots, but only the prospect of internment, and hopefully escape across the South of France to Spain. Thus, if Haas was really smuggling evaders into Switzerland, he was hindering and not really assisting the Allied war effort.

Undoubtedly Haas's tale of espionage and adventure on the Côte d'Azur cannot be an authentic story as has been claimed, and the flaws are so transparent one wonders how *The Doctor and the Damned* could have escaped scrutiny. Indeed, Haas is mentioned by David Schoenbrun in *The Soldiers of the Night* as a key figure in the French resistance, but his only source was Haas himself.[32] Although *The Doctor and the Damned* was written largely by his daughter-in-law, Sheila Haas, who usually edits medical texts, it is quite a puzzle to know how her publisher was persuaded to release the book as non-fiction. Meanwhile Dr Haas, who lives in Greenwich Village, New York, has completed a second volume of memoirs, *A Life Regained*, which concentrates on his very well-documented post-war medical career.

There remain a few other mysteries. David C. Smith, the surviving author of *The Search for Johnny Nicholas*, who still works as a journalist in Detroit, has been invited to produce whatever evidence he found to justify the claim that Nicholas had been an American intelligence agent. Similarly, Robert Vacha was offered an opportunity to explain the many inconsistencies in *A Spy for Churchill*, and James Leasor continues to insist from his home in Wiltshire that the spy he called *Nimrod*, hero of

The Unknown Warrior, really existed, despite the evidence to the contrary. The self-styled colonel, John Cottell, was asked to apply for a copy of the official record of his military career, but none has been forthcoming, which leaves readers to make up their own minds about the standards of accuracy and veracity adopted by these authors.

Notes

Introduction

1. Martin Gray, *For Those I Loved* (Bodley Head, 1971). Gray claimed to have joined the Polish Resistance and to have met two Poles (p. 186) who had been 'parachuted from London' to liaise with the *Armia Krajowie*. They were Jan Ponury and Captain Paczkowski (codenamed *Wania*). There is also mention of a third officer, Captain Mieczyslaw (*Bocian*).

   A total of 316 Polish military personnel were dropped into Poland during the war and the standard work on the subject, Jozef Garlinski's *Poland, SOE and the Allies* (Allen & Unwin, 1969), refers to all three officers mentioned by Gray (pp. 106, 111). Alfred Paczkowski (*Wania*) was arrested by the Germans in November 1942 near Dawidgrodek; *Ponury* was a codename ('grim' in English) and had been assigned to a Polish officer based in Warsaw; and Lieutenant Mieczyslaw Eckhardt, codenamed *Bocian* ('stork'), had died while under German interrogation in November 1942. None of the three people identified by Gray was alive when his book was published, and the references to each seem to have been deliberately transposed.

   His account of having been imprisoned at Treblinka is flawed. For example, the fake railway station he described as having seen upon his arrival in September 1942 was not built until at least December 1942. His descriptions of the gas chambers, buildings and paths do not accord with the recollection of other survivors. None of the labour processes he mentions, such as the sorting of human hair according to colour, ever took place, and certain passages appear to bear a striking resemblance to one of the very few books written on the subject, *Treblinka* by Jean-François Steiner (Simon & Schuster, 1967), itself a not entirely reliable guide to the camp which existed only between July 1942 and its destruction soon after the revolt of August 1943. Treblinka is the least well-documented of the Holocaust camps, from which only a relative handful are known to have survived.

2. M. R. D. Foot, *SOE in France* (HMSO, 1966), p. 430

3. *Ibid.*, p. 48
4. Elizabeth Denham, *I Looked Right* (Doubleday, 1956)
5. Maurice Buckmaster, *They Fought Alone* (Odhams, 1958), p. 82

1. *The Man Who Wouldn't Talk*

1. Quentin Reynolds, *The Man Who Wouldn't Talk* (Random House, 1953), p. 31
2. *Ibid.*, p. 20
3. *Ibid.*, p. 22
4. *Ibid.*, p. 44
5. *Ibid.*, p. 57
6. *Ibid.*, p. 103
7. *Ibid.*; p. 153
8. *Ibid.*, p. 156
9. *Ibid.*, p. 157
10. *Ibid.*, p. 159
11. *Ibid.*, p. 163
12. *Ibid.*, p. 177
13. *Ibid.*, p. 178
14. *Ibid.*, p. 183
15. *Ibid.*, p. 191
16. *Ibid.*
17. *Ibid.*, p. 138
18. *Ibid.*
19. *Ibid.*, p. 34

2. *Count Five and Die*

1. Barry Wynne, *Count Five and Die* (Souvenir Press, 1958), p. 73
2. *Ibid.*, p. 12
3. *Ibid.*, p . 24
4. *Ibid.*, p. 15
5. *Ibid.*,p. 34
6. *Ibid.*, p. 52
7. *Ibid.*, p. 42
8. J. C. Masterman, *The Double Cross System in the War of 1939–45* (Yale, 1972; reprinted Pimlico, 1995)
9. Wynne, *op. cit.*, p. 52
10. *Ibid.*, p. 43
11. *Ibid.*, p. 55
12. *Ibid.*

13. *Ibid.*, p. 66
14. *Ibid.*, p. 69
15. *Ibid.*, p. 75
16. *Ibid.*, p. 81
17. *Ibid.*, p. 86
18. *Ibid.*, p. 88
19. *Ibid.*, p. 102
20. *Ibid.*, p. 120
21. *Ibid.*, p. 122
22. *Ibid.*
23. *Ibid.*, p. 124
24. *Ibid.*, p. 124 n.
25. *Ibid.*, p. 124
26. *Ibid.*, p. 118
27. *Ibid.*
28. *Ibid.*, p. 126
29. *Ibid.*, p. 129
30. *Ibid.*, p. 131
31. *Ibid.*, p. 132
32. *Ibid.*, p. 140
33. *Ibid.*, p. 158
34. *Ibid.*, p. 88
35. *Ibid.*, p. 168
36. *Ibid.*, p. 170
37. *Ibid.*, p. 178
38. *Ibid.*, p. 174
39. Maurice Buckmaster, *Specially Employed* (Batchworth Press, 1952)
40. Maurice Buckmaster, *They Fought Alone* (Odhams, 1958)
41. Peter Dourlein, *Inside North Pole* (William Kimber, 1953)
42. Herman Giskes, *London Calling North Pole* (William Kimber, 1953)
43. Foreign Office Statement, para. 2, 14 December 1949, reproduced in full by Nicholas Kelso in *Errors of Judgement* (Robert Hale, 1988), pp. 225–9
44. Wynne, *op. cit.*, p. 179. In fact, this is a paraphrase of Churchill's *The Second World War*, vol. VI (Cassell & Co., 1954), p. 10, which actually reads: 'Our deception measures both before and after D-Day had

aimed at creating this confused thinking. Their success was admirable and had far-reaching results on the battle.' The specific 'confused thinking' Churchill referred to, but altered by Wynne, was Rommel and von Rundstedt's belief that the real invasion target was the Pas de Calais. Churchill makes no reference to any deception scheme for Holland, for there was none.

45. Frederick Winterbotham, *The Ultra Secret* (Weidenfeld & Nicolson, 1974)

46. Anthony Cave Brown, *Bodyguard of Lies* (W. H. Allen, 1976)

47. Robert Marshall, *All the King's Men* (Collins, 1988)

48. Charles Wighton, *Pinstripe Saboteur* (Odhams, 1959)

49. Jean Overton Fuller, *Double Agent?* (Pan, 1961)

50. M. R. D. Foot, *SOE in France* (HMSO, 1966), p. 308

51. *Ibid.*, p. 278

52. *Ibid.*

53. Colonel R. A. Bourne-Paterson, *The 'British' Circuits in France* (unpublished), p. 9

54. Foot, *op. cit.*, p. 328

55. *Ibid.*, p. 329

56. *Ibid.*, p. 350

57. *Ibid.*, p. 386

58. Wynne, *op. cit.*, p. 110

59. *Ibid.*

60. Carl Boyd, *Hitler's Japanese Confidant* (University Press of Kansas, 1993), p. 118

61. *Ibid.*, p. 188

62. *Ibid.*, p. 122

63. *Ibid.*, p. 125

64. Hans Spiedel, *Invasion 1944* (Henry Regner, Chicago, 1950), p. 33

65. *Ibid.*, p. 36

66. *Ibid.*, p. 51

67. *Ibid.*, p. 22

68. Juan Pujol, *GARBO* (Weidenfeld & Nicolson, 1985), p. 131

69. *Ibid.*

70. Wynne, *op. cit.*, p. 57

71. Barry Wynne, *The Empty Coffin* (Souvenir Press, 1959)

72. Roxane Pitt, *The Courage of Fear* (Jarrolds, 1957)

73. Roxane Pitt, *Operation Double Life* (Bachman & Turner, 1975)

74. Barry Wynne, *No Drums, No Trumpets* (Arthur Barker, 1961)

75. Barry Wynne, *The Day Gibraltar Fell* (1969)

3. Aline, the Countess from New York

1. Aline de Romanones, *The Spy Wore Red* (Random House, 1987), p. ix

2. *Ibid.*

3. *Ibid.*, p. 25

4. *Ibid.*, p. 23

5. *Ibid.*, p. 47

6. *Ibid.*, p. 56

7. *Ibid.*, p. 75

8. *Ibid.*, p. 83

9. *Ibid.*, p. 116

10. *Ibid.*, p. 84

11. *Ibid.*, pp. 87, 105, 189

12. *Ibid.*, p. 112

13. *Ibid.*, p. 260

14. *Ibid.*, p. 272

15. *Ibid.*, p. 294

16. *Ibid.*

17. *Ibid.*, p. 295

18. *Ibid.*, p. 297

19. *Ibid.*, p. 260

20. *Ibid.*, p. 277

21. *Ibid.*, p. 301

22. *Ibid.*, p. 83

23. Donald Downes, *The Scarlet Thread* (Derek Verschoyle, 1953), p. 128

24. Romanones, *op. cit.*, p. ix

25. *Ibid.*, p. 288
26. *Ibid.*, p. 127
27. Ladislas Farago, *The Game of the Foxes* (David McKay, 1971), p. 515
28. Romanones, *op. cit.*, p. 128
29. Jodl's evidence in *Nuremberg Trial*, vol. xv, p. 301
30. Romanones, *op cit.*, p. 128
31. *Ibid.*, p. 75
32. OSS Records, US National Archives, *Butch* file; report on Condesa Gloria Rubio de Furstenberg, 2 May 1945
33. *Ibid.*
34. *Ibid.*, Wedding of Prince Max Hohenlohe's Daughter, 19 June 1945
35. *Ibid.*, 6 July 1945
36. *Ibid.*, Editorial Biografica Española, 27 June 1945
37. Aline de Romanones, *The Spy Went Dancing* (Putnam's, 1990; *The Spy Wore Silk* (Putnam's, 1991); *The Well-Mannered Assassin* (Putnam's, 1994)
38. *The Well-Mannered Assassin*, p. 9
39. *Ibid.*, p. 78
40. *Ibid.*, p. 80
41. David Yallop, *To the Ends of the Earth* (Jonathan Cape, 1993)
42. Colin Smith, *Carlos: Portrait of a Terrorist* (Holt, Rinehart & Winston, 1976)
43. Ronald Payne and Christopher Dobson, *The Carlos Complex* (Hodder & Stoughton, 1977)
44. Claire Sterling, *The Terror Network* (Holt, Rinehart & Winston, 1981). For a convincing critique of her account, see Duane Clarridge, *A Spy for All Seasons* (Scribner, 1997), pp. 186–7

4. *The Search for Johnny Nicholas*

1. Hugh Wray McCann, David C.

Smith & David Matthews, *The Search for Johnny Nicholas* (Sphere Books, 1982), p. 5
2. *Ibid.*, dustjacket
3. *Ibid.*
4. *Ibid.*, p. vii
5. *Ibid.*, p. 322
6. *Ibid.*, p. 10
7. *Ibid.*, p. 5
8. *Ibid.*, p. 9
9. *Ibid.*, p. 51. There was no German military attaché in Port au Prince before the war. The local German chargé d'affaires was, at that time, Wolfgang zu Putlitz, an anti-Nazi member of the Foreign Ministry, who, coincidentally, was also a British agent. See Wolfgang zu Putlitz, *The Putlitz Dossier* (Allan Wingate, 1957)
10. *Ibid.*
11. *Ibid.*, p. 29
12. *Ibid.*
13. *Ibid.*, p. 28
14. *Ibid.*, p. 51
15. *Ibid.*, p. 30
16. *Ibid.*, p. 26
17. *Ibid.*, p. 142
18. *Ibid.*, photo, p. 178
19. *Ibid.*, p. 27
20. *Ibid.*, p. 236
21. *Ibid.*, p. 141
22. *Ibid.*, p. 236
23. *Ibid.*, p. 237
24. *Ibid.*
25. *Ibid.*, p. 30
26. *Ibid.*, p. 28
27. *Ibid.*, p. 25
28. *Ibid.*, p. 27
29. *Ibid.*
30. *Ibid.*, dustjacket
31. *Ibid.*, p. 83
32. *Ibid.*, p. 322
33. Philippe de Vomécourt, *Army of Amateurs* (Doubleday, 1961), p. 81

5. George Borodin, Surgeon Extraordinary

1. George Borodin, *No Crown of Laurels* (Werner Laurie, 1950), p. 21
2. *Ibid.*, dustjacket
3. *Pillar of Fire* (Macdonald, 1947; *Cradle of Splendour: The Song of Samarkand* (Staples Press, 1945)
4. *No Crown of Laurels*, p. 5
5. *Ibid.*
6. *Ibid.*, p. 20
7. *Ibid.*, p. 18
8. *Ibid.*, p. 35
9. *Ibid.*
10. *Ibid.*, p. 37
11. *Ibid.*
12. *Ibid.*, p. 40
13. *Ibid.*, p. 44
14. *Ibid.*, p. 49
15. *Ibid.*, p. 59
16. *Ibid.*, p. 65
17. *Ibid.*, p. 70
18. *Ibid.*, p. 71
19. *Ibid.*, p. 99
20. *Ibid.*, p. 101
21. *Ibid.*, p. 103
22. *Ibid.*, p. 102
23. *Ibid.*, p. 111
24. *Ibid.*, p. 118
25. *Ibid.*, p. 135
26. *Ibid.*, p. 143
27. *Ibid.*, p. 158
28. *Ibid.*, p. 175
29. *Ibid.*, p. 185
30. *Ibid.*, p. 189
31. *Ibid.*, p. 190
32. *Ibid.*, p. 203
33. *Ibid.*, p. 197
34. *Ibid.*, p. 203
35. *Ibid.*, p. 204
36. *Ibid.*, p. 220
37. *Ibid.*, p. 23
38. *Ibid.*, p. 21
39. *Ibid.*, p. 52
40. *Ibid.*
41. Nelson quoted in Charles Cruickshank, *SOE in Scandinavia* (Oxford University Press, 1986), p. 56
42. *No Crown of Laurels*, p. 87
43. *Ibid.*, p. 99
44. Professor R. V. Jones, *Most Secret War* (Hamish Hamilton, 1978), p. 69
45. F. H. Hinsley, *British Intelligence in the Second World War* (HMSO, 1979), vol. I, p. 508
46. *No Crown of Laurels*, p. 102
47. *Ibid.*, p. 116
48. *Ibid.*, p. 158
49. Ibid., p. 194
50. *Ibid.*, p. 203
51. *Ibid.*, p. 208
52. George Sava, *Secret Surgeon* (William Kimber, 1979)
53. *No Crown of Laurels*, p. 108
54. *Secret Surgeon*, p. 25
55. *Ibid.*, p. 27
56. *No Crown of Laurels*, p. 28
57. *Secret Surgeon*, p. 25
58. Letter to author, 27 August 1992

6. *A Man Called Intrepid*

1. William Stevenson, *The Bormann Brotherhood* (Arthur Barker, 1973), p. 18
2. William Stevenson, *A Man Called Intrepid* (Macmillan, 1976), p. 6
3. For detail of *The Two Bills,* see Tim Naftali, *Intrepid's Last Deception* (privately printed, 1991)
4. C. H. Ellis, *The Transcaspian Episode* (Hutchinson, 1963)
5. Stevenson, *op. cit.*, p. xxi
6. H. Montgomery Hyde, *The Quiet Canadian* (Constable, 1962). As a result of *The Quiet Canadian*'s publication, Montgomery Hyde was contacted by Elizabeth Pack to whom he had attributed one of the great espionage coups of the war: the seduction of Admiral

Alberto Lais, the naval attaché at the Italian Embassy in Washington, from whom she stole a copy of the Italian navy's ciphers. Allegedly this episode had enabled the Allies to calculate exactly the right moment to mount the airborne raid on Taranto and sink part of the Italian fleet. In fact, much of the story was a fiction, carefully manufactured to conceal Allied success in decrypting Italian ciphers. Hyde subsequently perpetuated the myth by writing *Cynthia*, which, he was to admit privately, was almost entirely fictional and written at the request of Elizabeth Pack, with whom he had enjoyed a passionate affair.

7. Cordeaux's question to the Attorney-General, Sir John Hobson, was recorded in *Hansard* (Col. 1123), but the reference to Sir Stewart Menzies was misspelled 'Sir Stuart Menzies'.

8. *The BSC History*, to be published by St Ermin's Press in 1998

9. Professor Tim Naftali, *Intrepid's Last Deception* (privately printed, 1991)

10. Stevenson, *op. cit.*, p. xxi

11. *Ibid.*, p. 24

12. *Ibid.*, p. 39

13. *Ibid.*

14. *Ibid.*, p. 42

15. *Ibid.*

16. *Ibid.*, p. 53

17. *Ibid.*, p. 55

18. *Ibid.*, p. 69

19. *Ibid.*, p. 105

20. *Ibid.*, p. 103

21. *Ibid.*, p. 109

22. *Ibid.*, p. 110

23. *Ibid.*, p. 156

24. *Ibid.*

25. *Ibid.*, p. 165

26. *Ibid.*, p. 376

27. *Ibid.*, p. 381

28. *Ibid.*, p. 389

29. *Ibid.*

30. *Ibid.*, p. 391

31. *Ibid.*, p. 381

32. See David Stafford, *Camp X* (Lester & Orpen Dennys, 1986)

33. See *School for Danger*

34. Stevenson, *op. cit.*, p. 415

35. *Ibid.*, p. 414

36. *Ibid.*, p. 415

37. *Ibid.*, p. 423

38. *Ibid.*, p. 428

39. *Ibid.*, p. 424

40. *Ibid.*, p. 427

41. *Ibid.*, p. 428

42. *Ibid.*

43. See M. R. D. Foot, *SOE in France* (HMSO, 1966), p. 67

44. James Leasor, *Green Beach* (William Morrow, 1975)

45. Professor R. V. Jones, *Most Secret War* (Hamish Hamilton, 1978), p. 403

46. Stevenson, *op. cit.*, p. 65

47. *Ibid.*, p. 66

48. *Ibid.*, p. 463

49. *Ibid.*, p. 465

50. *Ibid.*, p. 463

51. *Ibid.*, p. 466

52. *Ibid.*, p. 473

53. *Ibid.*, p. 463

54. *Ibid.*, p. 481

55. *Ibid.*, p. 236

56. *Ibid.*, p. 238

57. *Ibid.*, p. 236

58. *Ibid.*, p. 237

59. *Ibid.*, p. 244

60. *Ibid.*, p. 246

61. *Ibid.*, p. 247

62. *Ibid.*

63. *Ibid.*, p. 246

64. *Ibid.*, p. 250

65. Foot, *op. cit.*, p. 293

66. *Ibid.*, p. 338

67. Stevenson, *op. cit.*, p. 246
68. Jean Overton Fuller, *Madeleine* (Victor Gollancz, 1952), pp. 182, 189
69. Stevenson, *op. cit.*, p. 250
70. *Ibid.*

7. *A Spy for Churchill*

1. Robert Vacha, *A Spy for Churchill* (Everest Books, 1974), WARNING, p. i
2. *Ibid.*
3. *Ibid.*, p. iii
4. *Ibid.*, p. 51
5. SOE's Cairo headquarters is described as being 'in Sharia Suleiman Pasha' (*ibid.*, p. 9), whereas the correct address was in Sharia Kasr-el-Aini.
6. Vacha, *op. cit.*, p. 9
7. *Ibid.*, p. 17
8. *Ibid.*, p. 22
9. *Ibid.*, p. 89
10. *Ibid.*, p. 137
11. *Ibid.*, p. ii
12. *Ibid.*
13. Anthony Cave Brown, *Bodyguard of Lies* (W. H. Allen, 1976)
14. Winterbotham's assertion in *The Ultra Secret* (Weidenfeld & Nicolson, 1976, p. 108) that General Sir Claude Auchinleck had anticipated Rommel's every move was an exaggeration. Winterbotham claimed, incorrectly, that 'with the aid of ULTRA, which had told him where and in what strength Rommel was moving his forces, Auchinleck had outwitted him like a lightweight boxer with quick punches just where Rommel least expected them'.
15. F. H. Hinsley, *British Intelligence in the Second World War* (HMSO, 1979), vol. I, pp. 405, 298–9
16. Sir David Hunt, *A Don at War* (Frank Cass, 1990), p. xii
17. Winston Churchill, *The Second World War* (Cassell & Co., 1954), vol. 3, p. 1
18. Hinsley, *op. cit.*, p. 397
19. Martin Gilbert, *Churchill: Finest Hour* (Cassell & Co., 1983), p. 1080
20. Hinsley, *op. cit.*, p. 397
21. *Ibid.*, p. 399
22. *Ibid.*, p. 398
23. Baron von Weizenbeck's children held Czech passports. His stepson joined the Pioneer Corps and his stepdaughter became a nurse. Another German in the same theatre was the mysterious Kurt von Strachwitz, alias 'Adrian Hunter', a distinguished journalist who joined SIS in 1939, having fled from Austria. Reportedly he was operating in Algiers at this time. He returned to Austria after the war, where he died in 1959.
24. Vacha, *op. cit.*, p. 23
25. *Ibid.*, p. 25
26. *Ibid.*
27. *Ibid.*
28. Hinsley, *op. cit.*, p. 394
29. Vacha, *op. cit.*, p. 17
30. *Ibid.*, p. 89
31. Hinsley, *op. cit.*, p. 393

8. Tony Duke: The Spy in Berlin

1. Madelaine Duke, *Slipstream* (Evans Brothers, 1955), p. 242
2. Madelaine Duke, *Top Secret Mission* (Evans Brothers, 1954)
3. Colonel A. P. Scotland, *The London Cage* (Evans Brothers, 1957)
4. *Slipstream*, p. x
5. *Ibid.*, p. ix
6. *Ibid.*, p. 109
7. *Ibid.*, p. 88
8. *Ibid.*, p. 91
9. *Ibid.*, p. 132

10. *Ibid.*, p. 242
11. *Ibid.*, p. 110
12. *Ibid.*, p. 111
13. Madelaine Duke, *No Passport* (Evans Brothers, 1957), p. 190
14. *Ibid.*, p. 195
15. *Ibid.*, p. 197
16. *Ibid.*, p. 193
17. *Ibid.*, p. 194
18. *Ibid.*
19. *Ibid.*, p. 199
20. *Ibid.*, p. 207
21. *Ibid.*, p. 215
22. *Ibid.*, p. 196
23. *Ibid.*
24. SOE Personal File of Hans Felix Jeschke

9. *The Paladin*

1. Brian Garfield, *The Paladin* (Macmillan, 1980)
2. *Ibid.*, p. ii
3. *Ibid.*, pp. 10, 59
4. Ibid., p. 9
5. Ibid., p. 75
6. *Ibid.*, p. 16
7. *Ibid.*, p. 15
8. *Ibid.*, p. 22
9. *Ibid.*, p. 24
10. *Ibid.*, p. 30
11. *Ibid.*, p. 76
12. *Ibid.*, p. 104
13. *Ibid.*, p. 120
14. *Ibid.*, p. 136
15. *Ibid.*, p. 143
16. *Ibid.*, p. 150
17. *Ibid.*, p. 154
18. *Ibid.*
19. *Ibid.*, p. 163
20. *Ibid.*, p. 157
21. *Ibid.*, p. 182
22. *Ibid.*, p. 183
23. *Ibid.*, p. 233
24. *Ibid.*, p. 237
25. *Ibid.*, p. 284
26. *Ibid.*, p. 331
27. *Ibid.*, p. 75

28. *Ibid.*, p. 135
29. *Ibid.*, p. 133
30. *Ibid.*, p. 333
31. *Ibid.*, p. 327
32. *Ibid.*, p. 307
33. Ibid., p. 83
34. Ibid., p. 152
35. Ibid., p. 133
36. Christopher Creighton, *The Khrushchev Objective* (W. H. Allen, 1988)
37. Ibid., p. xi
38. Christopher Creighton, *OpJB* (Simon & Schuster, 1996)
39. *Ibid.*, p. 145
40. *OpJB* original manuscript
41. *Ibid.*
42. Garfield, *op. cit.*, foreword
43. Creighton, *OpJB*, p. 13
44. *Ibid.*, p. 12
45. *OpJB* original manuscript
46. Creighton, *OpJB*, p. 9
47. *OpJB* original manuscript
48. *Ibid.*
49. *Ibid.*, p. 14
50. Ralph Barker, *Aviator Extraordinary* (Chatto & Windus, 1969), p. 148. See also Patrick Beesly, *Very Special Admiral* (Hamish Hamilton, 1980), p. 137
51. Garfield, *op. cit.*, p. 140
52. *Ibid.*, p. 163
53. *Ibid.*, cf. *OpJB*, p. 19
54. *Ibid.*
55. *Ibid.*
56. Creighton, *OpJB*, p. 20
57. Terence Robertson, *Dieppe: The Shame and the Glory* (Hutchinson, 1961), p. 402
58. *Ibid.*
59. Garfield, *op. cit.*, p. 178
60. Robertson, *op. cit.*, p. 402
61. *Ibid.*
62. *Ibid.*
63. *Ibid.*
64. *Ibid.*
65. *Ibid.*

66. *Ibid.*
67. *Ibid.*
68. F. H. Hinsley, *British Intelligence in the Second World War*, vol. II (HMSO, 1981), p. 702
69. De Valera offered Hempel asylum after the war, see Carolle J. Carter, *The Shamrock and the Swastika* (Pacific Books, 1977), p. 82
70. Nigel West, *MI5: British Security Service Operations 1909–45* (Bodley Head, 1981)
71. Garfield, *op. cit.*, p. 231
72. Creighton, *OpJB*, p. 25
73. M. R. D. Foot, *SOE in France* (HMSO, 1966), p. 308
74. Larry Collins, *Fall From Grace* (Simon & Schuster, 1985)
75. Creighton, *OpJB*, pp. 13, 57
76. *Ibid.*, p. 91
77. *Ibid.*, p. 15
78. *Ibid.*, p. 117
79. *Ibid.*, p. 114
80. *Ibid.*
81. *Ibid.*, p. 129
82. *Ibid.*, p. 149
83. *Ibid.*, p. 216
84. *Ibid.*, p. 244
85. *OpJB* original manuscript
86. Creighton, *OpJB*, p. 74
87. *Ibid.*, p. 224
88. *Ibid.*, p. 137
89. *Ibid.*, p. 133
90. *Ibid.*, p. 15

10. *The Year of the Rat*

1. Mladin Zarubica, *The Year of the Rat* (Collins, 1965), dustjacket
2. *Ibid.*, p. 51
3. *Ibid.*, p. 57
4. *Ibid.*
5. *Ibid.*, p. 58
6. *Ibid.*, p. 63
7. *Ibid.*, p. 63
8. *Ibid.*
9. *Ibid.*, p. 106
10. *Ibid.*, p. 114
11. *Ibid.*, p. 197
12. *Ibid.*, p. 201
13. *Ibid.*, p. 211
14. *Ibid.*
15. W. Stanley Moss, *Ill Met by Moonlight* (Harrap & Co., 1950)
16. M. E. Clifton Brown, *I Was Monty's Double* (Rider & Co., 1954)
17. Stephen Watts, *Moonlight on a Lake in Bond Street* (Bodley Head, 1962)
18. Zarubica, *op. cit.*, p. 211
19. Ralph Ingersoll, *Top Secret* (Harcourt Brace, 1946)
20. Arthur Schlesinger in the *Herald Tribune Weekly Book Review*, 21 April 1946
21. Ingersoll, *op. cit.*, p. 87
22. *Ibid.*, p. 88

11. *Codename Badger*

1. John Cottell and Arthur Gordon, *Codename Badger* (William Morrow & Co., 1990), p. 148
2. *Ibid.*, pp. ix, 22
3. *Ibid.*, p. 36
4. *Ibid.*, p. 41
5. *Ibid.*
6. *Ibid.*, p. 44
7. *Ibid.*, p. 64
8. *Ibid.*, p. 70
9. *Ibid.*, p. 75
10. *Ibid.*, p. 154
11. *Ibid.*, p. 96
12. *Ibid.*, p. 118
13. *Ibid.*, p. 121
14. *Ibid.*, p. 128
15. *Ibid.*, p. 124
16. *Ibid.*, p. 129
17. *Ibid.*, p. 136
18. *Ibid.*, p. 152
19. *Ibid.*, p. 153
20. *Ibid.*, p. 167
21. *Ibid.*, p. 184
22. *Ibid.*, p. 192

23. *Ibid.*, p. 195
24. *Ibid.*, p. 200
25. *Ibid.*, p. 201
26. *Ibid.*, p. 212
27. *Ibid.*, p. 215
28. *Ibid.*, p. 283
29. *Ibid.*, p. 297
30. *Ibid.*, p. 307
31. *Ibid.*, p. 389
32. *Ibid.*, p. 390
33. *Ibid.*, p. 150
34. *Ibid.*, p. 10
35. *Ibid.*, p. 17
36. *Ibid.*, p. 150
37. *Ibid.*, p. 17
38. *Ibid.*, p. 21
39. *Ibid.*, p. 24
40. *Ibid.*, p. 286
41. *Ibid.*, p. 27
42. *Ibid.*, p. 35
43. *Ibid.*, p. 65
44. *Ibid.*, p. 75
45. *Ibid.*, p. 38
46. *Ibid.*, p. 21
47. SOE Adviser, 19 February 1990
48. Cottrell, *op. cit.*, pp. 137, 148
49. *Ibid.*, p. 361
50. *Ibid.*, p. 362
51. *Ibid.*, p. 70
52. *Ibid.*, p. 158
53. *Ibid.*, p. 135
54. *Ibid.*, p. 39
55. *Ibid.*, p. 38
56. *Ibid.*, p. 36
57. *Ibid.*, p. 136
58. *Ibid.*, p. 291
59. *Ibid.*, p. 326
60. *Ibid.*, p. 34
61. *Ibid.*, p. 35
62. *Ibid.*, p. 75
63. *Ibid.*, p. 148
64. *Ibid.*, p. 298
65. *Ibid.*, p. 297
66. *Ibid.*, p. 298
67. *Ibid.*, p. 149
68. *Ibid.*
69. *Ibid.*
70. *Ibid.*
71. *Ibid.*
72. Colonel Scotland, *The London Cage* (Evans Brothers, 1957), p. 61
73. Airey Neave, *Little Cyclone* (Elmfield Press, 1954)
74. *Spycatcher* (Werner Laurie, 1952); *Friend or Foe* (G. P. Putnam's Sons, 1953); *The Boys' Book of Secret Agents* (Cassell & Co., 1955)

12. *Churchill's Secret Agent*

1. Josephine Butler, *Churchill's Secret Agent* (Methuen, 1983), p. 195
2. *The Times*, 15 March 1982
3. Butler, *op. cit.*, dustjacket
4. *Mail on Sunday*, 23 May 1982
5. Butler, *op. cit.*, p. 14
6. *Ibid.*, p. 18
7. *Ibid.*, p. 19
8. *Ibid.*, p. 20
9. *Ibid.*, p. 22
10. *Ibid.*, p. 31. Squadron Leader Torr Anderson DFC was Director of Training at the Air Ministry.
11. *Ibid.*, p. 196
12. *Ibid.*, p. 23
13. *Ibid.*, p. 24
14. *Ibid.*, p. 28
15. *Ibid.*, p. 30
16. *Ibid.*, p. 34
17. *Ibid.*, p. 35
18. *Ibid.*, p. 54
19. *Ibid.*, p. 55
20. *Ibid.*, p. 57
21. *Ibid.*, p. 59
22. *Ibid.*, p. 58
23. *Ibid.*
24. *Ibid.*, p. 61
25. *Ibid.*, p. 62
26. *Ibid.*, p. 65
27. *Ibid.*, p. 75
28. *Ibid.*, p. 77
29. *Ibid.*, p. 79
30. *Ibid.*, p. 82

31. *Ibid.*, p. 91
32. *Ibid.*, p. 94
33. *Ibid.*, p. 95
34. *Ibid.*, p. 97
35. *Ibid.*, p. 109
36. *Ibid.*, p. 113
37. *Ibid.*
38. *Ibid.*, p. 115
39. *Ibid.*, p. 119
40. *Ibid.*, p. 130
41. *Ibid.*, p. 157
42. *Ibid.*, p. 134
43. *Ibid.*, p. 149
44. *Ibid.*
45. *Ibid.*, p. 152
46. *Ibid.*, p. 156
47. *Ibid.*, p. 158
48. *Ibid.*, p. 166
49. *Ibid.*, p. 195
50. *Ibid.*
51. *Ibid.*, p. 64
52. *Ibid.*
53. Josephine Butler, *Cyanide in My Shoe* (This England Books, 1991)
54. *Churchill's Secret Agent*, dustjacket
55. *Cyanide in My Shoe*, dustjacket

13. Lady Clarke Looked Right

1. Elizabeth Denham, *I Looked Right* (Doubleday, 1956), dustjacket
2. *Ibid.*, p. 31
3. *Ibid.*, p. 24
4. *Ibid.*, p. 31
5. *Ibid.*, p. 32
6. *Ibid.*, p. 41
7. *Ibid.*, p. 46
8. *Ibid.*, dustjacket
9. *Ibid.*, p. 42
10. *Ibid.*, p. 46
11. *Ibid.*, p. 45
12. *Ibid.*, p. 77
13. *Ibid.*, p. 86
14. *Ibid.*
15. *Ibid.*, p. 91
16. *Ibid.*, p. 96
17. *Ibid.*, p. 113

18. *Ibid.*, p. 114
19. *Ibid.*
20. *Ibid.*, p. 116
21. *Ibid.*, p. 117
22. *Ibid.*, p. 192
23. *Ibid.*, pp. 30, 62
24. *Ibid.*, p. 84
25. *Ibid.*, p. 17
26. Maurice Buckmaster, *They Fought Alone* (Odhams, 1958)

14. With My Little Eye

1. Edward Edlmann, *With My Little Eye* (The Adventurers Club, 1961), p. 5
2. *Ibid.*, p. 14
3. *Ibid.*, p. 17
4. *Ibid.*, p. 24
5. *Ibid.*, p. 27
6. *Ibid.*, p. 32
7. *Ibid.*
8. *Ibid.*, p. 38
9. *Ibid.*, p. 42
10. *Ibid.*, p. 50
11. *Ibid.*, p. 56
12. *Ibid.*, p. 59
13. *Ibid.*, p. 60
14. *Ibid.*, p. 65
15. *Ibid.*, p. 66
16. *Ibid.*, p. 67
17. *Ibid.*, p. 68
18. *Ibid.*, p. 71
19. *Ibid.*, p. 78
20. *Ibid.*, p. 84
21. *Ibid.*, p. 85
22. *Ibid.*, p. 90
23. *Ibid.*, p. 147
24. *Ibid.*, p. 157
25. *Ibid.*, p. 179
26. *Ibid.*, p. 177
27. *Ibid.*, p. 199
28. *Ibid.*, p. 202
29. *Ibid.*, p. 203
30. *Ibid.*, p. 204
31. *Ibid.*, p. 220
32. *Ibid.*, p. 206
33. *Ibid.*, p. 238

34. *Ibid.*, p. 199
35. *Ibid.*, p. 239
36. *Ibid.*, p. 5
37. *Ibid.*, p. 37
38. *Ibid.*, p. 40
39. *Ibid.*, p. 42
40. *Ibid.*, p. 43
41. *Ibid.*, p. 39
42. *Ibid.*, p. 41
43. *Ibid.*, p. 43
44. *Ibid.*, p. 44
45. *Ibid.*
46. *Ibid.*, p. 46

15. *The Courage of Fear*

1. Roxane Pitt, *The Courage of Fear* (Jarrolds, 1957), p. 88
2. *Ibid.*, dustjacket
3. *Ibid.*, p. 26
4. *Ibid.*, p. 30
5. *Ibid.*, p. 39
6. *Ibid.*, p. 89
7. *Ibid.*
8. *Ibid.*, p. 87
9. *Ibid.*, p. 151
10. *Ibid.*, p. 191
11. *Ibid.*, p. vii
12. *Ibid.*, dustjacket
13. *Ibid.*
14. *Ibid.*
15. *Ibid.*, p. 4
16. *Ibid.*, p. 40
17. *Ibid.*, p. 35
18. *Ibid.*, p. 83
19. *Ibid.*, p. 89
20. *Ibid.*, p. 83
21. *Ibid.*, p. 78
22. *Ibid.*, p. 154
23. *Ibid.*, p. 3
24. *Ibid.*, p. 232
25. *Ibid.*, p. 200
26. *Ibid.*, p. 133
27. *Ibid.*, p. 187
28. Roxane Pitt, *Operation Double Life* (Bachman & Turner, 1975), dustjacket
29. *Ibid.*, p. 9

30. *Ibid.*, p. 13
31. *Ibid.*, p. 26
32. *Ibid.*, p. 113
33. *Ibid.*, p. 174
34. The year of Roxane's marriage to Roberto Salviati can be deduced from her reference that in 'February, 1954' (p. 67) she had been parted from her husband 'for the last four years'.
35. *The Courage of Fear*, p. 8
36. *Operation Double Life*, p. 20
37. *Ibid.*, p. 22
38. *Ibid.*, p. 27
39. *Ibid.*, p. 53. In her first account of this flight, Roxane had said her plane had intended to land at Castel Vetrano, but had been forced to divert to Bicocca. 'My pilot, a reserved young man, had not spoken a word' (p. 159).
40. *Ibid.*, p. 88
41. *The Courage of Fear*, p. 202
42. *Operation Double Life*, p. 97
43. M. R. D. Foot, *SOE in France*, (HMSO, 1966), p. 91
44. *Operation Double Life*, p. 28
45. *Ibid.*
46. *Ibid.*, p. 24. In *The Courage of Fear*, Roxane had given a slightly different account of Romans's ordeal, referring to him as 'Jean Roucou' (pp. 76–7).
47. Philippe de Vomecourt, *Army of Amateurs* (Doubleday, 1961)
48. See Chapter 2
49. *Operation Double Life*, p. 28

16. *The Druid*

1. Leonard Mosley, *The Druid* (Atheneum, 1981)
2. Ladislas Farago, *The Game of the Foxes* (David McKay, 1971)
3. Sir John Masterman, *The Double Cross System of the War of 1939–45* (Yale, 1972), p. 3. Although Mosley relies heavily

on Masterman, he occasionally fails. For instance, Mosley's suggestion that Arthur Owens was imprisoned at Pentonville (pp. 17, 223) is contradicted by Masterman (p. 39), who records that he was in Wandsworth and then Dartmoor.

4. Leonard Mosley, *The Cat and the Mice* (Arthur Barker, 1958)
5. *The Druid*, p. 7
6. *Ibid.*, p. 8
7. *Ibid.*, p. 10
8. *Ibid.*, p. 11
9. *Ibid.*, p. 12
10. *Ibid.*
11. *Ibid.*, p. 13
12. *Ibid.*
13. *Ibid.*, p. 16
14. *Ibid.*
15. *Ibid.*
16. *Ibid.*, p. 17
17. *Ibid.*
18. *Ibid.*
19. *Ibid.*, p. 41
20. *Ibid.*, p. 44
21. *Ibid.*, p. 43
22. *Ibid.*, p. 44
23. *Ibid.*, p. 65
24. *Ibid.*, p. 67
25. *Ibid.*, p. 68
26. *Ibid.*, p. 103
27. *Ibid.*, p. 106
28. *Ibid.*, p. 103. Mosley incorrectly gives 1968 as the year of Harris's death in Majorca (p. 240), when in fact he died in January 1964.
29. *Ibid.*, p. 207
30. *Ibid.*, p. 225
31. *Ibid.*, p. 43
32. *Ibid.*, p. 118
33. *Ibid.*, p. 116
34. Terence Robertson, *Dieppe: The Shame and the Glory* (Hutchinson, 1961), p. 27
35. James Leasor, *Green Beach* (William Morrow, 1975), p. 144

36. Richard Deacon, *The British Connection* (Hamish Hamilton, 1979), p. 179
37. F. H. Hinsley, *British Intelligence in the Second World War* (HMSO, 1990), vol. v, p. 261
38. Dusko Popov, *Spy CounterSpy* (Weidenfeld & Nicolson, 1974), p. 203
39. Kim Philby, *My Silent War* (MacGibbon & Kee, 1968)
40. *The Druid*, p. 17
41. *Ibid.*, p. 97
42. *Ibid.*, p. 16
43. *Ibid.*
44. *Ibid.*, p. 141
45. *Ibid.*, p. 11
46. *Ibid.*, p. 141
47. *Ibid.*, p. 94
48. *Ibid.*, p. 76
49. *Ibid.*, p. 79
50. *Ibid.*
51. *Ibid.*, pp. 81, 145
52. *Ibid.*, p. 126
53. *Ibid.*, pp. 160, 165
54. Popov, *op. cit.*, pp. 203, 234
55. *The Druid*, p. 240

17. *The Unknown Warrior*

1. James Leasor, *The Unknown Warrior* (Heinemann, 1981), p. 78
2. See Chapter 6
3. Leasor, *op. cit.*, p. 78
4. *Ibid.*, p. 79
5. *Ibid.*
6. *Ibid.*, p. 89
7. *Ibid.*, p. 100. Cabourg is actually north of Bayeux. A Lysander aircraft had a cruising speed of 160 mph, which in two hours would bring the plane over three hundred miles. The distance between Tangmere and Bayeux is less than half that.
8. *Ibid.*, p. 127
9. *Ibid.*, p. 129
10. *Ibid.*, p. 174

11. *Ibid.*, p. 250
12. *Ibid.*, p. 254
13. James Leasor, *War at the Top* (Michael Joseph, 1959)
14. *The Unknown Warrior*, p. 254
15. *Ibid.*, p. 255
16. *Ibid.*, p. 256
17. *Ibid.*, p. 140
18. *Ibid.*, p. 107
19. *Ibid.*
20. *Ibid.*
21. *Ibid.*
22. *Ibid.*, p. 27
23. *Ibid.* p. 81
24. *Ibid.*, p. 46
25. *Ibid.*, p. 82
26. *Ibid.*, p. 83
27. *Ibid.*, p. 82. In fact, the term is 'fist', not 'wrist'.
28. *Ibid.*
29. *Ibid.*
30. *Ibid.*, dustjacket
31. *Ibid.*, p. 61
32. F. H. Hinsley, *British Intelligence in the Second World War*, vol. v (HMSO, 1990), p. 32
33. *Ibid.*, p. 101
34. *The Unknown Warrior*, p. 110
35. Ian Dear, *Ten Commando 1942–45* (Leo Cooper, 1987)

Conclusion

1. Leonard Mosley, *The Druid* (Atheneum, 1982), p. 17
2. Knut Haukelid, *Skis against the Atom* (William Kimber, 1974)
3. Roger A. Ready, *Operation Killer Mouse* (Eakin Press, 1985), p. vii
4. Albert Haas, *The Doctor and the Damned* (St Martin's Press, 1984)
5. *Ibid.*, p. 42
6. *Ibid.*
7. *Ibid.*, p. 46
8. *Ibid.*
9. *Ibid.*
10. *Ibid.*
11. *Ibid.*, p. 47
12. *Ibid.*, p. 49
13. *Ibid.*, p. 50
14. *Ibid.*
15. *Ibid.*, p. 46
16. *Ibid.*, p. 32
17. *Ibid.*, p. 294
18. *Ibid.*, p. 38
19. *Ibid.*, p. 39
20. *Ibid.*
21. *Ibid.*, p. 37
22. *Ibid.*, p. 46
23. *Ibid.*
24. *Ibid.*, p. 42
25. *Ibid.*, p. 45
26. *Ibid.*
27. *Ibid.*, p. 46
28. *Ibid.*
29. *Ibid.*, p. 47
30. *Ibid.*, p. 50
31. *Ibid.*
32. David Shoenbrun, *The Soldiers of the Night* (Robert Hale, 1981), pp. 403–5

Select Bibliography

Beesly, Patrick, *Very Special Admiral* (Hamish Hamilton, 1980)

Best, Sigismund Payne, *The Venlo Incident* (Hutchinson, 1950)

Blunt, Anthony, *Tomas Harris* (Courtauld Institute)

Borodin, George, *No Crown of Laurels* (Werner Laurie, 1950)

Buckmaster, Maurice, *Specially Employed* (Batchworth Press, 1952)

Buckmaster, Maurice, *They Fought Alone* (Odhams, 1958)

Butler, Josephine, *Churchill's Secret Agent* (Methuen, 1983)

Butler, Josephine, *Cyanide in My Shoe* (This England Books, 1991)

Cave Brown, Anthony, *Bodyguard of Lies* (W. H. Allen, 1976)

Clifton Brown , M. E., *I Was Monty's Double* (Rider & Co., 1954)

Cottell, John, *Codename Badger* (William Morrow & Co., 1990)

Creighton Christopher, *The Khrushchev Objective* (W. H. Allen, 1988)

Creighton, Christopher, *OpJB* (Simon & Schuster, 1996)

Dear, Ian, *Ten Commando 1942–45* (Leo Cooper, 1987)

Denham, Elizabeth, *I Looked Right* (Doubleday, 1956)

Dobson, Christopher, & Payne, Ronald, *The Carlos Complex* (Hodder & Stoughton, 1977)

Duke, Madelaine, *Top Secret Mission* (Evans Brothers, 1954)

Duke, Madelaine, *Slipstream* (Evans Brothers, 1955)

Duke, Madelaine, *No Passport* (Evans Brothers, 1957)

Edlmann, Edward, *With My Little Eye* (The Adventurers Club, 1961)

Elliott, Nicholas, *Never Judge A Man By His Umbrella* (Michael Russell, 1991)

Ellis, C. H. Dick, *The Transcaspian Episode* (Hutchinson, 1963)

Farago, Ladislas, *The Game of the Foxes* (David McKay, 1971)

Foot, M. R. D., *SOE in France* (HMSO, 1966)

Fuller, Jean Overton, *Madeleine* (Victor Gollancz, 1952)

Fuller, Jean Overton, *The German Penetration of SOE* (William Kimber, 1975)

Garfield, Brian, *The Paladin* (Macmillan, 1980)

Garlinski, Jozef, *Poland, SOE and the Allies* (Allen & Unwin, 1969)

Gray, Martin, *For Those I Loved* (Bodley Head, 1971)

Haas, Albert, *The Doctor and the Damned* (St Martin's Press, 1984)

Hinsley, F. H., *British Intelligence in the Second World War* (HMSO, 5 vols, 1979–90)

Hyde, H. Montgomery, *The Quiet Canadian* (Hamish Hamilton, 1962)

Hyde, H. Montgomery, *Cynthia* (Hamish Hamilton, 1966)

Hyde, H. Montgomery, *Secret Intelligence Agent* (Constable, 1982)

Ingersoll, Ralph, *Top Secret* (Harcourt Brace, 1946)

Johnson, Brian, *The Secret War* (BBC, 1978)

Jones, R. V., *Most Secret War* (Hamish Hamilton, 1978)

Jones, R. V., *Reflections on Intelligence* (Heinemann, 1989)

Langley, J. M., & Foot, M. R. D., *MI9* (Bodley Head, 1980)

Leasor, James, *Green Beach* (William Morrow, 1975)

Leasor, James, *The Unknown Warrior* (Heinemann, 1989)

Lovell, Mary S., *Cast No Shadow* (Pantheon Books, 1992)

McCann, Hugh, Smith, David C., & Matthews, David, *The Search for Johnny Nicholas* (Sphere Books, 1982)

Masterman, J. C., *The Double Cross System of the War of 1939–45* (Yale, 1972)

Masterman, J. C., *On The Chariot Wheel* (OUP, 1975)

Mills, Cyril, *Bertram Mills Circus: Its Story* (Hutchinson, 1967)

Minney, Rubeigh, *Carve Her Name With Pride* (George Newnes, 1956)

Mosley, Leonard, *The Druid* (Atheneum, 1981)

Moss, W. Stanley, *Ill Met by Moonlight* (Harrap & Co., 1950)

Neave, Airey, *Little Cyclone* (Elmfield Press, 1954)

Philby, H. A. R. (Kim), *My Silent War* (MacGibbon & Kee, 1968)

Pitt, Roxane, *The Courage of Fear* (Jarrolds, 1957)

Pitt, Roxane, *Operation Double Life* (Bachman & Turner, 1975)

Pujol, Juan, *GARBO* (Weidenfeld & Nicolson, 1985)

Ready, Roger A., *Operation Killer Mouse* (Eakin Press, 1985)

Reynolds, Quentin, *The Man Who Wouldn't Talk* (Random House, 1953)

Robertson, Terence, *Dieppe: The Shame and the Glory* (Hutchinson, 1961)

Romanones, Aline de, *The Spy Wore Red* (Random House, 1987)

Romanones, Aline de, *The Spy Went Dancing* (Putnam's, 1990)

Romanones, Aline de, *The Spy Wore Silk* (Putnam's, 1991)

Romanones, Aline de, *The Well-Mannered Assassin* (Putnam's, 1994)

Sava, George, *Secret Surgeon* (William Kimber, 1979)

Schoenbrun, David, *The Soldiers of the Night* (Robert Hale, 1981)

Scotland, A. P., *The London Cage* (Evans Brothers, 1957)

Simkins, Anthony, *British Intelligence in the Second World War* (HMSO, 1990)

Stafford, David, *Camp X* (Lester & Orpen Dennys, 1986)

Steiner, Jean-François, *Treblinka* (Simon & Schuster, 1967)

Stevenson, William, *The Bormann Brotherhood* (Arthur Barker, 1973)

Stevenson, William, *A Man Called Intrepid* (Macmillan, 1976)

Stevenson, William, *Intrepid's Last Case* (Villard Books, 1983)

Taylor, Eric, *Heroines of World War II* (Robert Hale, 1991)

Vacha, Robert, *A Spy for Churchill* (Everest Books, 1974)

Vacha, Robert, *Phantoms over Potsdam* (Everest Books, 1975)

Vomécourt, Philippe de, *Army of Amateurs* (Doubleday, 1961)

Watts, Stephen, *Moonlight on a Lake in Bond Street* (Bodley Head, 1962)

Whiting, Charles, *The March on London* (Leo Cooper, 1992)

Winterbotham, F. W., *The Ultra Secret* (Weidenfeld & Nicolson, 1974)

Wynne, Barry, *The Empty Coffin* (Souvenir Press, 1959)

Wynne, Barry, *Count Five and Die* (Souvenir Press, 1958)

Wynne, Barry, *No Drums, No Trumpets* (Arthur Barker, 1961)

Wynne, Barry, *The Sniper* (Macdonald, 1968)

Wynne, Barry, *Angels on Runway Zero 7* (Souvenir Press, 1968)

Yallop, David, *To the Ends of the Earth* (Jonathan Cape, 1993)

Zarubica, Mladin, *The Year of the Rat* (Collins, 1965)

Zembsch-Schreve, Guido, and Lalande, Pierre, *Special Agent* (Leo Cooper, 1996)

Index